The German Economy

BEYOND THE SOCIAL MARKET

Horst Siebert

PRINCETON UNIVERSITY PRESS

PRINCETON AND OXFORD

Copyright © 2005 by Princeton University Press
Published by Princeton University Press, 41 William Street,
Princeton, New Jersey 08540
In the United Kingdom: Princeton University Press,
3 Market Place, Woodstock, Oxfordshire OX20 1SY

All Rights Reserved

ISBN 0-691-09664-3

Library of Congress Control Number 2004112206

British Library Cataloguing-in-Publication Data is available

This book has been composed in Sabon

Printed on acid-free paper ∞

www.pupress.princeton.edu

Printed in the United States of America

10 9 8 7 6 5 4 3 2 1

Contents

Preface

GERMANY has experienced nearly six decades of a continuous rise in well-being. Gross domestic product per head of the population has risen by a factor of six since 1950. This increase in welfare has benefited a large spectrum of society, and there is a stable middle class. The work force is highly qualified, and German firms are competitive globally. In spite of occasional spurts of extremist parties in the parliaments of several federal states and a few flare-ups of xenophobia, the country has been politically stable and democracy is well established. Germany is fully integrated into the international community. Since World War II it has been able to participate in the international division of labor and has conquered a sizable share of the world market. An open economy, it has been a driving force in European integration, including the creation of the European Monetary Union and enlargement.

The peaceful and effective uprising of the people in East Germany in 1989 and the ensuing German reunification can be considered a quantum leap in Germany's post-war development, dealing a final blow to the communist approach and helping to reunite the East with the West, not only in Germany but throughout Europe. The battle between the free and democratic market economies of the West and communist central planning with its political oppression and extreme collectivism was finally won by the free and open societies.

However, this success story shows serious signs of faults and failures. Economic growth has been extremely slow since the mid-1990s, raising troubling questions regarding the long-run energy of this one-time European powerhouse. The German engine seems to be stalling. Germany has recently performed less well than most of its European neighbors and the United States. Unemployment has ratcheted upward in the last three and a half decades from full employment to a situation of high unemployment, reaching 10 percent—14 percent when the jobless who are hidden in governmental schemes are taken into consideration. The labor market institutions include severe disincentives leading to such high and persistent unemployment. The economy, rigid in its structures, does not seem to be able to digest negative external shocks easily, or to respond flexibly to a changed economic environment. The social security systems can no longer be financed in their present form, and the population will be declining and aging in future decades. Social absorption is affecting the economic base negatively, placing a severe strain on the economy's capacity to generate a sufficient value added. These policy issues are all interrelated as in a Gordian knot. The system of governance, with its reliance on intermediation, group participation and consensus, coupled with its timid approach to the market, does not seem to be able to solve the pressing problems. The issue is whether Germany's societal preferences for leisure and social protection have eroded the foundation of the country's once successful economic policy concept, the social market economy.

This book presents a realistic and undistorted portrait of the German economy. Such a portrait should neither embellish the given situation, glossing over the issues, nor exaggerate the troubles that face the country and its economy. My aim has been a dual one: to provide a sober representation of the German economy to an international audience in order to allow a better understanding of the country; and to hold a mirror to the German public and German politics so that they may recognize and solve the issues at hand.

This is not a historical appraisal, although it was necessary to put issues into a historical perspective. I conceived this book from the problems in Germany that need to be solved. Thus, readers will not find a chapter on German monetary policy, which has ceased to exist with the creation of the euro, or on the Deutsche Bundesbank, which is now just one member in the European System of Central Banks. My lead question in writing the book has been: What is Germany's future, and what are its long-run policy issues?

In this endeavor I deal with the issues that were discussed in the German Council of Economic Advisers, of which I was a member for twelve years in 1990–2003. The discussions with Chancellors Kohl and Schröder and the economics, finance, and labor ministers of their cabinets have provided a sense of how the German system operates. This also applies to the regular hearings that the Council of Economic Advisers holds with the trade unions, the employers' association, German industry, and the head office of the Chambers of Commerce, the Federal Labor Office, state governments, the Bundesbank, and others in the preparation of its annual reports.

I want to thank my colleagues in the Council—Juergen B. Donges, Wolfgang Franz, Herbert Hax, Jürgen Kromphardt, Rolf Peffekoven, Rüdiger Pohl, Bert Rürup, Hans Karl Schneider, Axel Weber and Wolfgang Wiegard —as well as the Council's staff for intensive discussions over the years. Equally, I have benefited from the fourteen years as president of the Kiel Institute for World Economics, where the implications of the international division of labor are discussed for Germany and where new solutions to economic issues are searched for. I am especially deeply indebted to Alfred Boss, Claudia Buch, Björn Christensen, Christophe Kamps, Gernot Klepper, Henning Klodt, Rolf J. Langhammer, Oliver

Lorz, Carsten-Patrick Meier, Frank Oskamp, Christian Pierdzioch, Klaus-Werner Schatz, Joachim Scheide, Rainer Schmidt, and Jürgen Stehn.

In the winter semester of 2003–04 I taught the course on "The German Economy" at Johns Hopkins University at Bologna. I am grateful to my students and to my colleagues Eirik Jones and Mike Plummer for critical discussions.

I also have received critical comments to different stages of the manuscript or parts thereof from my colleagues Martin Albrecht, Richard Baldwin, Axel Börsch-Supan, Friedrich Breyer, Günter Franke, Martin Gasche, Patrick Puhani, Ingo Walter, and Jens Weidmann. I have indicated in each chapter to whom I owe specific comments to that chapter. Four anonymous referees have provided many critical points.

In collecting the material, including tables and figures and institutional features, my research assistants at the Kiel Institute for World Economics and at the Bologna Center have been of invaluable help. These were at varying times Akram Esanov, Carolin Geginat, Eduard Herda, Matthias Knoll, David Moore, Christine Hübner, Terhi Jokipii, Tim Schmidt-Eisenlohr, and Bennedikt Wahler. I also am grateful for support to Wolfgang Gloeckler from the German Statistical Office. Ms Hübner prepared the reference index, Ursula Fett has arranged the figures. I also have received administrative assistance in preparing the manuscript from Jutta M. Arpe. Finally, I appreciate financial support from the Heinz–Nixdorf Foundation. Without all these helping hands and minds, and without my invaluable PC, the book would never have been finished. Unfortunately, all mistakes and shortcomings remain my own.

Horst Siebert

The German Economy

CHAPTER ONE

Basic Features of the German Economy

Germany is an open economy with a strong industrial base, producing about a third of its gross domestic product for export. It is also an economy in which social protection and the state play dominant roles. These two characteristics establish the central theme that will be encountered throughout this book.

Because of its openness, Germany is influenced both by the intense competition on the world product markets and by the competition among locations for the internationally mobile capital and technology that abound on the world's factor markets. Economic decisions in Germany are therefore subject to the country's need to compete in the world economy. This has been a fundamental economic law for Germany since the end of World War II. Openness means that, by and large, free markets for products prevail. The exceptions are regulations in specific areas and subsidies to sectors like coal mining and agriculture.

In contrast to this openness to competition, however, protection exists in many areas of the German economy, especially protection of the individual—e.g., through social security for unemployment, health care, nursing care, old-age pensions and by social welfare. About a third of GDP is allocated to the "social budget." Those in employment are also protected, with respect to both their jobs and their wage incomes, as negotiated by the social partners, the trade unions and the employers' associations. Germany's labor market is heavily regulated. The social partners have a strong position arising from legal stipulations; they have been granted the right to define norms and set the nominal wage rate. In addition, people are protected against the implications of competition by the institutional forms of governance in the German system. Reliance is placed on a non-market type of decision-making, as in the management of firms through codetermination by the employees' and union representatives in the supervisory boards of directors and in the workers' councils, the allocation of capital through a bank-based system with intermediated products, and the formation of human capital, especially in universities, via a governmental administrative planning approach. Codetermination restrains the influence of market forces in firms; mediated products are a substitute for market products in the capital market, and human capital formation is government dominated.

The government has a strong impact on the German economy in other areas as well: half of GDP (including social security) passes through it. In all of these domains, consensus plays a central role in the system of governance. The government itself is organized as a federal state, with tax revenue shared between the federal states (distributive federalism) and with two parliamentary chambers, one of which—the *Bundesrat*—represents the federal states (*Länder*). Many laws require the concurrence of both chambers, so that here too consensus is required.

THE HISTORIC ROAD TO PROSPERITY

With a population of 82 million inhabitants and a GDP of €2.1 billion, Germany is Europe's largest economy, producing nearly a quarter of the European Union's GDP and nearly a third of the GDP of the euro currency area (data for 2002). It is the third largest economy in the world, accounting for 6 percent of world GDP (2000)—one fifth the magnitude of the US share and less than half that of Japan. Accounting for 9.5 percent of world exports, Germany comes second in world trade after the United States.

GDP per capita is €26 000 in current values (2002), slightly above the EU-15 average (104 percent at current prices) and at about the same level as France, Italy, and the United Kingdom, but somewhat lower than some of the smaller EU members, e.g., Austria, Denmark, the Netherlands, and Ireland. GDP per capita at current prices and at the current exchange rate is about the same as that of Japan, but lower than that of other countries, e.g., the United States (at 142 percent of the EU level), Switzerland, and Norway. According to calculations of the World Bank,[1] Germany's relative ranking in GDP per capita in current prices stands at position 20, and in purchasing power parity at 21. Without question, Germany belongs to the rich industrialized countries of the world—in other words, the high-income countries.

Germany has experienced an admirable increase in prosperity. Its per capita GDP of about €4350 in 1950 rose by a factor of nearly six to €24 057 in 2002 in constant prices.[2] GDP growth rates were high in the first three decades after World War II, at 8.2 percent in the 1950s, 4.4 percent in the 1960s, and 2.8 percent in the 1970s. It also enjoyed a high growth rate in labor productivity per hour, with rates of 5.3 percent in the 1960s and 3.7 percent in the 1970s (table 1.1).

[1] World Bank (2002: table 11).
[2] DM8535.88 (in constant 1991 prices), equivalent to €4364.33.

TABLE 1.1
Growth rates of GDP per capita, GDP and labor productivity per hour[a]

	1950–60	1960–70	1970–80	1980–90	1991–2000	2000–2003
GDP/capita	7.1	3.5	2.6	2.0	1.3	0.2
GDP	8.2	4.4	2.8	2.3	1.6	0.3
Labor productivity per hour	4.7[b]	5.3	3.7	2.6	2.1	1.2

Source: Federal Statistical Office, Volkswirtschaftliche Gesamtrechnungen, Fachserie 18, Reihe 1.2.

[a] Calculated as an exponential growth rate for a decade, i.e., with 1980 and 1990 as the end point (10 periods).

[b] Productivity per capita.

The first three decades after World War II were devoted to the process of catching up with the United States. The country's institutional setup was beneficial for growth. In 1948 Ludwig Erhard freed prices, which ended the rationing of the product markets. Quickly, the economy was opened up to international competition. Nationalization of basic industries, especially coal and steel, was not pursued, although this had been considered, temporarily, even by the Christian Democrats. Establishing the Deutschmark as a stable currency made possible convertibility, first for foreigners and then for residents. Germans, hard-working and success-oriented, saw their dreams coming true—the first vacation abroad, the first motorcycle, their own home. In a way, in these years of the *Wirtschaftswunder* Germans experienced positive surprises, in that the economic system generated a higher income and a larger bundle of consumption goods than people had hoped for. Even wages increased by more in real terms than the social partners had negotiated; there was a positive wage drift through the market forces. This was a period of positive surprise. In such a period, today's success is the fuel for greater effort tomorrow.

A LOWER GROWTH PATH SINCE 1980

The two oil crises in 1973/74 and 1979/80, though causing a serious shock to the German economy with the two ensuing recessions, did not seem to have changed the pattern of growth, at first; three million additional jobs were generated in the 1980s, and many economic indicators improved in the second part of that decade. Nevertheless the year 1980, with the second oil shock, and the following recession in 1982 can be viewed as a turning point of Germany's economic development. The increase in GDP per capita became smaller, falling to 2.0 percent in the 1980s,[3] and the economy moved to a lower potential growth path of around 2.5 percent. Labor productivity was growing at a similarly low rate after 1980, by which time productivity growth had halved relative to the 1960s and was substantially lower than in the 1970s. The economic system had changed its economic properties without the politicians and the public really noticing.

Looking at economic growth for the united Germany from 1991 (the first year for which we have GDP data for the reunified country) onward, the annual growth rate for the period 1991–2000 was only 1.3 percent. This figure is somewhat distorted, since the high growth rates of 1990 (in West Germany) and of 1991 (in reunified Germany) are not included. If one were to take the 1990 West German GDP as the base value, the annual GDP growth rate for the period 1990–2000 would amount to 3.0 percent. However in this procedure, unification or the addition of East Germany to the German economy would be interpreted as growth. This rate would be way too high. If we include the West German growth rate of 1991 (5.1 percent), the growth rate for the period 1990–2000 would amount to 2.0 percent instead of 1.3 for the period 1991–2000. For 1995–2002 these statistical problems are no longer relevant; moreover, the deep recession of 1992 does not affect these data; for this period Germany's GDP growth rate was only 1.2 percent.

Over a longer duration of five decades, the high rates of about 8 percent or more in the years between 1951–56, 1959, and 1960 could no longer be reached. Since 1980, rates over 4 percent were registered only in 1990 and 1991, the years of the German unification boom (figure 1.1). The GDP growth rate continued its decline. Even if a recovery in 2004 and 2005 changes the bleak picture somewhat, there is a clear secular trend of a steadily decreasing growth rate.

AN OPEN ECONOMY

A widely accepted principle of German economic strategy has been the openness of its economy, that is, its free trade policy. In spite of the subsidization of some sectors such as coal mining and agriculture, protectionism

[3] Growth rates are calculated according to the formula

$$r = [(Y_{90}/Y_{80})^{(0.1/n)} - 1] \times 100$$

where n is the number of periods and, as an example, 90 and 80 are the end- and start-years of the period.

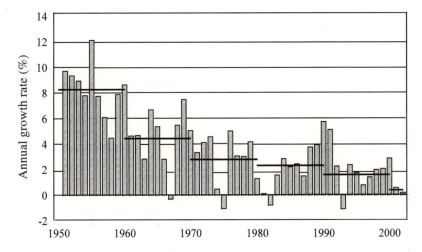

Figure 1.1 Annual growth rates, averages for decades. Until 1990, data for West Germany; since 1991, data for unified Germany. *Source*: Federal Statistical Office.

was never attractive in post-war Germany. Having joined the GATT in 1951, and with current trade policy being implemented at the European level, the principle of an open economy is by now well entrenched.

Germany has an export share of 35.5 percent of its GDP (2002). The overwhelming part of its exports—42 percent—go into the euro area and 55 percent are sold to the 15 EU countries (not all EU countries are part of the euro area); if the ten new member states of European Union enlargement are included, this share would be 64 percent. About 10 percent of exports are bought by the United States, another 10 percent by other industrialized countries, and still another 10 percent by the countries of central and eastern Europe (including the new EU members). Smaller portions are shipped to South East Asia (5 percent) and Latin America (2.5 percent) (2001).

The share of West German exports in its GDP increased steadily from the end of World War II, from 13.7 percent in 1950 to 18.0 percent in 1951, 19.0 percent in 1960,[4] 21.2 percent in 1970, 26.4 percent in 1980, and 32.1 in 1990 (figure 1.2). It then fell for the united Germany to 22.8 percent in 1993 before rising again beyond its 1990 level. Clearly, Germany has successfully integrated itself into the international division of labor. Free trade has been the vehicle by which it has managed to increase its well-being.

Germany's technology-based industry provides almost 90 percent of the country's exports, of which a large part is investment goods: 59

---

[4] There is a structural break in the data in 1960. Older data for 1960 show a larger share.

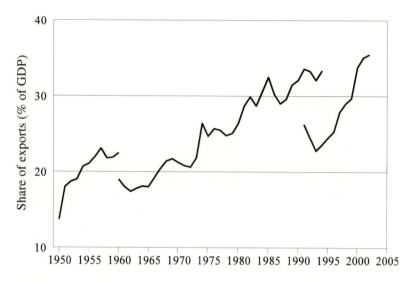

Figure 1.2 Share of exports, 1950-2002 (percent of GDP). Calculated as nominal exports to nominal GDP. At 1960 there is a structural break in the data. *Source*: Federal Statistical Office, Series 7 and 18.

percent of exports stem from four industrial sectors—machine building, automobile, chemicals, and electro-technical products; only 10 percent of exports are services.

Germany has hardly any natural resources except for coal, wood, and a few minerals. Its industrial base traditionally depended on the engineering ideas and innovative performance, on entrepreneurial spirit, on the organizational capabilities of its people, and on the skills and the effort of its workers. Raw materials and energy had to, and still have to, be imported; energy accounts for 5 percent of total imports. Foodstuffs make up 11 percent of all imports, 9 percent are intermediate products. The bulk of imports are consumer goods and investment goods. This holds especially for trade within the same sector (intra-industry or intra-sectoral trade), where many products, from cars to investment goods, are similar and thus represent both export goods and import goods. The coefficient of intra-industry trade at the two-digit level is at 0.74, higher than in for the United States (0.68) and Japan (0.45) (data for 2000).

The current account was slightly negative in the 1990s, but the balance has been in a surplus since 2001. A larger surplus, amounting to over 4 percent of GDP, was reached in the late 1980s when Germany was a net capital exporter like Japan. As a result of German unification, there was a swing in the external position, from a positive 4.6 percent of GDP in 1989 to a negative 1.2 percent in 1991.

The contribution of trade to growth can be interpreted from both the demand side and the supply side. In the short run, and viewed from the demand side, the contribution of trade stems from net exports, i.e., from a surplus in the trade balance. Positive net exports have a positive impact, as exports stimulate aggregate demand and offset imports, which represent a leakage in the traditional Keynesian analysis. From this point of view, a positive trade balance represents a positive contribution to the growth rate, its contribution being measured by the Lundberg component. A negative trade balance reduces the growth rate, and a balanced trade account has no demand effect on growth. Traditionally, in the German case an upswing in the business cycle is stimulated by an increase in export demand, which is then followed by a pick-up of investment and eventually leads to less uncertainty, in terms of employment, and to higher income, so that consumer demand increases as well. In the long run, and viewed from the supply side, trade has an impact on growth through different channels. Imports increase the set of available consumption goods; they also enlarge the production capacity of the economy by making intermediate inputs, investment goods and new technology available to the firms. Trade allows specialization gains and enhances the accumulation of growth factors.

THE ENTERPRISE SECTOR

Looking at the production side of the German economy, 22.2 percent of total gross value added came from industry in 2002, a further 6.8 percent from the other producing sectors, and 1.1 percent from agriculture. The bulk of gross value added, 70.1 percent, was generated in the service sector. Within the service sector, 30.4 percent came from financing, housing, and services to firms, 18.0 percent from retail, trading, hotels, and restaurants and 6.1 percent from public sector services.

Of the German firms, the larger German multinationals such as Allianz, Bayer, BMW, DaimlerChrysler, Siemens, and Volkswagen are recognized internationally. Out of the 20 largest firms as measured by their employees, 8 are in the export-oriented German industry, 3 of which are car producers (table 1.2); 4 are in the service sector; and another 4 in retail and trading. A few of these, like Lufthansa, are multinationals, but most are oriented toward the home market. Together with the two large energy suppliers on this list of the 20 largest German firms, the nontradable sector is strongly represented.

It is important to make a clear distinction between the performance of the German firms and the status of the German economy. The German multinationals generate a large part of their value added abroad; this

TABLE 1.2
The twenty largest German firms

Rank	Firm	Sector	Employment ('000)
1	Siemens	Industry	445
2	Deutsche Post	Service	372
3	DaimlerChrysler	Industry	356
4	Volkswagen	Industry	325
5	Deutsche Telekom	Service	256
6	Deutsche Bahn	Service	251
7	Bosch	Industry	224
8	Edeka	Trading	200
9	Metro	Trading	192
10	Thyssen-Krupp	Industry	191
11	Rewe	Trading	187
12	Tengelmann	Trading	183
13	Allianz	Financing	182
14	RWE	Energy	132
15	Bayer	Industry	123
16	EON	Energy	110
17	Karstadt-Quelle	Trading	106
18	BMW	Industry	101
19	Lufthansa	Service	94
20	BASF	Industry	89

Source: Frankfurter Allgemeine Zeitung, July 8, 2003.

production is not included in the German GDP, whereas production by foreign firms in Germany does count towards the German GDP. Likewise, employment by German firms is not identical to employment in Germany. Whereas German firms are efficient according to international standards, this does not imply that targets of economic policy such as full employment are met in Germany.

It would be misleading to attempt to understand Germany's enterprise sector by looking solely at these 20 large firms. Among the larger firms are other international players, such as Bertelsmann with 81 000 employees, Deutsche Bank with 77 000 employees, and MAN with 75 000 employees. The ranks of firms smaller in size are densely populated with, for instance, Boehringer Ingelheim at position 25 of the industrial firms in terms of revenue (32 000 employees), Freudenberg, a family-dominated enterprise (28 000 employees) at position 49, Braun (29 000) at rank 66, Miele (15 000) at position 80, and Brose Fahrzeugbau (7000), a firm producing car seats and car doors, at ranking 100.

Analyzing the structure of firms in more detail, and looking at it from the revenue side, 2.6 million out of 2.9 million enterprises, or

89.4 percent, have an annual revenue of less than €1 million (data for 2000); 300 000 enterprises, or 10.3 percent, have an annual revenue of between 1 million and 50 million euro; 7700 companies, or 0.3 percent, have a revenue of more than 50 million euro. From the point of view of employment, there are 2.15 million businesses[5] paying social security contributions for their employees (table 1.3). Of these, 18.2 percent are businesses with fewer than 10 employees, 60.2 percent businesses employing between 10 and 499 people, and 21.6 percent businesses employing 500 or more.

There is no doubt that small and medium-sized firms play an important role in the German economy. Enterprises with an annual revenue of less than €50 million account for 43.2 percent of total revenue of all firms; businesses with less 500 employees make up 78.4 percent of total employment according to the social security statistics. The role of small and medium-sized firms for total employment becomes even more apparent if employees exempted from social security, especially the self employed, are taken into consideration. Furthermore, small and medium-sized businesses train more than 80 percent of all apprentices and are also an important reservoir for upcoming entrepreneurs.

Small and medium-sized firms make up the *Mittelstand*. In a narrow interpretation, the Mittelstand may be defined as all those firms with an annual revenue of €50 million or less, or with fewer than 500 employees. In a broader interpretation, however, the concept of "Mittelstand" includes larger firms and implies other characteristics as well. One is that in these firms private ownership of the entrepreneur plays an important role, and that the owner-entrepreneur is the driving force of the enterprise. The legal form of such firms often is not a stock company, but another option of limiting liability, such as a limited liability company (GmbH) or the alternative with more personal liability, a non-incorporated company (e.g., a sole proprietorship or partnership with individual liability) where transparency requirements are less strict. As a rule, the more important firms of the Mittelstand are technological specialists in their field; they are built around a technological idea, often stemming from the owner-entrepreneur or developed further by him. Whereas some of the medium-sized firms are outsourced legal units of larger firms, or may be completely dependent on a single buyer as in the automobile industry,[6] quite a few have their own international independent position. This applies to, for example, medium-sized enterprises like

---

[5] The term "business" is here used for the German term *Betrieb*. *Betrieb* is the economic unit of an enterprise at a location. A *Betrieb* may be part of an enterprise, the legal unit, or it may be an enterprise itself.

[6] How important this group of the Mittelstand is, relative to the dependent firms, especially in the automobile industry, is hard to say.

TABLE 1.3
Businesses in Germany according to size, 2000[a]

Employees	Number of businesses	Number of employees	Percent of employees
Small businesses			
1–9	1 728 716	5 064 101	18.2
Medium-sized businesses	416 499	16 759 991	60.2
10–19	205 706	2 756 042	9.9
20–49	129 296	3 908 517	14.0
50–99	46 442	3 204 874	11.5
100–499	35 055	6 890 558	24.8
Large businesses			
500 and more	4 980	6 001 532	21.6
Total	2 150 195	27 825 624	100

Source: German Council of Economic Advisors (2002), Annual Report 2002/03, p. 220.
[a] Employees paying social security contributions in businesses.

the saw producer Stihl, the hydraulic systems producer Sauer-Danfoss, the investment good producer Trumph, the cigarette machine maker Hauni, the producer of furniture machines Homag, and the tunneling machines producer and operator Herrenknecht. These are all firms that employ between 7000 and 1200 people and have an annual revenue of between €1.5 and €0.3 billion per year. Most of them have a market niche in the world market for a very specific product, normally in machine construction.

The Mittelstand has been called the backbone of the German economy. Although it is hard to imagine German industry as consisting of the firms of the Mittelstand alone, without the larger players, the description of them as a backbone seems justified when one looks at employment. The Mittelstand is also unique in the sense that, instead of having hired managers, as in the incorporated large enterprises, entrepreneurial effort of the owner-entrepreneur plays a decisive role. Politically, this group is more sensitive to changes in taxation or regulation than, say, the managers of large stock companies. There tends to be a more direct response from the Mittelstand to changes in governmental policy such as taxation and regulation. Here indeed may lie an important difference between the reality of the German economy and the economic drawing board of quite a few governmental interventionists and governmental decision makers. But it seems that this reality, i.e., the existence of a large group of small and medium-sized firms with their entrepreneurs, is typical for other countries in Europe as well, including France, Italy, and the United Kingdom.

SOME MACROECONOMIC DATA

Viewing the German economy through the macroeconomic looking glass, consumption demand of private households accounts for 57 percent of aggregate demand on the expenditure side of GDP; consumption demand of government is 19 percent, and investment demand is 18 percent (data for 2002). Net exports or the trade balance,[7] the remaining components of aggregate demand, account for nearly 4 percent of GDP.

The major part of the €379 billion of investment in 2002 is in buildings (about 57 percent), while about 40 percent is for investment in equipment—the most volatile element of investment, and at the same time the driving force in the ups and downs of the business cycle. Investment here means gross investment, including the replacement of existing capital, financed from depreciation; net investment is normally one quarter of gross investment.

The tax share is 23.2 percent of GDP; taxes and contributions to the social security system make up 40.8 percent; and the share of government spending is 49.2 percent. The budget deficit has increased in recent years, amounting to 3.9 percent of GDP in 2003. Social absorption is high: the social budget, which encompasses all expenditures with a social objective, absorbs one third of what is annually produced. Government debt, at 64.2 percent of GDP in 2003, has doubled in the 1990s.

National income, i.e., GDP minus depreciations and production taxes plus subsidies, was €1.57 billion (2002), of which 82 percent went to labor (including the self-employed) and about 70 percent to the dependently employed; the remainder was interest income and profits of firms. The disposable income of households, i.e., national income minus direct taxes and net contributions to social security (contributions minus transfers received), is €1.3 billion. This goes on consumption and savings.

Households save 10.8 percent of their disposable income (2003). Drawing a rather broad picture and not going too much into the details, savings of the private sector (households and firms), including depreciation, amounted to 22.5 percent of GDP (€474.84 billion[8]) in 2002, whereas investment of the private sector was 16.5 percent (€346.85 billion). Excess savings of the private sector of 6 percent of GDP (€127.99 billion) finance a budget deficit of government of

[7] Note that net exports are not identical to the current account.
[8] *Statistisches Bundesamt*, Series l. 18, no. 1.2, table p. 25

3.6 percent of GDP (€76.19 billion), i.e., its dissaving, and the current account surplus of 2.4 percent (€50.39 billion). Note that the budget deficit of the government is used partly to finance government investment. The relationship described here reflects the external financing constraint of the economy, well known to students of international economics, namely $S - I - D = CA$, where S and I are gross savings and gross investment of the private sector, D is the government's budget deficit, and CA is the current account. In our figures for 2002, this equation reads: $22.5 - 16.5 - 3.6 = 2.4$. Note that, unlike the United States, Germany does not have a twin deficit in the public budget and in the current account.

EMPLOYMENT

Germany has 38.3 million employees, including 4.1 million self-employed (2003). That means that less than 50 percent of the population is working. The participation rate, calculated as those in work plus the unemployed as a proportion of the entire population, stands at 51 percent. The participation rate of women, calculated as the employed plus unemployed in the 15–65 age group as a proportion of the total number of women in that age group, is much lower than that of men (65 vs 80 percent, respectively). Therefore, there is a potential for an increase in the supply of labor. Of the 34.3 million who were dependently employed in 2003, 24.6 million were fully employed and 9.3 were working part-time, implying a part-time ratio of 27 percent.

Unemployment stood at 4.4 million in 2003, or 10.5 percent of all employable persons, according to the German definition of unemployment. This amounts to 9.3 percent under the internationally standardized EU calculation. Unemployment in eastern Germany was 18.6 percent. In mid-2003 unemployment was highest in the labor office district of Neubrandenburg in Mecklenburg-West Pomerania at 24.8 percent, while the lowest rate was in Freising, Bavaria, at 4.1 percent. The labor office district of Suhl in Thuringia had the lowest unemployment rate in East Germany at 13.8 percent; the highest unemployment rate in West Germany was in Gelsenkirchen, in the Ruhr area of North Rhine-Westphalia, at 15.4 percent.

In addition to the official unemployment rate, the German Council of Economic Advisers also considers as unemployed those persons who are in various governmental schemes, i.e., who are not active in the "first" labor market.[9] In this context, the Federal Labor Office funds job-creating measures, training programs, and early retirement. If these

[9] Council of Economic Advisers, 2003, table 26.

are included—1.6 million people in 2003—the unemployment rate jumps to 13.9 percent in 2003, and to about 25 percent in eastern Germany.

The unemployed tend to have a weak skill base; one-third of them have no formal training in an occupation, and some have not finished German high school. Some further individuals are unemployed because of illness. Unemployment has proven to be a persistent problem for Germany. The long-term unemployed, i.e., those unemployed for more than one year, account for 35 percent of the total unemployed (August 2003), 42.5 percent in eastern Germany and 31.3 percent in the West. If, instead of simply taking the numbers of the unemployed, one weights these numbers by the duration of unemployment, the long-term unemployed account for 64 percent of the total unemployed, and those who are unemployed for three months or less for 5 percent. From a policy point of view, therefore, it is necessary to be able to reduce long-term unemployment. The unemployment rate of those under 20 years of age is 5.4 percent, for those under 25 10.8 percent; among foreign workers, the unemployment rate is more than 20 percent.[10]

Sectoral Change

Germany has seen major changes in its economy since the end of World War II. A consideration of these changes helps us to understand how the German economy functions. One of the major changes was the country's integration into the world economy, as we have already seen in the significant increase in exports relative to GDP. Accompanying this higher degree of openness was a remarkable structural change, which is reflected in the relative decline of industry or manufacturing (*verarbeitendes Gewerbe*) from 38.1 percent of employment in 1970 to 22.4 percent in 2002; the percentage of value added is similar. The wider delineation of the producing sector or the production industries (*produzierendes Gewerbe*), also including mining, energy supply and construction, fell from 47.9 percent of employment or 12.5 million in 1960 to 27.8 or 10.8 million in 2002, whereas the employment in the service sector increased from 38.4 to 69.7 percent (figure 1.3). There has been a continuous shift away from the industrial economy, first to a service economy and lately to the information (IT) or knowledge-based economy. Employment in mining, which is part of the producing sector, fell from over 650 000 in the mid-1950s to 108 000 in united Germany. (The sector today includes the quarrying of stone.) Agriculture too has decreased in importance, with its current share in total employment standing at just

[10] 21.8 in July 2003.

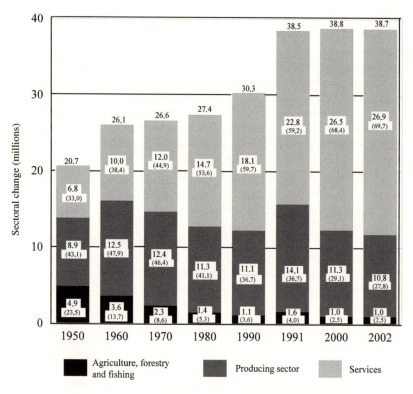

Figure 1.3 Sectoral change in employment (millions). Numbers in parentheses indicate percentage of total employment. *Source*: Federal Statistical Office, Series 1 and 18.

1 percent. It should be noted that part of this statistically observed structural change reflects the outsourcing of activities from industry, for instance to escape the branch labor contracts, but also to shift cost risks to other firms.

Such structural change is a necessary adjustment in an open economy, but it has meant that well-paid jobs have disappeared in the industrial sector. In 2001 the united Germany had more than half a million jobs fewer in industry than West Germany in 1990. This not only implies that labor demand has been reduced; it also reveals a need for drastic adjustment in the lives of workers, who can no longer rely on life-long employment in one job but must face up to the possibility of having to retrain and invest in new qualifications. Where this is not possible, and where the relative wage structure is not flexible enough, unemployment is likely to follow when a shock to the sectoral structure occurs. Moreover, the structural change means that labor relations have changed.

The dominant structural transformation from agriculture to industry, and then to the service sector, required by the high degree of openness of the economy affected the industrial regions, especially the Ruhr and the Saar, with their intense concentration on coal and steel. Baden-Württemberg and Bavaria, formerly ridiculed for their "dwarf schools" in the villages and as people in the backwoods (*Hinterwäldler*), went through a long-term catching-up process lasting three to four decades. Ultimately, they overtook the North, as northern Germany experienced a decline of its traditional heavy industry, especially in ship building; while this could be overcome in a city like Hamburg, with its new specialization in the media including television (moreover, Hamburg regained its traditional position as an economic center with German unification), other parts of northern Germany saw a relative decline.

Past Challenges and Shocks

After World War II Germany was separated into two different states, one belonging to the market-oriented Western world and one to the Eastern world of central planning and public ownership of firms. In both parts of Germany the economy had to be rebuilt, but the two states developed separately and quite differently. West Germany absorbed the refugees from the former eastern parts of the country equaling about 8 million, or one sixth of its population (data for 1949). The Erhard reforms paved the way for a market economy, for a system open to international competition, and for competition policy. Whereas economic success came about quickly in the West, East Germany experienced a major upheaval on June 17, 1953, with the uprising of construction and industrial workers who were unwilling to accept the more stringent labor norms and the changes in the food stamps decreed by the Politburo. These changes, including higher production quotas of farmers and the exclusion of still independent craftsmen, coupled with the worsened living conditions, led to extreme dissatisfaction. East Germany found that it could not retain its inhabitants, who were attracted to West Germany, as long as they were allowed to move freely to West Berlin: until the Berlin Wall was constructed in 1961, the German Democratic Republic experienced an exodus of 3.8 million people. Those who remained were then walled in, and thereby prevented from leaving the country; at the same time, they were restrained in their travel options internationally to the eastern bloc of the Comecon countries. In spite of the Wall, however, an exodus of about 22 000 people annually[11] continued, and in the late 1980s this swelled to reach nearly 400 000 in both 1989 and 1990.

[11] 616 000 people between 1961 and 1988.

The West German economy, meanwhile, was experiencing other major shocks and changes. A definitive turning point was the student revolts of the late 1960s, when the younger generation expressed its deep dissatisfaction with the West German way of life—with the demands, pressures, and constraints of Germany's economic system; its institutional setting, including the traditional and closed system of the universities; its political system; and the political orientation of its society. As in other countries, the Vietnam War was a major catalyst. Suddenly, as a new and noticeable political force, there was an opposition outside parliament, with a new preference function whereby leisure ("Make love...") and other hedonistic aspects were major goals.

All this affected Germany's political and cultural values. First, it led to a substitution of the political elites by the "sixty-eighters," who are now in political command and represent values quite different from those of the previous generation. At times there was a "Tuscany fraction"[12] in the Social Democratic Party and in parts of the Green Movement, expressing these new values. Second, politics reacted to the student unrest with reforms in an attempt to integrate the new sentiment. This gave rise to the reform policy under Brandt in the 1970s, but also to a strong expansion of the welfare state. Third, a specific response of politics to changing times was an increased participation of non-governmental groups in the decisions of society—for instance, of trade unions and workers in firms and of students in the universities. Fourth, the overall restraints of the economy were loosened in the public's perception, which implied that the steering of the economic system became less efficient. Only today it is it being rediscovered that Germany's preference shift for leisure, welfare, and participation has serious implications, for instance for future generations.

Independent of this, but partly related to it, a new topic of German politics has evolved with the issue of environmental policy, raised by academics as early as the 1970s (Siebert 1973) and then brought into the political arena by the Greens in the 1980s. This issue came to the fore in a country that is so densely populated that everyone is affected by air and water pollution. Although the high growth rates of the 1960s and 1970s were reached without the need to pay too much attention to environmental degradation, the Germans' high per capita income allowed them to take environmental quality into account. Environmental awareness redefined the abundance of the environment and of nature; and, of course, this involved adjustment costs for the economy as a whole.

In terms of macroeconomics, Germany has experienced four recessions, by the criterion that for a country to be in recession its annual

---

[12] This group of politicians was so dubbed because of their preference for vacations in the Italian province of Tuscany and its life style.

GDP growth rate has to be negative for at least one year (see figure 1.1). The 1967 downturn, with a negative rate of 0.3 percent and with an unemployment rate of just 2.1 percent, was only a minor recession compared with the dire situation in 2003, but it was the first recession in an environment in which everyone was accustomed to high growth rates. The Social Democratic economics minister Schiller applied the concept of macroeconomic stabilization according to the prevailing Keynesian mind-set of the time. The idea of a "concerted action" was born, which entailed an attempt to harmonize the actions of the social partners, the trade union, and the employers' association. The "Stability Law" was introduced with the aim of satisfying the four major targets of economic policy: price level stability, high employment, external equilibrium, and steady and satisfactory growth. This approach led to the establishment of the German Council of Economic Advisers.[13]

The next two recessions were linked to the two oil crises, i.e., two negative external supply shocks. In 1975 GDP fell by 1.05 percent. Oil prices quadrupled, thus making energy, an important factor of production, considerably more expensive. As in other oil-importing industrial countries, the existing capital stock of the German economy became partly obsolete, since it had been formed under the low oil prices of the 1960s. The marginal productivity of capital fell, and the production capacity of the economy was reduced. All this shifted the supply curve of the economy to the left. The terms of trade, i.e., the relative price between exportables and importables, deteriorated, and on the demand side real income was transferred from Germany to the oil producing countries. This meant an unrecoverable loss of purchasing power. The trade unions attempted to make up for this loss by demanding high wage increases, amounting for instance to 11 percent in 1974 for the public sector. There can be no question that under these circumstances the inflation rate was high: it reached 7.0 percent in 1974. At the same time, the unemployment rate started to rise. Two targets of economic policy were violated, and stagflation became the economic policy maker's new challenge.

In 1982 the repercussions of the second oil crisis hit the German economy, which saw a decline of GDP by 0.79 percent; it had increased by only 0.11 percent in 1981. The current account had turned negative in 1980, and the German mark saw a depreciation in nominal terms in the late 1970s as a result of the second oil crisis. Inflation went up, and unemployment rose once more, to top 9 percent in the aftermath of the recession in 1983–85. Again, Germany found itself in a stagflation.

[13] The Council uses this as an official translation of the Sachverständigenrat Council of Economic Experts. It seems to me that the translation is misleading.

The final recession occurred after the German unification boom in 1993, when the country experienced a negative growth rate of 1.09. The main reason for this was a general slump in the world economy in 1992; its impact hit Germany one year later because the unification boom had put the German economy under steam, representing a Keynesian demand pull.

In terms of economic growth, the second part of the 1980s can be considered a successful period for Germany (as, of course, was the catching-up phase that lasted up to 1970). The growth rate gained momentum, with an average of over 4 percent in 1988–90, and investment was strong. About 3 million new jobs were added in the 1980s once the recession and unemployment had receded in the second part of the decade. In spite of some moderation of wage demands by the trade unions, compared to those of the 1970s real income of workers increased. The inflation rate came down, so that price level stability was established. The budget deficit was balanced in 1989, a tax reform was implemented in several steps, and the current account reached a surplus of 4.9 percent of GDP. Two of the major policy players—the central bank and fiscal policy—had done their homework; the social partners were more employment-oriented than in the prior decade. Even with some criticism of the wage policy, this was a good example of how to approach the problem of assigning responsibilities to the different players. Germany has yet to match such a period of positive development since then.

GERMAN UNIFICATION

German unification was, of course, a stroke of luck in a historical sense, and it represented a major change in the economic conditions of Germany. For the former East Germany, it meant a drastic new environment for the lives of the inhabitants—the state-owned firms had to be privatized; production had to be oriented towards the markets of the West; and new capital stock had to be built up in the business sector, in the infrastructure, and in housing.

The transformation of eastern Germany did not go as well as had been initially expected. Hopes that the German *Wirtschaftswunder* of the early 1950s could be replicated did not materialize. In the first place, investment in eastern Germany was not a bottleneck problem, as had been the case in West Germany after 1945, when the repair of a single bridge over the river Rhine represented a huge productivity boost: in eastern Germany the whole capital stock had to be rebuilt. Second, there was a great deal of uncertainty with respect to the property rights in the first years of transformation. Third, the whole enterprise sector had to be privatized.

In addition to these challenges, serious policy mistakes were made. First, exchanging the East German mark 1:1 for the West German mark in the German Monetary Union implied an appreciation of the East German mark by some 400 percent. This adjustment was too much for any firm to handle, let alone inefficient ones used to central planning. Second, the exchange of 1:1 had a negative effect in that it formed the wrong expectations, with a devastating impact on wage negotiations; people assumed that social absorption could be financed without any repercussions. Third, applying the West German institutional arrangement of collective bargaining to eastern Germany and letting the West German unions and the West German employers' association do the wage bargaining meant that, together with the inflated expectations, wages quickly grew out of line with productivity; unit labor costs were at 140 percent of the West German level in 1991 and stayed above 100 percent thereafter (table 1.4). This meant that eastern Germany was less attractive for investment. Fourth, using the West German institutional arrangement in a transformation economy—not only for the labor market, but also for product market regulation, the university system, and taxation—was a serious mistake.[14] By imposing West German institutional conditions, East Germany was not able to adopt its own approaches to enhancing its competitive position, such as establishing a more competitive university system as a leapfrogging basis for a new technological production platform. It was not allowed to find its own solutions or to determine its own priorities. As a major example, wages were negotiated by the West German social partners, whose interests, namely to protect their own position by imposing a similar arrangement on the incoming region, were counter-productive for eastern Germany. Fifth, all four of the above issues, especially the exchange rate conversion and wage policy, were reasons for high consumptive transfers, i.e., transfers that will not end up in investment but in consumption. These took place within the government sector, including the social insurance system.

In terms of GDP per capita (of the population, which is different from output per employee), GDP per capita in eastern Germany, excluding Berlin, was 62.7 percent of the West German figure, also excluding Berlin, in 2001; it had started out at 33 percent in 1991. From a historic dimension, this is quite an achievement. In a policy oriented approach, however, it does not make sense to exclude Berlin from the East German region since it lies in the middle of eastern Germany. If it is included, the

---

[14] An exemption is the law on large transportation infrastructure projects, where legal restraints can be overruled by parliamentary decision of the East German Länder.

TABLE 1.4
East German wages, labor productivity, and unit labor cost (% of the West German level[a])

	1991	1992	1993	1994	1995	1996	1997	1998	1999	2000	2001	2002
Wage income[b,c]	49.3	61.9	69.2	72.6	75.2	75.8	76.1	76.3	77.1	77.2	77.3	77.6
Labor productivity[c,d]	34.9	48.3	59.4	64.2	65.0	67.0	68.0	67.7	68.4	69.2	70.7	71.5
Unit labor costs[c,e]	141.1	128.3	116.3	113.2	115.7	113.1	111.8	112.6	112.7	111.7	109.8	108.5

Source: German Economic Research Institutes (2003), p. 55.
[a] West Germany = 100 in each year West Germany including Berlin).
[b] Wage income including contributions to social security of employees and workers.
[c] Data for eastern Germany: new *Bundesländer* without Berlin, March 2003.
[d] GDP in current prices per person engaged in economic activity.
[e] Wage income per employee created (*Inlandkonzept*) in relation to the GDP, in current prices per person engaged in economic activity.

East German GDP per capita is now 66.2 percent of the West German level, or 71.2 percent of the overall German level. Taking into account that other German Länder such as the Rhineland-Palatinate, Lower Saxony and Schleswig-Holstein reach 80–85 percent of the West German level, eastern Germany has attained a remarkable level of GDP per capita.

The manufacturing sector in eastern Germany has exhibited sizable growth rates in its net output, reaching 10 percent in real terms in 1998–2000, albeit starting from a low level; in 2001 and 2002 the rates have been positive, at 4.7 and 2.8 percent respectively, despite stagnation in the German economy in these years. In branches where new plants have been built, e.g., car production, IT, communications, and aerospace, high growth rates have been observed since 1991. In machine building, in the construction of railroad cars, in ship building, and in leather and textiles the rates have been negative (Ragnitz et al. 2001); in part this is because these branches have experienced strong structural change in West Germany as well.

From 1997 to 2003, the GDP growth rate of eastern Germany has been below the unified German rate. This means that the convergence process has stopped, and that we have divergence instead of convergence. It should be noted that out-migration is an important adjustment mechanism, which for an economist is a normal way of adjusting to different income conditions. Since 1989 about 1.4 million people have emigrated from East Germany (net emigration), most of them before and shortly after the fall of the Wall. Young people in particular have sought jobs in the West. While emigration has decreased considerably since before and just after the Wall fell, eastern Germany continues to lose people to the West: in 2001 net out-migration came to 98 000, and a further 627 000 commuted from East to West. This, of course, means that the GDP growth rate is reduced because of a lower labor input; at the same time, per capita rates become more favorable.

German unification required, and still requires, public transfers to the East. It is estimated that only one quarter of total transfers (neglecting interest and debt repayment) were used for investment, either in the private sector or for infrastructure; three quarters went toward consumption. The magnitude of the transfers is hard to estimate; they constituted between 3 and 4 percent of the German GDP in 1995, when the flows of the different governmental layers were consolidated and when the interest burden for debt was included (see chapter 12); the amounts have become considerably smaller since then. Transfers were financed to a large extent through credits, leading to a doubling of government debt. This has had an impact on Germany's fiscal policy stance, negatively affecting the German economic position. In addition, the transfers were organized within the social security system, which increased labor costs and reduced the demand for labor.

With respect to East Germany, two other developments represented a negative impact on growth there, with some repercussion in the united Germany. One was the over-expansion of the construction sector. This was generated by public subsidies for housing and for investment in firms, as well as by transfers for the public infrastructure in the early 1990s, and it created a massive distortion which eventually had to be corrected. Construction firms had to shrink by laying workers off; some firms went bankrupt. All this had a negative impact on the GDP growth rate in eastern Germany. Construction firms in the West were affected as well, so that the construction sector in united Germany pulled the German growth rate downward. The excess supply of office and apartment space in East Germany, a result of the distorting stimulation of the real estate sector through tax breaks, affected the positions of German banks, requiring large write-offs and bank bail-outs. Banks became more cautious in issuing credits.

The other process was a real appreciation in eastern Germany. Owing to transfers, the relative price for non-tradables expanded, reducing the attractiveness of tradables, i.e., of import substitutes and the export sector. That is to say, eastern Germany experienced a "Dutch Disease" phenomenon with an over-expansion of the service sector, to the detriment of industry as well as economic growth. This led to a real appreciation of the Deutschmark as a consequence of unification, which weakened Germany's competitive position in the world market.

THREE MAJOR POLICY FAILURES

There is no doubt that German unification has been—in economic terms—a shock to the German economy. Germany has been financially constrained in part by funding the transfers. But it would be misleading to assume that Germany's economic position would be completely different if the issue of the East German convergence were solved. German unification occurred in an environment in which long-run trends were already leading to three major policy failures rooted in unresolved, severe structural problems. First, since 1980 the economy has been on much lower growth path than previously, except for the late 1980s, and since 1995 the increase in its production capacity is around 1.5 percent, notably below 2 percent. It can no longer unfold sufficiently strong dynamics. Second, unemployment has ratcheted upward since 1970, from virtually full employment to a situation in which over 10 percent of the population is out of work; if those who are in government programs and who cannot find a job in the labor market are added to the number of the officially unemployed, the rate is 14 percent. Third, the social security system and its social absorption, as well as other aspects of the social budget, clearly can no longer be financed. This issue of financing will become even more acute with an ageing population. Moreover, the financing of the social security system represents a tax on labor, which not only lowers the demand for labor, and hence creates unemployment, but also calls into question the very economic foundation of the economy.

These three issues—low growth performance, high unemployment, and the financing limits of social security—are interrelated, creating a vicious circle. Unemployment is a reason for low growth, and weak economic dynamics partly explains the high unemployment. The problems of financing social security are linked to low growth, but at the same time are responsible for high unemployment. We will study these issues in more detail in the following chapters.

CHAPTER TWO

The Social Market Economy

Germany has developed its own, unique institutional approach to running the economy, encompassed under the concept of the "social market economy." This must be understood as an economic order attempting to meld the market approach and competition with social protection and equity. Soziale Marktwirtschaft is seen as an institutional arrangement whose main targets are, on the one hand, individual freedom and choice, and efficiency through decentralized autonomy in a competitive order, and on the other, equity and social protection.

THE HISTORICAL ROOTS

Germany's "social market economy" has its roots in the country's historical experience. The immediate historical background can be found in the Orwellian dictatorship of the Nazi regime, which repressed individual preferences and individual liberty. It is no wonder that at the end of World War II the German people longed for individual freedom. This orientation came to light again in the demonstrations in East Germany in the autumn of 1989, when people reminded the politicians that *Wir sind das Volk* (We are the people).

Another aspect of the negative experience of Germans with the state was the economic interventionism of the state and the planning mechanism, which became dominant in the two war economies and in the interwar years of the 1930s. The hyperinflation of 1923 and the repressed inflation of 1936–48, which became apparent in the currency reform of 1948 when the Reichmark was completely devalued and then abandoned, are yet another major area where the state failed. Furthermore, the extreme poverty that persisted during the years just after the war created a certain willingness to look for new solutions.

A further root can be found in the catholic philosophy of social ethics prevailing, for instance, in the Rhineland, Bavaria, and other regions of western Germany as well in the ethics of the Protestant Church. In these approaches equity, distribution, and the protection of the individual in a *Gemeinschaft*, i.e., a community, were the focal point. This thinking, which can be interpreted as the churches' answer to the problem of the alienation of the worker in the nineteenth century, was a strong source of the intellectual basis of the Christian Democratic Party and the Christian Social Union in Bavaria. Together with the traditional orientation of the Social Democrats to workers as their prime voters at the start of German reconstruction, this produced an orientation in which non-individualistic or social elements—one might also say collective approaches—gained importance. In addition, social elements, i.e., the organization into groups of different kinds, had their century-long tradition in German history.

These two lines are not necessarily in harmony. Societies and econo-mies may be organized either along the lines of individual freedom or according to collective principles. Of course, collective rules can be understood to guarantee individual freedom; that is, they may be inter-preted as exercising some restraint on the maneuvering space of an indi-vidual, with the basic aim of retaining individual liberty. Individual freedom then is the primary value. Alternatively, the collective norm may be considered the starting point from which, once it is defined, the individual takes as freedom what remains from the collective approach. Individual freedom then is simply a residual. Thus, a permanent dialogue between these orientations can be expected within the concept of the social market economy. Conflicts are sure to show up in specific economic conditions and in changing economic environments, for instance when an economy is assailed by negative shocks.

Basic Principles of the Constitution

The two lines of individual liberty and social elements come to light in the German Constitution, the *Grundgesetz*, in which the value orientation prevailing at the time of its conception was laid down. The consensus of the founding fathers of the Constitution stressed individual freedom, human dignity, and the subsidiarity of societal organization—but also the protection of the individual.[1]

Individual Liberty

Drawing on the German experience of dictatorship, and in accordance with the constitutional history of other European countries, the first arti-cles of the German Constitution define the rights of the individual. The

---

[1] On some details of the concept of the founding fathers of the social market economy introduced in 1948, see Müller-Armack (1999, 1978); Röpke (1963, 2002); Giersch (1991); Watrin (1979).

"dignity of man" (Article 1), "inviolable and inalienable human rights" (Article 1), "the right to the free development of one's personality" (Article 2), "the right freely to express and to publish one's opinion by speech" (Article 5), the "freedom of movement" (Article 11), the "rights of ownership and inheritance" (Article 14), and many other provisions show that the Grundgesetz is founded on a respect for the decisions of the individual. In terms of economics, the basic presumption of the Grundgesetz is that individual preferences count, and that therefore it is for the individual to decide. One should be free to choose what to consume, whether to consume or save, whether to work or enjoy leisure, which job to take, where to live, where to travel, and what to produce for someone else. These rights of the individual are a restraint in the classical sense that they shall not affect others negatively in their rights: no one is allowed to violate the rights of others (Article 2).

Equity

In addition to Article 2, the constitution also restrains the individual. The federal republic is a "social federal state" (*Sozialer Bundesstaat*, Article 20). The rights of property and of inheritance, though guaranteed in Section 1 of Article 14, are restricted by Section 2 of the same article. Property implies obligations; its use should simultaneously serve the interest of all. This is the social binding of private property. If members of the society are dependent on the use of a property, the right of the owner to do with the property what he wants is restrained. This holds for real estate by limiting the right of a landlord to give notice to a tenant, and by capping house rents. Equity enters other stipulations in the Constitution, such as preventing regional disparities in living conditions (Article 72). Moreover, de facto, there is a strong material protection of the individual, especially through a net of mandatory social insurance systems including unemployment, disability, old age insurance, health, and nursing care.

The Competitive Order

The German economic system has to respect these two aspects. A system that ultimately is geared toward the preferences of the individual must have an institutional mechanism by which the individual can voice his preferences. Besides the ability to vote in the political process, the institutional vehicle is the market or set of markets: the competitive order. If a market economy is established by an adequate institutional framework, the individual can vote with his purse and with his feet. He can thereby clearly signal his opportunity costs, and his marginal willingness to pay, by giving up income to purchase a specific product rather than alternative products, and by choosing one place to live over another one. Moreover, by deciding how many hours to work or not to work, he can indicate his evaluation of work and leisure.

Economic decentralization gives firms autonomy on decisions regarding production and investment. Markets signal the incentives to produce and to search for efficient solutions; they represent incentives to collect and reveal information and to look out for new technical knowledge and new investments (Hayek 1968).

The competitive order is not explicitly written down in the Constitution. It may be questioned whether it is a principle in its own right,[2] as stated by Eucken (1990: 254), who regarded it as the only basic principle. One may also take the view that the competitive order is instrumental in allowing individual liberties. Decentralization allows personal choice and provides options. Thus, decentralization is part of an open society (Popper 2003). Still other writers may link the competitive order to the overall target of efficiency or the economic principle.

But regulations of the product market and the factor markets, especially the labor market, limit and impede the role of competition. Moreover, the competitive process is substituted by institutional arrangements for cooperative decision-making, for instance by letting the social partners set the wages. The market as an allocation mechanism is altered in order to attain results that are seen as socially acceptable. In these areas, the conflict between the two major goals of the social market economy becomes apparent.

Major Trends in the Constitution

The Constitution was not changed after German reunification. Formally, the new Länder became a member of Germany by Article 23 of the Constitution, which contained the option of East Germany joining the Federal Republic of Germany. Nevertheless, it may be assumed that the unified Germany has somewhat different political preferences from the former West Germany. To some extent it has become more "protestant," more Prussian, in the sense of accepting hierarchical structures (and thus less individualistic), and more collective, in the sense that the idea of social protection has been retained by East Germans from the communist era.

When agreed upon, the new European Constitution proposed by the Convention in 2003 will define rights and specify equity targets and redistribution goals in addition to the national settings. It is a constitution very much in the spirit of the welfare state, distant from the notions of the

---

[2] Germans tend to become very *grundsätzlich* (fundamental) on terms. For Eucken (1990: 252), a principle was a basic demand as a guide to action, not the goal itself.

ordoliberals such as Eucken searching for the order of a free society. In principle, the European Convention cannot invalidate the German Constitution. Nevertheless, it is likely de facto to develop its own momentum.

THE CONCEPT OF SOCIAL MARKET ECONOMY AS AN ECONOMIC ORDER

In Germany's concept of the "social market economy," the notion of the economic order plays a central role. This is to be understood as an institutional arrangement defining the rules for the decision making of households, firms, and politicians, including the restraints as well as the incentives.

The Economic Order

In a way, an economic order can be interpreted as a super principal-agent contract. In this paradigm of institutional economics, the principal sets the rules that influence the behavior of the agent; he cannot, however, fully observe the behavior of the agent, although it is the behavior of the agent that determines the outcome of the activities. In the constitutional context, the fathers of the Constitution were the principals. In addition, the legislature holds the function of the principal when it has the appropriate majority for making constitutional changes and the normal majority for making other legislative alterations. To some extent, the judiciary plays the role of the principal when the rules require additional interpretation. The individuals (the households and the firms) are the agents, responding to the incentive structure and the institutional framework developed by the principal; so the principal will devise rules to ensure that the optimality conditions of the agents are satisfied. The principal will want to attain a maximum in its targets of freedom, efficiency, and equity, for instance by maximizing one target subject to restraints from the other targets.

The description of the economic order as a super principal-agent problem, however, is not complete. Eventually, the voter will become the principal when he grows discontented with the institutional conditions prevailing and wants a change. However, in contrast to specific policy areas, the rules of the game require constancy, and should change only under rare conditions. This is especially true for constitutional change.

Hutchison (1981: 162) has come close to the German concept of an economic order by distinguishing between a Ricardian and Smithian mode of the competitive market economy (Vanberg 1988: 16f.). Whereas the Ricardian concept stresses "an abstract, purely economic model of competitive equilibrium presented as achieving some kind of Utopian 'maximum' or 'optimum'," the Smithian concept is "formulated in much broader terms, comprehending the political and social order" (Hutchison 1979: 433). The concept of the founding fathers corresponds to the Smithian concept.

Institutional Order versus Process Policy

Economic policy in a social market economy has two distinct roles which are crucially different: to establish and preserve the economic order (*Ordnungspolitik*, or institutional policy), and to influence economic processes ("process policy"). Process policy attempts to stimulate growth, i.e., to influence allocation in day-to-day or year-to-year or even longer-term operations, for instance providing social overhead capital, or smoothing the business cycle. Institutional policy refers to establishing property rights, setting incentives, and expressing restraints including the constitutional conditions. The ordoliberals who laid down the intellectual foundations of West Germany's economic order argued that the main policy task was *Ordnungspolitik*, i.e., to establish the institutional arrangements for a market economy. Process policy should be limited to special cases.

Eucken (1990) developed the constituent principles of the competitive order. Open markets, nowadays the most important ingredient of the concept of contestable markets, are a prerequisite for competition. Private ownership is both a guarantee of individual liberty and an incentive to minimize costs and reveal truly economic information. Freedom of contract is conducive to competition. Liability ensures that social costs are internalized. The constancy of economic policy helps to prevent a misallocation of resources over time, and price level stability (see below) is a *sine qua non* for the price mechanism to operate.

"Thinking in Terms of an Order"

The way in which an institutional setup affects the behavior of individuals and firms was a central issue for the German economic thinkers of the Freiburg school. *Denken in Ordnungen*—to think in terms of an order—was a central precept of the ordoliberals. An economic order for the economy as a whole may be taken as consisting of separate partial orders for specific functional areas (order for the competitive process, the monetary system, the labor market, and social order) or for specific policy areas (trade policy, business cycle policy, agricultural policy). A basic issue is how these partial orders can be made consistent with each other (Eucken 1990: 304; Kloten 1989: 11). One of the issues was how the social question could be integrated into the paradigm. A related problem is how macro policies can be integrated into the order of a social market economy.[3]

The "Social Question" and the Social Order

The late nineteenth and early twentieth centuries in Europe were dominated by the "social question." Industrialization, new forms of production, and the migration from the countryside to the industrial locations all gave rise to social problems. Socialist movements claimed to have found the answer to the problem of obtaining economic efficiency and progress along with personal freedom: by the public ownership of the means of production, and by central planning. The social ethics of the Catholic and Protestant Churches centered on improving the conditions of human life. From this historical perspective, any economic system has to provide an answer to the social question, both from an ethical point of view and from a practical one. There must be some consensus on the economic system. As history tells us, and as we will see later on, the approach to the social question affects the performance of the economic system.

The experience of a central collectivist planning system in Russia has been that this approach did not deliver the promises made, as anticipated by economists such as von Mises. It did not protect the worker as an individual: rather, it required an Orwellian-type control of the individual worker, for instance limiting his choice of workplace, controlling the type of work he did, rationing his food by food stamps. Thus, introducing the market economy in 1948 was in itself a social reform in Germany. The market system provided economic opportunities and choices.

Besides stressing this positive property of the market economy, the attribute "social" of "social market economy" refers to the basic position of at least some of the ordoliberals, i.e., that the allocation process by markets may lead to an income and wealth distribution that warrants correction (Vanberg 1988: 20). An important aspect of this can be found in the social insurance schemes that were started in the 1880s under Bismarck and have been further developed in the nearly sixty years of the Federal Republic. Moreover, the worker participated in economic growth in terms of his higher real income, and he was integrated into the system in economic terms by acquiring real and financial wealth, for instance by owning his own home. Finally, the issue of the position of the worker of the nineteenth century has changed. With 70 percent of the workforce in service activities and only 22 percent in industry, the social question of nearly two centuries ago has disappeared from center-stage.

[3] On the discussion in the 1960s, see Kloten (1989: 12–13).

Some Preconditions of a Market Economy

The social market economy as an institutional framework has a set of important requirements that need to be satisfied in order for the institutional framework to function. These conditions are the system (market) conformity of policy measures, the defense of competition, and price level stability.[4] These elements can be understood only with reference to the historical experience of Germany prior to 1945.

Market Conformity, No Interventionism

The German population, and the intellectual fathers of the social market economy in particular, had experienced an interventionist state, especially in the 1930s and during World War II. It was clear to the majority that a controlled economy—*une économie dirigée*—was appallingly inefficient. Therefore, decentralization and a competitive order were called for.

The interventionist experience of the 1920s and the 1930s had shown that one intervention would quickly lead to the next. This is especially true for price regulation; for example, capping the price of a standard loaf of bread would quickly spread like a cancer to all types of bread, including bagels and croissants—and then to the labor costs of the baker, to flour, to the milling process, to wheat, and to all other inputs, as well as to substitutes for the product. As a drop of oil dissipates into a groundwater system, the intervention pervades the whole economy. (This is the "oil drops theorem.") Whereas the actual problems are not that simple, agricultural policy in the European Union, the interdependence between product and factor markets, and the false incentives of the social security systems are cases in point (Siebert 2003).

Not only may a specific intervention affect other markets (via the interdependence of markets by the potential for substitution and by complementarity), but intervention may also have an impact on the market system itself, changing the basic properties of the allocation mechanism. Therefore, the intellectual founding fathers of the Soziale Marktwirtschaft (Eucken 1990; Müller-Armack 1978, 1999; Röpke 1994, 2002) demanded that policy actions should be compatible with the market economy (*marktkonform*, or market compatible). In a narrow interpretation, a policy decision should not induce a change or disequilibrium in another market such that a new intervention becomes necessary. In a broader sense, a policy measure should not change the property of the overall system. A

---

[4] I do not quite follow Eucken's four regulating principles. His fourth problem, namely inverse supply reaction, is not a major issue. His third problem, that prices correctly reflect scarcity, is a dominating issue.

small institutional change should not affect the overall system negatively after all the households, all the firms, and other agents such as the policy makers have reacted. In a cybernetic context, this is the question of how the system changes if the rules are slightly altered. It is analogous to the general equilibrium analysis for an institutional arrangement. The idea is similar to the concept of defining super-exogeneity in econometrics as the property that changes in a variable do not change the structure of the system. This concept is not very well understood by many economists abroad. Unfortunately, more and more German politicians too have given it up.

It has proven extremely difficult to describe the concept of market conformity precisely. In a static view, one can quickly see how the regulation of one market shifts demand or supply to another market; but in intertemporal decisions such as the choice of a location, capital accumulation, the creation of jobs, and the depletion of natural resources, it takes a long time to see the impact. Moreover, the concept of market conformity is extremely difficult to define with respect to the impact on the system as a whole (system conformity).

In contrast to the ordoliberals' line of thinking, the issue of the nationalization of basic industries and the imposition of a strong government influence was a prominent topic in the early days of West Germany. Although it still flares up occasionally, it is not an issue any longer, partly because of the severe inefficiencies of those German firms that are supposed to have been oriented toward the common weal (*Gemeinwirtschaft*) over the last sixty years, and of course also because of the experience of central planning in East Germany. But Germans still have a liking for a paternal state, so potential conflicts on this issue remain likely.

The State as the Guarantor of the Framework

Apart from the issue of interventionism, the state as a "constitutional state," restrained in its activities by a set of rules and procedures, has been assigned the role of protecting individual liberty and guaranteeing the institutional arrangement of the competitive order by the ordoliberals, for instance through competition policy (see below). Eucken (1990) and Miksch (1947) demanded a strong government that could defend the competitive order and suppress specific interests.[5] The state "is assigned a crucial role in monitoring the proper functioning of the competitive process, which, if left alone, is believed to degenerate due to monopolistic tendencies and growing disproportions of private power"

[5] "Es erwies sich, dass die Gewährung von Freiheit eine Gefahr für die Freiheit werden kann, wenn sie die Bildung privater Macht ermöglicht, dass zwar außerordentliche Energien durch sie geweckt werden, aber dass diese Energien auch freiheitszerstörend wirken können" (Eucken 1990: 53).

(Vanberg 1988: 19). According to Buchanan (1975: 68), the state has the role of providing public goods (or rules for public goods as in environmental quality management). Moreover, the German state has also assumed a dominant role with respect to the equity targets, in an attempt to establish fairness.

A Framework for Competition against Endogenous Tendencies to Monopolize

Competition is a necessary condition for effective decentralization. The spontaneity of the market, however, may be endangered endogenously by the behavior of firms. Profit-maximizing firms can improve their market position by reducing competition. They can form cartels and engage in other forms of cooperation to reduce competition; they can strive for a monopoly position by internal growth, or attain a monopolistic position via mergers. This was the experience in Germany during the three decades preceding World War I and at the time of the Weimar Republic, reflected in the debate in the late 1920s and early 1930s (Mises 1929; Rüstow 1932; Hayek 2001). These potential endogenous tendencies would severely affect the institutional setting of a market economy; at the same time, firms could engage in rent seeking and in influencing the institutional arrangements under which they operated. The result, an industrial complex interlinked with the state (*Vermachtung der Wirtschaft*), was an important issue for the ordoliberals (Eucken 1990: 169).

A necessary framework of the institutional arrangement of Germany's social market economy is therefore competition policy. This has now shifted to the European level for the more important cases. Its role is to guarantee that competition is not eroded endogenously, principally by ruling out cartels, controlling mergers, and curbing the abuse of a monopolistic position. Other important aspects include free market entry, to keep markets contestable, and an open economy, to allow competition from abroad. Openness increases the intensity of competition and protects consumers from firms' charging too high a price. It prevents resources from being wasted by inefficient production, is a driving force to find better solutions, and creates additional welfare.

Independence of the Central Bank against Inflationary Risks

Germany has gone through two major inflations: the hyperinflation of 1923, and the repressed inflation of 1936–48. Inflation generates severe repercussions, by distorting allocation and especially by hurting individuals with fixed nominal incomes, for instance pensioners and wage earners. Inflation can therefore be a danger to an economic system; it can lead to a political destabilization of society, and it violates the condition of constancy of economic policy. For these reasons, and from past experience, price level stability is an important policy target in the eyes of the German public. The Bundesbank was institutionalized as an independent central bank, and the European Central Bank (ECB) too is conceived as autonomous. EU national governments cannot monetize their budget deficits by taking recourse to the central bank, and they should not influence the ECB's interest rate policy.

The position of the Bundesbank was not defined in the Constitution, but only by a specific law. Its independent status, however, was rooted in a consensus of the population. It can be expected that the preference for monetary stability will remain an important factor in German public opinion, although the younger generation may have a less pronounced stand.

The Conflict between the Principles

There is a broad range of problems in which the basic principles of personal liberty and equity, together with the concept of the competitive order, stand in harmony. Thus, the competitive order is instrumental in allowing personal freedom and in contributing toward a solution to the social question. But there are a range of problems in which the basic principles are in conflict. Satisfying one principle exclusively may violate another principle. In sum, the principles define a solution space in which they partly restrain each other. Depending on the weight given to the principles, the solution space changes its form. Without going into a detailed discussion about the extent to which one of the principles dominates and the extent to which a value judgment must be made among conflicting principles, I would like to touch on the major areas in which principles are in conflict. Some of these conflicts will become more explicit in the later parts of the book.

Efficiency versus Equity

A major conflict exists between the two major goals of efficiency and equity. This relationship can be portrayed as a hump-shaped curve, with efficiency first increasing, and then falling, with equity (figure 2.1). Unfortunately, we do not know the exact properties of this curve; it can be viewed as a broad band whose width depends on many factors. It is likely that Germany is on the right arm of the curve, where more equity causes losses in efficiency. Reducing equity may bring efficiency gains.

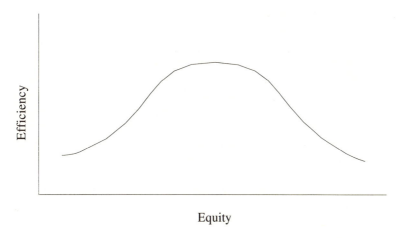

Figure 2.1 Goal relation between efficiency and equity.

Growth versus Equity

A related conflict is the one that exists between growth and equity with a curve similar to that seen in figure 2.1; the only difference lies in the fact that the GDP growth rate, instead of efficiency, appears on the vertical axis. Increasing equity beyond a threshold reduces the growth rate. With a lower degree of equity, more growth can be achieved.

Flexibility versus Protection of the Individual

Another major conflict can be seen in the labor market. The regulation of the labor market has its roots in the objective of protecting the individual. Labor market regulation consists of three basic aspects: governmental insurance schemes for people who are unemployed, ill, disabled, or retired; lay-off restraints; and the delegation of bargaining for the wage contract to the employers' and employees' organizations, with the bargaining solution de facto being mandatory for all employees, including non-union members.

This system of regulation implicitly defines the incentives to supply and demand labor. The incentives work in the direction of reducing the demand for labor and uncoupling employment and growth as well as investment and employment. This is a deficiency of the system. As is the case for any insurance, social insurance gives rise to moral hazard behavior of those insured. Lay-off restraints explicitly define exit conditions and implicitly stipulate entry conditions by influencing the demand for labor. Generalized wage bargaining, allowing an organizational integration of the employees, prevents differentiation of wages according to occupation, sectors, and regions. Moreover, the three types of regulation interact with each other; for instance, social security and lay-off regulations define the bargaining position of the trade unions.

In addition to problems of moral hazard behavior, a regulating system protecting the individual may also give rise to a different attitude in individuals: they may expect individual protection from the government and from the regulatory system, and so may tend to think in terms of entitlements from the government. There is a trade-off between the insider and the outsider; but, much more importantly, there is a trade-off between individual protection and the open society, characterized by Popper (2003: 186) as "competition for status among its members." Definitely, there is a conflict between individual protection and the efficiency or flexibility of the system.

Private Sector Freedom versus Government Regulation

A more practical conflict exists between the freedom of business and regulation. Regulation imposes restraints on the decision space of households and firms, for instance in licensing private activity, especially new products, or in introducing constraints for the protection of health or the environment. Here it is important to have clear criteria on whether, and to what extent, regulation is necessary. Since markets depend on property rights which in turn define economic power, a scenario has to be prevented in which firms engage in rent seeking. It is essential to recognize the linkage between property rights and market entry conditions when designing an institutional order.

Private Sector versus the Role of Government

Yet another conflict is what should and can be done by the private sector and by government, respectively. This refers to the nineteenth-century topic of private versus public ownership of the means of production, to the extent of public involvement in economic activities such as public utilities, to the size of subsidies, and to the share of government expenditures in GDP. The fact that half of German GDP passes through the government coffers is an indication that over the last sixty years Germany has opted for an intensive involvement of the state in its economy.

EROSION OF THE MARKET MECHANISM

In the original Erhard interpretation of the "social market economy," the underlying idea was to have an efficient institutional arrangement for the economy generating a high volume of production, and to distribute the benefits of economic progress widely so that the vast majority of people could enjoy them. The market mechanism was accepted as the basic institutional arrangement of allocation and of setting the incentives for effort, production, investment, and innovation. Social considerations, i.e., the equity target, were deemed as important, requiring a correction of the allocation outcome. But this correction was to be done in such a way that the most important incentives of the market mechanism would remain intact.

This concept of the social market economy has been seen to have won out over the communist philosophy of the public ownership of the factors of production and over central planning, and has served to bring about German reunification. But it has run into severe difficulties. The requirement of the "market conformity" of government activity has long been forgotten, and the actual institutional arrangement now contains incentives such that the growth process is stalling, a high unemployment rate results, and the systems of social security and other attempts to correct the market mechanism can no longer be financed and now endanger the economic foundation of Germany.

CHAPTER THREE

The Weak Growth Performance

Germany experienced a low GDP growth rate in the period 1995–2003. Whereas the stagnation of 2001–2003 was strongly influenced by the worldwide decline of economic activity, the poor growth performance for the period since 1995 as a whole has to be traced to other factors. The German economic engine seems to have lost its dynamics. The labor force is not being fully utilized; the rate of capital accumulation is slower than in the past; innovation is centered on improving existing products along traditional trajectories but is not focused on new technological horizons; human capital formation is not organized efficiently; and economic growth comes from existing firms rather than through new ones. The export position is weakening, and German enterprises are investing abroad instead of at home. A superstructure of the economy, the social security system, is exerting a negative impact on the economic system with its unsolved structural problems. And finally, German unification has affected the performance of the economy.[1]

The Loss of Economic Dynamics

Following the unification boom of the early 1990s, with GDP growth rates of 5.7 and 5.1 percent in 1990 and 1991, respectively, Germany experienced weak growth with the relatively low average growth rate of GDP of 1.2 percent in the period 1995–2003. Since 1994 this rate has been lower than the EU average in each year, and since 1998 Germany and Italy have brought up the rear of the European Union in terms of growth. The forecast for 2004 is for more of the same. In the period 1995–2003 Germany's growth rate was 2 percentage points lower than that of the United States (table 3.1). At present, the economic engine of the largest economy in Europe, contributing a quarter of the EU's output, is stalling (Siebert 2002a).

This picture does not change in substance if additional factors are taken into consideration. It continues to hold if we look at the GDP growth rate

---

[1] I appreciate critical comments to this chapter by Eduard Herda, Christophe Kamps, and Tim Schmidt-Eisenlohr.

TABLE 3.1
GDP growth rates[a]

	1970–1980	1980–1990	1991–2003	1991–1995	1995–2003
Germany[b]	2.8	2.3	1.3	1.3	1.2
France	3.3	2.4	1.8	1.0	2.2
Italy	3.6	2.3	1.4	1.3	1.5
EU-12[c]	3.2	2.4	1.8	1.3	2.0
UK	1.9	2.7	2.6	2.4	2.7
USA	3.2	3.2	3.2	3.1	3.3

Source: OECD Economic Outlook, no. 73, June 2003.
[a] Calculated, as in table 1.1, as an exponential growth rate.
[b] 1969–90, Western Germany; since 1991, with data for unified Germany.
[c] EU-15 excluding UK, Denmark, and Sweden.

per head of population, although population growth was somewhat higher in the countries of the euro currency area that were used for comparison than in those of the EU as a whole,[2] and consequently the growth differential is lower if population growth is taken into consideration. The difference is also lower with respect to the euro area if countries with a high convergence rate (Greece, Ireland, Portugal, and Spain— countries that are now catching up) are excluded from consideration. Statistical methods to measure real output, where a product such as a computer is evaluated by its parts (the "hedonic approach"), contribute to the growth differential with respect to the United States, although they explain only a minor part of that difference; these methods, however, are not relevant with respect to European countries.[3]

In comparison with a number of European countries, it can be argued that some of these countries, e.g., Italy and France, had to be restrictive in their fiscal policy in the early 1990s in order to satisfy the Maastricht criteria; then, after the European Monetary Union was founded, they were able to enjoy the advantage of their efforts in terms of a less burdening debt load and much lower interest rates.[4] This meant weaker growth for them in the early 1990s but stronger growth later on. Germany did not experience a similar tilt in its growth rate, so its growth rate has remained lower. However, in the euro area Germany has the advantage in its export markets of no longer being confronted with the depreciations of European currencies such as the Italian lira, which in 1992 decreased in value by about 30 percent. At any rate, this argument is not valid for the growth differential with respect to the United Kingdom and the United States.

[2] See table 49 in German Council of Economic Advisers (2002).
[3] In France, the hedonic approach plays some role.
[4] They have lost the possibility to devalue their currency.

Another argument is that a still-independent Bundesbank would have given Germany lower interest rates than the ECB has delivered (Posen 2003: 16). Such a statement may attract attention, but it is really not convincing. First, it is contra-factual and therefore rather speculative: it cannot be substantiated empirically. Second, interest rates in the euro currency area are extremely low. The short-term rate of 2 percent is zero in real terms. Long-term rates are low as well in a historical comparison— below 5 percent in 2002 and below 4.5 in 2003, and at nearly the same level as in the United States. Therefore the speculation has little empirical foundation. Third, in accordance with the low interest rates, while the money supply grew below the ECB's reference value in the winter of 2000/01, its growth rates were very high in 2002 and 2003, at 7.2 and 8+ percent, respectively. It is unlikely that the Bundesbank would have had such high rates of money growth. According to the Taylor rule, the interest rate was slightly above the corridor in the winter 2000/01, but it should have been higher for 2002 and 2003 (Institut für Weltwirtschaft 2004: 7).

In order to determine whether there is a more or less permanent loss of economic dynamics in Germany, we have to know whether, and to what extent, the low growth performance is the result of the business cycle situation, or whether Germany has indeed moved to a much lower growth path. There is no question that the stagnation in the period 2001–2003 is due in part to the impact of the worldwide downturn, particularly in countries like Germany that are very open to international trade. The methodological difficulty is that we cannot easily distinguish empirically the business cycle situation from the growth path. The growth path has to be measured by an increase in the production potential, i.e., by the potential growth rate. This, however, cannot be observed directly but must be determined indirectly. One approach would be to specify the production potential by a macroeconomic production function; the difficulty then arises as to what extent such a function can be estimated satisfactorily by econometric methods. An alternative approach is to use a filter such as Hodrick-Prescott to estimate the growth trend. But this is a more or less ad hoc method, with the value of the trend depending on the smoothing factor and the value of the trend for the most recent period being a function of the quality of the forecast for future years. Although we have to be cautious in estimating the extent of a more or less permanent loss of economic dynamics in Germany, the long period of low growth at a time when other countries were doing much better is sufficient justification for the hypothesis that weak economic growth is one of the characteristics of present-day Germany. This hypothesis will not be refuted if a recovery occurs after the 2001–2003 stagnation, because such a recovery does not necessarily mean that the economy has reached a higher growth path.

Let us look now at the factors that can be expected to have an impact on the growth process and that may explain Germany's low growth rate. Ideally, we should have an econometrically tested model of growth expressing the precise relevance of each growth determinant; then we would be aware of each factor's exact contribution to the GDP growth rate in a given period. For instance, we would know the production elasticities of all the factors of production—labor, physical and human capital, and technology—as well as of institutional arrangements.[5] I will here follow a less demanding approach and discuss those factors that may represent a cause of weakness or of strength.

THE IMPACT OF GERMAN UNIFICATION

Unification is the first factor that comes to mind as a specific condition influencing the German growth rate. In principle, unification was a new frontier in economic growth or a positive supply shock, i.e., an investment opportunity, adding labor and (an unfortunately obsolete) capital stock to the German economy. This promised a catching-up process with high growth rates that would stimulate economic dynamics in the whole of Germany and augment the overall German growth rate. In practice, it did not turn out that way, as already described in chapter 1. Too many mistakes were made: exchanging the East German mark 1:1 for the West German mark; raising wages out of line with productivity growth; applying the West German institutional arrangement—e.g., of the labor market, of product market regulation, of the university system, and of taxation—to a transformation economy; generating an over-expansion of the construction sector by public subsidies for housing, office space, and factories which eventually had to be corrected; and relying mainly on consumption transfers.

From the point of view of economic growth, there are positive signals in eastern Germany. In a historic context, a substantial amount of progress has been achieved. The East German region excluding Berlin started out at 33 percent of the West German GDP per capita in 1991[6] and reached 62.7 percent of the West German level in 2002. This is quite an achievement, considering that some West German Länder are only at 80–85 percent of the overall West German level: eastern German GDP per capita was 71.2 percent of the level of unified Germany in 2002. The public infrastructure in the East has been rebuilt, and is now more modern than in quite a few parts of western Germany. Strolling through the beautified old cities of Weimar, Dresdner Neustadt, or Leipzig, visitors will indeed see a "blossoming landscape."

[5] For such an approach, compare German Council of Economic Advisers (2002: 205ff.).
[6] In this calculation of West German GDP, Berlin is also excluded.

The main concern, however, is that unemployment stood at 18.6 percent in 2003, and that from 1997 to 2003 the growth rate of eastern Germany was lower than the overall German rate. This means not only that the convergence process has stopped, but that we do indeed have divergence. This is due partly to a decline in the construction industry as a correction to an earlier over-expansion in that sector following from public subsidies. As examples of successful regional restructuring and a successful quick convergence process (e.g., Ireland and Pittsburgh) show, important prerequisites for regional growth are initiative and a mood of optimism. The latter mood, although apparent in quite a few groups and in some regions, is not an overwhelming sentiment in eastern Germany; the PDS party, successor to the previous communist SED, alludes to people feeling like deprived second-class citizens, and this party collected up to 20 percent of the votes in the Länder elections up to 2002.

German unification required, and still requires, annual public transfers from the West to the East of the country of 2 percent of West German GDP (see chapter 12). The transfers within the governmental system, between the federal level and the Länder as well as among the Länder, have been financed mainly through credits, with other transfers being funded to a large part through additional contributions to the social security system. It is quite apparent that these transfers have made an impact. The government transfers, resulting in a doubling of government debt, have affected Germany's fiscal policy stance negatively. The maneuvering space for tax reductions has been severely reduced by the interest load for new debt. Thus, even after the 2001 tax reform, the tax rates for German firms remained higher than those in the other EU countries. The transfers within the social security systems, financed by higher contributions, have led to an increase in the tax on labor, with a negative impact on employment in Germany as a whole. The attempt to control the increase in the contributions by using the receipts of the eco-tax to finance old-age pensions means distortions and negative effects elsewhere, since the eco-tax has a negative impact on productivity.

In addition, there was a real appreciation of the Deutschmark as a consequence of unification in the early 1990s, which affected Germany's competitive position in the world market (see below). This follows from a model with tradables and non-tradables: transfers to East Germany increased domestic absorption and implied a rise in the price of non-tradables relative to tradables.[7] There was also an appreciation in the context of exportables and importables, since consumption transfers to

[7] Eastern Germany itself has experienced a "Dutch Disease" phenomenon. Because of transfers, the relative price of non-tradables expanded, reducing the attractiveness of tradables (manufacturing).

eastern Germany meant an increase in the absorption of goods that would have been exported otherwise.

There is no doubt that, in economic terms, German unification has been a shock to the German economy. Western Germany has been somewhat restricted by the financing of the transfers. But it would be misleading to assume that this is the only reason for the country's poor growth performance. German unification occurred in an environment in which ongoing long-run trends were leading to unresolved severe structural problems. Western Germany does not have a sufficiently dynamic economic system to sustain a strong carry-over to eastern Germany.

Let us now look at these issues in some detail. We have to ask how the traditional growth determinants, including labor, physical capital, technology, and human capital, have shaped the process of growth.

LEAVING LABOR IDLE

From 1995 to 2002, Germany's labor force increased at an annual rate of 0.3 percent when measured by the number of persons, i.e., "heads," owing to an increase during 1998–2001; but it declined at a rate of 0.3 percent when measured in total hours worked. Looking at total hours worked, this means a (slightly) negative contribution to the GDP growth rate from this factor of production, assuming a given labor productivity.

The change in the labor force is determined by two main factors: population growth and incentives, defined by the institutional arrangement of the labor market. For population growth, we have to go back some twenty years for *birth rates* that will be relevant to an increase in the labor supply today. But population stagnated in the 1980s; consequently there has been/will be no increase in the labor supply in the first decade of the twenty-first century stemming from that potential source. *Immigration* is also likely to have a direct effect on the labor supply. The immigration rate stood at 400 000 persons in 1995 when calculated net (immigration minus emigration), but declined to 270 000 persons in 2000. As immigrants at present account for less than 1 percent of the labor force, this has not been a stimulating factor for growth in recent years. The *participation rate*, another relevant aspect of the labor supply, remained constant in the 1990s, with the participation rate of women falling in the East and increasing in the West.

Of course, a primary issue is *unemployment*. Germany does not use its labor force fully. About 4.4 million were out of work in 2003, and an additional 1.6 million were in governmental schemes, i.e., in "hidden unemployment," according to the concept of the German Council of Economic Advisers. If 6 million were fully employed in the "first" labor market (i.e., not including the secondary labor market of governmental support schemes), and if they had only half the average productivity of the employed,[8] and if they only worked half time, GDP could still be higher by about 2 percent. Of course, this would be one-off effect, not an annual increase in the growth path. But it would augment the flexibility of the economy and improve conditions for investment, which would influence the growth rate positively.

Over the three decades since 1970, the German labor force has more or less stagnated when calculated in heads (except for an increase of 1 percent per year in the 1980s) and has fallen at a rate of 0.5 percent per year when measured in total hours worked. Assuming constant labor productivity, the sheer number of workers has not contributed to the GDP growth rate, and total hours worked imply negative growth. In contrast, other countries, e.g., the United States, show an increase in the total hours worked so that there has been some growth even if there was no increase in labor productivity. (*Note*: in the above rates the one-off increase resulting from German unification has not been included.)

By international comparison, Germany has maintained the relatively low level of 1443 effective working hours per worker per year (including the self employed) (in 2003). Hours worked per head in Germany are the lowest among the industrial countries—6 percent lower than in France, 14 percent lower than in the United Kingdom, and 20 percent lower than in the United States and Japan (in 2000). The average number of hours worked per year by the dependently employed was 1361 (2003). The norm is now the 35 hour work-week in, say, the metal industry; the effective work-week for the fully employed in the economy, however, is slightly higher at 37 hours. Germany enjoys many holidays, most of them religious. Holidays occurring in the middle of the week, especially religious ones on a Thursday, are extended with an extra day of leave to create a long weekend. The legal minimum number of leave days is 24. In labor contracts, as a rule, 30 working days are paid leave days. It has become customary for Germans to take two two-week vacation trips per year.

A Declining Share of Investment

In Germany the share of investment in GDP fell from 23 percent in 1995 to 18 percent in 2002. Investment is an important engine of growth, as empirical studies show.[9] Assuming a production elasticity of capital of 0.3 and a capital-output ratio of 2.5, a fall in the investment share by

[8] Here assumed to be €28 000 (average labor cost) per person employed.
[9] German Council of Economic Advisers (2002: 299).

5 percentage points leads to a lower growth rate of 0.3–0.4 percent.[10] However, it may be misleading to consider such a short period in the case of investment. In the first place, the early 1990s represented an investment surge arising from German unification, so the level of investment was extraordinarily high. Second, the low level of investment in the years 2001–2003 reflects the stagnation in that period.

In a longer run perspective of the last four decades, the investment ratio fell from 26.5 percent of GDP in the 1960s to 19.4 in 2000–2003.[11] Clearly, there is a trend of a declining investment ratio. This trend is consistent with the convergence hypothesis. According to this approach, a country that is catching up exhibits high growth rates when its capital stock is still small and, consequently, the marginal productivity of capital is high. When more capital is accumulated, the marginal productivity of capital and the growth rate fall. The country moves down its marginal productivity of capital curve. This approach applies very well to Germany inasmuch as the capital stock, partly destroyed after World War II and far too small for the huge influx of refugees in the 1950s, had to be rebuilt, initially producing a high return. It should be noted, however, that Germany's actual share of investment in GDP is not too different from that of other industrialized countries, for instance France and Italy: it is 2–3 percentage points higher than that of the United States and of the United Kingdom, but lower than that of Japan.

An indicator of the profitability of capital is the profit-revenue ratio as calculated by the German Council of Economic Advisers.[12] This was 8 percent in the 1970s and fell to around 2.5 percent in the 1990s—in spite of the investment opportunity presented by German unification. Thus, the poor growth performance and the weakness of investment are two sides of the same coin. It is relevant here that the annual increase in labor productivity per hour has declined, from 5.4 percent in the 1960s to 1.5 percent since 1995 (see below, figure 3.1). This indicates a decline in the productivity growth trend.

Looking at the components of investment, the share of investment in buildings has remained constant since 1970 with the exception of a surge resulting from German unification; it is now not too different from what it was in 1970. Government investment, i.e., investment in buildings and equipment, fell from 4.8 percent of GDP in 1970 to 1.7 percent in 2001,

---

[10] This follows from

$$\hat{Q} = \alpha \frac{1}{Q} \cdot \frac{Q}{K}$$

where $\hat{Q}$ is the GDP growth rate, α is the production elasticity of capital, I is investment, Q output, and K the capital stock.

[11] It was 24 percent in the 1970s, 21 percent in the 1980s and 22.5 percent in the 1990s.

[12] German Council of Economic Advisers (1996: 301).

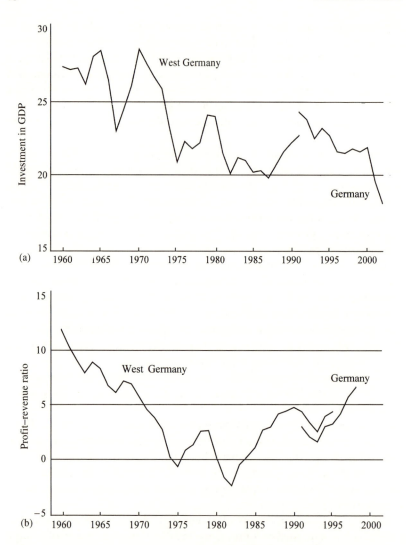

Figure 3.1   Investment as a percentage of GDP, 1960–2002, and profit–revenue ratios, 1960–1998. (a) Investment in GDP (%). (b) Profit–revenue ratio. *Source*: German Council of Economic Advisers, Annual Report 1996/97, updated.

receding about one percentage point per decade. The relatively high figure in the 1970s can be explained by the expansion of the government sector under Social Democratic and Liberal Democratic governments. The fall since 1990 partly reflects the privatization of government activity such as telecommunications and the postal service. Nevertheless, there is a sizable change in the investment share. With respect to infrastructure in transportation and telecommunications, where the public and the private sectors overlap, Germany has modernized its infrastructure in eastern Germany. This also applies to the communications sector for the whole of Germany. However, there have been only minor attempts to modernize the transportation infrastructure, for instance by new railroad tracks between Cologne and Frankfurt.

The Innovative Performance

Another possible reason for Germany's low growth performance may be a lack of dynamics in innovation. Technological progress—new products, new processes of production, and new methods of organization—has been shown in empirical studies to be an important factor in growth.[13] In order to consider the impact of innovations on growth, the productivity increase has to be measured. Here, however, we run into difficulties, for a number of reasons. First, a higher productivity may be embedded in factors of production such as labor and capital, so that a factor-neutral technical progress does not fully reflect the innovative performance. Second, factor-augmenting technical progress is faced with the difficulty of separating the change in the quantity of a factor, for instance capital accumulation, from a change in its quality. Third, a macroeconomic production function is needed in order to measure factor-neutral or factor-augmenting technical progress; but only too often technical progress has been interpreted as a residual, i.e., as a contribution to growth that cannot be explained otherwise. Moreover, the difficulty is to determine quantitatively the initial level of technological knowledge from which the rate of progress can be calculated. But in part, technological knowledge is embedded in another factor of growth, namely human capital (see below). We therefore have only a limited basis on which to evaluate Germany's innovative performance and link it to economic growth.

Patent figures, which might be considered a output measure, do not show Germany at a disadvantage. Germany granted about the same proportion of triad patents, i.e., those registered in the United States, Europe, and Japan, per inhabitant or per employee, as the United States, somewhat less than Japan but more than the other large European countries (*Bundesministerium für Bildung und Forschung*, 2003, table 4-2). Unfortunately, patents do not sufficiently measure the contribution to growth.

A different approach, this time input-oriented, is to analyze how much of GDP is spent on research and development (R&D). In the 1960s

[13] German Council of Economic Advisers (2002: 209).

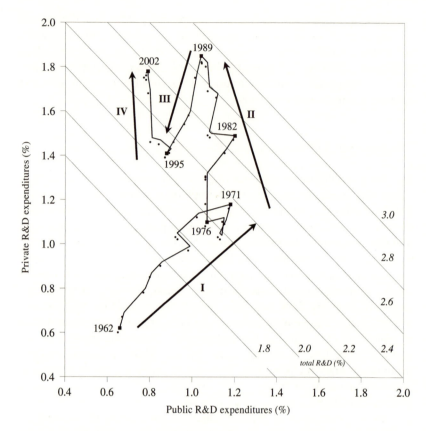

Figure 3.2 Phases of private R&D expenditure (% of GDP). Data since 1999 is preliminary. *Source*: Bundesministerium für Bildung und Forschung 2003, table 4-2. See also Fier (2002).

(phase I in figure 3.2) both public and private R&D expenditure in Germany rose; however, from the mid 1970s to the end of the 1980s (phase II), although private spending in Germany continued to rise, public spending remained more or less constant. R&D expenditure reached 2.8 percent of GDP in the late 1980s, then fell to 2.3 percent in the mid 1990s for six years, the first part of the 1990s having seen a fall in both public and private spending on R&D—public spending by 0.2 percentage point and private by 0.4 percentage point (phase III). From 1997 (phase IV) private spending increased again, and public spending ceased to decline, and by 2001 it had regained the level of the early 1980s.[14] In 2001, then, Germany's expenditure on R&D was

[14] France increased its share slightly; the share in the UK fell.

2.5 percent of GDP, somewhat less than that of the United States (2.8 percent) and Japan (3.0 percent), but more than that of France (2.2 percent) and the United Kingdom (1.9 percent). Germany did not manage to keep its high share of the early 1980s whereas Japan as one of its competitors increased its share over the last twenty years by 0.7 percentage point.

Other approaches adopted to study innovative performance use additional indicators. Looking at technical progress from the product side, Germany's technology-based industry is strong in innovation in its main industrial export sectors—machine building, automobiles, and chemical products (see below on export performance). Outside these traditional technological areas, however, innovative capacity is less pronounced (Siebert und Stolpe 2002). Thus, although comparative advantage exists in the upper segments of mature technology, there is a comparative disadvantage in high-tech products (see below on the export position). Germany's balance of payments for technological services is negative (see below).

The typical pattern of technological development in Germany incorporates incremental improvements along established trajectories, mainly in the above-mentioned export oriented industries. This means that there is a technological sophistication in the production processes of a broad range of continuously upgraded engineering based products. New internationally available technologies like IT are quickly applied to the existing product set in these industries. Germany's approach has been compared to the optimization of extant railroad tracks that were laid in the nineteenth century: in the same way, the four important export sectors of today—machine building, automobiles, chemical products, and electro-technical goods—have their roots in the academic achievements of German universities in the nineteenth century. Clearly, this paradigm does not represent a technological leapfrogging with a shift to a completely different and new technology. Incidentally, the same approach of marginal improvement was applied to the problem of bringing eastern Germany up to West German levels.

Examples of technological leapfrogging that did not succeed are the Siemens-Nixdorf saga in computers and the early foray of Hoechst into biotechnology. Also, German producers of mainframes were ill prepared when the PCs arrived. And there is the anecdotal story that a forerunner of the fax machine was invented by Hell in Kiel as early as the early 1960s, long before the Japanese invented the fax; when Siemens, then dominant in teletypes, acquired Hell in 1981, it seems not to have recognized the potential of the new technology, a rival to its own well selling product.

The approach of incremental technological improvement is reflected in Germany's institutional setup. Germany's capital market is bank-based and relies on intermediated products (see chapter 10). Commercial banks have a close relationship with their customer-firms as *Hausbanken* and shy away from financing large risks; most of the risk-prone R&D funding of the private sector typically comes from firms' retained earnings. The venture capital market is less developed in Germany than elsewhere. The institutional setting of the capital market is thus geared to technological development along traditional lines.

There are other aspects of the institutional setup in Germany that are not conducive to innovation. Codetermination policies and workers' councils tend to seek a consensus on the firm's established technological trajectories, and may find it more difficult to leapfrog to a new technology. These consensus approaches are seen as an alternative to competition; they can be expected to have slowed implementation even on a given trajectory (chapter 14). A lack of labor market flexibility is another case in point. Finally, the university system is less competitive and does not seem to generate enough new technological knowledge (see below).

Public attitudes towards new technology have an impact on the choice of the technological trajectory. It is a fact that Germany is less inclined than other countries to experiment with new technologies and to take on technological risks; in France, for example, one can observe an underlying readiness, even a preference, for new technological solutions. Germany, on the other hand, seems to be averse to unfamiliar technologies. Public technophobia and a very strict law on genetic engineering place narrow constraints on experiments, so that several projects were halted in the courts, whereupon the firms moved elsewhere with their research. Product market regulation (e.g., with respect to the licensing of new pharmaceutical products) represents an impediment to growth. The exit from atomic energy, in which Germany was internationally competitive, with a closing plan for the existing power plants over two decades, is yet another example of German political preferences regarding technological risks. Sometimes it seems as if important segments of the German society have what doctors call "neophobia"—a fear of new and unknown things.

In addition, compensation for taking risks in terms of higher risk premiums is called into question in public discussions in which the issue of "a distorted income distribution" (*Schieflage*) pops up regularly. Members of the public tend to judge profits ex post, i.e., when they have been made, and when the risks that were taken have already been forgotten or simply have not materialized. Such a mood is not conducive to investment and innovation, for which it is preferable for profits to be evaluated ex ante, when the risks are still clear.

The regulatory approach described above is part of the government's technology policy. Other aspects of the policy relate to the "making" of new technologies, to subsidies, to the conditions for generating new technological knowledge, and to the organization of diffusion. Two of the missionary technologies of the state—the fast breeder nuclear reactor and the Transrapid—have been failures, at least so far. The coal industry is heavily subsidized; subsidies continue until 2012, albeit on a declining scale. Here tax money is being spent on an old industry. However, environmentally friendly energy generation, e.g., windmills, is also strongly supported by the government. Here tax money is spent on what is thought by quite a few to be a good cause, as some decades ago coal mining was thought to be. The German government's approach to organizing the conditions for basic research and the universities is wanting (see below).

The diffusion of new technology from research organizations to firms is a central aspect of German technology policy. Incentives for people to move from the public sector to private research are less pronounced in Germany than in other countries, possibly because Germans have a preference for a secure job in government. At the same time, it is unusual for people to move back from the private to the public sector. The process of turning basic research into a marketable product is therefore less developed. Moreover, the economic system is less prepared to accept entrepreneurial activities as a researcher's sideline. In the light of these missed opportunities for knowledge and technology diffusion by *markets*, it is understandable that German technology policy focuses instead on public institutions as a means of diffusion (Siebert and Stolpe 2002: 117).

Another important mechanism for diffusion is on-the-job training, which serves to equip the workforce with new technological knowledge. Regarding this aspect of diffusion, German firms have been quite successful. They have even succeeded in assimilating the "guest workers" into German standards and German work ethics. The approach adopted consists mainly in enhancing the technology-specific and firm-specific knowledge of workers. In this context, lifetime employment is instrumental. Again, this is consistent with improving existing technology.

There have been some changes in the institutional conditions in Germany since the mid-1990s. The role of business startups has been recognized, and political preferences changed somewhat in the 1990s. The government started a Bio-Regio contest in 1995, whereby regions compete for government funding. The sum of €77 million is set aside for three winners, who also have preferential access to the biotechnology program of the Federal Research Ministry (Dohse 2000). Regions can make a collective application involving a mixture of firms, research institutes, universities, chambers of commerce, and municipalities. This induces them to develop a joint effort. Several consecutive contests are envisioned. In the previous contest, 17 regions participated. This approach can be seen as an attempt to help regions identify their interests and choose a common target. It improves communications in a region and is instrumental in establishing networks. It may also help in speeding up permits as far as regional authorities are involved, since they are thereby alerted to the interest of the region. The winners are picked by a jury. This raises the question of whether the criteria are appropriate and—as an overriding issue—whether committees and the government have sufficient information to pick the winner.

Over-regulation of the markets, which did play a role in 1980s in biotechnology, seems to have been partially overcome. Another important change is a new institutional framework for the network industries, allowing more competition and less government influence in telecommunications, the postal service, public enterprises of municipalities, airlines, airports, railroads, electricity, gas, and water (see chapter 8). Here efficiency gains were realized.

Human Capital

According to the paradigm that underlies the traditional theory of economic growth, a study of the augmentation of labor, the accumulation of capital, and technological progress should enable us to understand Germany's slow growth performance. This approach, relevant for the industrial and service economies, does not hold for the information and knowledge economy, where human capital becomes the major determinant of growth and where traditional labor (excluding human capital) may have a production elasticity of only 0.3–0.4, whereas human capital, together with physical capital, may reach an elasticity of 0.6–0.7 according to international panel studies (Mankiw, Romer, and Weil 1992).[15] In any case, even in the traditional approach of economic growth, the quality of labor is a decisive factor.

As with technological knowledge, an issue of measurement arises. A potential indicator of human capital may be seen in labor productivity, which has fallen from 5 percent in the 1960s and nearly 4 percent in the 1970s to 2.5 percent after 1980 and to 1.6 percent after 1995. However, these data reflect many other factors, such as the slower pace of the convergence process, a reduced rate of capital accumulation, less technological progress, a loss of economic dynamics according to the governance system, and even an erosion of the competitive position. As with technological progress, we have to look for other, unfortunately softer, factors. Thus, the number of students in engineering and natural sciences, i.e., 693 per 100 000 of the population in 1999, was only half that of France and of the United Kingdom and much lower than that of Japan

[15] That is, 0.37 for the OECD countries, 0.28 worldwide.

and the United States (*Bundesministerium für Bildung und Forschung* 2003, table 2-7). The number of engineering graduates in machine building nearly halved in the 1990s, and the number in electrical engineering also fell considerably.[16]

Another approach to evaluating Germany's human capital formation is to look at the inputs and the institutions of that process. The German system of preparing the young for practical professions, both in the apprenticeship system of the crafts and in industry, deserves top marks in human capital formation. This dual system is a combination of practical training on the job and vocational schooling over a three-year period. Although systems can always be improved and made more responsive to change, the German approach equips the young with the necessary technological knowledge and qualifications, instills in them the norms of the work ethic, and also represents an important vehicle of social integration. It is part of the German approach to focus on a broad dissemination of knowledge and on a transfer of experience between the generations. In addition to this approach to training the young, firms give their regular employees on-the-job training. Both procedures lead to a broad qualification of the workforce. This qualification of the young and regular employees seems to be centered to some extent on the dissemination of the existing technology and its marginal improvement. It also relies on firm-specific knowledge.

The two other institutions of human capital formation—schools and universities—are wanting. The international comparisons of German schools, e.g., in the TIMMS (Third International Mathematics and Science Study of the International Association for the Evaluation of Educational Achievement) and PISA (Program for International Student Assessment of the OECD, studies, both from 2000, have been disappointing. Econometric analysis of the conditions influencing the quality of schooling indicates that the institutional incentives for the school system are at the root of the problem (Wößmann 2002). It seems that the attempt to use the schools to produce equal, i.e., non-differentiated, qualifications, instead of providing equal starting conditions and then allowing for a differentiation of results, has made for an inefficient school system. Thus, even the inadequacy of the German school system has to do with the equity target or the social market economy, i.e., with some ideological position of the political parties and society.

The university system is also deficient. This is a public, tax financed system, with some private universities now arising at the fringe of the system. The basic approach for this government-run system is one of administrative planning at the Länder level, with some federal restraints and some mixed financing between the federal and the Länder level.

---

[16] Bundesministerium für Bildung und Forschung 2003, figure 2-7.

Whoever has obtained the "Abitur" at the end of the German *gymnasium* has the right to enter a university. There are no admission fees, and students are allocated to universities by a set of administrative procedures including capacity norms (determining the maximum student load for a university), admission norms (determining what happens if more students want to go to a specific university than student places are available), and historically oriented budget allocations to the universities. It may be hard to understand internationally how the right to a place in a university as written into the Constitution could have led to the existing central allocation procedure. At present, all students for a specific discipline, say medicine, apply to a national office; the scarce student places are then allocated according a set of criteria including, besides quality and how long the student has been waiting for a place. Up to now Germany has not dared to deregulate this system and use competition as the guiding principle for university entrance and placement.

Moreover, the universities and research institutes operate according to the labor market regulations and the rules of codetermination, and the political system is not prepared to open the system up to competition. This is a severe impediment to the fostering of an innovative environment. The institutional setup, i.e., the procedures steering the universities and the labor market rigidities, signifies inertia relative to the United States, and inhibits the German academic institutions from keeping up with the international pace.

Sectoral Change and Digesting Shocks

Sectoral change is a mechanism of growth. Old sectors die away, new ones are born. It has been postulated that the service sector has a lower productivity growth than industry and that sectoral change towards a service economy means lower overall growth for a country. Such a hypothesis, however, seems outdated for the modern information society. In any case, the hypothesis does not hold for Germany, where since 1973 the productivity increase has been the same for both manufacturing and service sectors (Klodt et al. 1994: 125). Klodt's study uses a wide delineation of the service sector. In another analysis, the astonishing result was arrived at that in the 1990s the manufacturing industry had not contributed positively to the German growth rate (German Council of Economic Advisers 2002: table 19): its contribution to the growth rate was in fact slightly negative. This is consistent with another observation. From 1991 to 2003 the German manufacturing industry, which is practically synonymous with the export sector, lost 2.8 million jobs. This is a sizable loss relative to the 7.7 million employees in that sector. The reduction of jobs occurred in the main pillars of the German export sector—in the electro-technical industry, machine construction, and the chemical industry. Looking at plants with 20 employees and more, West German industry lost 1.75 million jobs[17] relative to the 5.6 million employees in that sector.[18] Admittedly, part of this adjustment was caused by the outsourcing of service activities such as firm-owned transportation, cafeterias, and cleaning services. Nevertheless, there is a sizable structural change away from manufacturing.

Another aspect of structural change concerns the over-expansion of the construction sector in eastern Germany. After unification, housing and office space were heavily subsidized, which led to over-expansion early on. When the overcapacity became apparent and prices fell, the over-expansion had to be corrected by laying off workers. The adjustment crisis contributed negatively to the growth rate of eastern Germany. Moreover, the structural issues of construction firms also affected enterprises in West Germany, where, in addition to these problems, a decline in demand (including governmental demand) occurred, which had a negative impact on the construction industry.

Shock absorption is another aspect that affects growth, in the sense of how long it takes an economic system to absorb an economic shock. This applies to labor demand, which needed longer to pick up after the 1990s recession than after the shocks of the 1970s and 1980s. It seems that the institutional setup, together with changed economic conditions, has reduced the German economic system's capacity to absorb a shock.

THE ENTERPRISE SECTOR

Dynamics in the enterprise sector can be a clue to the growth performance of the economy. In a very dynamic enterprise sector with high market exit and market entry rates, strong productivity growth can be expected. Market exit of obsolete firms means that untenable positions are given up and inefficiency is reduced. But in order to have growth, high entry rates have to compensate for the loss of activity arising from the high exit rates. When we compare market entry rates with market exit rates for Germany in the 1990s, where the rates are defined as the number of entries or exits in relation to the number of existing firms, the sketchy data hardly suggest a strong dynamics in the German enterprise sector;[19] in fact, it looks more like stagnation, or even decline. Market entry, measured as the number of new firms per 10 000 workers in the economy

---

[17] Structural break in the data.

[18] Germany has 6.2 million employees in that category.

[19] See the innovation panel of the ZEW (Rammer 2002).

(employed plus unemployed), takes place in consumer-related services and in retail and construction. Since 1993, entry in technology- and knowledge-oriented services increased up to the year 2000 and declined in the years of economic stagnation, 2001–2003. Entries in the research-based industries declined. Insolvencies, again measured per 10 000 workers, have increased in both East and West Germany since 1992. They relate mostly to construction, retail, and consumer-oriented activities.

In absolute figures, insolvencies can be said to tell the story of Germany's historic development. The number of insolvencies fell continuously from 1955 until the early 1970s. They started to rise after the first oil crisis, from their annual level of 3000–4000 to 10 000 in 1981, and to 19 000 in 1985. After falling again in the second part of the 1980s, they increased markedly from a level of 13 000 in the united Germany in 1992 to 37 620 in 2002 (Creditreform 2003).

Unfortunately, we do not have sufficient data on the net entry of firms over a longer horizon. A specific problem is that the figures on exit and entry need to be weighted, for instance by revenue or by the number of people employed. Comparisons with the United States indicate that US entrants are more open to experiment than in Europe, that the entering size of firms is smaller, that labor productivity is lower, and that employment expansion is much stronger in the initial years when entrants are successful (Scarpetta et al. 2002). This is consistent with the empirical observation that German entrants have difficulty in surpassing an employment threshold; employment in newly established firms is less than proportional. This is due to the regulations of the German labor market. Moreover, product and capital market regulations have a negative impact on entry (see below).

Besides market entry and exit, the internal growth of firms is an indicator of dynamics in the enterprise sector. Unfortunately, we do not have sufficient information on that topic. If we take into account anecdotal evidence, it is difficult to find examples of German garage firms that have recently become large players. An exception is SAP, the provider of business software.

There are, however, a few examples of German firms that have reinvented themselves by performing a market exit in a traditional product line and a market entry in a new product. One such metamorphosis is Mannesmann, a typical German industrial firm of the Ruhr area with a former focus on steel pipes for the oil and gas industry; it transformed itself into a mobile telephone company and was then taken over by Vodafone, the British communications firm. Another example is Preussag, a steel firm, which became a tourist company under the new name of TUI. In both cases, a structural change from industry to the service sector was performed.

As a rule, technological change in Germany is taking place within existing firms. Thus, the German export producers in the machine building industry have implemented new technologies such as electronics and IT software into their traditional investment goods—so that, for example, they are now able to rectify some of the defects in running machines worldwide from a command post in Germany. In another transformation, a firm like Siemens has restructured internally within the given shell. Other enterprises, such as AEG, a well established household name for white goods of all sorts, have disappeared from the market; this can be seen as a reflection of international competition in the "volume business" of the electro-technical industry. The restructuring of firms has been occurring in other areas as well. One example is the merger of Thyssen and Krupp, which has to be regarded as an attempt to improve efficiency in a declining sector, namely steel. Reorganization has also taken place as a response to changes in product market regulation and in privatization. Thus, EON was formed out of VEBA, the energy supplier, which gave up its oil business and took over Ruhrgas, the natural gas provider.

In the context of an internal change of firms, the takeover by heirs, i.e., the intergenerational transformation in ownership, is an important aspect, especially under the German conditions, where, in the small and medium-sized firms of the Mittelstand, the principal owner tends to be the driving force of a firm. It cannot be taken for granted that the heirs of today's businesses are going to be willing or able to perform the same role as their parents. They may be tempted to exit, to retire to Mallorca, if they feel crowded by political red tape with respect to taxation or regulation; or they may simply not be prepared to devote the same energy to the business, preferring to play golf. Generational change within the firms is therefore a constant topic in Germany's economic policy.

An Erosion of the Export Position?

Germany continues to be the world's second largest exporter behind the United States. It was even number 1 with the weak US dollar in 2003. Its export share of GDP is about one third. Of course, in a changing world market with fierce competition, the position of vice-champion of world exports is always under threat. However, there are some signs that the position is rather fragile and may be changing (Siebert 2002c). Let us take a closer look at Germany's competitive position.

Germany's world market share, calculated in US dollars, has declined since 1990 by 2.5 percentage points, from 12.0 to 9.5 percent in 2002; it rose to 10 percent in 2003. This is below the long-run average of 10.6 percent for the period 1975–89 (figure 3.3a). Of course, it is normal for

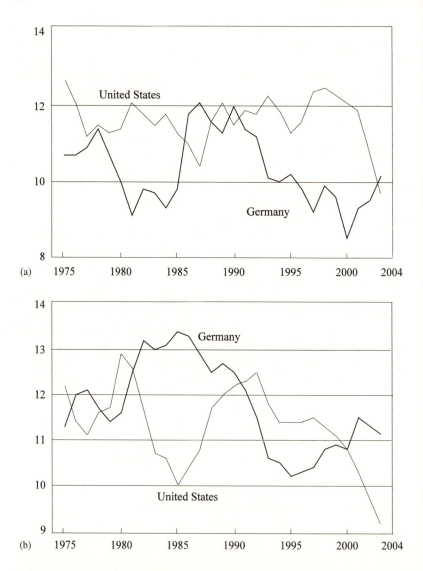

Figure 3.3 Germany's share of world exports and competitiveness, 1975–2001.
(a) World market share in US dollars (nominal): current prices and exchange rate.
(b) World market share in constant prices: nominal exports divided by export unit
values with 1995 = 100 for export unit value. (c) Price competitiveness: index of
German price competitiveness relative to 19 industrial countries on the basis of
consumer prices. *Source*: For market shares: IMF International Financial Statistic,
Data Stream, May 2004; for price competitiveness, Deutsche Bundesbank
Zeitreihe YX900D.

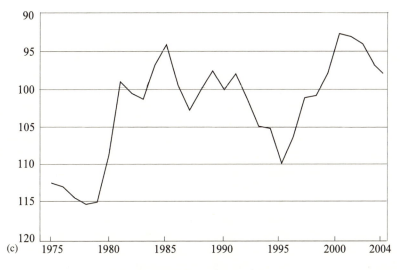

Figure 3.3   *(continued)*

industrial nations to lose world market share as developing countries successfully integrate themselves into the international division of labor. However, the United States has succeeded in holding onto its world market share, except for 2002 and 2003. Germany's share of industrial goods exports of all OECD countries was receding also relative to France and the United Kingdom in the same period, especially in the early 1990s. It should be noted that the above results hinge on calculating German exports in dollar terms. This implies that a high valued US dollar will artificially reduce German exports by sheer conversion, although it will make German exports cheaper and thus stimulate demand for them. This artificial reduction occurred in the first part of the 1980s and again in the 1990s. The stronger euro in 2003 increased Germany's world market share in US dollar terms.

If we measure the share of exports in real terms, dividing nominal exports by export unit values, the loss of market share in the 1980s disappears (figure 3.3b); but the decline in world market share in the first part of the 1990s remains. Export unit value as calculated by the IMF is a quantity weighted ratio of actual prices of German commodity exports to prices in a base year.[20] It is thus the value of exports in constant terms, and it indicates the extent to which the world market is willing to pay previous prices. The base year is 1995. The quantity weight for the country series is the 1995 value of exports (in US dollars). It seems that

---

[20] Export unit value is a Laspeyres index $\sum p_t q_t / \sum p_0 q_0$.

Germany has indeed lost world market share after unification. This is consistent with a reduction in the export share of GDP from 31.5 percent in 1989 to 26.3 percent in 1991, and to a further decline to 22.8 percent in 1993. (The export share then rose to 35.5 percent in 2002.) Western German firms were keen to sell their products to the new eastern German market at their doorstep instead of shipping them to the global market. Internal demand for German exportables increased, so that the relative price of export goods rose. This means that there was a real appreciation of the Deutschmark in the first part of the 1990s as a consequence of German unification, and this appreciation hurt exports. The inverse of the real exchange rate can be used as an indicator of price competitiveness. This indicator is illustrated in figure 3.3c, where a downward movement means a decrease in price competitiveness because of the inverted scale (and a real appreciation as measured by the effective real exchange rate). Competitiveness is here measured against nineteen other industrial countries on the basis of the nominal exchange rates and consumer prices. As already mentioned, this same result is obtained in an alternative approach in which tradables and non-tradables are distinguished instead of exportables and importables. In this approach the real appreciation of the Deutschmark at the beginning of the 1990s can be traced back to the large consumption transfers in the aftermath of German unification.

Another indicator of competitiveness is profits, and the maneuvering space for cost pass-through. Germany traditionally has had a quality edge in its products, implying a low price elasticity of demand. That is, German firms have been able to charge a higher price without losing export volume. However, there is anecdotal evidence that a sector like the electro-technical industry has been complaining about falling export prices. For instance, Siemens, with a total revenue of €40 billion, claimed an annual revenue loss of €2.5 billion in some years in the late 1990s. Indeed, the index of export prices of commercial products increased by only 0.8 percent per year in the period 1991–2002;[21] it rose by 2.7 percent in the 1980s. Export unit value, the value of German commodity exports in constant prices (as defined above), fell by 26.5 percent in 1990–2002. This value had risen continuously from the 1960s to 1992, even in the recessions of the 1960s and 1980s. With the exception of a small decline during the 1970 recession, it had not previously experienced such a fall. According to a recent study, Germany's export prices have remained fairly constant since 1987 against a base of 100 in 1975, whereas relative unit labor costs have increased (Brauer 2003: figure 22). Furthermore, unit labor costs rose more in the 1990s (until 1998) in Germany than abroad, and increased more than the domestic price (Brauer 2003: figure 14). A similar picture holds for Japan, including a loss of world market

[21] Council of Economic Advisers (2002: table 56*).

shares, whereas the relative unit labor costs and the relative export price for the United States fell and US world market share increased. All this indicates a narrowing of maneuvering space for German product prices and for shifting costs, i.e., for pass-through. The relative decline of foreign unit labor costs corresponds to an appreciation of the Deutschmark. When relative unit labor costs rise more than the relative export price, this translates into a squeeze on profits; firms react by scaling back investment and labor demand.

Additional insight into Germany's export position is obtained by looking at the product structure of exports. Industry, with 23 percent of employment and of gross value added in the German economy, produces 89 percent of Germany's exports (2001). Four sectors of industry account for 59 percent of total exports: machine building goods (18.1 percent), cars (17.7 percent), chemical products (12.4 percent), and electro-technical products (11.1 percent). Services contribute only 10 percent to German exports, whereas they make up 28 percent of US exports.[22]

Germany is traditionally strong in some important branches of the industrial sector. Looking at RCA coefficients,[23] by which we can measure comparative advantage (a positive value indicates an advantage), machine building, car production, and the chemical industry have a high comparative advantage (table 3.2); so do measuring instruments and medicinal goods. Small and medium-sized technology-based firms, and also somewhat larger family owned or family dominated enterprises, have established themselves in niches of the world market, giving them maneuvering space for cost pass-through, for example Linde (refrigeration), Stihl (saws), and Trumph (investment goods). But since the early 1970s electro-technical products (electrical machinery, apparatus, and appliances), telecommunications instruments, and optical equipment, including photographic apparatus and watches, have lost their comparative advantage—photographic apparatus even earlier, in the 1960s. In the electro-technical sector, the so-called volume business, i.e., mass production of electronic and household appliances (e.g., "white goods"), has more recently migrated to the developing countries, whereas comparative

[22] A similar percentage applies to the UK (28.4 in 2000); 19.9 percent of the exports of France are in services.

[23] Revealed comparative advantage. The RCA coefficient r_i represents revealed comparative advantage for a sector. It measures a sector's exports relative to its imports against the sum of all exports relative to the sum of all imports. Intuitively, exports and imports of all sectors are taken as a norm; the coefficients indicate whether a specific sector performs better than the norm. Positive values indicate an advantage revealed by trade, negative values a disadvantage. The coefficient is defined as

$$r_1 = \log\left[\frac{x_i^G/M_i^G}{\sum_i x_i^G / \sum_i M_i^G} \right].$$

TABLE 3.2
Trends in Germany's comparative advantage[a]

	1970	2001
54 Medicinal and pharmaceutical products	48.9	22.7
59 Chemical material and products	37.7	33.0
72 Machinery specialized for particular industries	89.3	88.6
74 General industrial machinery and equipment, parts	59.8	47.4
76 Telecommunications and sound recording apparatus	25.5	−27.9
77 Electrical machinery, apparatus, and appliances	8.5	−11.3
78 Road vehicles	76.0	56.0
88 Photographic apparatus, optical goods, watches	8.7	−23.3

Source: Own calculation.
[a] RCA coefficients.

advantage for large-scale industrial machines (power generation) and more complex products has been retained. The pharmaceutical sector also seems to be eroding, so that Germany no longer can claim to be the pharmacy capital of the world: BASF has sold its pharmaceutical branch to Abbot Laboratories, and Hoechst has ended up in the new international firm Aventis with its headquarters in France, now taken over by the French firm Sanofi. The traditional chemical sector does not seem to be able to participate in the technological race for the pharmaceutical products of tomorrow on the basis of its biotechnology. The new innovative IT and biotechnical products have to be imported.

Germany has a strong comparative advantage in medium-technology products, whereas it exhibits a comparative disadvantage in high-tech goods relative to the United States, France, and the United Kingdom, again using RCA coefficients (figure 3.4). In this approach the level of technology is defined in terms of R&D expenditure relative to the product price. German firms, including the medium-sized firms of the "Mittelstand," have been successful with sophisticated and human-capital-intensive medium technology in niches of the world market, especially machine building. With respect to the technology intensity of exports, Germany has a similar pattern of specialization to that of Japan.

This result is consistent with other observations. Germany's share in R&D-intensive products in total world exports fell from 18.5 percent in 1991 to 15 percent in 2002 (*Bundesministerium für Bildung und Forschung*, 2003: xvii). The balance of payments for technological services, including patents, R&D services, engineering services, and data processing, is negative by €5.9 billion (2002),[24] and has been negative in each year throughout the 1990s. There is anecdotal evidence that a

---

[24] Deutsche Bundesbank: Statistical time series EU 2069–EU 2071.

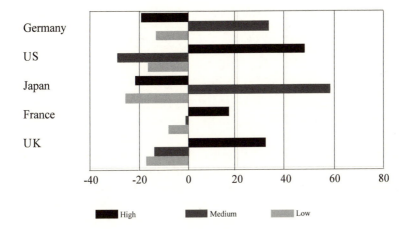

Figure 3.4 Competitiveness according to technology intensity, 2001 RCA coefficients according to technology intensity. The figures for Germany are for 2000.

new telephone for a German multinational was engineered completely in China, and a new dialysis instrument in Lahore, India. In 2001 German firms spent 36 percent of the research budget abroad, a much higher percentage than in the past (Belitz 2004); however, foreign firms spent about the same amount on research in Germany.

To sum up: so far, Germany has fared well with its exports. But there are some signs that the maneuvering space for price setting and for the pass-through of costs has been reduced. It is an open question whether the existing comparative advantage in medium-technology products will be sufficient to compensate for the lack of competitiveness in the new sectors as a propellant for investment, growth, and employment.

INVESTING ABROAD

Accumulating capital abroad can be viewed from two opposing standpoints in the context of economic growth. On the one hand, it can be seen as a sign of strength that a country is running a current account surplus that can be used to invest elsewhere; it can also be viewed as a sign of continuing strength, since subsidiaries will mean future exports of intermediate goods, as foreign direct investment and future exports are seen as complementary. On the other hand, investing abroad may be regarded as an alternative to investing at home; then foreign direct investment is seen as a substitute for future exports. In any case, a distinction has to be made

TABLE 3.3
Foreign direct investment of German industry (percent of gross investment)[a]

	Outbound	Inbound
1991–1995	11.5	−0.5
1995–2000	39.1	7.5
1996–2000	42.8	8.6

[a] For data see Siebert (2002b).

between the point of view of the firm and the point of view of the economy. From the firm's point of view, having a portfolio of investments in different countries opens up options, reduces costs, increases the profit potential, and spreads risks. From an economy's point of view, capital exports may be seen as a normal process: a mature economy uses its current account surplus to finance investment opportunities with a higher marginal productivity of capital abroad. As a compensation for supplying capital now, it receives dividends later. The exit of capital may also, however, be viewed in the context of locational competition, according to which countries compete for the mobile factors of production (Siebert 2000b). A country losing capital or unable to attract capital has a lower production potential and a lower labor productivity. In this context, the outflow of capital has negative implications; employment is affected negatively.

In this debate, the magnitude of the outflow may be relevant. It is astonishing that outbound foreign direct investment (FDI) of German industry remains relatively strong. In the period 1995–2000 outbound FDI of German industry made up 39.1 percent of annual gross investment of industry; the inflow was relatively weak (table 3.3). German industry has 13.4 percent of its capital stock abroad (in 2000). For some sectors, the gross outflow relative to gross investment at home is even higher, for instance 80.3 percent for metal products and machine construction, 70.3 percent in vehicle construction, and 55.9 percent in the chemical industry in 1995–99.

Admittedly, foreign direct investment in vehicle construction was strongly influenced by the Daimler-Chrysler merger in 1998, and there is a strong inflow of investment in the chemical industry. Moreover, FDI represents not greenfield investment, but overwhelmingly equity investment. Whereas greenfield investment increases the capital stock directly and also has a direct capacity effect in the country in which investment takes place (and a more or less direct withdrawal effect in the country in which investment is not forthcoming), equity investment brings new management and organization as well as a new technology; this has a more indirect effect on the production potential of an economy. Nevertheless, German firms have a portfolio of locations abroad, and they can react to changes in their environment, including policy-induced new conditions in Germany, by reallocating production and investment worldwide. They can avoid national policy measures. Some larger German firms now have half of their employees abroad. Of the 10 million cars produced by German firms in 2002, 4.5 million were produced abroad. Even the smaller and medium-sized firms of the Mittelstand have diversified their locations through subsidiaries abroad. Foreign direct investment may very well reflect the structural change that we have discussed, i.e., the relative loss in importance of industry and the possible erosion of the export position. If this trend continues with the same magnitude, the hypothesis that FDI today will lead to exports in the future is questionable.

Taking together the competitive position on the product markets and German direct investment abroad, one can conclude that German industrial firms are efficient and competitive in selling products in the market, but from the perspective of employment in the economy they are not efficient in creating jobs. As already mentioned, 2.8 million jobs have been lost in industry in the 1990s so that there is definitively an erosion of the job basis.

The Role of Government

Without any doubt, government absorption of about half of GDP, as in Germany, exerts an influence on the growth performance of the economy. With respect to the size of governmental absorption, it can be argued that the GDP growth rate is a function of the size of the country's government, i.e., of its share in GDP. Under ceteris paribus conditions, we can expect a bell-shaped curve. Starting from a low level of government activity, the GDP growth rate (on the vertical axis) can be expected to increase with a larger share of government in GDP (on the horizontal axis), for instance by spending on a reliable legal frame for the market, on internal security, or on infrastructure. An extremely low share of government in GDP may be associated with deficiencies in the legal frame of the market, causing high transaction costs because of the uncertainty of contracts. This has a negative effect on the productivity of the private sector that outweighs the negative effect of taxes. After passing a threshold, the negative effect on work effort and entrepreneurial effort begins to dominate (Bleaney, Gemmel, and Kneller 1999; Fölster and Henreksen 2001; Kamps 2004). Thereafter the growth rate of a country declines with an increasing share of government in GDP. Apparently, government activity includes not only allocation, i.e., providing public goods and financing them through taxes, but also distribution, including the social security system. It may well be that a 50 percent share of government consumption from GDP, as in Germany, is an impediment to growth.

Besides the size of expenditures, the type of governmental absorption plays a role. Panel studies of the industrialized countries show that governmental investment has a positive impact on growth.[25] While the output elasticity of public capital is positive for most OECD countries, the impact varies with the type of financing; lump-sum finance ensures the largest effect, while credit financed public investment is the least desirable from a growth perspective (Kamps 2004). Under ceteris paribus conditions, a declining share of governmental investment in infrastructure such as roads, airports, and harbors, as can be observed in Germany, means a lesser impact on growth. Of course, the transportation infrastructure has been modernized to some extent; this represents an improvement and extension of existing facilities. But except for those associated with German unification, examples of completely new infrastructure facilities are hard to find—one is the airport in Munich, which took thirty years to complete from its inception; another is the new railroad track between Cologne and Frankfurt which opened in 2002. Unlike in France with the TGV, there is no technological leapfrogging in the German infrastructure. It should be noted that government investment has a much lower productivity and contribution to the growth rate than private investment.

Governmental consumption, the overwhelming part of governmental expenditures, although having a short-run positive effect on the demand side, withdraws resources from the private sector and has a negative impact on growth. It is the withdrawal effect through taxation that affects growth. Specifically, subsidies can be expected to have a retarding influence. Subsidies require sizable financial resources and imply distortions and efficiency losses. They tend to protect and favor old and declining sectors such as agriculture, coal, and shipbuilding, and they impede structural change. Their financing puts a burden on the other sectors of the economy. It can be expected that subsidies amounting to €156 billion per year, or 7.5 percent of GDP (Boss and Rosenschon 2002), will have a negative impact on growth.

Government also exerts an influence on growth from the financing side. Taxes have a negative impact, mostly through their effect on private investment. Indirect taxes have a weaker negative effect than direct taxation. Germany's tax share in GDP remained relatively stable for over forty years, but had risen to 25.4 percent by 2000; it stood at 23 percent in 2002. Social security contributions have a negative impact as well. Social absorption does not have a direct productivity effect, and contri-

---

[25] For a detailed analysis, see German Council of Economic Advisers (2002: 209).

butions represent a tax wedge, which serves as a disincentive for effort. They have increased considerably over time. Moreover, the budget deficits and the level of public debt show a negative impact in empirical studies; public debt too has gone up. Thus, the financing side of government has had a negative effect on economic growth.

In addition, the government influences growth by defining the institutional design of the economy. A regulation-growth linkage shows up in empirical studies for the OECD countries, with economy-wide indicators of regulation and privatization and industry-level indicators of entry liberalization exhibiting a positive impact on multifactor productivity (Nicoletti and Scarpetta 2003). Strict product market regulation is one factor contributing to lower growth performance; the institutional arrangement of the university sector is another.

A Newly Declining Economy?

A number of factors occur to anyone considering potential reasons for Germany's low growth performance. Among these are both temporary factors and long-run phenomena.

A first hypothesis is that German unification has changed the economic data set, especially the fiscal policy stance, and that this is the reason for slow growth; accordingly, the intensity of the problem will ease over time and the issue will fade away. There is no doubt that the transfers weaken growth, but this is not the overriding reason for the poor performance. Moreover, the hope that the issues will disappear by themselves is misleading.

A second theory is that Germany is a mature economy, and mature economies grow at a slower pace. By this interpretation, Germany can be compared to Japan. It has a similar pattern of export specialization with respect to the technology intensity of products; new avenues of specialization are not being opened up; and capital accumulation is finding fewer and fewer investment opportunities.

A third explanation, the erosion hypothesis, goes further. As we will see in the next two chapters, this idea links low growth to high unemployment and the failure of the labor market, as well as to unsolved problems in the social security system. These issues were already present before German unification. It seems that the superstructure of the "social market economy" affects the economic base negatively, in that the set incentives represent distortions and lead to lower efficiency, to a loss of economic dynamics, and to high unemployment. This is a systematic problem, a structural issue, and it will not fade away. The superstructure was developed at the end of the 1960s and in the 1970s in a situation of strong growth rates and high productivity increases, which no longer prevail today. Together with the regulation of the product markets, the institutional design of the capital market, the system of human capital formation, i.e., the governance system of the economy, and the setup of the political processes, the superstructure of the generous social security system implies that the economic base of the economy can no longer expand as in the past. As a result, the economic base is weakened. External shocks to the economy become harder to digest. The factors endogenous to growth become weaker. There is an erosion of economic strength, as discussed by Olson (1982). According to this hypothesis, there is again a similarity with Japan, which extends to the governance system both countries, relying heavily on consensus. A major difference, however, is that Japan has already had to come to grips with a financial bubble that burst in 1989, severely affecting the balance sheets of banks, insurance companies, and firms in the producing sector (Siebert 2000a).

A fourth hypothesis, that of newly declining countries, puts Japan and Germany into the historical category of countries that have fallen behind in their economic development. They would then be the NDCs, the "newly declining countries," following in the footsteps of Sweden in the 1970s and 1980s, the United Kingdom in the three decades after World War II, and Argentina in the twentieth century. According to this view, a mature economy can no longer solve major economic policy issues; it has become immobile with respect to institutional modernization, its structures so rigid that institutional adjustment can no longer take place. The political process in such countries has lost its problem-solving capacity

It is too early to determine the extent to which this fourth hypothesis may be valid. But the third hypothesis seems to fit. If we accept that idea, then the future development is not predetermined, but can be shaped by economic policy. However, it would seem that the three issues of low growth, high unemployment, and unsustainable social security systems are intertwined. To unravel them and solve Germany's economic problems, an institutional Big Bang may be needed. We will look at this problem in more detail in the following chapters.

CHAPTER FOUR

The Labor Market: High and Sticky Unemployment

The poor growth performance of the German economy from 1995 to 2003 is partly linked to the high unemployment the country experienced during this period, with 4.4 million officially unemployed in 2003 and 1.6 million more in labor market schemes of different sorts. An important economic resource—labor and human capital—was being wasted, and the economy's production capacity was not being fully utilized. Unemployment has ratcheted upward since 1970. Apparently, Germany reacts to shocks with an increase in persistent unemployment. The institutional setup for the realm of labor is malfunctioning. This is at the heart of Germany's economic woes.

THE STEPWISE INCREASE OF UNEMPLOYMENT

Unemployment increased from 0.7 percent in 1970 to a peak of 11.4 percent in 1997.[1] It stood at 10.5 percent in 2003 (figure 4.1)—or 9.3 percent according to the EU-standardized rate—and amounts to an increase in West Germany from 100 050 to 2.8 million persons. In each of the three recessions in the 1970s, 1980s, and 1990s, roughly one million were added to the unemployed in West Germany, and the numbers unemployed were not significantly reduced during the intervening boom years; therefore each recession started from a higher level of unemployment than the one before. It can be expected that the same thing will happen in the next recession. Unification added the structural unemployment problems in eastern Germany, shifting the unemployment curve still further upward. Although unemployment in eastern Germany is severe, at 18.6 percent in 2003, however, the German unemployment problem has evolved over more than three decades, and its root cause does not lie in unification.

Long-term unemployment, that is the proportion of those unemployed for more than a year, has also ratcheted upward, from about 5 percent of

[1] I appreciate critical comments on this chapter from Björn Christensen, Eduard Herda, Patrick Meier, Frank Oskamp, Patrick Puhani, and Jens Weidmann.

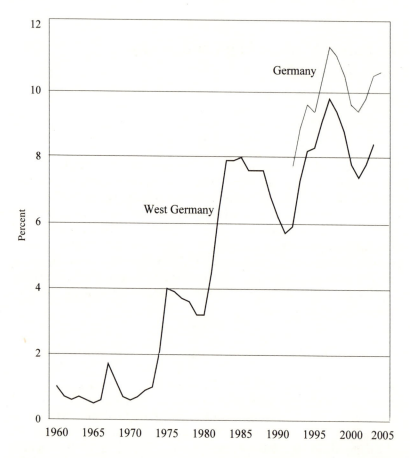

Figure 4.1 Unemployment rates in Germany, 1960–2003 (% of all civilian employees). *Source*: Federal Labor Office (2003); German Council of Economic Advisers.

total unemployment to more than 30 percent. Again, in each of the three recessions long-term unemployment moved upward and increased persistently. There are three loops in which the proportion of the long-term unemployed fell somewhat—in the late 1970s, the late 1980s, and the late 1990s—but this improvement was only temporary, and the unfavorable trend was quickly resumed (figure 4.2). It now extends to the middle-aged unemployed (aged 35+).

The stepwise increase in unemployment is linked to negative shocks that have hit the economy. Demand for exports can fall abruptly, stag-

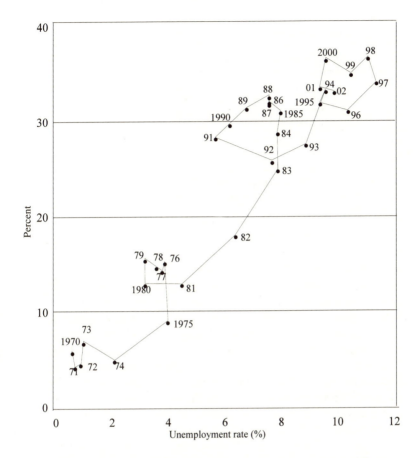

Figure 4.2 Long-term unemployment. *Source*: Federal Labor Office.

nate, or simply increase below trend in a downturn of the world economy (demand shock), i.e., when a financial crisis breaks out in other countries, when important global policy instruments such as fiscal or monetary policy are changed, when sectoral crises such as global over-investment require adjustments, or when secular sectoral shifts have an impact. Alternatively, and simultaneously, the price of an important resource such as oil can jump when a scarcity of the resource occurs or when the property rights for extraction change, as in the 1970s (supply shock). It is normal for such shocks to occur, and they hit other countries as well. However, the German economy reacts to these shocks somewhat differently from other economies. Whereas in the United States job creation sets in shortly after a recession begins, in Germany it takes much longer for employment to pick up. Moreover, it now takes longer than in

TABLE 4.1
Job creation: annual growth rate of employment (percent)[a]

	1970–1980	1980–1990	1991–2003	1991–1995	1995–2003
Germany[b]	0.4	1.0	0.0	−0.7	0.3
France	0.5	0.3	0.7	−0.2	1.1
Italy	0.7	0.1	0.3	−1.6	1.2
EU 12[c]	0.4	0.6	0.6	−0.6	1.2
UK	0.2	0.7	0.6	−0.2	1.1
USA	2.4	1.8	1.3	1.5	1.2

Source: OECD, OECD Economic Outlook.
[a] Calculated as in table 1.1 as an exponential growth rate.
[b] 2003 forecast.
[c] 1969–90: West Germany; since 1991: data for unified Germany.
[d] EU 15 excluding the UK, Denmark, and Sweden.

the 1970s and the 1980s for employment in Germany to start to rise after a recession; it was five years after the 1993 recession before employment began to increase again, whereas in the recessions of the 1970s and the 1980s employment started to increase after two or three quarters.[2]

The response of the Germany economy to shocks, therefore, seems to have changed over time. It can be argued that Germany is relatively open compared with economies such as the United States; therefore it is affected by international phenomena more intensively. Moreover, Germany's openness, as measured by the share of exports in the German GDP, has increased, from 22 percent in 1970 to about 35 percent in 2003. This means that global change has a stronger impact on the economy. But other countries, especially small ones, exhibit an even greater openness, and face similar shocks. The shocks of the 1990s may have been asymmetric for Germany; this definitely applies to the impact of unification on the fiscal policy stance. But this argument is not convincing with respect to unemployment if one looks at the long-run and step-wise increase of unemployment in West Germany since the 1970s. Finally, the nature of the German economy may have changed, so that it can no longer digest shocks so easily; or other countries may have altered their institutional setup, so that an external shock that was symmetric in the past is now felt more in Germany than in other countries.[3]

There has been minimal net job creation in Germany since the 1970s except for the jump in employment figures resulting from German unifi-

[2] German Council of Economic Advisers, Annual Report 2000, figure 40.
[3] The participation rate, i.e. the share of the labor force in the population, increased from 1970 to 1990 by roughly four percentage points and remained constant in the 1990s; this change in labor supply is not a sufficient reason for unemployment.

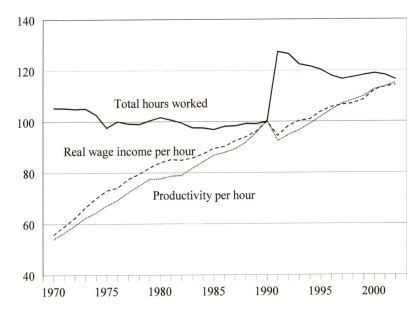

Figure 4.3 Real wage income, labor productivity, and labor demand (hours worked), 1970–2002 (1990 = 100). *Source*: Federal Statistical Office, Volkswirtschaftliche Gesamtrechnungen, Revidierte Ergebnisse, 1970 bis 2001.

cation. The size of the labor force stagnated in the 1970s and 1990s; it increased only in the 1980s (table 4.1). Total hours worked, another measure of aggregate labor demand, decreased in the three decades at a rate of roughly 0.5 percent per year;[4] only in the late 1980s and the late 1990s did Germany experience an increase in total hours worked (figure 4.3). This is in stark contrast to the United States, where net job creation was higher by two percentage points in the 1970s and by one percentage point in the 1980s and 1990s. More jobs were also created in the European countries since 1990.

Part of this difference can be explained by population growth—including immigration, which turns into an augmentation of the labor force. Another aspect of the low rate of job creation is a potentially different response to negative shocks. Low growth performance is yet another factor, because as a rule employment is related to growth. Sectoral change, for instance from industry to services, is a further explanation.

---

[4] 1.0 percent per year in the 1970s, 0.3 percent in the 1980s, and 0.5 in the 1990s (1991–2000). Calculated with the formula

$$r = (Z_t/Z_o)^{(1/n)} - 1$$

where r is the rate of change, Z_t is the total number of hours worked at t, and n is the number of periods.

As we have seen in chapter 3, German industry reduced its workforce by 2.7 million people in the period 1991–2002,[5] i.e., by nearly one third. Apparently, other countries experiencing similar sectoral changes have managed to create more new jobs in the service sector. In any case, the weak performance in job creation is the flip side of increased unemployment. To determine the causes of unemployment, we need to know why job creation is low.

The stepwise ratcheting upward of unemployment signals that Germany's institutional design for labor is malfunctioning. There are three major aspects of this problem: the institutional design of wage formation, the role of the reservation wage, and a systematic weakening of the demand for labor. I will address these issues now.

WAGE POLICY

The term "wage policy" may be surprising to international, and especially Anglo-Saxon, readers who are used to the notion that wages as a price for labor are determined in the market. But in Germany "wage policy" plays a decisive role; wage formation is not left to the markets but is determined by the social partners—the trade unions and the employers' associations—in a sector-wide bargaining process. The typical procedure is to start wage negotiations for a specific sector in a specific region, and then to apply the negotiated wages to all the other regions of the same sector. Normally, negotiations are started in economically strong regions. The sector-wide wage contracts are usually mimicked in the other sectors of the economy, including the public sector. As a result, the bargaining process is de facto nationwide. The length of wage contracts varies: its duration tends to be one year at least, sometimes two years. Since the length of the contract of individual unions varies, different unions may start the wage round. Usually one of the larger unions, either the metalworkers' or the service sector union, begins the negotiations.

Besides the branch or industry contract between the trade unions and the employers' association, trade unions can also contract with individual firms (firm contract). About 21.5 million workers were covered by 2731 branch contracts in 2002, about 3.5 million workers by 4853 firm contracts. This means that roughly 70 percent of the dependently employed are covered by contracts.[6] It is estimated by the Institute of

---

[5] This figure relates to plants with 20 employees and more.

[6] According to the 2001 IAB panel of 15 000 firms, representative for 2.1 million firms, 63.1 percent of the employees are covered by industry-wide contracts in West Germany and 44.6 percent in East Germany. With respect to businesses (*Betriebe*), the respective figures are 22.1 and 5.5.

the Labor Office that the contracts serve as an orientation for another additional 15 percent of the workforce. In addition to the 7584 wage contracts, there are 23 961 contracts referring to conditions of the work contract such as working hours and days of vacation.

The negotiated wage is not necessarily identical to the market wage. Whereas in the 1950s and 1960s there was a positive wage drift, in the sense that the effective wage increase determined by the market was higher than the increase in the negotiated wage, that could no longer be observed in the 1990s. This suggests that the negotiated wage increase became more and more binding on a macroeconomic scale. It may be argued that the unions could get a noticeable pay rise more easily in the first decades of the last half century, when productivity growth was strong, without negatively affecting employment, and that it may have become harder for them to obtain such an increase later on.

Trade unions have not accepted the proposal of the German Council of Economic Advisers as an orientation for union wage policy. According to the Council's concept, the decisive clue to a higher employment rate is the ratio between the increase in the real wage that the firm has to pay (*Arbeitnehmerentgelt*), including the social security contributions paid by employers—i.e., the change in labor costs, or the producer's wage—relative to the productivity increase.[7] When the producer's real-wage cost per hour rises more than productivity per hour, i.e., when there is wage overshooting, labor demand is likely to fall; if the wage rate rises less than productivity, i.e., if there is wage moderation, labor demand increases. Whereas in a situation of full employment real wages can increase with the growth rate of productivity without generating unemployment, when unemployment is high, wages should not be raised according to the observed trend in the growth of labor productivity per hour: instead, the wage increase should remain below that trend, in order to bring the unemployed into employment. That means that a discount should be applied to the trend of productivity growth. Put differently, the expected increase in labor productivity is different from the observed past trend when unemployment is high. The expected increase in labor productivity should be calculated not simply by dividing output by the hours worked by those employed, but by also including in the numerator of the productivity measure the potential hours of the 6 million who are in official and hidden unemployment.

Admittedly, wage policy becomes more difficult for the trade unions when the contributions to social security rise. These contributions are part of the labor costs from the point of view of the firms; and, together

---

[7] The correct measure is marginal productivity per hour. For simplification, I here use average productivity per hour.

with the gross wage income before tax, they must be covered by productivity. If the government is forced to raise contributions to social security, as during German unification, this will absorb part of the productivity growth. The remaining potential for pure wage increases is then squeezed.

Of course, labor demand is influenced by a whole set of factors, for instance the business cycle situation, the growth rate, the institutional setup, and a general trend of reduction in weekly working time and an increase in part-time work; but, in general, a relationship exists between wage overshooting and the weakness of labor demand measured in hours worked. From 1970 to the end of the 1980s, real wage income per hour was at a higher level than productivity, setting the variables for 1990 equal to 100 (figure 4.3). Labor demand, measured in total hours worked, declined. Only at the end of the 1980s did the productivity level come closer to labor income; then labor demand rose. In the first part of the 1990s, labor income in Germany was at a higher level than productivity. Again labor demand declined, although admittedly this was due in part to the restructuring in eastern Germany. Since the mid-1990s, the productivity level has been higher. This picture is more or less confirmed if a base year other than 1990 is chosen. Note that the sharp increase in total hours worked, and the decline in productivity and the real wage per hour in 1990, both reflect German unification.

Looking at the rate of wage moderation on an annual basis, i.e., the productivity increase per hour minus the augmentation of real labor income per hour, the early part of the 1970s shows strong wage overshooting, especially during the first oil crisis (figure 4.4). There is wage moderation in the second part of the 1970s, but overshooting again in 1980-81 during the second oil crisis. It seems that the real wage overhang continued to have an impact into the mid 1980s. There was wage overshooting again in 1987, 1992, and to a smaller extent in 1995, 1999, and 2000 (see below).

Looking at Germany's wage policy from 1970 to 2002, periods of overshooting and wage moderation follow each other. There are five periods of wage overshooting. One may argue that there is no increasing trend in wage overshooting and that the areas above and below the 0-line seem to balance out over time, but this is not sufficient to eliminate unemployment. Since, given the German institutional setup of layoff constraints, hiring a worker is a long-term decision, like an investment, for a firm, each wage overshooting represents a negative shock to the labor market and an incentive to the firm to reduce its demand for labor. The impact of such a negative shock is not compensated by a short period of wage moderation. Firms need some stability in their expectations of wage moderation. Cycles in wage policy with overshoot-

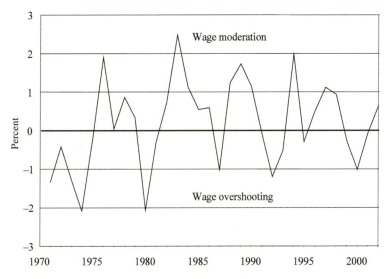

Figure 4.4 Wage moderation Not adjusted for unemployment; aggregate data for Germany since 1991. *Source*: See figure 4.3.

ing and moderation are not helpful in this respect; such cycles have a negative impact on employment. With unemployment rising, it is telling that wage moderation of more than 1 percent was applied only in the years 1976, 1983/84 (in and after the recession), 1988–90, 1994 (after the recession), and 1997. Of these moderations of at least 1 percent, only the moderation in the late 1980s lasted for a longer period, i.e., three years: it showed a positive impact for employment.

Comparing increases in the statistically observed productivity and in labor income is, however, a distorting measuring rod for wage policy, since part of the observed productivity increase is due to the rise in unemployment. An increase in unemployment means a move up the marginal productivity curve of labor; consequently, labor productivity increases when unemployment rises. Ironically, productivity would be highest if only one person in the economy, say the German chancellor, worked. Consequently, the measured annual productivity increase must be adjusted downward in order to account for the rising unemployment.[8] When this is done, there is less wage moderation and the curve of wage moderation shifts downward (figure 4.5). The employment-adjusted productivity growth as a guideline for wage policy is lower for those

---

[8] The annual wage moderation has been recalculated for the change in unemployment. It has been assumed that workers who are laid off have a lower productivity than those who are employed; their productivity is here assumed to be only 0.7 that of those who are employed.

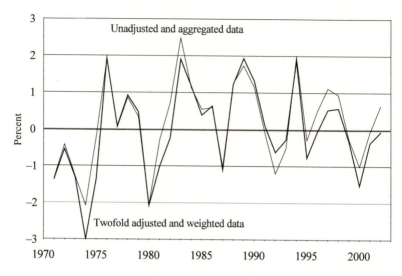

Figure 4.5 Wage moderation, unadjusted and adjusted. *Source*: See figure 4.3.

years in which more people are laid off; during unemployment it is higher for years in which unemployment is reduced. In the 1970s and the early 1980s, the adjusted wage overshooting was higher and lasted longer than the unadjusted overshooting; the adjusted wage moderation in the early 1980s was lower.

The present analysis, in which we use data for the German economy as a whole since 1991 for the employment levels and data since 1992 for the measured productivity rates, includes yet another distortion. Eastern Germany was hit by a structural transformation shock; consequently unemployment skyrocketed, especially in the early 1990s. The rates of wage moderation for eastern Germany in 1992 and afterwards would not adequately account for the structural break. We therefore have two options for adjusting the productivity growth: either to calculate the wage overshooting for the year 1990, or to adjust the data for 1992 and thereafter for the structural unemployment.[9]

Whereas a full employment situation implies that marginal productivity is equal to the real wage, there was a serious wedge between these two variables in eastern Germany in 1990 and after. Define f as marginal productivity per hour, w as the nominal wage, and p as the price level (with w/p as the real wage); then the equation

[9] Note that the approach of wage moderation applied here presupposes an initial situation of full employment as in 1970.

$$f(1 + \alpha) = \frac{w}{p}$$

holds, where the wedge is defined as

$$\alpha = \frac{(w/p) - f}{f}$$

Simplifying and using data for average instead of marginal productivity, the wedge α was 0.41 in 1991 in East Germany; in other words, the real wage was 1.41 times the productivity. This wedge is nearly identical to the wedge in wage income, the gross wage per head, and unit labor costs of East Germany relative to West Germany. Put differently, East German productivity per hour was 42 percent of the West German level, and wages per hour were 59 percent. This is a sizable gap.[10] In figure 4.6 the data for productivity and wage denote the East German level, setting the West German level equal to 100 in each year.

Such a high wedge between the real wage and productivity is, of course, a strong incentive to reduce jobs. Furthermore, the observed growth rate of productivity in a given year does not represent the permissible rate for the wage increase. On the contrary, a reduction must be made in order to melt down the initial wedge. Let us therefore assume that this wedge is to be reduced over a period of 12 years. If this correction in the calculation of wage moderation is made, it affects the total German picture only partially, since eastern Germany accounts for only about one fifth of the West German total hours worked in the early 1990s. But as a result, the curve of wage moderation is shifted downward (figure 4.5).

The overall result is that wage policy in Germany has contributed to the unemployment situation. It has failed to adjust productivity growth to the increase in unemployment by applying a discount factor to the measured productivity increase. The unemployment adjusted productivity increase is lower for years in which unemployment rises; correspondingly, it is higher for years in which unemployment falls. Wage policy is thus one of the factors accounting for the increase in unemployment.

In terms of economic growth, the second part of the 1980s can be considered a successful period for Germany, its first since the catching-

[10] Note that these data differ somewhat from the variables per head in table 1.2, with productivity per head at 34.9 and wages at 49.3. One reason is that in table 1.2 eastern German productivity relative to that of western Germany is calculated in nominal values, whereas here it is calculated in constant values with 1995 as the base year. Another reason can be seen in the total number of hours worked versus the total number of employees; whereas typically the individual worker works more hours per week, which should make the productivity per hour lower, more of the employees may work part-time, so that productivity per head is reduced. In any case, both measurements tell the same story. In both approaches, "eastern Germany" means without Berlin.

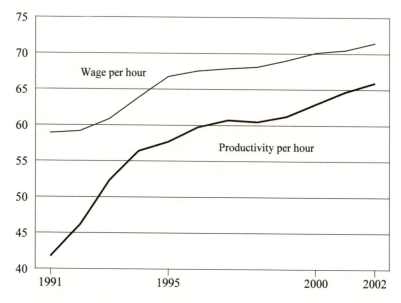

Figure 4.6   The productivity gap in East Germany West Germany = 100 for each year. *Source*: See table 4.3.

up phase that ended in about 1970. The growth rate gained momentum, with an average of over 4 percent in the period 1998-90, and investment was strong. About 3 million new jobs were added in the course of recovery from the recession, and unemployment receded by two percentage points in the second part of the decade. In spite of some wage moderation by the trade unions and a more employment oriented wage policy than previously, real wages and incomes of workers increased, albeit less than in the 1970s, given the lower productivity growth. Inflation fell, so that price level stability was established. The budget deficit went to zero in 1989, and a tax reform was implemented in several steps. The current account then reached a surplus of 4.9 percent of GDP. Two of the major policy players, the central bank and fiscal policy, had done their homework; the social partners were more employment oriented than in the decade before. Even with some criticism of the wage policy, this was an example of how the assignment of responsibilities between the different players has to be approached. Never again has Germany seen such a period of positive development.

Wage Structure

Another impact of the trade unions' wage policy is the absence of German wage differentiation. An economy needs a differentiated wage structure so that the profiles of qualification supplied by workers and the profiles desired by firms can be matched and an equilibrium between supply and demand attained. It is realistic to expect that the 34 million German employees will exhibit different degrees of qualification; the labor supply of an economy can be viewed as representing a productivity staircase, where each step represents a different productivity level. Moreover, there is a strong shift in the structure of labor demand reflecting the sectoral change in the economy from the industrial sector to the service and information sectors. This means that the existing qualifications are re-evaluated. Human capital can become outdated, and this will show up in a decline of the relative wage. If employees whose qualifications become obsolete cling to their previous wage, some of them will lose their jobs. The wage structure must adjust to the changes in the structure of labor demand.

In addition, the characteristics of the wage contract have changed, requiring more differentiation. In contrast to traditional industry, with standardized production on assembly lines, the service sector requires a different type of labor input, where individual effort in a personal relationship with the customer becomes more important. Instead of a standardized labor contract whereby labor input can be easily measured, there is now a result-oriented labor output to assess, and individual effort is much harder to measure. This is especially true for the information society. Thus, the nature of the labor contract is changing from a standardized contract which is fairly similar for all employees to more individualized one. Instead of input, it is output that is more relevant. In addition, incentives require that the employee take over part of the economic risks. Therefore the new contracts no longer fully reflect the traditional pattern of risk allocation between the firm and the employee, in which the firm more or less guarantees a fixed income and so takes over the market risk for the employee. Instead, employees are tending to take over some of the commercial risks. Even in industry, effort-oriented contracts are beginning to prevail, in that groups of people are being made responsible for their production result. All this requires a change in the orientation of the wage structure.

Looking at these developments, it has to be admitted that we do not know the precise set of wages or the exact wage structure for the economy as a whole that could bring about equilibrium in the labor market. However, there are some indications of a serious misalignment in the German case.

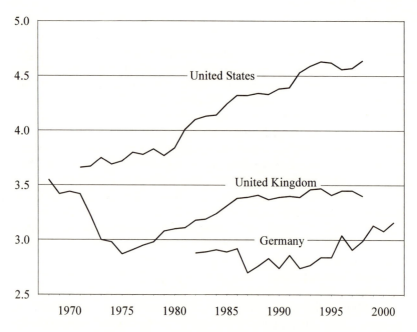

Figure 4.7 Relative earnings. Highest decile of gross labor income to lowest decile. *Source*: OECD Labor Market Statistics; for Germany, own update for 1997–2001.

First, wage differentiation, measured as the relation of the highest to the lowest decile of wages, is low in Germany compared with the United Kingdom and the United States for the 1980s and the 1990s. (There are no more recent internationally consistent data.) Moreover, in the Anglo-Saxon world the spread has increased over the last twenty years (figure 4.7). It is now agreed in the field of economics that all industrial countries have been affected by a relative decline in the demand for low-skilled labor.[11] However, whereas other countries have responded by increasing the spread of wages, Germany's wage structure has remained relatively stable. This is not only surprising given the background of the international experience, it is all the more surprising since Germany experienced an expansion in its labor force following unification. This increase in labor supply was not in highly qualified labor but labor accustomed to working with obsolete physical capital. Thus, German unification should have been an additional reason for the development of a more differentiated wage structure.

[11] For instance in Germany industry axed 1.8 million jobs in 1980–2000, of which 1.6 million were less qualified positions. The service sector has expanded employment by 3.7 million, of which 2.8 million are qualified (Siebert 2003: 115).

Second, there is a disequilibrium between the high and rising unemployment rate of the low-skilled and their relative wage. The low-skilled, i.e., those without a formal school diploma, had an unemployment rate of 22 percent in 2000[12] following increases in the 1990s in both western and eastern parts of the country; yet the wage structure with respect to qualification has remained constant for western Germany since the early 1980s and for eastern Germany since 1993[13] (Christensen 2003). This means that the low-skilled are exposed to an increasing unemployment risk, but their relative wage cannot respond to ameliorate the situation. This result has been obtained from the data set of the 2001 Socioeconomic Panel, comprising more than 10 000 individuals in about 5000 households who were interviewed in waves in the period 1984–2001;[14] a wage equation including age, marital status, the level of qualification, and other factors (West and East) was estimated empirically. Earlier results for the period 1984-95 indicated a slight decline in the spread, in terms of qualifications (Christensen and Schimmelpfennig 1998; Schimmelpfennig 2000). This means that, taking into account the relative decline in the demand for low-skilled labor, this segment of the labor force is being priced out of the market; the relation between wage structure and qualifications is not adequate. This has resulted partly from a wage policy favoring the lower income groups, negotiating for them an over-proportional increase in previous years. Moreover, the lowest wage group, in industry, was discontinued. In addition, the expansion of the welfare state (to be discussed later) has increased the reservation wage, which in turn has led to an increase in the informal minimum wage, so that the lower segment of the labor market has dried up.

Third, the wage structure in Germany seems to be compressed from above. This is indicated by an empirical study in which relative wage rigidity is measured as the relative wage compression of high-skilled versus low-skilled wages (Puhani 2003: figure 4). Such a compression is almost inevitable when the floor of the wage structure is too high and, at the same time, the financial means to compensate the negative effects of the wage structure, in terms of unemployment and social welfare, is through taxes on higher-income labor: in that case, effort and the incentive to build human capital are reduced, and the inducement to move to the underground economy is strengthened. Insufficient wage differentiation is thus linked to the welfare state, as will be discussed later, but at the same time it is connected with the low dynamics of the economy.

[12] 19.4 in western Germany and 50.3 in eastern Germany in 2000.

[13] There was an increase in the spread over 1990–93.

[14] For this specific analysis of unemployment, the data set comprised 2893 persons in western Germany and 1332 in eastern Germany persons (means, for the period 1984–2001).

To sum up, wage differentiation in Germany is not adequate. The trade unions' argument that the multitude of wage contracts gives sufficient flexibility in the wage structure of the economy, relating wages appropriately to the productivity level, does not hold.

THE PHILOSOPHY OF REDUCED WORKING TIME

Germany had long pursued the idea of reducing working time. Total hours worked per year have been reduced by about 0.5 percentage point per year since 1970. In 2003 they stood at 55.3 trillion hours for the united Germany, against 52.0 trillion for West Germany alone in 1970. The average number of hours worked per year fell from 1956 per head in 1970 to 1443 in 2002 (including the self employed). This is extremely low compared with other industrial countries, even accepting that an increase in part-time work has been a factor in the reduction. The share of those working part time has increased from 6.3 percent in 1970 to 27.0 percent in 2003, but the average working time of the part-time employed fell from 989 hours per year to 642 in 2003, whereas hours worked by the full-time employed fell from 1939 to 1635 hours.

The reasons for this reduction are diverse. The increase in unemployment and the rise of the shadow economy are two factors. Moreover, there may be a preference among Germans for leisure time, as shown for instance when a holiday occurs on Thursday and the Friday is used as a "bridge-day," allowing a four-day weekend. Additionally, it is a reflection of the inefficiency of the German university system, where it is not unusual for students to take their final exams at age 27 or older. But the overwhelming reason is political. The trade unions used the reduction in working time as a strategy to solve the unemployment problem. Their underlying philosophy started from the premise that the volume of work in the economy is independent of the wage rate and the wage structure, and that more people can be employed if they all work fewer hours, a concept readily welcomed by nearly every clergyman. The reasoning was as simple as the rule of three: if 34 million dependently employed Germans are working 55 trillion hours per year over eight hours per day, how many additional jobs could be created if each of them worked only seven hours a day? Of course, this philosophy is quite naïve. The volume of labor is not a given constant, but depends on the wage level and the wage structure, among other things. The reduction in working time included various governmental measures for early retirement; it was an attempt to solve the unemployment problem to the detriment of the public old-age pension system, and required higher contribution rates which aggravated the unemployment problem. The trade unions thus attempted to shift part of their responsibility to the state and the general public, including the workers.

Whereas trade unions were successful in reducing working time, they failed in their specific campaign for a 32-hour work week in West Germany. In addition to the above mentioned naivety, it may have become apparent to the public that a 32-hour work week represented a constraint, which would limit the decision space in the economy and thus reduce potential productivity gains, thereby affecting the competitiveness of firms. For instance, R&D in Germany could hardly be competitive internationally with such a time constraint. This also applies to those functions of a firm that are essential in the sense that, if they are not performed, serious organizational bottlenecks arise. Maybe people sensed this, and resisted the demand of the trade unions for reduced working hours. In addition, Germans were feeling extremely uncertain about the future because of the risks of unemployment so perhaps they were not prepared to sanction the experiment. The norm for the working week is now 35 hours, and the effective hours worked is somewhat higher for the fully employed. The unions also failed with their strike for a 35-hour work week in eastern Germany in 2003 (see below).

A related continuous demand of the trade unions is to reduce overtime, but firms need this as buffer of flexibility, and workers like overtime, especially in certain phases of their life cycle, for instance when they have young families and mortgages for their newly built homes. Another failure of the trade unions, again most dominant of IG Metall, was the demand for a reduction in the retirement age to 60, a claim that was still actively being advanced in 1999 and 2000. This demand collided with the necessity of adjusting the pay-as-you-go pension system to the conditions of an aging population, so that eventually it was given up.

Apart from the general reduction in working time, there has been quite a bit of progress with respect to working time flexibility, both in the branch treaties and at the firm level. One major breakthrough was at Volkswagen, where the working week can now be reduced to 28 hours with a (less than proportional) reduction in pay when sales run low; similar schemes have been applied in other firms. This approach helps to keep people employed in a slump because it allows firms to reduce their labor costs. In addition to this downward flexibility, there is an upward flexibility in branch contracts and firms' practice, in that additional hours can be worked above the 35 hours per week if overtime is paid at a higher rate or is compensated by leaves later on. Firms also have introduced a rich variety of working time options (in agreement with the workers' councils) from which workers can choose, for instance a four-day work week with 9 hours a day, or two or even three shifts per day (including a shorter night shift) and shifts on Saturdays.

Another important innovation is the time budget of a year. According to this concept, the total hours for a year are fixed, but can be spread flexibly depending on the sales conditions of the firm. For instance, more hours per week can be worked in a period of high demand, or fewer hours when demand is weak. Some firms have now started lifetime accounts of working hours; this allows employees to take sabbaticals or to retire earlier. All these measures have increased labor productivity. The productivity gains have been used to improve the competitiveness of firms, and to increase the real wage of employees.

Since I am critical of the workers' councils and trade unions in another context, it should be acknowledged that quite a bit of working time flexibility has been obtained through them in a pragmatic way. Thus, Germany has been able to ward off the rather bitter debate on the 35 hour work week that France had. Nevertheless, there remain many constraints on working time, with the overall result that the average number of hours worked per head in Germany is low, and that strategic human resources like research capacity is restrained.

TRADE UNIONS ARE LOSING MEMBERS

In the wage formation process, as well as in many other aspects of the institutional setup of the German labor market, trade unions play an important role. The German Federation of Trade Unions (DGB), the umbrella organization of the sectoral trade unions, had 7.4 million members in 2003. Verdi, the Unified Service Sector Union, and IG Metall, the Metalworkers' Union, with about 2.6 and 2.5 million members, respectively in 2003, are the dominating sectoral unions. Of the total workforce, 17.3 percent are organized in DGB-affiliated unions; sometimes a higher figure of 30 percent is mentioned. However, about 20 percent of trade union members are retired, so only 6 million are actually of working age. This means that, relative to the 34 million dependently employed in 2003, the degree of organization is low, as mentioned above. It may seem ironic, but the trade unions have about the same number of members as the number of the unemployed (including those in hidden unemployment).

Trade unions are losing members. This is especially apparent in the 1990s. From 1991 the DGB lost 4.4 million members, more than a third (table 4.2). IG Metall has lost more than one third of its members, and the unions making up Verdi lost 40 percent. However these figures give a somewhat misleading picture, because the trade unions attracted many new members from eastern Germany, accustomed to trade union membership under the Communist system; thus, the high level of

TABLE 4.2
Decline in union membership, 1991–2003 (millions)

	DGB	IG Metall	Verdi
1991	11.8	3.62	4.32[a]
2003	7.4[b]	2.53[c]	2.61
	−4.4	−1.09	1.71

[a] The number represents the members of the unions that formed Verdi in 1991.

[b] The number includes the 451 000 members of the clerks' union (DAG) integrated into the DGB in March 2001 (preliminary estimate).

[c] The number includes the 183 000 members of the textile union as well as the 133 000 members of the wood and plastics union integrated in 1998 and 2000 into IG Metall.

membership in 1991 is somewhat of a distortion, owing to German unification.

Taking a longer-run perspective, membership in 2003 is lower than in 1980 in spite of an increase of 10.5 million in the (dependently employed) labor force over the same period (table 4.3). The degree of organization fell from 26.4 percent of the dependently employed in 1980 to 17.3 percent; it had been 31.9 percent in 1950. (Again, for this calculation it was assumed that 20 percent of trade union members are pensioners.)

In order to become more effective, unions have been consolidating since the 1990s. In part this reflects the structural change in the economy, i.e., the relative decline of employment in the producing sector and the rise of the service sector. It has proved to be more difficult to organize employees in the service sector, especially in the New Economy, where the traditional standardized work contract does not apply and where effort-oriented and profit-sharing arrangements are typical.

The consolidation of unions also is a response to declining membership. In 1998 the 183 000 members of the textile union integrated into IG Metall; in 2000 the 133 000 members of the wood and plastics union also joined IG Metall. In March 2001, five unions of the service sector merged to form the new union Verdi, among them ÖTV, the Public Services, Transport, and Traffic Union with 1477 million members; DAG, the clerks' union, with 451 000 members; IG Medien, the media union, with 175 000 members; HBV, the commerce, banking, and insurance union with 441 000 members; and DPG, the Postal Workers' Union, with 446 000 members. Thus, the clerks union, which was separate from the DGB, came under the umbrella of the German Federation of Trade Unions.

The power of trade unions arises not only from their membership. They also have political influence in a country where it's the done thing to be a

TABLE 4.3
Union membership in Germany[a,e] ('000)

		1950	1960	1970	1980	1990	1991	2000	2003
DGB	German Federation of Trade Unions	5451	6379	6713	7883	7938	11800	7772	7363
IG Metall	Metalworkers' Union	1352	1843	2223	2622	2727	3624	2763	2525
IG BCE	Chemicals, Energy and Mining Union					[1041][b]	[1425][b]	892	801
GCGPK[b]	Chemicals, Glass, Paper, and Ceramics Union	410	520	599	661	676	877		
Verdi	Unified Service Sector Union					[2826][b]	[4317][b]	[2989][b]	2614
ÖTV[c]	Public Services, Transport, and Traffic Union	726	963	977	1150	1253	2138	1477	
DAG[c]	German Salaried Employees' Union	307	450	461	495	505	585	451	
DBB	German Public Servants' Federation	190	650	721	819	799	1053	1200	1258
Estimated union density in Germany[d]		31.9	25.2	24.1	26.4	24.9	28.5	17.9	17.3

Sources: DGB; Ebbinghaus (2002); Federal Statistical Office; German Council of Economic Advisers, *Annual Report* 1990/91 and 1997/98.
[ ]: The brackets show the hypothetical size of the union before its later formation.
[a] 1950–90: data for West Germany; 1991–2002: data for unified Germany.
[b] IGCGPK joined IG BCE in October 1997.
[c] ÖTV and DAG joined Verdi in March 2001.
[d] Without DBB.

member of the trade union. For instance, Chancellor Schröder and part of his cabinet are trade union members. Of the 251 Social Democratic members of the Bundestag in 2002–06, 186 members or 74 percent belong to a trade union, and some are still active in some function of the union in spite of their parliamentary membership. For the PDS, the Socialist Party, the percentage is 50, for the Greens 24, for the Christian Democrats 4, and for the Liberal Democrats 2.

Union power also depends on the willingness of firms to remain members of the relevant employers' association, although non-organized firms can be forced into a firm contract. If firms leave their association, the trade unions lose their counterparts and collective bargaining becomes less relevant. Anecdotal evidence suggests that smaller and medium-sized firms are less willing to be members of an employers' association. Some of the associations have split up into two, only one of which has the role of wage negotiation. Data of the IAB panel of 15 000 businesses[15] considered to be representative of 2.1 million businesses indicate that the number of those employed covered by collective contracts is falling—for instance, for the branch contract, from 72.2 percent in 1995 to 63.1 percent in 2001 (West Germany); in eastern Germany only 44.4 percent of those employed are covered by branch contracts in only 22.1 percent of the businesses. Branch contracts are especially relevant in coal mining, construction, banking and insurance, and among government employees.

Although the trade unions have only a small proportion (less than 20 percent) of the active workforce as members, nearly 70 percent of the employed are covered by a union contract. It would seem therefore that trade unions continue to have a decisive influence on wages and the wage structure, even when they are losing members. They also have a strong impact on economic policy and the government; in a way, they can block major changes in the institutional setup of the labor market and other regulations. This is a puzzle, at least at first sight.

The Institutional Design for Wage Formation

The power of the trade unions is rooted to a large extent in Germany's institutional setup. Let us take a closer look at some of the legal regulations that define the role of the collective contract and that of the unions. The social partners, i.e., the trade unions and the employers' associations, have been granted the right to negotiate a collective wage contract relating to wages, working time, holidays, fringe benefits, and other

---

[15] "Business" is used here for the German word *Betrieb*.

aspects of work. The unions have the right to strike, and thus to force such a contract onto the firms, if they have sufficient support from their members and the public. Membership is voluntary, but the result of collective bargaining is binding for the members. Thus, the negotiated wage applies to all firms that are member of the employer's association and to all workers who are members of the trade union. That means that the social partners are legally entitled to regulate labor relations as if they had parliamentary power to pass laws (wage autonomy, or *Tarifautonomie*). The collective contract is defended by the courts; it even applies to the unemployed union members who can take a job only at the union wage. For collective bargaining to be binding, both workers and firms must be members of their respective organizations. In practice, however, the collective contract has an impact beyond membership. De facto, firms do not differentiate wages according to union membership or non-membership of workers. As a matter of fact, they would not be allowed to ask their employees whether they are union members. Firms apply the negotiated wage to non-union members as well; otherwise they fear they might motivate workers to join the unions and thus make the unions stronger. Trade unions that have a high degree of organization in a firm can force the firm to agree to a union contract; this then is not a branch contract but a firm-specific arrangement. Moreover, the negotiated wages set the standard for the non-unionized firms as well.[16] Thus, negotiated wages represent the norm for the economy, even for the unemployed. Trade unions are further empowered because they participate in co-determination on the supervisory boards of companies and in workers' councils. The social partners also enjoy functions assigned by law, either explicitly or implicitly. For example, they have the right to regulate in a binding way many aspects of how the work process is organized in the firms; and retirement savings plans negotiated by the social partners receive a preferential treatment in terms of taxation.

Limitations on the Deviation from the Collective Contract

The clue to the German setup is the fact that the negotiated collective wage contract is legally protected by a number of provisions. These mechanisms prevent market forces from bringing about an equilibrium with less unemployment. They protect the insiders in their jobs with respect their negotiated wage income, the security of their jobs, their working hours, holidays, and fringe benefits; but they effectively discriminate against the outsiders,

---

[16] For instance, the local labor offices mediate jobs for the unemployed according to the local customary wage, which is influenced by the negotiated wage.

the unemployed. Discrimination occurs for the simple reason that, the more protected is the economic position of the employed, the lower is the incentive for firms to hire additional workers. These regulations define a wage cartel, giving trade unions and employers' associations the right to set wages but not making them institutionally responsible for the outcome in the labor market, i.e., increased unemployment.

Constitutional Freedom of Coalition

Article 9, sec. III, of the German Constitution defines the right to form a coalition. This positive freedom of coalition, the cornerstone of all other legal stipulations with respect to the labor market, is limited in that nobody can be forced to become a member of a coalition (negative freedom of coalition).

Giving the social partners the right to set wages does not guarantee an outcome of full employment. Of course, there is moral suasion, in that they should take into consideration the impact of wages on unemployment. But apart from moral suasion there is no explicit mechanism that prevents a wage policy from resulting in high unemployment. No formal responsibility has been defined for the social partners, and it would be extremely difficult to specify such a responsibility. For instance, the social partners could have been obliged to increase wages in regions with high unemployment by *less than* the national average; or they could have been asked to finance the unemployment benefits from their membership dues; or a condition could have been established that the unemployed should have some say on the collective bargaining results, at least where unemployment is extremely high. In any case, if one is not prepared to rely a little more on the market, the dependencies are somewhat blurred so that the responsibilities cannot be easily defined in legal terms. Nevertheless, the Constitutional Court has ruled that the social partners—although having norm-setting rights—do not have a norm-setting monopoly. Parliament may intervene in the *wage autonomy* of the social partners if other constitutional rights are violated. Reducing mass unemployment allows more individuals to enjoy their constitutional right of freedom of occupation (Article 12) and to develop their personality (Articles 1 and 2). Thus, Article 9 and the positive right of coalition do not imply that some limits cannot be put on wage autonomy.

Limiting the Individual's Option to Deviate

One basic legal principle, the *Günstigkeitsprinzip* (the principle of the most favorable condition— para. 4, sec. 3 of *Tarifvertragsgesetz*), stipulates that as a union member the individual worker can deviate from the negotiated union wage contract if such deviation is favorable for him. "Favorable," however, is interpreted in a narrow sense by the labor courts as relating to a higher wage than that defined in the collective contract or shorter working time. The risk of becoming unemployed or losing the security of the job cannot legally be part of a worker's decision to deviate from the union contract; this has been explicitly decided by the highest labor court (*Bundesarbeitsgericht*) in 1999. The reason given is that, according to this decision, wages and working time on the one hand, and the security of a job on the other, cannot be compared. But any freshman of economics knows that in economic reality the three variables—wage level, working time, and job security—are strongly correlated. Moreover, all three variables can be expected to be relevant factors in the utility function of workers. Limiting the individual's choice means creating rigidity in the labor market; it also contributes to the low degree of wage differentiation. Allowing the risk of losing the job to be taken into consideration or giving individual workers the right to decide for themselves whether to deviate from the union contract would meet the strong opposition of the trade unions, which fear the loss of organizational power.

The favorable implication of these provisions for the employed is that the unemployed can enter the labor market only according to the rules of the collective contract, unless the social partners have introduced provisions allowing for the unemployed to start a job at below the collective pay scale. For instance, such a provision holds in the chemical sector, with a dispensation of 10 percent below the collective wage in the first year of employment. But in general, the existing collective wage is protected against the competition from the unemployed. Of course, such protection of the insiders represents a hindrance to market entry.

Limiting the Firm's Option to Deviate

Another legal provision is equally essential in establishing the role of the collective contract and the power of the unions. It stipulates that firms cannot deviate from the union contract unless this is permitted in the contract itself (para. 77, sec. 3, of the Business Constitution Act, or *Betriebsverfassungsgesetz*). Thus, even if workers of a firm would agree by an overwhelming majority to work more hours per week, or to accept a lower wage, in order to make their jobs safer, this is *verboten* (forbidden). This regulation applies even to those firms that are not members of an employers' association.[17] Labor contracts guaranteeing job security as well the wage have advantages both for the workers and the firm. In that

---

[17] It thus de facto violates the negative "freedom of coalition" guaranteed by the Constitution, i.e. that no one should be forced into a union membership.

sense they are efficient contracts: they allow a higher welfare than the union contract. Moreover, they give important signals to the market. But such efficient labor contracts are not legally feasible in Germany. Admittedly, firms and workers have disregarded this stipulation to some extent; but legal battles in the courts have sustained the law preventing efficient labor contracts. Again, the trade unions oppose a change in this regulation for fear of losing power.

Other Mechanisms Strengthening the Collective Contract

Firms are free to leave their employers' associations. However, they continue to be legally bound for the duration of the contract and even until a new contract is established. For contracts that specify the framework of labor relations, for instance with respect to holidays or extra pay, and that tend to have a duration of five to seven years, this is a long time. Besides this legal aspect, trade unions can force a firm that has left the employers' association, and thus walked away from the branch contract, to sign a firm-specific contract if the trade union has enough organizational power in that firm. Therefore firms may be reluctant to leave their employers' associations.

Moreover, the labor minister has the right to declare a wage as mandatory if this is deemed to be in the public interest. This instrument has been used in the construction sector and in low-paid occupations like window cleaning—labor-intensive and wage-sensitive activities. A mandatory setting of wages in these areas is one of the reasons for the observed constancy of the relative wage of the low-skilled in the last two decades in spite of the relative decline in the demand for this type of labor.

Finally, a more recent law has enacted a minimum wage for the construction sector. This was intended to reduce the impact of low-skilled labor from other countries of the European Union such as Portugal and from the countries of middle and eastern Europe. Another recent law requires private firms to honor the results of collective bargaining, irrespective of whether they are member of an employers' association, if they are carrying out construction work for the government or are providing local transportation services. By this law, even product market regulations are used to enforce the collective contract.

Layoff Constraints

Another aspect of German wage formation is that layoff restraints and the practice of getting around them with high severance pay represent an exit constraint that is anticipated by the firms in their demand for labor. Layoffs are permitted only under specific conditions. Besides the case of individual misbehavior, a layoff is allowed if it is warranted by a firm's economic situation. In that case a set of social criteria have to be observed. From 2005, these criteria have been limited to four: the duration of employment in the firm; age; obligations to support other people, i.e., spouses, dependent children, and aged relatives; and physical handicaps. Moreover, employees with outstanding performance can be exempted from the law; management and the workers' council can present a consensus list of those protected from the layoffs. A severance pay has to be made, varying with the length of employment in the firm and amounting up to one year's salary as a general rule and up to 1.5 year's salary for an employee with 20 years' service. In the case of mass layoffs, severance pay is negotiated with the workers' council in a social closing plan. The layoff rules are subject to interpretation, so disputes are typically settled in the labor courts. The labor courts have developed the legal setting further (judge's law). Consequently, firms face uncertainty in the case of layoffs. In order to reduce the number of court cases, from 2005 the employer may offer as severance pay half a month's salary per year of employment with the firm to anyone laid off because of the economic conditions of the firm. If an employees agrees to this proposal, he voluntarily renounces his right to go to court.

The layoff constraint for those employed is an exit constraint and represents an entry barrier for the unemployed; it weakens the demand for labor. The restraint is especially binding when in times of crisis wages and working time are sticky downward for the individual firm.[18] Up to 2004 only firms with fewer than 5 employees were exempt; from 2004 the layoff constraint applies to firms with fewer than 11 employees, if these employees have taken up employment starting on or after January 2004. This change is part of the reform in the Agenda 2010 of the Schröder government. But this reform only reintroduces a stipulation that was in effect when the Red-Green coalition came into power in 1998 and was then done away with immediately. Thus, the change does really not deserve the title "reform."

Restraints on Contracts with Limited Duration

Work contracts with limited duration are possible only if they are justified by the limited type of work, for instance a research project with limited funding. There some exemptions to this rule. One is the above mentioned case of very small firms, where layoff restraints do not apply so that the work contract can be limited de facto. Another is that contracts that do not stipulate giving a reason for the termination are allowed, but they

---

[18] Downward flexibility in working time with a reduction of pay can reduce the impact of layoff constraints.

have to be limited to two years at most. Clearly, this reduces flexibility in the labor market. Yet a third exception applies (as of 2004) to newly founded firms, which can have contracts with limited duration of up to four years without giving reason.

Codetermination and Workers' Councils

The power of trade unions is also rooted in the codetermination on the supervisory boards of firms with more than 2000 employees, and in workers' councils. The board is the supervisory, not the operating, body of a firm. In incorporated firms[19] with more than 2000 employees, half of the board's seats are taken by the capital owners, the other half by the employees; there are six for each side in firms with less than 10 000 employees (see chapter 14). One of the seats on the employees' side is earmarked for a managerial employee; two of the six (or proportionately more for larger firms) are reserved for the trade unions. The chairman of the board has two votes. In the coal and steel industry 50 percent of the employees' seats are allocated to the trade unions. Here the chairman does not have two votes, but there is an additional "neutral" member. In firms of other legal forms, employees must make up a third of the members of the board according to Business Constitution Act. The members of the board on the employees' side are elected by an electoral board. Trade unions have the right of nomination for their positions.

The workers' council has a set of decision rights where its consent is mandatory according to the Business Constitution Act. These include the day-to-day operations such as working conditions, the organization of working time and the work process, as well as the introduction of new production processes. The council is involved in layoffs, the closing of firms requiring a social closing plan, and all social issues of the employees. Its decisions are binding for all employees. Its members are elected; they are not necessarily representatives of the trade unions, although the unions play a dominant role.

Rules on Strikes

Trade unions have the right to call a strike, provided that a collective wage contract does not exist or has expired. They do not have the right to strike during the contract period (although wildcat strikes may occur illegally) or during a period of grace after the contract has expired and when negotiations are taking place. They also are not allowed to strike during a media-

---

[19] Including limited liability companies (GmbH).

tion period, which either side may call for after negotiations have broken down. The proposal of the mediator has to be accepted by both sides; if it is not, a strike may be called. A strike is allowed only if 75 percent of the trade union members agree to it; the negotiation result is final if at least 25 percent of the members accept it. Striking union members receive a strike compensation from the union; non-union workers who are out of work because of the strike (for instance honoring the picket line) forgo any pay. In the legal interpretation, the strike is the last possible means to come to a contract (the "ultima ratio"). The government has few legal means to prevent a strike. Firms are allowed to lock out all their workers (not only those on strike), but this instrument has not been used lately as it is becoming less and less acceptable in public opinion; moreover, it hurts those of their employees who are not on strike.

Recently, the unions have resorted to the strategy of "warning strikes" or "pinprick strikes" preceding negotiations. In this form of strike the union harasses strategically selected firms, say, because they produce essential intermediate inputs whose non-availability will hurt other firms; the union fluctuates between the firms concerned. These strikes are allowed by the labor courts with the specification that a ratio between those on strike and those who could be threatened by a lockout in a bargaining district is not out of proportion, i.e., where a small number of strikers cannot effectively put a large number of people out of work. This is a rather unrealistic requirement, since a lockout rarely finds public support and thus is not effective against pinprick strikes which take advantage of intensively networked firms. Consequently, employers do not seem to have much countervailing power against such strikes.

This strategy backfired for the union in a strike in the eastern German metal industry in the summer of 2003, when the union attempted to get a 35-hour work-week. Since products produced in eastern Germany are intermediate inputs for the western German automotive industry, the strike eventually shut down western German automobile production, laying off far more workers than those on strike in eastern Germany. The strike had to be called off, the second time in the history of strikes and the first since the 1950s; this led to a severe internal struggle in IG Metall and to a loss of support for the trade unions. It may prove to have been an event similar to UK Prime Minister Thatcher's fight against the miners' union in 1984–85 and US President Reagan's struggle with the air traffic controllers in 1981, the only difference being that the blow to the trade unions was self-inflicted.

A strike does not invalidate the labor contract between the firm and the employee; the contract is merely inactive. The firm is not obliged to pay the salaries, not even for those employees who are not on strike, if it is impossible for the enterprise to continue the operation. The firm may close its operation or parts thereof without formally locking out the employees. The workers then have to live off their savings or on social welfare. The firm also has the right to continue its operations with the labor of those not on strike, and it may even pay them a premium. The firm against which the strike is directed cannot use labor market instruments like support for short-time work. Employees, whether on strike or only without work owing to the strike, do not receive unemployment benefits; their social security coverage, however, continues. Strikers and the trade unions have the right to erect a picket line that working employees have to cross. The strikers are allowed to try to persuade the non-strikers to join them, but they are not entitled to block the entrance to the firm with force. Nor can they block deliveries.

Until 1985, the Federal Labor Office paid unemployment benefits to workers who became unemployed because of a strike in other regions of the affected sector, because intermediate inputs could not be obtained for production. Since then,[20] the Federal Labor Office is required be neutral in case of a strike. That means that employees of the same sector who are laid off as a ramification of the strike can no longer collect unemployment benefits; it is a permanent request of the trade unions that this ruling be repealed. It is a different story if the impact of the strike is felt in more distant firms, however; then unemployment benefits are paid.

Labor Courts

A feature of the institutional setup of the labor market are the labor courts that deal with all sorts of labor issues, including disputes on the stipulations regarding collective wage bargaining, the rules for strikes, layoffs, etc. The court system is structured vertically with three tiers, the Supreme Labor Court having the final say except for constitutional issues. The labor courts are a specific form of the administrative courts. They have developed legal rules in addition to the written law (the "judges' law").

THE RESERVATION WAGE AND THE LOWER SEGMENT OF THE LABOR MARKET

An important aspect of the labor market in Germany is the institutional arrangement for those who cannot find a job or who are unable to work because of illness or for other reasons. This setup protects people, but at the same time it influences the search behavior of the unemployed and their willingness to accept a job offer. All this has an impact, especially on the lower segment of the labor market.

[20] Para. 146, Sozialgesetzbuch III.

Unemployment Benefits

Germany has developed two types of unemployment support, in which some changes become effective from 2004 onward.

Unemployment benefits of type I (*Arbeitslosengeld*) constitute 67 percent of the previous net income after tax (for an unemployed person with at least one child).[21] Until 2003 the duration of benefits varied with age with a maximum of 32 months for those over 44 years of age. In 2002 1.9 million persons received this type of benefit. From 2004, benefits have been reduced to one year; for those aged 55 and over the duration will be 18 months. Unemployment benefit of type I is an insurance benefit. A person unemployed can receive benefits if he and his employer have paid contributions for at least 12 months in the two years prior to unemployment. This duration of employment was tightened from a three-year period which applied until 2003; moreover, the benefits no longer automatically increase with wages, as had previously been the case. The reduced duration of benefits is to be phased in gradually, and will apply to those who become unemployed on or after February 1, 2006. With this new law, Germany returns to the duration of benefits that applied until the mid-1980s. It follows the proposal by many economists (German Council of Economic Advisers 2002) for those under 55, for whom the period for unemployment compensation is twice as long as the duration in the United Kingdom and the United States.

Unemployment benefit of type II has been redefined in the reform laws agreed upon by the Bundestag and the Bundesrat in December 2003. The old type of benefit (*Arbeitslosenhilfe*) is still effective for those who have been receiving it so far: it amounts to 57 percent of the net wage,[22] is paid when unemployment benefits of type I expire, and is provided indefinitely. It is linked to the previous working income, albeit with a weakening link. This type of benefit, which was paid to 1.7 million people in 2002, requires means testing for neediness. "Neediness" is currently defined more strictly than previously, for instance with respect to the income of a married couple if one of them receives a high market income; some aspects of wealth are also taken into consideration.

As of 2005, this type of benefit will be changed considerably for new recipients, for whom the unemployment benefit of type I expires. They will receive a monthly amount of €345 (in western Germany—€331 in eastern Germany), plus a transfer for housing, plus a supplement for two years. The supplement depends on the level of the previously received employment benefit: it is capped at €160 per month in the first year, plus

---

[21] 60 percent for singles. Benefits are adjusted according to wage increases; they require a minimum time of contributions paid.

[22] With at least one child—53 percent in other cases.

up to a further €160 for the spouse and €60 for each child; in the second year the supplement is reduced by 50 percent. Thus, the level of the new type of unemployment benefit II has been separated from the applicant's previous income. Recipients will be allowed to earn an additional market income without losing all of the unemployment benefit of type II. In the income bracket of up to €400 per month an additional 15 percent can be earned without losing benefit; in the range €400–900, 30 percent, and for €900–1500, 15 percent. This is in line with proposals to introduce better incentives to move to the "first" labor market, i.e., the labor market governmental support schemes. Except for the supplement, the unemployment benefit of type II is at the level of social welfare; it is thus lower than the previous transfer for most of the recipients. As of 2005, this type of benefit will also apply to those social welfare recipients who are capable of working (see below).

Short-Time Working Benefits

Employees of firms experiencing structural adjustment problems can now receive special support when working fewer hours for a period of just 12 months, instead of 24 months before 2004.

Sickness pay

Sickness pay is provided at 100 percent of the previous gross wage for the first six weeks and at 70 percent thereafter.[23]

Social welfare benefits

Social welfare benefits (*Sozialhilfe*) represent payments to allow a dignified lifestyle for those who cannot earn their own living. This includes the elderly without sufficient income, although this group has no relevance for the labor market; those of working age who are unable to work; and those who cannot find a job and/or for whom the unemployment schemes do not apply or whose unemployment benefit is lower than the standard set by social welfare. This benefit is highly relevant for employment and unemployment. Social welfare benefits require evidence of neediness, meaning insufficient income and no wealth. Social welfare is defined by minimum requirements for living and is means-tested. Benefits consist of a regular monthly payment, plus specific payments for housing rents and heating costs, both of which are covered up to a limit. A lump-sum payment is also made for the purchase of household goods. For those

---

[23] It cannot surpass the net wage income. For the same illness it is limited to 78 weeks in a three-year period.

recipients who are not covered by public health insurance, medical costs are covered. Payments are differentiated according to marital status and the number of children and their respective age.[24]

Conceptually, benefits are linked to a price index for low-income groups though they are not automatically indexed to it. Their actual increase is coupled to the augmentation of pensions. For a married worker with one child, the benefits amount to 68.5 percent of the lowest net wage in industry, 75 percent of the going wage in the sector, and 100 percent of low-paid professions such as jobs in catering. For a single person they amount to 42 percent in industry and up to 67 percent in catering (Boss 2002).

Although these data paint the general picture, a court case of August 2003 in the second level of the administrative court may be telling to the international reader. A German living in Florida, named "Florida Rolf" by the press, had been receiving German social welfare benefits for three years, including the monthly rent of $875 for his apartment near the beach in Miami.[25] A medical expert had testified that the recipient, who had lived in Florida for twenty years and then become poor, could not live in Germany because of the risk of falling into an incurable depression. The court case concerned the fact that the German authority administrating social welfare decided that $600 would be sufficient for the apartment rent; the court, however, ruled that the higher payment had to be continued for six months in order to give the recipient the opportunity to find a new apartment in Florida. Without evaluating this individual case, the case shows that social welfare is understood as an entitlement that is supported in the German court system. It should be mentioned that the cost of the lawyer is taken over by the state if a person is poor; a "service industry" has come into existence illustrating the possible ways to gain such an entitlement.

Out of the 2.7 million people who received social welfare payments at the end of 2001, 1.6 million were between 15 and 64 years of age, when most people tend to be working. One third of those capable of working were under 30 years of age. Some of them were unable to work because of illness or handicaps; some were in training; 140 000 did have jobs, but at a wage that was lower than welfare benefits;[26] and 700 000 were regis-

---

[24] As of July 1, 2002, the standard payment to the head of a household in western Germany averages €292 per month. The standard payment for the spouse is 80 percent of this amount. Depending on their age, children will receive 50–90 percent of the payment made to the head of the household. Certain groups of individuals with special needs can receive additional support.

[25] Frankfurter *Allgemeine Zeitung*, August 20, 2003.

[26] Of those social welfare recipients registered as unemployed, some received unemployment benefits as well; these benefits were supplemented because they were lower than welfare.

tered as unemployed. Thus, 800 000 is the rough number of those who were unemployed but able to work. In the 15–64 age group the average duration of social welfare receipt was 27 months. Recipients of welfare tend to have a lower level of qualification. More than 40 percent of the 1.4 million households receiving welfare were single people. The number of recipients doubled from 0.9 million in 1980 to 1.8 million in 1990 and then rose to its most recent figure in 2001.

The Reservation Wage

The government unemployment benefit and social welfare benefit provide an income when people are not working. This income defines the reservation wage, i.e., the wage that an unemployed person expects from his next job; and this in turn influences his search intensity and his willingness to accept a job. The higher the income provided by government, the higher the reservation wage. Empirical analysis of the unemployed in Germany shows that the reservation wage is at 120 percent of the wage received by the out-of-work when previously employed (Christensen 2001). This is unusually high compared with other countries. Empirical analysis also shows that the reservation wage is not reduced with the duration of unemployment (Christensen 2002). This means that search intensity is lower and willingness to accept a job is reduced. The labor market dries up from the supply side.

At the same time, the arrangements described above imply that neither workers nor their unions will accept a wage rate below the reservation wage. Thus, welfare benefits of the German type define a floor to the wage structure. Whereas the reservation wage is a variable defined for each individual, the wage floor is an institutional variable; it represents a de facto minimum wage. In other words, there is an implicit minimum wage even though there is no formally defined minimum wage. This means that wage differentiation is restricted. The lower part of the demand curve for labor is truncated. There is no effective labor supply or demand below the minimum wage. Such an economy loses the lower segment of the labor market; the labor market simply dries up. Unemployment is the consequence. Moreover, a minimum wage has an impact on labor market equilibrium because it determines wage bargaining behavior of unions.[27] Finally, since the minimum wage implies higher outlays of the social security system, which de facto have to be financed by taxes on labor income, it compresses the wage structure.

[27] See German Council of Economic Advisers (2002: box 9).

Changes in Social Welfare

In 2005 social welfare benefits will change. Those not capable of working, i.e., the elderly and the ill, will receive social welfare benefits as previously. The monthly basic amount will be the same as the unemployment benefit of type II, i.e., €345 instead of the monthly standard payment of €292 that has prevailed to date in western Germany; in eastern Germany the amount is €331. It will thus be higher than in the past; but special payments, e.g., for clothing, will be changed into somewhat lower lump-sum transfers. Furthermore, the payment of social welfare payments to Germans living in a foreign country have been restricted. These benefits will continue to be administered by the municipalities as in the past.

Changes also come into effect for those 800 000 welfare recipients who are capable of working; they will receive unemployment benefits of type II, including the supplementary payment described above. The idea is to integrate the two means-tested support schemes, the social welfare payments and unemployment benefits of type II, into one policy instrument. This benefit will be higher than previous social welfare transfers as a result of the supplement. Moreover, a person's contributions to the pension system will now be paid systematically when he is unemployed. As explained above, recipients will be allowed to earn an additional market income without losing all of the unemployment benefit of type II; however, the transfer has not been reduced, and the conditions for entitlement have not been changed, as had been proposed by economists (see below). Preliminary simulation results indicate that the reservation wage will not actually be reduced for persons with low skills, i.e., those who were receiving a low market income before unemployment (Christensen 2004). This would seem to indicate that the problems concerning the low segment of the labor market continue to exist.

Moreover, the new law will change the organizational allocation of responsibilities between municipal and federal levels for those recipients of social welfare who are able to work. Whereas social security standards are defined nationally, the welfare system has traditionally been administered and financed by the municipalities according to the subsidiarity principle. The new system, however, is to be administered by the Labor Office,[28] which belongs to the federal level. Support of the children of social welfare recipients and their housing remain with the municipalities. This arrangement has serious shortcomings. In the first place, it entails national financing. A task that is to be performed by local government, because the local community is better informed as well as more directly concerned and affected by the expenditures, is shifted to the national

---

[28] The *Bundesanstalt für Arbeit* changed its name to Bundesagentur für Arbeit in 2004.

level. This is a false incentive, and it will prove extremely difficult to control costs with such a national approach. Considering how difficult it is to control increases in costs in other areas of social security, for instance health insurance, one can only wonder why politicians have chosen this centralized approach over the tried and tested decentralized methods by which experience has been garnered in the past.

As a compromise with the Christian Democratic Union in the Bundesrat, municipalities are to be given the option, until August 2004, to declare their competence to continue to manage the social welfare system; they then have to renew their declaration every three years thereafter. In this way they could remain in charge of the welfare recipients who are capable of working. It is however difficult to see what incentive a mayor would have to declare his municipality competent if the federal government then took over the task, with the high risk of failure that such a transfer carries.[29] At the time of writing (May 2004) this was not yet put into law; no agreement could be reached on the compensation that municipalities should receive for taking over the responsibility for the unemployed welfare recipients.

The government had intended to link the receipt of a governmental benefit to the union or local wage. This would have meant explicitly introducing a minimum wage. We know very well from theory and from practical experience, for instance in France, that such a wage is a major cause of falling employment in the bottom segment of the labor market. Moreover, it increases the power of the unions. In the compromise reached with the Bundesrat, a minimum wage was prevented.

Mini Jobs

There are exemptions from contributions to social security and from taxation for "mini" jobs paying up to €400 per month as of 2003. The employee in such a job pays no income tax and no contribution to social security. This income can be earned in addition to other income, for instance a regular job. The employer pays a flat rate of 25 percent, for health (11 percent) and retirement insurance (12 percent), and taxes (2 percent). There are special provisions for an income range between €401 and €800. In midyear 2003, 5.9 million mini jobs existed, 1.7 million more than under the previous, more restrictive, arrangement which was effective until March 2002.

This figure illustrates that a labor market can very well function in Germany. But it should be noted that these are jobs for pupils, students,

[29] Admittedly, the final outcome will depend on the details of the new institutional arrangement, for instance the extent to which the states will supply funds to the municipalities, and whether this will initiate institutional competition between the municipalities.

retirees, and housewives; often they are a second job. The occupations are in distribution and trade, the housing sector (e.g., janitors), and catering. Also, the jobs require some level of qualification; consequently this law, though establishing some degree of flexibility in the labor market, does not solve the problem of the less qualified in the lower segment of the labor market.

Social Security Contributions: A Tax on Labor

In addition to the two discussed institutional features of collective bargaining and the high reservation wage, yet another reason for the high unemployment in Germany is that the demand for labor is systematically weakened because the social security system is financed by contributions from labor income, paid by firms and by workers on a half and half basis. This creates a significant wedge between the gross and net wage. Taking together the tax on work income and the contributions to the social security system, the marginal tax plus the rate of social security contribution amounts to 58 percent of gross income for the average earner if he is married and to 67 percent if he is single.[30] A large proportion of this is accounted for by the contribution rate for the social security system. For instance, from the 58 percent of deductions from gross labor income for the average married wage earner, 34 percentage points represents social security contributions; the same proportion applies to the average single wage earner.[31] This wedge has increased considerably over time, as we will see in chapter 5.

A more detailed analysis shows the specific impact on labor demand and labor supply. In a way, the workers take a part of their incomes not as net wages after contributions and before tax, but as a "social wage," i.e., as a degree of insurance protection. On the demand side, and from the point of view of the firms, both the net wage and the social wage must be covered by labor productivity. When the gross wage is higher than labor productivity, firms will attempt to bring it into line with productivity. They can do this by a set of adjustments: by laying off workers so that those remaining employed have a high enough productivity to cover the net wage plus the social wage; by not filling vacant positions; by substituting capital for labor; by looking for labor-saving new technologies; and by shifting production abroad. From the point of view of firms, social security contributions shift the labor demand curve downward (figure 4.8). When all adjustments have taken place in a general equilibrium,

[30] German Council of Economic Advisers (2002: 243).

[31] In the German system, there is an income limit for mandatory health insurance beyond which the individual can choose to be privately insured.

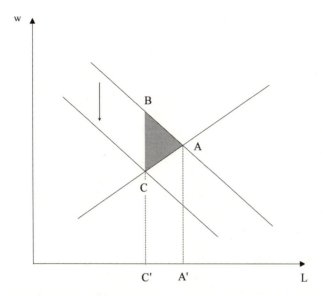

Figure 4.8 Social security contributions as a tax on labor.

employment is reduced from point A′ to point C′ and unemployment results. Thus, the worker bears the burden of adjustment. There is an efficiency loss in terms of production forgone in value terms, as represented by the Harberger triangle ABC. This presentation would become more complex if the impact on the supply curve were also taken into consideration. Taxes on wage income and contributions paid by the worker can be seen as reducing net income and thus shifting the supply curve to the left.

Thus, the contributions to the social security system have a similar effect as a tax on labor: they weaken the demand for labor. Whereas the reservation wage affects the labor supply negatively and truncates the lower segment of the labor market, mandatory contributions increase firms' costs, which shifts the labor demand curve of the economy as a whole downward or to the left.

On the supply side, and from the point of view of the workers, such high marginal rates create the wrong incentives for work effort and human capital accumulation in the workforce. The negative impact on human capital accumulation is especially relevant in an information society where human capital and knowledge are the dominant sources of economic growth. The existing arrangement thus hurts the growth dynamics and may well be a reason for the poor growth performance. Moreover, it is an incentive for high-earning Germans to take up official residence in low-tax places such as London. This affects locational advantage and is relevant for the modern service sectors (banking and insurance) and research activities. Finally, it is an invitation to move to the underground economy. The supply curve of labor is shifted to the left (not shown in figure 4.8): this represents an additional efficiency loss. The combined effect of the leftward shift of the demand and the supply curve is a reduced level of official employment.[32] Note that the leftward shift of the labor supply curve affects the elasticity of the economic system and indirectly the dynamics of the economy; it thus indirectly influences the demand for labor as well.

There also is an impact on the role of the minimum wage. Consider just the usual market diagram without indirect effects on dynamics. If the leftward shift in the demand curve is stronger than the leftward shift of the supply curve, the excess supply of labor is increased. This means higher unemployment.

Since the early 1970s, the political parties in Germany have expanded the systems of social security in order to attract political votes. But, simultaneously, they have raised the contribution rates and in this way have reduced the demand for labor and increased unemployment. Ever increasing public benefits and the stepwise increase of unemployment were considered to be two different phenomena, but in essence they are two aspects of the same problem. The unemployed have had to foot the bill. It is about time to acknowledge this interdependence.

The Interplay of the Institutional Factors

To describe the institutional setup of the German labor market, four different layers must be distinguished (figure 4.9). With regard to the first layer, the systems of social protection provide an income when people cannot or do not work. This influences the reservation wage on the supply side and simultaneously represents a tax and contribution wedge, especially on the demand side. In the second layer, legal rules— for instance the constitutional norm of Article 9, the legal defense of collective bargaining, and other labor market regulations such as layoff constraints—define the institutional arrangement relevant for the system. This setup specifies the incentives of the system and the mechanics of the wage formation process which make up the third layer. All these factors determine the negotiated wage, which influences the wage level and the wage structure together with—in the fourth layer—the capital stock, labor productivity (i.e., the production function), and product prices. The final outcome is the level of employment and unemployment. Looking at this institutional arrangement, it is easy to see how far away the

---

[32] The impact on the net market wage can go either way.

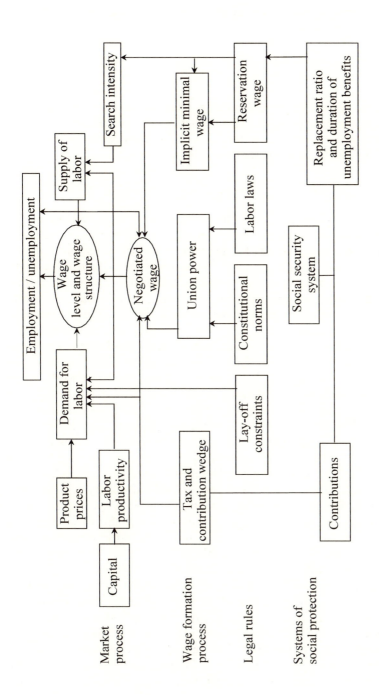

Figure 4.9   The institutional setup of the German labor market.

German system is from the market process that operates in the Anglo-Saxon countries.

THE NEED FOR REFORMS

Reforms of the German labor market relate to the three areas discussed: the institutional design of wage formation, the influence of unemployment insurance and social welfare on the reservation wage, and the tax on labor for financing social security.

Reforming the Institutional Design of Wage Setting

With respect to wage setting, the political task is to re-evaluate present institutional arrangements and to reappraise the degree of protection received by the employed. The protection of workers has evolved from the nineteenth century to prevent them from being exploited. Traditionally, the root of labor market problems has been seen as residing in the conflict between capital and labor, or between the firms' owners and the workers. At the same time, it is recognized that flexibility of the work contract, for instance of working time, generates productivity gains that may be to the benefit of the firm as well as the worker. Moreover, job security, or alternatively a smaller risk of losing one's job, is an important aspect for an employee. In an open economy, and in a world where external shocks prevail, firms and workers are confronted with a similar risk. They are both in the same boat. Whereas in the classical work contract the firm carried the revenue risk, guaranteeing the worker a more or less fixed income and—within limits—a secure employment, the modern work contract attempts some form of risk sharing based on a common interest of both sides. This relates especially to the risk of a loss in income for the worker—above, say, a threshold guaranteed by the firm, except in the extreme case of a layoff. Therefore, the balance between protection and flexibility must take into account the welfare gains in terms of real income for the worker and the long-run job security that are made possible by greater flexibility.

The main conflict, however, now lies elsewhere. The increased protection of the employed in a welfare state has given rise to a new clash, a conflict between the protection of the employed and the discrimination of the unemployed. The real political task is to appraise that conflict. The answer is that the protection of those employed should be reduced to such an extent that discrimination of the unemployed disappears.

The solution to this problem lies in allowing more decentralized autonomy in the collective labor contract, both for the individual worker and for the workers of a firm as a group. Germany has to move in the direction of a market solution.

With respect to the individual worker, more decisions should be allocated to him by allowing him to deviate from the collective contract if this can make his job more secure, for instance by securing a commitment from the firm that there will be no layoffs in, say, the following three years. This requires a legal redefinition of the *Günstigkeitsprinzip*, inserting a rule that the security of a job should be an aspect in the decision of whether or not a deviation is favorable for the individual worker. A more radical solution would be to give the right to decide on such a deviation to the individual. Such a right would also apply to the unemployed, who then would be allowed to enter the labor market below the collective wage. At the same time, more individual, result-oriented, elements should be introduced into the work contract without being linked to the collective contract.

With respect to the workers of the firm as a group, they should be granted the right to deviate from the collective contract if a majority of the group so desires; if no majority exists, then the union contract should hold. If it is considered desirable to protect the collective treaty, the threshold of the necessary majority could be set high, for instance at two thirds. This would mean changing para. 77, Sec. III, of the Business Constitution Act (*Betriebsverfassungsgesetz*). In the legal sense, this alteration would refer to union members only. The decision to deviate would be their decision. This follows from the positive freedom of coalition: union members cannot be forced by non-union members into a contract they do not want. Non-union members would not therefore have a vote on the union contract. But of course they and management would be free to enter into a non-union contract. In all these cases, the workers' councils play a role; they can become part of a practical solution in finding a majority. It should be noted, however, that each employee is bound by law to the decisions of the workers' councils, so that wage setting by the councils would to some extent represent even more collectivity than wage setting by the trade unions, whose membership is voluntary. Therefore, workers' councils should enter into wage formation only in the form of a recommendation,[33] on which then individual contracts can be made.

These are the two central changes needed in the German labor laws in order to allow a greater decentralization of wage formation. They were not on the agenda of the Schröder government; they are not part of the "Agenda 2010." The Christian Democrats and the Liberal Democrats, who at first had requested the provision of a deviation from the collective

---

[33] Betriebsabreden instead of Betriebsvereinbarungen.

contract in firms as a precondition for accepting the reform package in the Bundesrat in December 2003, eventually gave up their demand. Apparently, each of these reforms would reduce the power of the trade unions; consequently, the trade unions oppose the changes vehemently. But the organizational interest of the trade unions cannot be the overriding factor determining the intensity of Germany's labor market reform.

Adjusting the Reservation Wage

Since the high reservation wage depends on the benefits provided by government for those not working, the reservation wage can be changed only if the benefits are redefined. Unfortunately, some ill advised incentives were introduced by the compromise of December. Moreover, part of the package only undoes what had been introduced some years ago by the same government, such as a softening of the layoff constraints.[34] Whereas in some aspects of the package the grand coalition of the Red–Green government and the coalition of the Christian Democrats and the Liberal Democrats in the Bundesrat have moved in the right direction, for instance shortening the duration of unemployment benefits of type I, the overall package does not go far enough when measured against what is needed and what has been proposed for the solution of the problems of the lower segment of Germany's labor market.

The most far-reaching proposal is to discontinue this type of support altogether (German Council of Economic Advisers 2002). Those who do not find a job and whose unemployment benefit has expired will then receive social welfare. This would have prevented the false institutional incentives that now have been introduced for those social welfare recipients capable of working. To limit the duration of the unemployment benefit of type II to one or two years, or to scale down the benefit over a three-year period, would have been a better alternative.

The adjustment of social welfare itself is a most complex issue. One approach would be to apply the existing criteria of eligibility for social welfare more strictly. Thus, the actual legal rule that welfare payments can be reduced if a job offered by a municipality is not accepted could be enforced more stringently. Moreover, the rules could be changed administratively, for instance with respect to the level that the rent costs are picked up. In addition, the procedure for the annual increase in benefits linked to a price index for low-income groups, or following the increase in pensions, could be changed. Benefits could be set lower for those capable of working than for the elderly and those suffering from chronic illnesses. All this would represent a "psychological" redefinition of the

---

[34] Compare also the repeal of the demographic factor in the pension formula.

income floor in the welfare system and thus of the level income that people require from the government.

The approach to differentiating social welfare for those who are able to work from social welfare for others uses economic incentives. The concept is to reduce the level of social welfare of those who are able to work by, say, 25 or 33 percent, and at the same time to let those recipients who can earn a living in the market lose only a proportion of their benefits with each additional euro earned. That means that, as with the US Earned Income Tax Credit and the UK Family Tax Credit, social welfare benefits can be phased out with increase in income. The double-sided approach of reducing benefits and granting a subsidy is intended to correct the false incentives that now exist. Specific proposals differ. The German Council of Economic Advisers wants to limit this measure to those who are receiving social welfare under his new proposal. This would mean that the measure would relate to 800 000 in social welfare (capable of working) and to a further 800 000 who were receiving unemployment benefit II before and will now receive social welfare. Since these groups overlap somewhat, this amounts to 1.4 million people for whom an incentive problem exists. The proposal of the Ifo Institute (Sinn et al. 2002) goes much further: while reducing the benefits of social welfare recipients, benefits are not formally limited to these recipients but are paid to the employed as a wage subsidy when income falls below a certain level. Consequently, there is a wider phasing-out range, so that the program extends to 4.5 million people already employed plus 2 million newly employed.[35] This is a large group to solve the incentive issue originally relating to the 1.4 million recipients of social welfare according to the concept of the Council of Economic Advisers.

To what extent such proposals will solve the incentive problem depends on a set of factors. One is that trade unions must be prepared to reduce the implicit minimum wage: if they are not, the measure will be ineffective. Unfortunately, trade unions may acquire a lever with which they can play a strategic game against the government. After all, with the new arrangement the government will be footing the wage subsidies bill if the trade unions do not find or accept the equilibrium wage in a differentiated structure according to the qualifications of the workers. People may get used to the idea that the government is obliged to make up the difference between the desired wage and labor productivity. This is quite a contrast to the Anglo-Saxon world. It shows that the lower segment of the labor market cannot be reformed without some reform of the wage setting arrangement. Another issue is whether the Constitutional Court

[35] Table 3.5.

will accept the automatic reduction in social welfare for those who are able to work. Related to this constitutional problem is the question of what to do if someone who is capable of working does not find a job in the private market. Apparently, the constitutional issue would be less severe if the municipalities provided jobs. This, however, has its own shortcomings, because it is not the function of government to provide jobs.[36]

Of course, the idea of a tax transfer mechanism stems from Friedman's (2002) concept of a negative income tax. Here a warning is in order, because such a tax will not function in a continental welfare state. Assume that a welfare recipient could retain 50 percent of the additional market income that he earns, and neglect the criterion of neediness: this will establish a wide range over which income is not taxable. Empirical analysis of the German tax system shows that this range contains a third of the German workforce (Gern 1999; Siebert 2003). It would not be possible to resolve an incentive issue for as many as 1.4 million welfare recipients. In the continental system, therefore, it is unlikely that the benefit level can be reduced to the level of the Anglo-Saxon world.

Reducing the Tax on Labor

The third major task is to lower the tax on labor significantly. This, in turn, requires the reformation of the welfare state, a topic already touched upon in the context of the reservation wage. The reform of the welfare state is the issue of the next chapter.

Preventing New Errors

The policy approach to unemployment in Germany has been on the wrong track more than once, for instance in attempting to solve the unemployment problem at the cost of the pension system, or in having recourse to the strategy of reducing working time. In the autumn of 2003 labor market politics was again barking at the wrong tree. In recent years there has been a shortage of apprenticeship positions, which were set to fade away at the end of the year. The Social Democrats now intend to introduce a "non-apprentice fee," to be levied on those firms that do not offer enough apprenticeship positions. Such a proposal does not suggest a solid knowledge of how firms react and how the economy operates. How would a norm on the number of apprenticeship positions for a firm be determined, for instance, in a declining sector? And would the norm not effectively reduce the number of apprenticeship positions, since expanding firms may only live up to the norm? And would firms not have a new incentive to reduce their total employment if the number of total employment were the criterion for the number of apprenticeships to supplied? And would such a political measure therefore not introduce an additional incentive to reduce jobs in the economy? It is possible that this stance became part of the party platform to get the agreement of the more radical wing to the reform package of 2003. But the fact that such a notion could find its way onto the party program shows how easily the direction of German labor market politics may take a new regressive step. And it demonstrates how poorly rooted German thinking is in terms of market solutions to its main poblems.

CHAPTER FIVE

The Social Security System under Strain

The reform of the social security system and the welfare state is Germany's other major structural policy issue (along with the reform of the labor market). Clearly, the social security system has hit a financing constraint. Even without the problems of an ageing population it would not be sustainable in its present form, and it definitely can no longer be financed in an ageing society. Moreover, it has a negative impact on the labor market, i.e., on labor demand, on labor supply, and also on the equilibrating mechanism that has to bring labor demand and labor supply into balance.[1]

BENEFITS PROVIDED BY THE SOCIAL SECURITY SYSTEM

Germany is characterized by a generous social security system representing one of the aspects of the social market economy and making up an important element of the social budget. The social security system consists of four major elements: the old age pension system, nursing care (also called long-term care) insurance, health insurance, and unemployment insurance with two types of unemployment benefit. The bulk of the expenditures of the social security system are financed by contributions paid half and half by employees and employers; about one fifth is financed from tax revenue. The financing of the social security system is thus linked mainly to the labor contract. The basic elements of this insurance system are as follows.

Old-age Pensions

The old-age pension system provides a retirement income amounting to 69.9 percent of the net average wage income before retirement (2003).[2] This is the pension accruing to a full-time employee with average earnings who retires at age 65 and who has a record of

---

[1] I appreciate critical comments on this chapter from Axel Börsch-Supan, Alfred Boss, Friedrich Breyer, Martin Gasche, Carolin Geginat, Matthias Knoll, and Oliver Lorz.

[2] Council of Economic Advisers, Annual Report 2003, table 76*.

paid contributions for 45 years during his working life. It amounts to €1176 per month before taxes and contributions in western Germany and to €1034 in eastern Germany. For each year in which the employee and his firm have paid contributions, he receives "credit" points (*Entgeltpunkte*), which are determined by the ratio of the individual's wage income to the average wage income. A shorter working time means fewer credit points; a lower income while working also means fewer credit points.

In 2003 a minimum level of pensions was introduced for those who are due to receive a pension below the level of social welfare. Previously, such pensioners had to rely on social welfare benefits, and the government could ask their children to finance the welfare payments if they had a sufficient income. This obligation has now been abolished. The old-age insurance includes a disability insurance covering individuals who become physically unable to work; it also includes an insurance for surviving dependants covering widows/widowers and orphans.

Payment into the old-age insurance scheme is compulsory for all dependent employees except civil servants. Contributions are proportional to wage income; the contribution rate was 19.5 percent of the gross wage in 2003. This payment is mandatory up to an income ceiling. Employees with an income above this limit pay contributions on the ceiling income. This ceiling normally rises in relation to the increase in income but is not indexed in a strict sense; in 2003 it was raised in a discretionary fashion and by a large amount (13 percent): at the time of writing it stands at €5100 per month, well above the average monthly labor income of €2217 per month. The ceiling for eastern Germany is lower, at €4250 per month. Regular government employees are insured in the same system as all other employees. Civil servants, however, i.e., government employees with official governmental functions, such as teachers, judges, law enforcement officers, and specific administrators, although dependently employed, are not included in that system and have their pensions paid out of tax revenue. There is a specific old-age insurance for coal miners. The self-employed can opt to pay into the public system. Other groups with special, and partially funded, pension systems are lawyers, physicians, and architects, regardless of whether they are dependently employed or self-employed.

The pension system is a pay-as-you-go (PAYG) system in which the benefits of the pensioners are financed by the contributions paid by those currently employed and their employers. In fact, there is no capital fund in this system: the reserve requirements were lowered in 2002 from one month's to half a month's expenditures in order to meet payment obligations. In the fall of 2003, the government lowered the reserves still further, to two-tenths of the monthly expenditures. According to a new law passed in March 2004, the reserve is to be increased to one and a half month's expenditures.

In 2002 a capital-funded supplementary voluntary system was introduced as a second pillar of the pension system. Under this system the insured can save an additional amount of up to 4 percent of their wage incomes in a private pension plan, subsidized by a tax transfer scheme. The maximum of 4 percent applies from 2008 onwards, when the voluntary system is fully phased in. Contributions for this insurance can be deducted from income up to an amount of €2100. For those on lower incomes, who cannot take advantage of the expenditure deduction, the government will pay a transfer, the amount of which declines with rising income and depends on family status and the number of dependent children. The supplementary private insurance is voluntary; from time to time the question is raised as to whether it should become mandatory.

The new voluntary pension law that became effective in 2002 favors employer-provided or firm-provided pensions as a third pillar of the pension system. In addition to the support for the new voluntary capital-funded private insurance already described, contributions to this pension plan are exempt from contributions to the public social security system, for both employees and employers. Thus, such pensions receive a preferential treatment relative to the voluntary capital-funded system that is government-subsidized. Employees can spend part of their income on contributions to this type of insurance and thereby avoid part of the state pension contributions and also save on taxes. It can be argued that this helps to promote the idea of private retirement insurance; but since the firms' pension systems are typically a matter of wage negotiations, it can also be argued that the government intended to strengthen the position of trade unions in this way. With the introduction of the supplementary system, the benefit level of the PAYG system will be reduced from 70 percent (it was 69.9 percent in 2003) to 68 percent of the net wage in 2030, according to government projections of 2001—assuming for instance an annual wage increase of 3 percent.[3] Together with the pensions from the supplementary systems, 75 percent of the net wage is expected to be reached when the pensions are provided by both systems for the first time, according to this same government forecast.

The introduction of the privately funded system on a voluntary basis was definitely a step in the right direction; a funded system allows workers to accumulate interest and thus represents efficiency gains relative to the PAYG system, gains that will reduce the costs of old age. However, it

---

[3] Council of Economic Advisers, Annual Report 2001, table 32.

is surprising that a major reform of a pension system that tackled the problem of financial constraints and is considered an important step towards the sustainability of the pension system in an ageing society should have ended up with a pension level that is even higher than what the previous system could provide. New calculations show that the pension level will be at 60.2 percent of the net wage in 2030, or 41.8 percent of the gross wage.[4] The government is now putting the focus on the gross pension instead of the net pension, with the deliberate intention of blurring the exact magnitude of the reduction in the pension level. The gross pension level is defined as the pension (before taxation) minus the pensioner's contributions to health and nursing care insurance in relation to the gross average income of the employed, with all social security contributions deducted. It applies to a pensioner with 45 years of contributions. Note that the pension reform of 2001 does not prevent a rise in contribution rates. They were expected to remain below 22 percent of the gross wage in 2003 at the time the 2001 reform was passed; thereafter, it was estimated by the Rürup Commission in 2003 that the rate would rise to 24.2 percent.

Annual adjustments of pensions are made according to a formula that contains the increase in the gross wage income in a modified form. This increase, expressed as the ratio of the gross wage income of the previous period to the gross income of the period before the previous period, is adjusted by a factor including the change in the contribution rate to the pension system.[5] A rise in the contribution rate implies a lower augmentation of pensions. In a similar way, an increase in the tax-subsidized rate of voluntary contributions to the government-supported privately funded

---

[4] 63.9 or 40.6 percent, respectively, in 2040: Deutsches Institut für Altersvorsorge Köln, according to Frankfurter Allgemeine Zeitung, August 27, 2003.

[5] The monthly pension (MP) is determined by individual factors: namely, the credit points (CP) according to the years of insurance; the entry factor, i.e., earlier or regular retirement (EF); the type of pension (TP), i.e., (old age, dependent person); and the general factor of the pension value (PV),

$$MP = CP \cdot EF \cdot TP \cdot PV$$

According to the new formula introduced in 2002, the pension value will be determined by

$$PV_t = PV_{t-1} \cdot \frac{GW_{t-2}}{GW_{t-3}} \cdot \frac{0.9 - CR_{t-2} - VCR_{t-2}}{0.9 - CR_{t-3} - VCR_{t-3}}$$

starting with the year 2011. The formula applies to adjustments in July. The variables are defined as follows: GW is gross wage sum per worker, CR is the average contribution rate to the public pension fund, 0.195 in 2003, and VCR is the contribution rate to the voluntary funded system with government support, 0.04 in 2008. Until 2010 pensions will be determined by a formula with 1 instead of 0.9:

$$PV_t = PV_{t-1} \cdot \frac{GW_{t-2}}{GW_{t-3}} \cdot \frac{1 - CR_{t-2} - VCR_{t-2}}{1 - CR_{t-3} - VCR_{t-3}}$$

system reduces the increase in pensions. Note that contributions to health insurance, unemployment insurance, and nursing care insurance are not deducted; nor are income taxes. Thus, the pension formula is linked not to the net wage but to a modified gross wage; one might call it a *modified net wage*.

Subtracting the contribution rates links the increase in pensions to the financing side. In that sense, the ageing population is included in the pension formula. However, the contribution rates are politically determined variables: they do not represent an objective basis for the calculation of pension. In order to make the pension system independent of political decisions, the increase in pensions should be coupled with an objective variable, especially demographics.

For 1999, a demographic factor taking into account the increase in life expectancy was legally introduced into the pension formula by the Kohl government. This factor reduced the size of pensions as the population aged.[6] However, this law was suspended by the Schröder government of 1999 and 2000 immediately after it won the 1998 election, in fulfillment of an election promise. The demographic formula was discontinued completely when the above-described new pension formula was introduced in 2001.

With a law passed in 2004, a new formula including a sustainability factor will become effective in 2005[7]. This formula includes the ratio of pensioners to contributors.[8] In addition to reproductive behavior and life expectancy, this factor recognizes immigration and changes in the participation rate. When this ratio increases, the increase in the pension is automatically reduced. Since the "demographic factor" of the Kohl government was politically tarnished, the new term "sustainability factor" was introduced in its place. With this formula, the gross pension level will be reduced to 43 percent of the gross wage in 2030. It is now

---

[6] The demographic factor reduces pensions according to the ageing of the population, here expressed as the life expectancy at age 65:

$$PV_t = PV_{t-1} \cdot \frac{GW_{t-2}}{GW_{t-3}} \cdot \frac{NRW_{t-2}}{NRW_{t-3}} \cdot \frac{NPR_{t-2}}{NPR_{t-3}} \cdot [(\frac{LE_{t-9}}{LE_{t-8}})/2 + 1]$$

The variables are defined as in footnote 5; additionally, NRW is the net ratio of the wage, NPR is the net pension ratio, and LE is the average life expectancy at age 65.

[7] The sustainability factor is expressed by the term in brackets:

$$PV_t = PV_{t-1} \cdot \frac{GW_{t-2}}{GW_{t-3}} \cdot \frac{1 - CR_{t-2} - VCR_{t-2}}{1 - CR_{t-3} - VCR_{t-3}} \cdot \left[\left(1 - \frac{PR_{t-2}}{PR_{t-3}} \right) \frac{1}{4} + 1 \right]$$

where PR is the ratio of pensioners to contributors.

[8] Alternatively, a "generation factor" specific to each cohort could be used so that reductions would apply only to new cohorts of pensioners. This might be seen as a discrimination of the individual cohorts and so might not be accepted by the Constitutional Court, although it would be fair in so far as these generations would enjoy a longer life.

estimated that, with the 2004 reform, the contribution rate can be limited to 22 per cent of the gross wage in 2030. In order to obtain the votes of all the social democratic and green members of the Bundestag, a provision was introduced that the government has to examine measures when the pension level falls below 46 percent. The suspension of the demographic factor by the Schröder government was clearly a mistake. Germany has lost six years in its reform process.

The statuary retirement age is 65 years for men and, from 2005, also for women, with some phasing-in adjustments. The effective retirement age, however, is 60.8 years in western Germany (in 2001) and 58.6 years in eastern Germany. The difference between the statuary and the effective age of retirement is due to a variety of factors. Whereas the statuary retirement age of 65 applies in the case of a contribution period of at least five years, earlier retirement is possible under certain conditions. First, the lower retirement age is due in part to the fact that the average retirement age for the disabled is 51.4 in western Germany. Second, the legal retirement age for disabled persons until recently was 60 (now been raised to 63). Third, persons who have paid contributions for a minimum of 35 years can take early retirement on full pension at age 63; a deduction of 3.6 percent of the pension per year (0.3 percent per month) of earlier retirement is made for each year of earlier retirement for men. Fourth, the retirement age for women was 60 until 1999; it is being raised to 65 in several steps. Fifth, earlier retirement is possible if a person is unemployed at age 60 or over; again, the above deduction is applied, for instance 18 percent for a retirement at 60. According to a new law passed in 2004, early retirement before 63 will not be possible in the future even if a reduction of pensions is accepted.

In addition to the early retirement rules for the unemployed, there are stipulations favoring an exit from the labor market for those who are under 60 (pre-retirement age), which changed in 2004. The unemployed aged 58 and older no longer have to be actively seeking work; they do not have to show up at the Labor Office each quarter, as do the other unemployed. After signing a declaration that they no longer intend to look for work, they are entitled to receive unemployment benefits until they are 60 and pensions afterwards, with the above mentioned pension reduction of 3.6 percent per year of earlier retirement. Thus, someone could exit from the labor market at 58 and receive benefits for seven years—two years of unemployment benefits and five years of pensions—with a reduction of 18 percent of the pension; this reduction will apply for the rest of the pensioner's life. Since the retiree does not pay contributions during this time, the reduction is actually higher. By the end of 2003, 377 000 people had received unemployment benefits of this type, after signing a declaration that they were no longer available and wanted to start their pension at age 60; 607 000 pensioners received a reduced pension arising from a pre-retirement contract.

In short, the pension system has been used to reduce the labor supply and thereby, supposedly, solve the unemployment problem. Under the new ruling, unemployment benefits are provided for only 18 months; the older recipients are obliged to accept job offers even if the new job pays less than the former; and the earliest possible age to receive a pension is now 63. Moreover, employees aged 55 and older can switch to a half-time job for a five-year period, during which they will work full-time for the first part of the period and get paid in the second half without working. These contracts are subsidized by the Labor Office if the employer fills the empty position in the company with a new employee. The sudsidy consists of an income increase and a contribution to the pension insurance. Under the new ruling, such contracts can be started only at the age of 58, with the individual receiving his pension at 63.

These arrangements all provide incentives to take early retirement; as long as pensions are not reduced on an actuarial basis, early retirement programs imply that there is an implicit tax on labor when working prior to retirement; people are, in fact, being punished if they work. It is debated to what extent the deduction of 0.3 percent per month (or 3.6 percent per year) of retirement between 60 and 65 years is on an actuarial basis, even without all these special cases of earlier retirement, and whether it would have to be higher if it were calculated according to actuarial principles. From the point of view of the insurance, a deduction is actuarial if the present value of the pensions of an early retiree plus the present value of lost contributions resulting from early retirement are identical to the present value of retirement at age 65. Apparently, these calculations depend on the assumptions about future benefits, the assumed institutional setting, the sustainability of the status quo, and many other factors. Some calculations indicate that the deduction is not actuarial (Institut der Deutschen Wirtschaft 2003[9]). A different slant on the actuarial property of the deduction for the insurer is the incentive effect for the insured. Here, the individual's time preference rate comes into play. The incentive effect and the impact on the labor market may therefore differ from the actuarial property. Usually, in most of these calculations the gross rates of return are calculated without looking at taxation. Taking into account taxation and the institutional arrangements for early retirement prior to the age of 60, the implicit tax on labor before retirement, or the preferential treatment of early retirement, has been estimated to be equivalent to roughly 35 percent of the net wage earnings from working an additional year (Gruber and Wise 2002:

[9] Quoted according to Frankfurter Allgemeine Zeitung, January 7, 2004.

55).[10] Even if these calculations do not reflect all institutional changes that are actually already in effect, and even if some changes have been raising the effective retirement age, there remain strong mechanisms operating in favor of early retirement.

The pension system so far has been generous to academics in counting three years of education in high school or the universities as three contribution years. This will be discontinued in 2005.

A new law passed in June 2004 will bring a change in the taxation of pensions. Whereas pensions have been only partially taxed so far, the full pension will be subject to the income tax in the future. Contributions, however, are tax exempt. This approach will have to phased in over a long period in order to make sure that pensioners do not have to pay taxes for pensions that were obtained without contributions being exempt from taxation.

Nursing Care

In nursing or long-term care insurance, introduced in 1995, benefits include payments for those in nursery homes and, to a smaller extent, for those who are taken care of by their families. Contributions amount to 1.7 percent of the gross wage. When the nursing care insurance was introduced, a religious holiday was abolished in order to gain an additional working day and thus reduce overhead labor costs. The state of Saxony chose to keep the holiday; in order not to augment labor costs for firms, the original contribution of 1.0 percent of gross wage in Saxony is footed completely by the employees; the increase in the rate of 0.7 percentage point is financed half and half.

Health Care

The public health system covers costs for medical treatment by physicians and hospitals, and for prescription drugs except for a flat fee per prescription. Health insurance covers all dependent family members of the insured, including children. Where both husband and wife are employed, contributions are calculated for each individual in proportion to his wage income. Children are insured with the highest earner. Coverage applies to the employed, the unemployed, and the retired. When a person is unemployed, the unemployment insurance picks up the contributions to the health insurance. For those who receive social welfare, the municipalities pay the contributions; for those recipients of social welfare who are not

---

[10] This relates to the pre-Riester reform. According to Gruber and Wise (2002), the present value of future benefits in Germany falls by 18 percent if retirement is postponed for five years from age 60 to age 65.

covered by health insurance, the municipalities pay the health costs directly. In principle, there is no time limit for insurance coverage; people with longer illnesses and/or unsuccessful rehabilitation receive disability insurance. Medical costs are therefore covered until someone is allocated to the disability insurance program. For civil servants, the government pays between 50 and 80 percent of health costs, depending on marital status and the number of children and varying with the federal states.

Health insurance also pays sickness benefit amounting to around 70 percent, and not more than 90 percent, of the insured person's gross wage, starting with the seventh week of illness. From 2006 on, this sickness benefit will no longer be financed half and half by employers and employees. The employees will pay 0.5 percentage point of their wage—which, however, is not sufficient to finance the sickness benefit completely. During the first six weeks of illness, the employee's full gross wage is paid by the employing firm. Moreover, a maternity benefit is provided by the public health insurance as a substitute for the worker's gross wage six weeks before and eight weeks after giving birth. A maternity benefit is also provided as part of social welfare benefits.

Health insurance is mandatory for all who are dependently employed. Above an income threshold of 75 percent of the contribution ceiling to the pension insurance (insurance ceiling), there is an exit option from the public system; in 2003[11] this mandatory insurance ceiling stood at €3825 per month. There also is a cap on income of €3450 per month for which contributions are calculated (the contribution ceiling). The contribution rate is around 14.4 percent of the gross wage (2003). Some 88.5 percent of the population is covered by the public health system, 8.9 percent by private insurance, 2.4 percent by other systems in case of illness, for instance social welfare. Only 0.2 of the population has no health coverage.

Unemployment Insurance

The benefits of the unemployment system have already been described in the last chapter. Membership is mandatory for all the dependently employed. The contribution ceiling is €5100.

---

[11] Contribution ceilings and insurance ceilings (ceiling for compulsory contribution) are not identical in the different branches of social security (see table 5A-1). In 2003 the contribution ceilings of the old-age pension system and the unemployment system were raised from €4500 to €5100. (There is a somewhat lower ceiling in eastern Germany.) The insurance ceiling for the health system stands at 75 percent of the contribution ceiling of the public pension system (see Appendix 5A-1).

Accident Insurance

In addition to the above four types of insurance, social security also includes a mandatory *insurance for accidents* occurring at the workplace and an insurance for health hazards associated with work. This type of insurance was first established in 1884 under Bismarck in order to limit costs to firms in the case of legal disputes. Two other branches of social security also came into existence under Bismarck: the health insurance in 1883 and the old-age and disability insurance in 1889. Unemployment insurance was added in 1927 and nursing care insurance in 1995.

Institutional Features

A specific feature of the German social security system is that it is self-administered. For instance, unemployment insurance is administered by the social partners, i.e., the trade unions and the employer' associations, and the health system by the public insurers and the Association of Statuary Health Insurance Physicians. The voting procedures of self-administration are specified by law.

Another institutional feature of social insurance, as well as of the other aspects of social assistance, is that there are social courts that deal with legal issues, especially claims against the social insurance system or the government. The court system is structured vertically with three tiers, on the local, state and federal level, with the Federal Social Court having the final say. The social courts are a specific form of the administrative courts.

SOCIAL WELFARE

Another important element of Germany's social system is social welfare (*Sozialhilfe*). As already discussed in the previous chapter, 2.8 million people in 1.44 million households received social welfare payments in 2002, that is 3.3 percent of the population (Federal Statistical Office 2003c). The percentage of recipients in the population differs considerably between the federal states, from 1.7 percent in Bavaria to 9.4 percent in Bremen. The level of entitlements stipulated by a national law is not completely uniform between the federal states. Regional differences in the percentage of recipients may be due to different structural conditions; for instance, larger cities tend to have more welfare recipients. It may also be a matter of implementation. Expenditures for social welfare amount to €24.7 billion in 2002, that is 1.2 percent in relation to GDP. In addition to the social welfare system, asylum seekers receive transfers according to a specific law; in 2001 their number was 314 000.

Whereas the standards for the social welfare system are defined nationally, the system is administered and financed by the municipalities. This corresponds to the subsidiarity principle. As explained in chapter 4, the new law passed in 2003 will change the organizational allocation for recipients of social welfare who are able to work. They will now receive the unemployment benefit of type II from the Labor Office, to be financed nationally. This is a new false incentive in Germany's social system; a task that was performed at the local level—and the local community is better informed as well as more directly concerned and affected by the expenditures—has been shifted to the national level.

Social welfare payments define an income floor for those not working and are therefore a crucial variable in Germany's system. They influence the reservation wage, the informal minimum wage, and the wage structure, as I described in chapter 4. In addition, social welfare benefits play a vital role in the system of taxation. The minimum income deemed necessary for living as defined by social welfare is the threshold for taxable income. Whereas this threshold can exceed the upper income limit of welfare payments, it is not allowed to fall below it.[12] This issue becomes relevant when social welfare benefits begin to be phased out gradually with rising income, so as to give people the incentive to move to the private sector. A further problem arises with respect to old-age pensions. Since social welfare provides an income for the elderly and the retired who are no longer paying contributions, there is a limit to any reduction in the benefit level of the PAYG pension system when pensions hit the floor provided by social welfare. People are reluctant to pay contributions if they can receive the benefits anyhow. Consequently, there is a limited maneuvering space in which to introduce a capital-funded system (see below).

THE SOCIAL BUDGET

Besides social security and social welfare, there are other programs with a social dimension. These include programs for specific purposes, such as support for juveniles (youth support), and a variety of transfers, including child allowance, education allowance for families with children, and housing subsidies for lower income groups (see "Social assistance in a broad sense"[13] in table 5.1 and figure 5.1).

Youth support (*Jugendhilfe*) sponsors programs for young people and includes extra-curricular educational activities, sport, leisure, and social activities for younger people as well as family and youth support in

---

[12] Decision of the Constitutional Court, November 11, 1998.

[13] I deliberately deviate from the official classification by the Economics and Labor Ministry; cf. table 73* in German Council of Economic Advisers Annual Report 2003/04.

TABLE 5.1
The Social Budget: type of expenditure, 2001

By institution	€bn	By function	€bn
Public Insurance Scheme	420.2	Old age	250.5
Public Pension Insurance	225.1	Old age	241.9
Health Insurance	137.1	Surviving dependants' provisions	8.5
Nursing Care Insurance	16.8	Health	227.6
Accident Insurance	10.9	Prevention/rehabilitation	12.3
Unemployment Insurance	64.9	Sickness	154.0
Social Assistance in a broad sense	86.4	Work related accidents	13.3
Social Assistance in a narrow sense	26.3	Disability	48.0
Youth Allowance	17.1	Family	98.7
Child Allowance	0.1	Youth	66.2
Education Allowance	3.9	Married couples	28.0
Housing Benefits	4.5	Pregnancy	4.4
Family Allowance	31.9	Employment	61.4
Programs provided by private employers	55.6	Professional education	14.2
Programs for government employees	50.9	Mobility	12.2
Pensions	34.6	Unemployment	35.0
Others	51.5	Others	25.5
Total Social Budget	663.7	Total Social Budget[a]	663.7

Source: Council of Economic Advisers Annual Report 2003/04, tables 73* and 74*.
[a] The difference between the sum total of expenditures by institutions and the Total Social Budget figure results from non-consolidation of government contributions of some of the above categories.

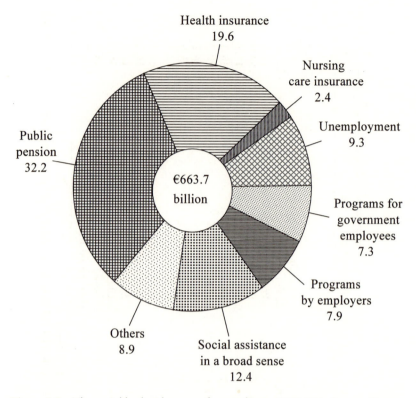

Health insurance
19.6

Nursing
care insurance
2.4

Unemployment
9.3

Public
pension
32.2

€663.7
billion

Programs for
government
employees
7.3

Programs
by employers
7.9

Others
8.9

Social assistance
in a broad sense
12.4

Figure 5.1   The social budget by type of expenditure, 2001 (%). *Source*: German Council of Economic Advisers Annual Report 2003/04, table 73*.

specific cases. As a rule, transfers are made to public and private institutions that provide pedagogical and social services for the young. In specific cases, housing and income subsidies for young people who go to school and cannot live with their parents are provided. Moreover, contributions to social security are paid under specific circumstances. Youth support is provided mainly by the municipalities and in 2001 amounted to €17 billion, or 0.8 percent of GDP.

Child allowance (*Kindergeld*, or burden-sharing for families with children) represents a subsidy to families with children living at home. For each child, the sum of €5808 can be deducted from the annual taxable income of a married couple; for a single parent the amount is €2904. If taxable income is low and the tax deduction doesn't amount to very much, a monthly transfer of €154 for every first, second, or third child and €179 for every additional child is paid. The child allowance of €2904 extends to children up to 16 years of age, 21 years if they are unemployed. The allowance also applies to children up to 27 years of age in education and training if they earn less than €7188 (2003). The age limit of 27 years shows how generous the German welfare state is. In 2002 this program took €34.5 billion or 1.6 percent of GDP.

Education allowance (*Erziehungsgeld*) is provided to families to encourage one parent to stay at home and dedicate all her or his efforts to looking after the child/children; it amounts to €307 per month for two years' absence from work or €460 per month for one year. An income threshold reduces the allowance. This threshold is differentiated according to the marital status and the number of children; it is higher for the first six months. For instance, for a couple with one child the income threshold lies at €51 130 per year, decreasing beginning with the seventh month. If the income is below the income threshold, the allowance will be paid for full two years. If it is higher, it is reduced starting with the seventh month.[14] Some states pay an additional allowance. The program also is valid for refugees and persons to whom asylum has been granted. Expenditures totaled €4 billion in 2001.

The education allowance concerns not only expenditures. It legally implies a leave of absence from work for a three-year period, so that the existing work contract continues. This includes an entitlement to return to the previous job. Since the couple has a choice about which of them will opt for the child allowance, either the husband or the wife can exercise this option in their job. If the employer agrees, the leave of absence can be extended to eight years. Both parents have the right to part-time work during the three-year period. After this period, both parents have the right to return to their pre-allowance working time.

A housing transfer for rent payment (*Wohngeld*) is provided, depending on the size of the family and its income. In some cases this transfer also includes heating subsidies. Housing subsidies come to €295–630 for a four-person family depending on the type of municipality, the age of the house, and the kind of housing. For singles, the range is €160–370. The income limit stands at €1830 and €830 per month respectively. Transfers are reduced with income. Housing transfers amount to €4.5 billion.

Taking those programs that fall under the heading of "social assistance" in a broad sense and including €26 billion of social welfare, government expenditure on them all amounts to €86.4 billion, or 4 percent of GDP.

Other items of the social budget relate to pension programs for civil servants (governmental employees with an official status), including their retirement pension fund (€35 billion) as well as assistance to health costs. Still other benefits are provided by firms, including wage payment during

---

[14] The income thresholds for education allowance in 2003 are as follows: for the first six months (from month 7 on in parenthesis): married with one child €51 130 (€16 740); single with one child €38 350 (€13 198), each additional child for both periods €3140.

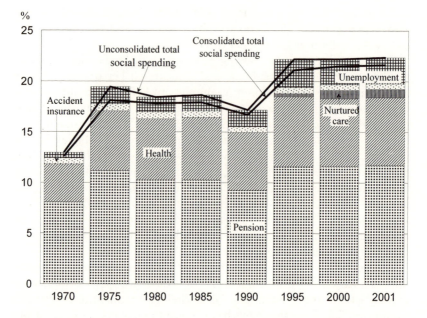

Figure 5.2 Components of spending on social insurance in relation to GDP, 1970–2001. *Source for data*: Federal Statistical Office and Council of Economic Advisers Annual Report 2002/03.

the first six weeks of illness (€27 billion) and firm-sponsored pension plans (€14 billion).

All expenditures for social purposes are summarized in a "social budget"; they amount to €663 billion, or one third of GDP (32 percent). This includes expenditures of the social security system, which accounted for 22.6 percent of GDP in 2002 or 65 percent of the social budget, the largest proportion arising from the pension system and health insurance (figure 5.2). On the financing side of the social budget, employers' and employees' contributions of €435 billion represent 60 percent of the system's revenue, and tax-financed transfers, 36.9 percent (table 5.2). This percentage has increased by three percentage points since 1995. Employers provide the larger part of contributions. The totals of the social budget expenditure side and revenue side are not identical because entries of expenditures and revenues for a specific purpose may differ in time.[15] All the systems are interdependent in many ways.[16]

[15] For instance transfers from the European Union. Note that some of the categories are not consolidated.

[16] It is beyond the framework of this book to portray the flows between the different systems. For instance, unemployment insurance pays contributions to the health insurance and old-age insurance for the unemployed.

TABLE 5.2
The financing side of the Social Budget 2001 (€bn)[a]

Contributions to social security		408
of insured	176	
of employers	232	
Transfers from the public budget		249
Other revenues		19
Social Budget		676

Source: Council of Economic Advisers Annual Report 2003/04, Table 75*.
[a] Consolidated flows; data are provided from the social insurers, and include e.g., imputed liabilities of employers for pension liabilities; they deviate from data in the macroeconomic

TABLE 5.3
Budget of the social security system, 2002 (€bn)

Revenue	458.0	
of which:		
Interest income and similar		1.9
Social security contributions		368.4
Transfers (tax revenue)		87.7
Deficit	−6.8	
Expenditures	464.8	

Source: Federal Statistical Office.

The social security system accounts for two-thirds of the social budget. Whereas the overwhelming part of the expenditures of the social security system are financed from contributions of firms and employers, about one-fifth are transfers from the government; this part is tax-financed (table 5.3). The most important items are in the pension system, where the federal budget carries about 31 percent of the social security expenditures for pensions (2002);[17] this amounted to €72.1 billion in 2002. Moreover, the Bund picks up the deficit of the Federal Labor Office, €5.6 billion in 2002, or about 10 percent of the expenditures of the Labor Office. When the nursing care insurance was introduced, the Bund took over half of the contributions of pensioners to that insurance (€1.7 billion in 2001). Moreover, but strictly speaking outside the social security system, the unemployment benefit of type II, €15.0 billion, representing 28 percent of the total expenditures of the Labor Office, is financed through the federal budget.

[17] These are the usual and additional transfers from the federal government to the pension system, the transfer for the miners' insurance, and special benefits for recipients, e.g., for the education of children.

Expansion of the Welfare State

In the 1970s there was a major expansion of the German welfare state. Entitlements were defined more generously.

In the pension system, the 1972 reform raised the pension level relative to the net wage from 60 percent in the 1960s to 70 percent, in several steps. A flexible age limit was introduced that allowed individuals to retire at 63, i.e., two years earlier, without allocating the costs of earlier retirement to them on an actuarial basis. Another new benefit was a minimum pension corresponding to a hypothetical minimum life income. Even in 2003, a new form of a minimum pension was introduced—yet another step in the expansion of the welfare state.

These expansions in benefits were possible only by considerably loosening the budget constraint of the pension system in 1969 and reducing the role of capital as a reserve. Up to 1969 it had been required that, at the end of a ten-year period of rolling financing, the reserves in the system had to amount to the previous year's expenditures. This requirement was abolished in 1969. The new constraint for a projection period of 15 years was that the reserves in three consecutive years should not be lower than the expenditures of three months (Schewe et al. 1975). This new rule allowed for an increase in pensions by giving up reserves. Today the reserve requirement is down to 0.2 month's expenditure. With the benefit of hindsight, loosening the reserve requirements was an irresponsible decision when sustainability of the system and the interest of future generations are taken into consideration.

As long ago as 1957, sustainability was pushed into the background when the capital fund, which amounted to one and half years of expenditures, was given up so that pensions could be raised considerably. The claims-backed approach (*Anwartschaftsdeckungsverfahren*), by which claims were backed by some type of fund of accumulated contributions, was substituted by the period-backed approach (*Abschnittdeckungsverfahren*), by which a financing constraint was introduced for a financing decade, as described above. The focus of the system was shifted away from individual claims and toward a functional constraint for the system.[18] This allowed Adenauer to win the 1957 elections. Since 1959, pensions were annually adjusted to economic development.

In this context, it should be mentioned that the generous increase in benefits were already having to be corrected in the 1990s. Since 1992, the adjustment of pensions was changed from a link to the gross wage to a

---

[18] The Constitutional Court upheld in a decision in 1980 that equivalence between contributions and benefits exists in the narrow sense that the rank order of benefits must be consistent with the rank order of contributions.

link to the net wage, the reason being that the reference to the gross wage could no longer be afforded in a situation where the income tax as well as social security contributions were being raised; otherwise pensions would have increased at a much higher rate than net wages, thereby violating the financing constraint. That Germany found itself in such a situation was due to unification in the early 1990s. But for a similar reason, the link to the net wage would have been inadequate in the situation in which taxes were reduced in the late 1990s, because then pensions were again raised, to a higher rate, and financing problems might have arisen. Indeed, in 2001 the pension formula was changed again, this time into a modified wage formula.

Early retirement was resorted to in several laws to reduce the labor supply without properly assigning actuarial costs to the retired. Thus, the early retirement law of 1984 (*Vorruhestandsgesetz*), effective until 1998, stipulated that employees who were 58 and older could take early retirement in principle without a deduction from their pension; firms paid the retirees 65 percent of their gross wage, but the government picked up 35 percent of the expenditures of the firms plus the firms' contributions to social security for the early retirees. This law was used by firms to send their older employees into retirement and thus to attract a younger workforce. Two other laws, one from 1988 and another passed in 1996 allowing part-time work, described above, gave similar incentives for early retirement.

In health insurance, the insurance ceiling was raised in 1970 and adjustments were linked to economic development. The ceiling had already been increased several times. A sickness benefit for workers had been introduced in 1957 and 1961, including a contribution from the employer. In 1970 workers received the same treatment as clerks; the employer was required to pay the sick person's wage for the first six weeks. A maternity benefit was newly set in 1965 and 1967. As already mentioned, nursing care insurance was introduced in 1995.

Unemployment benefits, i.e., benefits of type I (*Arbeitslosengeld*),[19] were increased in 1975 from 62.3 to 68 percent of the net wage for a married person; it has remained at 67 percent since 1994. For a single person, the benefits were raised from 42.8 to 63 percent, and have stood at 60 percent since 1994. Simultaneously, a family allowance of DM12 per week for each dependent family member was abandoned, but a child allowance was introduced. In sum, this meant an increase in benefits for the married unemployed. In the mid-1980s the maximum duration of benefits was increased from 12 to 32 months with the duration varying with age. Moreover, in 1985 a new law was introduced, stipulating that

---

[19] More precisely: the main component.

unemployed people 58 years and older can receive unemployment benefits even if they are no longer are actively seeking work. Unemployment
benefits of type II (*Arbeitslosenhilfe*) was raised from 52.5 to 58 percent
(today it is 57 percent). Unemployment benefits of type I and II were
indexed to the net wage increase (they no longer are since 2003). In
1969 the Labor Office, the Bundesanstalt für Arbeit, was established—
ironically, at a time when Germany's unemployment stood at 179 000.
Today the Employment Office has half that number as employees. The
office was restructured in 2003.

The child allowance was extended to families with two children instead
of three in 1961; benefits were again raised in 1965 and 1974. Social
welfare was extended in 1974, with respect to both the benefits and the
persons that are entitled to receive them. The law on the housing allowance, introduced in 1960 and extended in 1965, was extended again
1974. The law on social courts—special courts for social problems, and
a branch of Germany's administrative courts from 1954—was revised in
1974. A major new law on the voting procedure in the self-administration
of the social security system was also introduced.

In addition, governmental employment was risen by one million in the
1970s after it had increased by a million in the 1960s as well, starting out
from a level of 2 million in 1960. It eventually reached a maximum of 4.3
million in western Germany in 1992. As a result of unification, the
number of government employees rose to 6.1 million (including part-
time workers). After privatizing the telecommunications and postal
services and the railroads, consolidating the budget, and scaling back
government employment in eastern Germany, the number of government
employees stood at 4.8 million in 2001.

Taking all these developments together, a variety of measures especially
in the 1970s markedly extended the social dimension of the social market
economy and expanded the welfare state.[20] German politicians handed
out goodies. But this development was no free lunch. The contribution
rate to social insurance rose from 26.5 percent of the gross wages in 1970
to 42.1 percent in 2003, reaching a maximum of 42.2 percent in 1998
(table 5.4). A newly introduced tax on energy consumption ("eco"-tax)
prevented this trend from continuing, but in 2003 the contribution rate
was at the same high level as in 1998, in spite of the €17.2 billion revenue
of the eco-tax in 2002.[21] Without the eco-tax, the contribution rate would
have been 1.7 percentage points higher. According to the macroeconomic
accounts, the German state absorbs nearly half the gross wage income in
the form of income taxes and contributions to social security.

---

[20] See Schewe et al. (1975).

[21] Note that only part of this revenue is directly transferred to the pension system.

TABLE 5.4
Contributions to social security and tax load

	Contribution rates to social security (% of gross wage)	Tax and contributions to social sercuity (% of gross wage income[a])
1970	26.5	33.8
1980	32.4	41.4
1990	35.6	43.5
1998	42.2	48.6
2000	41.1	48.1
2001	40.9	47.1
2002	41.3	47.2
2003	42.1	47.8

[a] Macroeconomic accounts.

The share of government spending on social security in GDP increased from 12.6 percent in 1970 to 22.3 percent in 2002. The increase comes from all branches of social security (figure 5.2). Note once more that there are transfers between the branches; for instance, unemployment insurance pays contributions to the pension system during unemployment. Therefore, the sum of all unconsolidated spending is higher than the consolidated spending of the social security system.

On the financing side, the share of the contributions in GDP has increased from 11.1 percent in 1970 to 17.5 percent in 2001. The shortfall between expenditures and contributions is financed by transfers from the government budget (4 percentage points) and a deficit of the social security system (0.1 percentage point).[22] Whereas in 1970 the difference between the expenditure on social security in GDP (12.6 percent) and the contribution share (11.1 percent) was only 1.5 percentage points, it had increased to 4.1 points by 2001.

In an international comparison, German expenditure on the three main social security branches (pensions, health, and unemployment) relative to GDP are similarly high as those for France and Italy. Each of these three countries spends nearly 20 percent of GDP, more than the United Kingdom and nearly double that of the United States. Unfortunately, more recent data are not available (figure 5.3).

As a result of all these developments, the share of government spending in GDP rose from 39.1 percent in 1970 to 48.8 percent in 1981 (figure 5.4). It was reduced to 44.0 in 1989, but went up again in the 1990s, reaching 50.3 percent in 1996; in 2003 it stood at 49.2 percent. Social expenditures in cash and social expenditures in kind are the major reason for the increase.

[22] German Council of Economic Advisers 2002, table 34*.

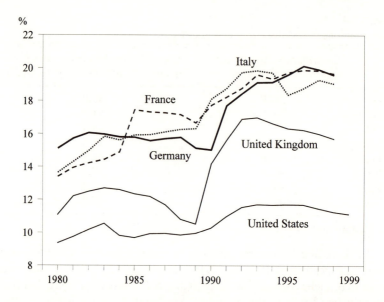

Figure 5.3 Expenditure for pension, health, and unemployment insurance in different OECD countries, 1980–2000 (% of GDP). *Source*: OECD Social Expenditure Database.

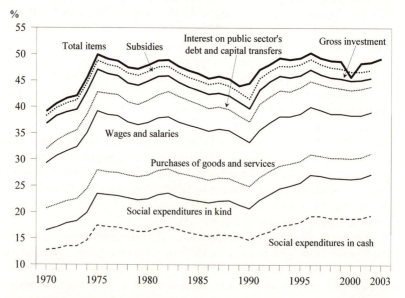

Figure 5.4 Government share in GDP: the expenditure side, 1970-2002 In current prices; until 1990: West Germany. *Source*: German Council of Economic Advisors Annual Reports 1998/99, table 33* and 2002/03, table 34*.

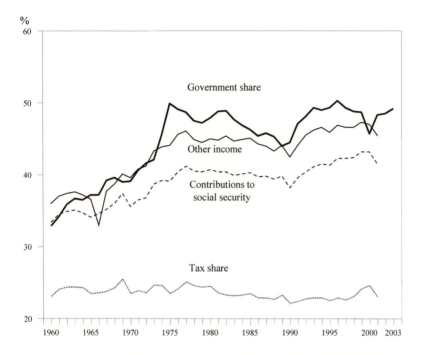

Figure 5.5 Government share in GDP: the financing side, 1960–2002 In current prices; until 1990: West Germany. *Source*: German Council of Economic Advisors Annual Reports 1998/99, table 33* and 2002/03, table 34*.

The rise in government spending had begun as early as the 1960s; in 1960 the share of government spending in GDP was just 32.9 percent (figure 5.5). Whereas the tax share of GDP remained nearly stable for over forty years, it is contributions to social security that have been responsible for the increased expenditure. Thus, the rise in the government share of GDP can be explained by the expansion of the social budget, i.e., by the rise of the welfare state.

The rise of the welfare state in the 1970s was accompanied by an increase in new debt. The budget deficit amounted to about 3 percent of GDP in the second part of the 1970s. The consequences of the expansion of the welfare state became apparent only many years later, when the interest burden became evident and the additional debt had to repaid. The expansion of governmental employment will be felt only in the coming years, when the increased number of civil servants will retire and receive their pensions from the tax revenue of the time.

When the expansion of the welfare system took place in the 1970s, the politicians still were used to the high real growth rates of more than

5 percent of labor productivity of the 1960s. When these high rates of labor productivity could no longer be sustained, Germany's catching-up process came to an end, and the two oil shocks delivered a further blow to the German economy. Whereas the rate of increase in labor productivity of nearly 4 percent in the 1970s was still sizable, in the 1980s it declined to 2.5 percent, and fell still further—to 1.6 percent—since 1995. Thus, the economic basis of the welfare state changed at the very moment that its expansion took place.

Administration of the social budget involves a heavy expenditure. The cost of administering the social security system in 2002 are estimated at €20.85 billion, that is 5 percent of the total expenditure for the social system.[23] The public pension system employs 150 000 persons, the Labor Office 90 000, and the public health insurance system 74 000. The system gives rise to its own bureaucracy and the groups supporting it, for instance the trade unions and employers' associations, the interest groups with respect to social policy, those involved in qualifying the unemployed, and the politicians who take a deep interest in and specialize in social policy. Thus, the system has its own political pressure groups resisting major changes because their own situation is affected.

THE REDISTRIBUTIVE EFFECT OF THE SOCIAL BUDGET

The social budget and its main component, the social security system, can be considered an important element of the social market economy. They provide social assistance, but they create opportunity costs. In the following sections we look at their impact.

One important aspect is that the social budget has implications for equity and income distribution. After all, the main focus of social assistance relates to equity and distributive considerations. However, there is not a simple one-to-one relationship between the social budget and equity. In the context of social security and the social budget, equity can refer to four different aspects. First is the access to insurance benefits; this is distribution in kind. Second is the distribution in the financing of insurance coverage; this is the distributive aspect of contributions. Third is the distribution of income, i.e., the change between market income and post-distribution income; this is monetary distribution or distribution of purchasing power. Finally, there is the distribution in the access to goods other than insurance coverage, be they private, public, or merit goods; this is distribution in kind, in contrast to access to insurance coverage.

---

[23] The sum consists of administrative costs for the pensions (€3.52 bn in 2002), the health system (€11.95 bn in 2001), nursing care (€0.58 bn in 2002), and the employment office (€4.8 bn in 2002).

With respect to the policy instruments used, we can distinguish between the distributive impact of the rules for social insurance, including contributions, of tax-based transfer mechanisms, and of tax-subsidy mechanisms.

Social security provides insurance against risks; it can be interpreted as risk coverage. For instance in health insurance individuals are characterized by different health risks, and health insurance can be considered risk sharing. Assume that people are under a veil of ignorance considering their future health. Insurance then allows them to be protected against risks that they cannot cover individually. In a sense, health insurance has redistributive aspects, but it is in essence an arrangement of risk allocation.[24] In the insurance against disability, risk allocation works in a similar way. Risk allocation is also present in other insurance branches, for instance unemployment insurance, but to a lesser extent. Although workers risk the possibility of being laid off, they can influence this possibility to a large extent, for instance by building up their human capital, increasing their effort, or moving to another region with better jobs. There is even less risk involved in providing an income in one's old age. This can be interpreted as consumption smoothing or precautionary saving, which means that risk coverage can be more differentiated. Looking at the aspect of carrying risks collectively, we can derive an important principle: the smaller the risk component of an insurance, the more justifiable it is to individualize the benefits and the contributions. This means that old-age insurance, except for disability occurring before old age is reached, can be individualized.

The financing side of insurance exhibits the redistributive aspect more clearly. This is especially relevant when contributions are linked not to the risk covered, but to the income of the insured, as is the case in Germany. For instance, in health insurance access to the coverage is identical for everyone, but contributions are proportional to income. Thus, there is a redistributive impact beyond the pure sharing of health risk. In other branches of social security there is some link between the access to coverage and the level of contribution. In unemployment insurance, for instance, contributions and benefits are coupled to wage income. In the old-age pension system, pensions are again linked to contributions, albeit more loosely. It is typical of the existing social security system that it is only vaguely based on the equivalence principle, which would require that contributions are proportional to the benefits of insurance coverage, i.e., that they are risk equivalent: instead, contributions are generally defined in proportion to income. In other words, these

---

[24] In health insurance, risk coverage cannot be individualized: it must be some average, for instance the average health risk of all insured or the health risk of a cohort.

systems contain strong redistributive elements, especially by differentiating contributions according to income.

However, it is difficult to specify the redistributive impact of social security. One reason is that defining the reference point from which redistributive effects can be determined is a complex process. Theoretically, the frame of reference would be an insurance based on the actuarial equivalence. But this frame of reference cannot be clearly defined. We have encountered this argument already, when considering the tax or contribution wedge of social security in chapter 4. A second reason for the difficulty is that we simply do not have sufficient data. Thus, we unfortunately have no empirical evidence of the magnitude of the redistributive dimension of these systems.

Other aspects of the social budget, such as social welfare, unemployment benefits of type II, youth support, and child and housing allowances, are explicitly tax-based transfer mechanisms. In these cases, the government provides an income transfer to households; the transfer is financed by taxes or implicitly by tax allowances. The redistributive effect of both the expenditure side of transfers and the financing side of taxes and the overall effect all show up in the distribution of income.

The social budget does not include all redistributive activities of the government. This holds for taxation. Thus, the choice of tax rates and the definition of the tax base, including tax allowances for the income tax, have a redistributive impact. Similarly, different rates of the value added tax for different categories of products have implications for the distribution of consumption possibilities; for instance, lower rates apply to foodstuffs. There is no value added tax for housing rents, which absorb more than a proportional part of the income of low-income groups relative to the population average. Moreover, subsidies are very often motivated by social considerations, for instance the construction of housing for lower-income groups, the public transport system, or sectors with adjustment problems. They may serve to keep labor income at a higher level, for instance by covering production costs, and they may keep domestic firms competitive in the face of international competition. Subsidies may also be used to reduce product prices, so that consumers can afford these goods more easily.

The social budget also includes items that cannot be shelved under the heading "redistribution." Thus, pensions to civil servants can be regarded as part of the wages the government has to pay its employees, with the proviso that this part of the wage is paid at a later stage of life for work already done.

Moreover, government expenditures may de facto be directed towards specific groups of society to give these groups a preferential access to goods; for instance, government expenditures on the public university system favor those families who send their children to the university, and not (in general) workers' households (see chapter 11). Expenditures on universities have a regressive distribution effect instead of the intended redistribution effect.

IMPACT ON THE ECONOMIC BASE

The flip side of the coin of social protection is an unfavorable allocation effect caused by the social security system.

Moral Hazard

Any insurance, whether privately or publicly organized, can generate moral hazard effects. In technical terms, "moral hazard" refers to the behavior of the insured person in not undertaking measures to reduce the probability of insurance damage arising. This is not to say that the insured is deliberately negligent: he may simply have little incentive to prevent such damage. This problem arises in cases where the insurer cannot observe or control the behavior of the insured. It becomes especially relevant when the risks covered cannot be clearly specified ex ante; when, in addition to risk sharing, other aspects such as distribution dominate, as is the case with the public social security system, and when there is no restraining incentive for the individual to restrict his demand for coverage.

Beyond these technical considerations, there is a moral hazard problem at a higher level, namely for society as a whole. People rely on protection against risks by governmental systems, and their incentives to prevent insurance damage are underdeveloped. Since the benefits provided are not related to the contributions paid, insurance coverage has the property of a semi-free good, so that it tends to be overused, like the commons in the middle ages. The individual does not receive a price signal for the scarcity of this good "insurance coverage," and over-exploitation is the consequence. Moreover, the supply is determined by the political process, and the majority of beneficiaries can dominate the contributors if the beneficiaries represent the majority in voting and if financing can be dissipated through non-actuarial contributions or general taxation. In addition, the policy-maker has an incentive to extend the benefits if the beneficiaries are his voters. There is a clientele for the extension of the social security program (Lindbeck et al. 1994; Saint-Paul 2000). People who are used to the system take it for granted and eventually increase their demands on the government. A further aspect is that courts will require equal treatment, which is another mechanism by which favorable arrangements are extended. Quite a few decisions of the Federal Social Court as well as of the Constitutional Court go in this direction. Thus, there is an inherent tendency of the system to extend itself, and thereby expand the welfare state. Eventually, the cost of social absorption becomes uncontrollable.

Misleading Incentive Effects for Labor

As described in chapter 4, the high marginal rate of income taxation and contributions to the social security system (58 percent of gross labor income for the average married wage-earner and 67 percent for the average single wage-earner) creates misleading incentives for work effort as well as for human capital accumulation in the workforce. In addition, it encourages individuals to move to the underground economy. It is also an inducement for high-skilled employees to take up residence in lower-tax places such as London, and for firms to direct their location decisions accordingly, a relevant phenomenon for the service sectors (banking and insurance) and for research.[25] Moreover, from the point of view of firms, the financing of social security acts like a tax on labor, reducing their effective demand for labor.

Additionally, the benefits of the social security system define a reservation wage that influences search behavior of the unemployed, the supply of labor, and the functioning of the labor market in the lower segment of the workforce.

Looking at these impacts on the supply and demand sides of the labor market, it becomes clear that the existing arrangement negatively affects employment and is thus an important reason for unemployment.

Negative Impact on Growth Dynamics

Social security and the social budget affect resource allocation and growth negatively. There is a welfare loss if a more efficient form of insurance can provide the requisite risk coverage. In addition, there is a trade-off between social protection and growth. The production potential of the economy could be higher with a lower level of the social budget; the economy could be on a higher growth path. Raising the level of contributions for social security and the social budget and financing part of the welfare state by taxes places negative effects on work effort and also on investment. This in turn affects the growth potential of the economy negatively. Moreover, imposing a tax on labor and not fully using labor as an important resource lowers the growth dynamics of the economy.

---

[25] This argument does not apply to people above the insurance ceiling.

THE LIMITS OF FINANCING

Besides its negative influence on moral hazard behavior, unemployment, and growth, it must be accepted that the social welfare system in Germany has reached its financing limits.

Actual Financial Difficulties

After the German election of 2002, the government took a variety of stop-go measures, such as reducing the reserve of the pay-as-you-go pension system from 0.8 month of expenditures to 0.5 month (in 2001 it had already been lowered from one month); in 2004 it is 0.2 month. The contribution rate to the old-age pension system had to be increased from 19.1 percent of the gross wage to 19.5 percent. The contribution ceiling for the PAYG system was raised; this automatically also increased the insurance ceiling of the public health insurance, limiting the exit option from the mandatory public health insurance to private insurance. Nevertheless, the system ran a deficit of €6.4 billion in 2003. These ad hoc measures indicate that the social security system clearly is in a financing calamity.

An Ageing Society

The financing issue becomes even more pressing in an ageing society. Germany is going to be severely affected by the ageing of its population, even more so than France, the United Kingdom, and the United States. The median age of the German population will increase from 39.8 years in 1999 to over 50 years in 2050, assuming an annual net immigration of 200 000 persons. In such a scenario, there will be considerable pressure on the expenditure side of social security; the system will gradually cease to be sustainable (see chapter 6).

Searching for New Sources of Financing

A way out of this dilemma is seen by some to lie in new sources of financing, accessed by broadening the group that contributes and by widening the contribution base. One of the approaches explored is to enlarge the group of those who are required to contribute in the hope of increasing the size of financial contributions, for instance by including the self-employed. This, however, would force into the governmental system more people, who will then claim benefits in the future. Even more important, it would reduce the chance of creating a voluntary privately organized system. For instance, individual retirement saving by the self-employed will become less important. Adjusting the insurance and contribution ceiling with the rise of income has already been done in the past. If the ceiling can be kept in line with the increase in labor income, it will not crowd out the private sector and thus will not impede the option to develop a private-sector solution to the problem. If these ceilings are raised abruptly, as in 2003, the option to move out of public sector insurance and into the private sector is restricted. This approach of broadening the base of the contributory group has the disadvantage of hindering private solutions, so that eventually society will forget about the market alternative to the public system of social welfare.

Another approach to broadening the contribution base would be to include non-labor income, for instance capital income, in the base. Whereas I will argue later that it is indeed a promising approach to uncouple social insurance from the work contract, it would be inappropriate to do this without introducing a change in the overall system. Broadening the contribution base would increase the distributive dimension of social insurance, thereby magnifying the existing undesirable incentives of the system and the ensuing distortions. It would be a move in the wrong direction. Generating additional revenue from a broader base would not solve the core of the problem.

Raising other taxes or increasing general taxation in order to finance social security would create tax wedges somewhere else in the economy and establish new distortions. Germany has introduced an energy tax in order to reduce the contribution rate for the pension system. It has been argued that there is a double dividend here, in the sense that the tax raises revenue for the PAYG pension system and at the same time improves environmental quality. I am extremely skeptical about this argument, as I will discuss in chapter 9.

Increasing the rates of the value added tax in order to raise revenue for social security would bring its own negative effects. It would induce market participants to move to the shadow economy, a phenomenon especially relevant in construction, house repair, and the crafts. Moreover, it would reduce purchasing power. Indirect taxes represent a distortion of incentives and imply a larger deadweight loss if the given level of benefits is kept up.

The overwhelming argument against additional taxes, however, is that this approach would not go to the heart of the problem. It would introduce greater distribution into the social security system, would not correct the false incentive effects, and would enable the present system to keep going for a while longer, thereby preventing any real reform of the system.

Strategies for Reform

Several strategies are necessary to help solve the dilemma of the German social security system.

Making the Intertemporal Financing Constraint Explicit

There is no mechanism in the present system to guarantee that an intertemporal budget constraint of the social security system is satisfied; i.e., there is no arrangement that brings promised future expenditure in line with expected future revenue. Thus, the long-run impact of entitlements as they exist today is not taken into consideration. One way out of this situation is to make the implicit debt of the system explicit and to show the public and the political decision-makers the system's projected impact on future generations. Generational accounts have been proposed to document the burden for future generations (see chapter 6).

However, explicit consideration of the existing debt in an intertemporal budget constraint is not sufficient to bring about a solution to the pension crisis. Such a line of action would be merely an informational instrument, albeit an important one. A more promising approach is to give the intertemporal budget constraint some teeth. For instance, such a constraint would have to specify that at any given moment the expected stream of future expenditures must be in line with the stream of future contributions. In more formal terms, the present value of all future benefits should not exceed the present value of expected revenues, given the institutional setting (i.e., the contribution rate). Were this condition to be violated, there would have to be a mechanism in place that would prevent an excessive rise of the implicit debt. This means that the system would need to adjust its benefits in accordance with the intertemporal budget constraint.

For the pension system, the problem is to find a formula that gives expression to the intertemporal financing constraint. This can be accomplished through different factors in the pension formula, e.g. the demographic factor, the generation factor, or the sustainability factor. However, these factors are only instruments to determine the pensions of individuals: they do not guarantee that the pension system respects the intertemporal budget restraint. Whether or not this condition will be fulfilled is determined in simulations whose results depend on many assumptions, including the ones on productivity growth.

A simple law specifying the intertemporal budget constraint would not be sufficient to provide a credible restriction; it could be changed too easily with a simple majority. Thus, we would need a constitutional rule that would protect future generations and limit the benefits of today's pensioners, taking into account that the young generation has to accumulate private entitlements in a capital-funded system in addition to financing the PAYG system.

The issue of an intertemporal constraint also arises for health insurance. The public health system is a PAYG system similar to the pension system. No precaution is taken at present with respect to future higher health expenditures, partly because of expected technical progress in health care and partly because of increased longevity. In contrast, it is necessary to introduce individualized funded pension reserves, as these are customary for private health insurers. This means that each individual would pay contributions when young in order to cover his health costs later on. Such reserves will become ever more necessary in an ageing population.

Redefining the Risks: Large versus Small

The increase in expenditures in all the branches of the social security system, especially in health care, has been a concern of past governments in Germany. In health, administrative measures such as capping the contribution rates have been used to control increases in costs. Another measure in health care involved capping the total amount of expenditure of physicians and applying a credit point system by which payment to each individual physician was determined ex post. Through such measures the cost increase was halted for a year or two, but eventually the increase resumed. Moreover, these stop-go measures produce unwanted incentive effects and distortions. It can be expected that administrative measures will not be able to control the cost increases for much longer. Therefore we need to look for other approaches.

A major solution in reforming social security in Germany consists in determining what are large risks and what are small risks for individuals. Large risks are those that cannot be borne by the individual, for example a long-term illness or permanent disability. These risks have to be taken over by society. Small risks, however, like having no income during the first days of unemployment or illness, can be borne by nearly everyone, for instance via precautionary savings. Only if the income of an individual is too low to have permitted individual savings to accrue should the government have to step in. It should be the guiding principle in any reform of the welfare state to cover large risks by social security and to individualize the small risks.

The distinction between large and small risks has to be made for the different branches of the social welfare system. In so doing, one has to take into account the different dimensions involved in allocating core risk among the various social security departments, and even the different dimensions of specific benefits in each of the departments. By making such a distinction, the benefits of the social security system can be newly defined. The insurance system then would apply only to the core risks; peripheral risks would be covered by private insurance. Following this approach, mandatory contributions to social security could be reduced. This would mean a lower tax on labor and fewer distortions. The negative impact on the demand for labor and on growth could be ameliorated. Moreover, the now apparent impossibility of financing the systems would be overcome. Additional options for individual contributors would also be available. They can decide themselves whether they want to be covered against small risks (and so would be prepared to pay higher premia) or not to cover these small risks (and thereby economize on the premia). For each individual, there would be a strong incentive effect to bring benefits and premia into line. This means that the insurance coverage for small risks in the economy would then be determined by the choices of all individuals, and not by the political process.

The distinction between large and small risk would yield different results for the different systems of social insurance. For unemployment insurance, some risks could be privatized if one really wanted to reduce the contributions—for instance receiving benefits during the first week of unemployment. As for the old-age pension system, the risk of not having an income in old age could be more or less individualized; benefits would then have to be linked to contributions. The governmental PAYG system can cover only part of the pensions; the rest will have to be covered by the individuals and by a capital-funded private insurance. In health insurance, benefits not directly linked to an illness (contraception, dental care, eyeglasses, private accidents, sport accidents) may no longer be provided. Along similar lines, the risk of lost income during illness after the six weeks paid by the employer will be covered by contribtions of the insured to the public health insurance only, as now has been implemented starting in 2006. However, the coverage of the health risk cannot be completely individualized. There must be (some) risk and burden sharing for the core health risks. But even in health insurance, the redistribution present in linking contributions to income can be shifted to the tax transfer mechanism; this would mean that greater equivalence would be established in the German social security system.

In a minor reform of the health system that was agreed upon by the two large political parties in the fall of 2003, and has been passed in parliament with the support of the Christian Democrats, only dental prostheses and sickness benefits will be taken out of the traditional catalog of the public health insurance system. From 2006 on, these will have to be covered by a mandatory insurance with contributions paid by the employees only. Other elements, such as the coverage of private accidents (e.g. in sports and in households) remain in the public health insurance system. Moreover, some fees were introduced. Individuals now have to pay 10 percent of allowances in kind (capped at €10) for each visit to a doctor (capped at €10 per quarter of the year), for each medication (capped at €10) plus €10 per day in a hospital (capped at 28 days). All payments are capped at 2 percent of the patient's income. It is fair to say that it will be complicated to administer the new fee rules. It docs not address the more basic issues of health insurance.

Reducing Demands on the State

An important point in the reform of social security is that the obligations on the state must be reduced. This requirement, which relates to all systems of social security and to social welfare, is not the same as the need to distinguish between large and small risks. One major feature is that, in pension insurance, the part of his lifetime in which an individual has to pay contributions is to be increased. This means extending the age of compulsory retirement to 67 years and to reduce the exemptions from statuary retirement. But it also implies that it cannot be considered normal that university education lasts until the age of 27, as it very often does, and the study of an additional discipline cannot be supported. Therefore, irrespective of increasing the retirement age to 67, the link between benefits and contributions would be strengthened by requiring that employees have to have paid contributions for 45 years before the full benefits can be paid out. Actuarial deductions would then be calculated not from the reference point of 65 years of age, but from the reference point of 45 years of contributions. Another major issue is that social welfare can no longer be maintained for those who are of working age and are physically able to work. As discussed in chapter 4, the incentives to move such individuals into the labor market have to be improved by letting recipients keep part of their welfare payments if they are earning in the market and by reducing the level of welfare payments for those who are able to work. This will reduce the reservation wage and the minimum wage and is thus a precondition for establishing a better functioning lower segment of the labor market.

The Role of an Income Floor

In reducing the level of benefits in the PAYG system in order to make room for a funded system, the problem is that social welfare provides an income floor below which the benefits of a contribution-based PAYG system cannot fall. You cannot expect people to pay contributions for 45 years of their working life and then let them have only the same monthly benefits they would have received as social welfare benefits. The relevance of this becomes apparent when we compare the level of pensions and of social security payments. Plans are under discussion to reduce the net pension benefit of 69.9 percent of the net wage over a working life (in 2003). Social welfare payments, however, make up roughly 44.2 percent of the income for single individuals in the lowest wage group in industry; for a married couple without children (single-earner household[26]) in this lowest wage group it is 58.9 percent. It would seem that reducing the benefits from the PAYG system would very quickly hit the lowest segment of welfare recipients. Thus, in restricting the PAYG system it will be necessary to rearrange the income floor provided by social welfare.

With an income floor of social welfare benefits assumed as given, there is only a limited space in which to lower the basic pension of the PAYG system. This constraint has become even more relevant after provision was made in 2003 for a basic pension for everyone to act as a lower floor for old-age income. Such a pension is financed by general taxes. The motivation was to prevent "old-age poverty", especially for those who had not been regularly employed in their lifetime and had "broken" or incomplete work histories. The basic pension introduces an income floor in addition to means-tested social welfare benefits; this will make the reform of the pension system more difficult and less likely.

Letting Competition Play

A decisive prerequisite in the reform of social welfare is to make greater use of competition. One aspect of this objective is the role of the regional associations of statuary health insurance physicians. These involve the mandatory membership of doctors. In a way, they are the doctors' trade unions, the only difference being that membership in trade unions is voluntary. The doctors have the right to negotiate the honorarium scales with the public insurers in a bilateral monopoly. This arrangement prevents contracts between insurers and doctors in integrated systems. If greater use of competition is to be initiated, an alternative solution will need to be found to this bilateral monopoly. Integrated systems of insurers, patients, physicians, and hospitals must be made possible. Competition between pharmacies, not now possible in terms of prices (and even not on the internet and not European-wide), should be allowed. Competition between public insurers should be intensified by introducing capital-funded individual reserves and by making them portable, so that the insured can change insurers. Care must be taken that reforms do not lead to a situation in which the public insurers drive out the private ones.

TAKING REDISTRIBUTION OUT OF SOCIAL SECURITY

The approach to redefining the risks that are covered by social security and to move to the equivalence principle wherever possible can be

---

[26] Childless couples.

strengthened by taking redistribution completely out of the social security system and shifting it to a tax transfer mechanism. People with low income could receive a transfer, for instance to pay their contributions to health insurance. Family support could then be undertaken not in the form of lower contribution rates, but by government payment of the contributions. Whereas distributive measures are now hidden in the four branches of social security and we do not know how much distribution there is in the actual system, a separation of insurance and distribution will make the redistributive dimension explicit. The advantages of this approach are several. Equity can be targeted better with a tax-transfer mechanism. The costs of financing will become more apparent. The social choice of the level of social protection will thereby become more rational. A decentralized mechanism will be established by which the financing constraint will impact on the individuals. In addition to transparency, deceptive incentives and distortions are reduced. Such an insurance concept would more or less automatically take contributions away from labor income as a basis for payment. People would tend to consider their total income as a determinant of their insurance coverage.

POLITICAL ECONOMY ISSUES

While the ideas of distinguishing between large and small risks, and of extracting the redistribution objective from the social security process and transferring it to the tax transfer mechanism, are attractive from a long-run point of view, the political process may propose partial steps and even conflicting solutions.

Regarding the pension system, it is suggested from time to time that the whole system be rearranged and that pensions be financed through taxes. The argument in favor of this is that, owing to the income floor discussed above, the pension level of the contribution-based PAYG system cannot be reduced much further, because people will not be willing to pay contributions for a benefit that they can get anyway in form of social welfare (provided they qualify). The problem with such a tax-financed basic pension, however, is that the motivation and the incentives inherent, at least to some extent, in the actual system, i.e., the relationship between contributions and future pensions, would be completely lost. Without such a partial equivalence, which keeps the tax wedge at least lower, people would lose their sovereignty (Breyer et al. 2004). The role of government would become even more dominant with a tax-based "citizen insurance," and of course the mechanics of political economy, with all its pressures, would gain additional relevance. The system would then become less incentive-compatible; it would be moved away from a market solution and would very much resemble the model of the Scandinavian social democratic *Volkshuset*, or folks' home. This could easily result in an expansion of the welfare state.

There is an overwhelming reason why this approach would not be a solution to Germany's social security problem. Given the country's institutional conditions and the electorate's preferences, it would be politically impossible to reduce the basic pension in Germany to a level as low as that pertaining in the Anglo-Saxon world, where individuals are accustomed to having to save enough to provide, to a large extent, for their own retirement. Moreover, a basic pension means that the government provides income for old age. Taking into account that in an ageing society people can enjoy twenty or thirty years of their life in retirement, the basic pension implies that the government is providing an income for a quarter or even a third of an individual's life. Individuals could receive a governmental income without any effort for as much as 45 years. They would not be induced to take responsibility for their old age. This is hard to imagine in a market economy. Old-age income should somehow reflect the result of precautionary individual saving during people's life. When this individual income is not sufficient, social welfare should then step in. In any case, a basic pension would require more financial means from the government than the present transfers. Depending on how the level of the basic pension is reduced, the government would have to finance between two thirds and one half of the actual expenditures of the public PAYG system instead of one third. This increase in expenditures would result in an expansion of the welfare state itself, in addition to creating the wrong incentives as described above, even taking into account that the insured would no longer pay contributions for the basic pensions but would pay taxes instead. Admittedly, the income floor of social welfare limits the scope for reducing social absorption, but even if the welfare level for the elderly remained unchanged, the psychological importance to society of that floor would be considerably reduced if the social welfare benefits for those who are able to work were adjusted downward. This has not been attempted by the new type II unemployment benefit for this group which has just been introduced. To conclude: Introducing a tax-based basic pension is not a promising option.

Another issue of the pension reform is the extent to which the voluntary additional funded system that is to augment the PAYG pension system should be made mandatory. So far, the new voluntary funded system, which receives preferential treatment, has not been as widely accepted as expected. By mid 2003 only 2.8 million new insurance contracts had been taken out since the introduction of the voluntary system, and there are 2.2 million occupational pension contracts. One reason for the relatively low number of new pension insurance contracts is that the favorable tax treatment applying to them will become fully effective in only 2008. Another is that the company contracts received an additional incentive, because insurance premia for those contracts are exempt not only from taxes, but also from the contributions to social security until 2008; employees can transfer part of their salaries into insurance premia without having to pay taxes and social security contributions. It is too early to tell whether the voluntary system will pick up additional momentum.

For health insurance, the concept of "citizen insurance" has been proposed, with contributions being based not only on labor income but on all sources of income, including dividends, interest payments, and rental income. Moreover, it is suggested that the insurance be extended to all groups of society, i.e., to those, such as the self-employed, who now have private health insurance. It is true that the contribution base of the existing public system would be enlarged by the inclusion of income components other than labor income, and in this way the financing problems of the actual system would be temporarily solved. But at the same time, the distributional component of the existing system would be enlarged and its inefficiencies would be perpetuated. In the long run, the implicit tax of the social security system would distort both savings and the labor supply. Moreover, it is to be feared that the exit option from public insurance to the private insurance, linked to the insurance ceiling of the public insurance, would become less accessible, and individuals would gradually forget how a private insurance functions. By only broadening the contribution base, the urgency of reform will lessen and so will be postponed. Moreover, the more fundamental reforms needed in ageing society will not be undertaken.

As an alternative, the Swiss model is being considered for Germany. This approach starts from the premise that a society has to allocate a health risk to all its members. Under such an arrangement, total health costs are assessed and are then divided by the number of the people in order to determine an individual's contribution to the system. This contribution would reflect the average health risk and would be independent of income, and thus also independent of labor income. The solidarity of this system consists in a sharing of the health costs. For those who are not able to pay the premia, distribution must be arranged through the tax transfer mechanism. Note that, in contrast to precautionary savings for old age, an individual has fewer options to protect himself against health risks. Thus, sharing the risks is more appropriate for health care, whereas precautionary individual savings is appropriate for old age income. The German Council of Economic Advisers (1996, 2002), the Rürup Commission, and the Herzog Commission all are in favor of separating income distribution from the social insurance system and dealing with distribution in the tax system. The Christian Democrats have now introduced this concept into their party program. However, the Christian-Social Union, the Bavarian arm of the Christian Democrats, seems set to block such a change. Their argument is that you cannot convince the public that a taxi driver should have to pay the same contribution as a bank director.

The efficiency of such a cost-sharing approach depends very much on the size of expenditures. These have to be clearly controlled; otherwise the costs are likely to explode, since the system has an incentive problem for its users similar to that of a restaurant bill, where all split the cost regardless of what they have eaten. Moreover, the sharing of costs is similar to a cost subsidy for the health sector, implying a disincentive for the service providers to over-expand. Therefore, a definition of essential health measures, i.e., to cover large risks, is crucial for this approach.

APPENDIX

Tables 5A-1, 5A-2, and 5A-3 show the contribution and insurance ceiling, the contribution rates of the pension scheme, and the reserves in the German social security system.

TABLE 5A-1
Contribution and insurance ceilings

	Contribution ceiling	Mandatory membership	Mandatory insurance ceiling
Public old-age pension insurance	€5100 (West); €4250 East	Dependently employed	None
Public health insurance	€3450	Dependently employed up to the insurance ceiling	75% of the contribution ceiling of the old-age pension system $0.75 \times €5100 = €3825$
Unemployment insurance	€5100	Dependently employed	None

TABLE 5A-2
Contribution rates of the pension scheme

Pension scheme for workers and employees[a]	Contribution rates (% of the income liable for contributions)[b]
1891–1911	1.7
1912–1916	2.1
1917–1923	2.6
1924	2.7
1925–1926	4.1
1927–1942	5.0
since July 1, 1942	5.6
since June 1,1949	10.0
since April 1, 1955	11.0
since March 1, 1957	14.0
since January 1, 1968	15.0
since January 1, 1969	16.0
since January 1, 1970	17.0
since January 1, 1973	18.0
1975	18.0
1980	18.0
1985	18.7/19.2
1990	18.7
1991	17.7
1995	18.6
1996	19.2
1997	20.3
1998	20.3
1999	19.5
2000	19.3
2001	19.1
2002	19.1
2003	19.5

Source: Council of Economic Advisors 2003/04, table 76*; Schewe (1975); and own calculations.

[a] Between 1891 and 1942, the numbers for the pension system represent workers' pensions only.

[b] Contributions are for all years, for employers and employees together, and are applicable from January 1 onwards with the exception of 1957 (March 1 onwards), 1983 (September 1 onwards), and 1985 (18.7 until end of May; 19.2 from June 1 onwards).

TABLE 5A-3
Reserves in the German social security system

Years	€bn	Months
1975	22.0	7.4
1976	18.3	5.4
1977	13.0	3.3
1978	9.3	2.2
1979	8.4	1.9
1980	9.6	2.1
1981	11.1	2.4
1982	10.5	2.1
1983	7.7	1.5
1984	5.0	0.9
1985	5.7	1.0
1986	9.1	1.6
1987	10.8	1.8
1988	11.9	1.9
1989	13.2	2.0
1990	17.9	2.6
1991	21.9	2.6
1992	25.1	2.6
1993	38.7	1.9
1994	33.5	1.5
1995	22.0	0.9
1996	14.2	0.6
1997	14.3	0.6
1998	9.2	0.7
1999	13.6	1.0
2000	14.2	1.0
2001	13.8	0.9
2002	10.0	0.7

Source: Council of Economic Advisors Annual Report 2003/04, table 78*.
Note: Data for the time before 1991 only cover Western Germany.

CHAPTER SIX

Ageing as a Challenge over the Next Forty Years

Germany is one of the countries that will be most profoundly affected by the ageing of its population, even more so than France, the United Kingdom, and the United States. This will markedly change the country's economic conditions in the coming decades. The social security system will be put under additional strain. A growing conflict between the generations will have to be resolved. With a decrease in the labor supply and possibly an increasingly risk-averse society, the prospects for economic growth will deteriorate. As a result of these conditions, Germany's political economy will change.

THE POPULATION FORECAST

According to Germany's tenth official population projection, from June 2003, the German population is expected to shrink considerably over the next forty years in spite of an increase in life expectancy. In a scenario with an increase in life expectancy (up to 2050) of four years for newly born males and five years for newly born females and a net immigration of 100 000 people per year (*scenario 1*), the population in Germany would shrink by 15 million, to 67 million (figure 6.1); with an increase in life expectancy of six years and again a net immigration of 100 000, the population would fall to 68 million. If we assume a net annual immigration of 200 000 persons, and again an increase in life expectancy of six years (*scenario 2*), the population would fall to 75 million. If, from 2011 onwards, there were 300 000 immigrants per year and an increase in life expectancy of six years (*scenario 3*), the population would increase to 84 million in 2020 and then fall to 80 million. A major assumption of these forecasts is that the reproductive behavior remains at the present rate. Historically, however, we know that there have been unexpected baby booms following changes in the reproductive behavior, so such surprises cannot be ruled out.

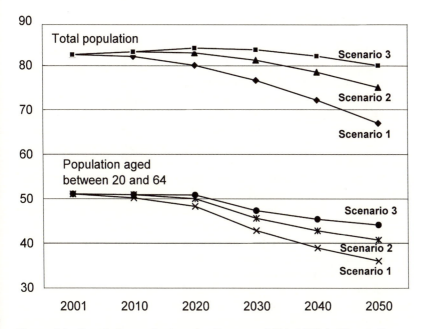

Figure 6.1 Population projections for Germany, 2001–2050 (millions). *Source*: Federal Statistical Office, 10th Official Population Forecast.

Ageing is an issue not only of the decline in the total population, but also of the changing age structure of the population. Thus, the median age will increase considerably, from 40.6 years in 2001 to over 50 years. The elderly ratio, i.e., the ratio of those aged 65 years and over to those aged between 20 and 64, will double under scenario 1 (with a four-year increase in life expectancy and 100 000 immigrants), from 27.5 to 56.4 percent. Taking into account the actual labor market participation rate, this means that there would be nearly one elderly person for every person of working age. This coefficient has already increased considerably in the last decade—it was 24 in 1995. In the two other scenarios the ratio of elderly to working adults will be only marginally lower: 54.5 percent in scenario 2 and 51.5 in scenario 3. Thus, immigration cannot positively affect the age structure very much.

The forecast for some of the other OECD countries over the next fifty years, for example Italy, is similar. Japan will be the country most subject to population ageing. The forecast for France, the United Kingdom, and the United States is somewhat less grim: according to OECD data, population in these countries will stagnate. Nevertheless, the average age in their populations will increase. Even the population of China is expected to age markedly.

IMPLICATIONS FOR SOCIAL SECURITY

Ageing will change the conditions of Germany's system of social security substantially. The working population, and with it the contribution base of the pay-as-you-go (PAYG) system for old age and for health, will shrink, while at the same time the number of recipients of pensions will increase dramatically and expenditures on health and nursing care are likely to rise. This will have two different effects. First, there will be more older people in relation to those working, assuming a given life expectancy, since fewer will be born and people will be living longer; consequently, the social security systems, which even today can be financed only by resorting to questionable methods, will encounter dramatic financing problems. Second, the rising ratio of elderly to working adults will cause labor demand to shrink systematically, because of the effect of rising contributions to social security as part of the labor costs, and thus will contribute to increased unemployment.

In the public discussion, the focus has been on the effects of ageing population on the public old-age pension system. In the 1970s three dependently employed persons were supporting one pensioner in the PAYG pension system via their contributions: today the ratio is more like two to one, with 34 million dependently employed and 23 million pension recipients (not counting government officials). By 2030, the point will be reached where one person in work will have to support one in old age. As for health insurance, with 72.6 million people or 88.5 percent of the population covered by the public health insurance system (including pensioners) (the data refer to 1999 and are likely to hold for 2003 as well), there are just 34 million working adults to support them all. This ratio between those retired and those working will worsen in the future, not only because there are fewer young and more older people for a given life expectancy, but also because of increasing longevity.

The pension system contains a massive implicit debt. Together with some other factors representing obligations to the future, such as the pensions of government officials which is to be financed out of taxation, the implicit debt is estimated to be 270 percent of GDP (Council of Economic Advisers 2003). It is expected that the contributions to the pension system will increase to 24 percent of the gross wage in 2030 with present institutional arrangements; if the recommendations of the Rürup commission are fully implemented, the contribution rate will be 22 percent. Unfortunately, these forecasts have often turned out to be wrong. For instance, when the Riester reform was implemented, according to the projections of 2001 the contribution rate in 2030 would remain below 22 percent; however, only two years later even the official forecasts were assuming that it would rise to 24 percent.

Ageing will also have an impact on health insurance. Not only will the ratio between the active population paying contributions and the recipients of insurance coverage shrink for a given life expectancy, reducing the contribution base; but also, medical costs will be higher. It has been observed that on average health costs rise with age, with the cost of a person's final year absorbing an overwhelming percentage of the total health costs of his lifetime.[1] Accordingly, a longer life implies that the increase in health costs, including those for the final year, are shifted forward, and that more years are going to have to be insured at higher average costs. Additionally, with a longer life more illnesses are likely to be contracted; i.e., the probability of multi-morbidity will increase. For these reasons, health costs will rise more than proportionally in an ageing society.

For public health insurance, forecasts of the contribution rate in 2030 or 2040 range from 23 percent (Breyer and Ulrich 2000a) to 34 percent (Deutsches Institut für Wirtschaftsforschung 2001); not taking into account the small changes in health insurance implemented in 2002 and 2003. In addition, expenditures on the nursing care insurance will rise.

INTERGENERATIONAL CONFLICT

Depending on the reforms to be undertaken, future working generations will have to contribute a sizable part of their incomes to the social security system. Summing up the forecasted contribution rates for the separate insurance systems—and even assuming just half of today's contribution of 6.5 percent to unemployment insurance, because unemployment can be expected to be lower if labor supply is reduced—a contribution rate of 50 percent of the gross wage cannot be ruled out.[2] In addition, the employed will have to pay taxes to keep the government going and to finance the public infrastructure. At the same time, the tax base from value added is likely to increase much more slowly, or even to shrink, with fewer people working.

A further problem looming in the public budgets concerns the state's pension obligations for retired government officials. These pensions are currently financed from tax revenue. Part of the additional pension load today is the result of the increase (by 1 million) in government employees in the 1970s, many with the status of official civil servants. It should not

---

[1] The health costs of the final year of life fall, however, with increasing age after 65.

[2] The sum of the contribution rates mentioned in the text would actually amount to 51.65 percent assuming the lower forecast for health, a doubling of the actual percentage of 1.7 for nursing care and a halving of the actual percentage for unemployment.

be forgotten that about 31 percent of social security expenditure on pensions, amounting to 69.1 billion in 2001, are already financed by tax revenues, i.e., transfers from the federal budget.[3] This means that the present generation is already financing a large part of pensions through taxes. Moreover, tax revenue of the Bund picks up the deficit of the Federal Labor Office—5.6 billion in 2002, or about 10 percent of Labor Office expenditure. In addition, the federal budget finances the unemployment benefit of type II to the tune of 15.0 billion, or about 28 percent of total expenditure of the Labor Office. If this tendency continues, future working generations will have to cover a sizable amount of social security costs in their tax load; if it is discontinued, contributions to the social security system will have to rise for that reason alone.

Thus, future generations of working adults will have to bear an immense burden, and one that will not leave them with many options. They may become unwilling, or even unable, to pay the contributions that are necessary to keep the PAYG systems going at its existing level. We can therefore expect to see a conflict arising between the generations with regard to the concept and implementation of the social welfare system. As a matter of fact, one such discussion has already flared up, in the summer of 2003.

In the past, politicians have attempted to calm the public's fears that future pensions might be at risk. Thus, in the 1990s you could read on bill boards the promise of the then Social and Labor Minister Blüm of the Kohl government that "The pensions are safe". His Social Democratic successor Riester made similar statements. But when such political utterances are being made, it is a sign that the confidence of the citizens is already lost.

The issue of equity between the generations is set to become a major topic in German politics. Equity cannot be defined only in the context of the status quo. Equity considerations have to take into account how a distributive measure will influence the decisions of economic agents and the result that will be obtained after all the adjustment processes had played out in the economic system. For economists, this is the idea of a change from one general equilibrium to another. In any such considerations, the interest of future generations is now introduced more explicitly, so that their utility and preference functions are taken into account. Put differently, if adjustments are needed in the public systems, the issue is how to split the burden of adjustment between the generations. Society and the political process must find an answer to what is fair between the generations. Political parties are now raising this issue in their programs.

---

[3] This includes the usual and the additional transfers from the federal government to the pension system and transfers to the miners' insurance and special benefits, e.g., for the education of children.

A guideline to finding a solution is the distinction between the impact of a different ratio between the retired and those in work for a given life expectancy, i.e., when fewer are born, and the impact of an increased longevity. With greater longevity, each cohort will receive higher benefits under the status quo. This means that either they will have to pay more in contributions (for the same number of working hours over their total lifetime, or by working more years), or they will have to accept lower benefits. This aspect of adjustment does not represent a conflict between generations, since benefits and contributions relate to the same cohort. Accordingly, this solution represents an important aspect of the issue of fairness. With a higher ratio of elderly to working adults, assuming a given life expectancy, the conflict between the generations arises because those working in the future will have to pay more, because there are more older people. Here the issue of fairness has to be resolved.

One of the instruments to be used in the context of equity between the generations relates to the generational accounts, in which the debt that is inherent in the actual systems of social security is made explicit. In these accounts, the flows of future benefits and future contributions are determined so that the present value of debt can be calculated. The method hinges on the correct evaluation of future flows as well as on the interest rate that is used to discount these flows. Whereas the generational accounts are an instrument for information, other policy instruments explicitly redefine contributions and future benefits. One of these is the pension formula, on which the demographic change is modeled, to some extent. In principle, this formula has to express two different phenomena: the increase in life expectancy, and the changed ratio between the young and the old for a given life expectancy, as discussed above.[4] This will allow us to disentangle the fairness issue. Another instrument concerns the individually accumulated funds for old age, introduced so that the importance of the public PAYG system is diminished. Analogously, funded individualized reserves in health insurance constitute an instrument that can be used to prepare the system for the increased expenditures of old age.

An additional factor in the social security system complicating a solution to the problem of an ageing population is that the PAYG system has not yet been switched to a funded or a partly funded system whereby each cohort will have to increase its savings in accordance with its higher life expectancy. Such a switch will now have to be made while the population is ageing. In principle, the switch from the PAYG system for pensions, health, and nurtured care to a partly funded system with private accounts

---

[4] The pension formula proposed by the Rürup commission does not distinguish between these two effects.

should generate efficiency gains (Feldstein 1995; Siebert 1998b). Thus, a switch from one steady state or general equilibrium (with a PAYG system) to another (with a partially funded system) is to be recommended. However, the switch cannot be carried out instantaneously, because today's working generation will have to build up its capital in the form of individualized funds, and this will take time. In addition, the workers will have to pay the pensions and finance the health costs of those who are older. Thus, today's young will have to bear a double burden until the new steady state is attained. It is debated in the literature whether today's young generation can also benefit from the move to a new steady state or whether they will just have to accept the additional burden so that the country can change to a more efficient, partly funded, system.[5] Whereas models may show that it is possible to make the shift without any loss for today's young, it seems realistic to start from the premise that the additional burden they will be required to bear will be a matter for policy discussion in the future. This means that present-day pensioners and those set to retire in the next two or three decades will have to accept lower pensions. This then raises the issue of fairness, discussed above. It is clear, therefore, that the issues of generational equity will be a major concern of German politics in the years to come.

IMPACT ON LABOR, CAPITAL, AND DEMAND

The conflict between the generations will have to be resolved, and the changes in the system of social security made, in an economy with an ageing society, which will quite likely have a weaker economic base. This holds for the supply side of the economy, where the augmentation and accumulation of factors of production follow a different pattern, as well as for the demand side. The endogenous forces of economic growth will be weaker. Moreover, fiscal policy and the political economy will change.

One immediate effect of population ageing is that the labor supply, in quantitative terms, will shrink. Measuring the rate of change of the labor supply by the population in the 20–64 age bracket, which is equivalent to assuming a constant participation rate, the labor supply in Germany is expected to shrink in scenario 2 above, i.e., with a net annual immigration of 200 000, by 0.2 percent annually in the period 2010–20, by 0.9 percent in 2021–30, and by 0.6 percent in 2031–40. All other conditions being equal, labor will become more scarce, its productivity will increase as a result of the greater scarcity, and real wages for the smaller labor force will rise. Capital will become relatively more abundant as a result of

[5] See Feldstein (1995) for an affirmative answer, but Breyer (2001) for a negative one.

labor being more scarce. Consequently, real interest rates should fall. Relative factor prices will shift, ceteris paribus, in favor of labor. Technically speaking, this can be interpreted as a movement along the factor price frontier[6] of the economy.

Further, the age structure of the labor supply will change. Labor is not homogeneous. Older workers will see their accumulated experience become obsolete more quickly than nowadays, given the fast pace of technological progress, especially in the information and communications industries. Many of these workers will find it difficult to acquire the new skills needed to keep up with this progress, or to cope with the new technologies. This could slow down the acceptance of such technologies. In order to deal with these possibilities, it is important to know just how the accumulation of experience proceeds in the life cycle, at what age the learning process stops, and when productivity starts to decline. Experience refers to existing or refined technologies and is linked to vintage capital; it does not relate to a shift in technologies. Consequently, it is likely that older workers will not have the skills that will be in demand. This problem will be exacerbated by the fact that the legal and the effective retirement ages in most countries are going to have to be increased by several years in order to secure the financing of old-age pension systems. To deal with these problems, older workers will need to be given better ongoing training. Human capital formation will thus become more important. Further, ways must be found to allow older workers to work on a part-time basis in order to work longer. Wage contracts relying on the seniority principle will have to be rewritten.

As a population ages, returns on capital investment will tend to become smaller. The capital stock will be too large for the smaller number of people and thus will have to be melted down by reducing investment. Moreover, investment opportunities will generally be less abundant in ageing societies because aggregate demand will be weaker. More specifically, the structure of the capital stock will change. Capital stock will become obsolete in those areas where demand falls. Of course, there will also be new investment opportunities, as older people will want to have larger and better appointed dwellings, more tourism opportunities, and better health care services.

Because of the smaller returns on capital investment in an ageing society, less capital will tend to be accumulated. There are secondary or countervailing effects arising from this. Thus, the real interest rate will fall because of the reduced investment opportunities, and the lower rate will stimulate capital formation. In addition, the relative increase in the cost

---

[6] The factor price frontier is the locus of maximally possible real wages and real interest rates as determined by the production side.

of labor will engender the substitution of capital for labor in capital-intensive areas. Moreover, with a longer life expectancy, more money has to be saved by individuals. In addition, with a change from the PAYG system to a funded system, workers will be putting more money away for their retirement, which again implies increased savings (Siebert 1998b: figure 3). None of these secondary effects, however, will be able to compensate for the diminished impact that decreasing returns will have on capital formation. Unless technological progress can open up new investment opportunities, capital formation will weaken.

This interest rate effect in the real economy has an analog in the financial markets. When the older generation sells its financial assets on the market in order to finance its old-age consumption, asset prices are likely to fall. There will be an asset melt-down for land prices, shares, and bonds.

Consumption demand will also change, because workers will have to set aside greater amounts of income for retirement; i.e., they will have to consume less when they are young in order to be able to even out their consumption in later life. Further, the consumption structure will shift in favor of products consumed by older people, e.g., leisure, tourism, and health services. These are labor-intensive products, for which a productivity increase is more difficult; thus, a sharp rise in prices is likely.

AGEING AND GROWTH DYNAMICS

Conditions for economic growth are thus different in an ageing society. Because of the nature of such economies, an important growth factor, i.e., the labor supply, is diminished. If one weights the forecasted rate of decrease in the labor supply for Germany with a production elasticity of 0.7, the GDP growth rate will, ceteris paribus, be lower by between 0.6 percentage point in 2021–30 and 0.4 percentage point in 2031–40. A second growth factor, i.e., capital formation, will become weaker, since the capital stock will shrink. Ageing societies thus move along a lower growth path.

The third growth factor, and one that is subject to different conditions in ageing societies, is technological progress. Ageing societies may be more risk-averse. If so, entrepreneurs will be less daring as regards innovation, and political parties and the responsible administrators in these societies will be less willing to approve new products and new production processes. Product innovation may therefore become more difficult. In addition, demand for new products, apart from those intended specifically for older people, such as new medical products, could weaken. The willingness of the population to accept new products could also decrease if older people, as either workers or consumers, feel they cannot cope with them given the human capital they have accumulated.

But technological dynamics does not depend only on the adoption of new technologies. Consider a world or model in which new technology is generated by the young generation and applied by the older, experienced, generation. In such a context, in which neither entrepreneurs nor workers are homogeneous, an ageing generation will produce a weaker flow of technological innovations. If however the alternative hypothesis—i.e., that the engine of technological progress is the accumulation of experience—is assumed, ageing societies may even have an advantage.

On the whole, there will be a strong tendency in ageing societies for growth to be lower.

The Impact on Foreign Trade

An ageing population will have considerable consequences for foreign trade. The shift in demand in favor of leisure and health services will stimulate the production of internationally non-tradable goods. This specialization will not motivate the domestic market to develop an export base for new products. The demand for tourist services abroad will probably exacerbate the foreign trade situation. On balance, prices for non-tradable goods will increase relative to prices for tradable goods; i.e., there will be a real appreciation. This would mean that a current account deficit would be more likely. In the euro area, this change in relative prices would affect especially Germany and Italy; it would be less pronounced with respect to euro area as a whole, as the impact in countries with a higher average age of the population will be somewhat ameliorated by those member states with a younger population. Nevertheless, Europe may in the future be faced with endogenous forces increasing the demand for non-tradables, thus leading to a current account deficit.

If retirement provisions have been made by accumulating wealth abroad, this current account deficit can be financed by importing capital. If they have not, however, a real depreciation of the domestic currency will be necessary in order make the non-tradable goods less attractive. This would require a nominal devaluation of the euro, consistent with a less dynamic region of the world economy. Such a scenario can also be explained as follows: capital flows in the world are diverted to economies with young populations, whereby these economies become more dynamic, thus moving further onto the economic center-stage.

The Political Economy

Besides affecting the economic constraints of an economy and its economic base, ageing will have an impact on the political process. This relates to fiscal policy, but also to the political process and its outcome.

Public budgets will be affected in numerous ways. In the first place, weaker economic dynamics will cause tax revenues to drop. In addition, the working members of the population will constitute a considerably smaller tax base. Expenditures, however, will increase for a number of reasons, for example because heavier demands will probably be placed on the social security system. This will be the case not only because of increased retirement and welfare expenditures for older people, but also because of increased health insurance expenditure, which will rise as the average age of the population rises. The magnitude of these effects will, of course, depend on how successfully the social security and health systems are redesigned in years to come, and how sustainable such reforms are. In addition, the pensions of public servants, whose numbers swelled considerably in the 1970s as the welfare state was being expanded, are a time bomb that is ticking away in public budgets. Government expenditures could also rise because the infrastructure (schools, transportation systems, administration buildings) is oversized for the new situation and cannot be downsized quickly enough, i.e., because the costs incurred by the existing infrastructure cannot be cut immediately.

If expenditure adjustments are not made, public budget deficits will become even larger relative to GDP than today. Thus, if fiscal policymakers do not address the issue of cutting expenditures, massive budget imbalances will occur. Numerous calculations demonstrate that future generations not only will have to pay higher social security contributions, but also will have to bear a greater net tax burden. It is not known whether the future working generation will renege on the contract between the generations, and it is thus questionable whether public finance systems, along with their transfer systems, will be sustainable. Their being sustainable, however, is a precondition for monetary stability. This is the motivation for the stability pact in the euro area, putting a lid on public debt (see chapter 13).

Moreover, in an ageing society the political process itself will change. Older voters have their own preferences. They may be more risk-averse and this may be expressed in their voting behavior. Political parties will have to change their basic platforms in such a way that policies on the whole will change. And this may create a climate that is not conducive to innovation. Taking all these points together, Germany's economic and political processes are likely to change considerably over the next forty years.

In order to minimize the negative impact of ageing on the economic base, the challenge for Germany is to initiate the necessary adjustments before the process of ageing really begins to gain momentum after 2010. Time is running out. It is important that conditions be created which will make social security systems sustainable. This requires a reduction in the benefit level of the social security systems, for instance in the pension level of the PAYG pension system, a later retirement age, and the introduction of more private insurance elements, as already discussed. Further, it is important that conditions be created that will allow ageing societies and their institutional systems to carry out the structural adjustments that will be necessary in the future. Flexibility of the economic systems and the labor markets is a critical issue. Above all, it is important that conditions be established that will counteract the stagnation of economic growth in ageing societies. Thus, economic policy strategies should give priority to creating a setting that is conducive to innovation. Taxes, infrastructures, and institutional systems should constitute a good business climate. Workers need to have excellent job qualifications, which means that there need to be institutional arrangements that are conducive to human capital formation throughout individuals' working lives. Finally, it is all-important that the basis for innovation, i.e., higher education and research facilities, are completely redesigned if ageing societies are to be made dynamic.

Germany: an Immigration Country

In an ageing society like Germany, immigration is an important issue. Immigrants can make up for the decrease in the workforce, augment the contribution base of the social security system (and so, of course, receive benefits from it), ease bottlenecks in the labor market, and fill those jobs that Germans are no longer willing to take. But there is also the issue of how integrated foreigners are into German society, and how much integration Germany as an immigration country requires from its immigrants. This issue is at the heart of Germany's debate on its immigration policy. In a way, Germany simply let immigration happen in the past: it did not have an explicit immigration policy, and sought only to correct unsatisfactory outcomes ad hoc. Thus, it now has to make up its mind about its immigration policy for the future.[1]

IMMIGRANTS IN GERMANY TODAY

About one-tenth of the population in Germany are foreigners. The actual percentage for the whole of the country is 8.9 (December 2002). Since there was less immigration to East Germany in the past (the former German Democratic Republic being less open), West Germany has a larger proportion of foreigners in the population: 10.4 percent (December 2000). This is the same percentage as the foreign-born population in the United States (in 2000) and double that of European countries like France (5.4 percent in 1999) and the United Kingdom (4.0 percent in 2000). In addition to 7.3 million foreigners, there are about 430 000 asylum seekers who receive benefits according to the asylum law. Thus, it is fair to say that in an international comparison Germany is an immigration country, despite public discussion in Germany which creates the impression that there is still a choice in the matter.

One quarter of the foreigners in Germany are from the EU-15 countries (1.9 million), most of them from Italy (610 000; data for 2002[2]). More

---

[1] I appreciate critical comments on this chapter from Matthias Knoll and Rainer Schmidt.

[2] German Council of Economic Advisers, Annual Report 2002, table 15*, updated.

than one quarter (2 million) are from other European countries, including the former Yugoslavia (590 000) and Poland (320 000). A further one quarter are from Turkey (1.9 million), and the remainder come from Asia (12 percent or 877 000), Africa (4 percent or 300 000), and the Americas (3 percent or 220 000).

Foreigners do not stay permanently in Germany. There is quite a bit of out-migration to their former home countries. Thus, in the boom year 2000 gross immigration was 841 000 but gross emigration was 674 000, so that net immigration was 167 000. Net immigration in the period 1995–2002 was 211 000 annually; this is 2.5 persons per thousand of the population.[3] The average duration of stay in Germany is 15.6 years (end 2002). This means that, in contrast to a traditional immigration country like the United States or Australia, a sizable part of immigrants to Germany eventually return to their home countries. It is therefore important to look at the net immigration figures.

THE HISTORY OF IMMIGRATION

After World War II, West Germany absorbed a huge number of refugees from the former German territories and also from East Germany—until the wall was built in 1961. In 1949, the year of the foundation of the Federal Republic of Germany, 7.9 million refugees were living in West Germany; with a population of 48 million, this constituted a ratio of 16 percent. In East Germany the ratio was higher, at 19 percent, or 3.6 million refugees out of a total population of 18.8 million. Between 1950 and 1961, however, 3.8 million people migrated from East to West Germany, while only 400 000 moved in the other direction.

Immigration of foreigners into Germany started in the late 1950s, when German industry recognized a shortage of labor and began to attract foreign workers, first from Italy and then from Spain, Greece, Turkey, and Portugal (the first immigration wave). Formal agreements were signed with the emigration countries (Italy in 1955, Spain and Greece in 1960, Turkey in 1961, and Portugal in 1964). During this first immigration wave the German Labor Office actively recruited foreign workers from the Mediterranean countries. This was a demand-pull migration, where the initiative came from Germany as the immigration country. The foreign workers manned the assembly lines in the car producing firms or other enterprises of the German export industry, and on Sundays the Italians and Spaniards used the railway stations as piazzas or plazas,

[3] For comparison, the United States had an immigration of 8.9 per 1000 of the population from 1881 to 1890, Australia, 17 in the same period. In 1945 and 1946, West Germany took in 49 and 39 refugees per 1000 of the population, respectively (Siebert 2003).

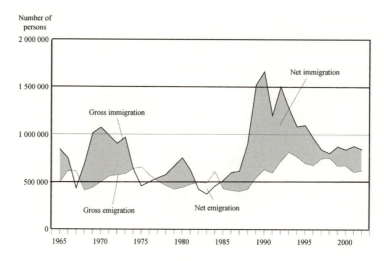

Figure 7.1   Immigration, emigration and net immigration, 1965–2002 ('000).

the meeting places they were so used to in their home countries. At first only the workers came to Germany; later they would bring their wives and families, or they would marry a German girl. They joined the local glee clubs or excelled in the town's sport team. Many immigrants created their own businesses, and nowadays an Italian pizzeria or a Turkish kebab stall can be found in every German town.

Following the first immigration wave in 1958–66, there was a second in 1968–73 prior to the oil crisis (figure 7.1; in the appendix). During these two waves, the number of foreign workers increased from 127 000 to 2 600 000. Only in the recession of 1966–68 was there a temporary stop for new foreign workers, when many existing contracts were not extended. Thus, the foreign workers acted as a buffer in this recession, as they were the first to be laid off. When the economy began to gain pace again, the demand for labor rose and attracted new immigrants. When the immigration surged, and when at the same time the first oil shock hit the German economy with the consequence of a major recession, the recruitment drive was halted in 1973. Since then, workers from non-EU countries have been allowed to immigrate only when an employer can demonstrate that he cannot fill a position from the labor force existing in Germany. This has to be certified by the Labor Office. Family members were allowed to follow the workers to Germany except for children older than 18 years; this age limit was reduced to 16 years in 1981. Meanwhile, the initial demand-pull migration had changed to a supply-driven migration, with the initiative now coming more from the migrant countries than from Germany.

When economic activity picked up again, a third immigration wave took place in the late 1970s and 1980. But again, following this surge and the onset of the 1982 recession, and ten years after the cessation of the immigration recruitment drive, a new law was introduced in 1983 in an attempt to limit immigration by providing an inducement for workers to return to their home country.

Germany experienced a fourth wave of immigration in the late 1980s and early 1990s, both before and after the fall of the Iron Curtain. In contrast to the other waves, this was a migration of people wanting to be free from the dictate of the state (before the wall had fallen), and wanting to seize the new opportunities that became available (when the wall had come down). Gross immigration rose in 1989 to 1.5 million, in 1990 to a peak of 1.7 million, and was 1.2 million in 1991, including immigration from East to West Germany. Net immigration reached 0.98, 1.03, and 0.6 million, respectively, in these years. When the migrants from East Germany and other Germans from the previous communist countries, for instance those whose parents had settled in parts of Russia, are excluded from these numbers, net immigration into West Germany was considerably lower, e.g., only 329 000 in 1989. Thus, the fourth wave was to a large part driven by Germans.

Concern arose that, besides the freedom seekers, who came just before and after the fall of the Iron Curtain, and besides those who were truly being prosecuted in their home countries, a new type of migration was arising: social welfare migration. There were indications that a number of migrants had discovered that they could participate in the benefits of the German welfare state, e.g., receive social welfare payments. Thus, after the fourth surge in immigration and another recession—and ten years after the previous law attempting to reduce immigration—an asylum law was passed in 1993 limiting the benefits provided to asylum seekers (see below). The new law speeded up the procedures for asylum applications, and severely limited access to the asylum system by requiring that applicants who passed through safe third countries en route to Germany had to apply for asylum there, rather than in Germany. Since Germany is surrounded by safe third countries, the only ways for asylum seekers to enter the country without passing through them were by air or by sea. The new regulation was intended to limit welfare migration.

To sum up, there has been a pattern in past immigration. Immigration has picked up when the economic conditions in Germany seemed promising. (Of course, other aspects like the fall of the wall also played a role.) After each surge of immigration, Germany initiated laws—in 1973, 1983, and 1993—attempting to limit the flow. Immigration can also be seen to have responded to the recessions: after each recession except for that of 1992, there was a net emigration (table 7A-1); and after the 1992 recession, net immigration fell to 47 000 by 1998.

The Integration of Foreigners

The extent to which foreigners are integrated into German society is a point that is heavily debated. Admittedly, an evaluation of this issue depends, among other things, on one's personal orientation. Looking at anecdotal evidence, some groups of foreigners are better integrated into the German economy than others. Thus, many people from the Mediterranean countries who still live in Germany are active as small entrepreneurs in the service sector, running their own barber shops, restaurants, or, as can be increasingly observed of the Turkish community, their fruit and vegetable stores or IT shops. As a matter of fact, Germany's restaurant menus would be dull without the Mediterranean specialties. Many jobs in German industry would remain unfilled if they were not manned by foreigners. In addition, immigrants' children have entered German universities with a fair degree of success, although they are still underrepresented considering the proportion of immigrants in the total population. Moreover, some of the immigrants have moved into the metropolitan areas where they help to ease bottlenecks in the labor market, especially in filling jobs that Germans are no longer prepared to take.

On the other hand, foreigners are concentrated mainly in the larger cities; here they tend to congregate in their own enclaves, where they can continue with their original customs and languages, and often don't even need to learn German. It is here that the lives of native Germans are most affected by the influx of immigrants, sometimes to the extent of being driven away. For example, in some of the larger cities classes in schools have a majority of foreign pupils, so that teaching cannot be conducted adequately in German. This reduces the employability of such pupils, both Germans and foreigners, in the labor market later on. Admittedly, Germans on low incomes are most affected by competition with foreigners, because they are economically closer to the immigrants' situation as regards housing, and to some extent jobs. To a large extent, people on higher incomes are not in competition with the incomers. It is therefore not surprising that open signs of xenophobia have been most pronounced in eastern Germany, where income per capita is low and unemployment is high, even if the proportion of foreigners is actually much smaller there than in western Germany.

Looking at macroeconomic data, foreigners have a larger proportion in the 15–64 year age group: they account for 12.0 percent of this group in western Germany (December 2000[4]) while making up 10.4 percent of its total population. They constitute a relatively lower proportion of 8.4 percent of those employees who have to pay social security contribu-

---

[4] Own estimate.

tions.[5] This may partly reflect the fact that some of them are self-employed. Other figures indicate that the foreigners are not well integrated into the labor market: their unemployment rate, i.e., the number of unemployed foreigners in relation to the total workforce of foreigners, in western Germany is 18.4 percent (August 2003), double the rate of Germans in the West; in eastern Germany the rate is 39.1 percent—in Germany as a whole it is 19.9 percent. The immigrants account for 17.4 percent of the total unemployed in western Germany, much more than their share of the population. The proportion of the long-term unemployed immigrants is 16.7 percent in western Germany and 11.1 percent in Germany as a whole (September 2002). All unemployment percentages, therefore, are higher for immigrants than their share of the population. Finally, their share in the recipients of social welfare benefits is 22.1 percent (December 2000). In addition to the 595 000 foreigners receiving social welfare (December 2000), 430 000 obtain benefits according to the law of asylum seekers.

This poor integration of foreigners into the labor market reflects the fact that the lower segment of the German labor market, so important for immigrants trying to get an economic hold in their new environment, has dried up because of the informal floor of income provided by the government. Whereas in the United States an immigrant is forced to earn his living in the labor market and so does not have too many outside alternatives to accepting the market-clearing wage, the informal minimum wage that exists in Germany does not exert the same pressure on job-seekers to enter the labor market. Thus, clearly, Germany does not have an adequate labor market for an immigration country. Moreover, whereas in the Anglo-Saxon world an immigrant cannot rely on a generous welfare system as a fallback option in terms of governmental programs, this is different in Germany once the foreign worker has been granted official entry. This raises the issue of welfare state migration, i.e., of migration that is driven explicitly or implicitly by the difference between the net wage at home and the welfare benefits provided in Germany.

In order to reduce this incentive, since 1994 asylum seekers are no longer entitled to receive social welfare benefits. By law, they are now provided with housing instead of financial support, and are given coupons for food and articles of basic need and a small pocket money. However, once they have been granted asylum, their status changes and they can receive social welfare benefits. They then are allowed to work if the job cannot be filled by a German or an EU worker. It is normal for legal battles to be fought in the administrative courts on the question of whether asylum should be granted. When the process of asylum seeking

[5] In June 2002 the percentage was 7.2 percent.

exceeds three years, applicants are entitled to receive social welfare benefits. Since these trials take time, such welfare benefits may be obtained
more or less automatically. Asylum seekers admitted into another EU
country cannot automatically receive asylum support just by moving to
Germany. Whereas the entitlements of asylum seekers have been reduced,
however, the rigidity of the lower segment of the labor market has not
been addressed.

Actual Rules for Immigrants from non-EU Countries

Immigrants from non-EU countries who want to come to Germany need a
permit to stay and another permit to work. There are several different forms
of permits to stay in Germany. *Applicants seeking asylum* are given a very
restricted permit of stay. There are special permits for *students*: during their
studies they are also allowed to work, with certain restrictions. In addition,
there is an *unlimited permit to stay*. This is given only upon the fulfillment of
very strict conditions: the applicant has to have lived in Germany for at least
eight years and must have a regular job, sufficient to finance his living. Those
who have a permit for an unlimited stay do not need a work permit. *Work
permits* generally are given only when it can be shown that the job cannot be
filled by a German or EU citizen.

The family of a foreign worker is allowed to follow him to Germany.
The breadwinner has to prove that he is able to house and support his
family in Germany. There are exceptions for humanitarian cases. Moreover, for non-EU citizens a few opportunities to work in Germany have
been created in the context of treaties limiting the total number of guest
workers per year from specific countries. This applies especially to seasonal workers in the agricultural sector.

The *green card law* was an attempt to open up immigration to qualified
people and to give the political discussion on immigration a different
focus. The idea is to attract qualified people into the country. The law
also allows foreign students of information and communication technology to take jobs in Germany after they have passed their exams and
received the German diploma. IT experts from non-EU countries can
utilize a simple mechanism to obtain a work permit for Germany. Basi-
cally, the only condition is that the employer has to guarantee a salary of
more than €39 600 to the IT expert; if he has no university degree, the
employer has to guarantee a minimum salary of €51 000. The green card
system was intended to attract 20 000 employees—and up to 10 000
more, should there be an even higher demand—but results have so far
been disappointing. Up to June 31 2003 only 15 000 people had applied
for a green card. One reason for its poor reception is the recent burst of

the IT bubble, which has diminished the demand for IT engineers. Another is that the green card limited employees to a stay of five years in Germany, and there were other restrictions—for example, the wife of the employee was allowed to start work in Germany only two years after moving here. These served to diminish the competitiveness of the program compared with other countries seeking such talents. The initial idea was to limit the green card mechanism until June 2003, when it was to have been replaced by a new migration law. As this law has not been finalized, the green card mechanism was prolonged until the end of 2004.

FREE MOVEMENT IN THE EUROPEAN UNION

Citizens of EU member states are free to choose the country in which they want to work. The free movement of people is one of the four basic freedoms of the European Union (along with the free movement of goods, services, and capital). It includes the right to take residence, the free movement of workers, and the right to establish a business everywhere in the European Union, i.e., the *right of establishment*. In addition, the free movement of services implies the free movement of workers if the services are embedded in persons. Discrimination based on nationality is to be abolished. The free movement of people also applies to citizens of the European Economic Area (Switzerland, Norway, and Iceland), who are free to work in Germany. It does not apply to nationals of third countries who have the legal right to reside in one member state.

A citizen of the European Union has the same entitlement, with respect to the German social security systems, as a German, and the same preconditions apply. For instance, to receive unemployment benefits contributions have to have been paid for at least twelve months of employment within the previous two years. For health insurance, coverage starts with the first day of insurance, which means the first day of work. This also applies to accident insurance for accidents at the workplace. Foreign students have to pay into the public health insurance scheme. Pensions require a minimum of 15 years' contributions. EU citizens seeking a job have the right to stay in Germany for three months, provided they have health insurance. This three-month rule is under scrutiny by the European authorities.

With respect to social welfare, the basic rule is that EU citizens can receive social welfare when they come to Germany. This also holds for citizens of states with some type of privileged access, such as the United States and Japan. EU citizens and citizens of countries with privileged access can receive social welfare only if they have to rely on it for reasons outside their control, for instance if they are laid off when they were previously employed, and if they were already living in Germany.

A more complex issue is the free movement of asylum seekers within the European Union, for instance of boat people who come to Italy and then want to move on to Germany. Asylum seekers have to apply for asylum in the country through which they enter the European Union while minimum standards with respect to the procedure of the asylum application are sought. During the asylum application procedure, the asylum seeker is restricted in his spatial mobility, usually being limited to a district in the country of application. Those who have been granted asylum in a specific country then in principle have the right of free movement; however, like for nationals of third countries who can legally reside in one member state, the rights and conditions under which they can then move to another member state have yet to be defined. Like EU citizens, they cannot automatically receive social welfare just because they have come to Germany. Since the right of movement differs for asylum seekers and for those to whom asylum has been granted, one member state of the EU can be affected by the asylum policy of another member. Therefore, there is an attempt to either harmonize such procedures, or not to cede those instruments by which the flow of asylum seekers (and also those who have been granted asylum) can still be influenced nationally. While the EU member states respect international rules on asylum, asylum policy is subject to unanimity according to Article 67 of the EU Treaty. According to the Treaty of Amsterdam, the procedure of co-decision with qualified majority will apply to this issue as of 2004, if agreed upon unanimously by the heads of state. If the Convention is passed, member states will retain the right to set national entry levels for third-country nationals.

Since foreigners from EU-15 countries make up 25 percent of the all immigrants and only 2.5 percent of the population, this group can in no way be regarded as constituting a policy issue. Language barriers and cultural differences do represent a strong home bias in the European Union, limiting the spatial mobility of workers. However, some people fear that the 2004 enlargement of the European Union will lead to mass migration from the new member countries to the West. I consider this unlikely. The systematic reason is that the migration of people depends, among other factors, not only on actual, but also on expected income differences, and on expected opportunities for employment (and therefore also on unemployment). It is true that actual income differences between the accession countries and the EU are still high. Using purchasing power parity as a measure, Poland has 40 percent of the EU per capita level of GDP (Eurostat estimate for 2003); for Hungary the relative level is 59 percent, for the Czech Republic 61 percent, and for Slovenia 75 percent. In contrast, for Bulgaria the figure is only 27 percent, and for Romania 26 percent, of the EU level. When GDP per capita is compared in current prices and nominal exchange rates, the Czech Republic enjoys only 30 percent of the EU average, Hungary 29 percent, and Poland 22 percent (Eurostat data for 2002). However, some regions in some of the accession countries are already attaining income levels that are not too far off the EU average or are even higher. Thus, in Prague the GDP per capita is 115 percent of the EU level, in Bratislava it is 99 percent, and in Közep Magyarorszag in Hungary, 72 percent (in current prices). For people in these areas, on average, emigration is unlikely to pay.

Moreover, it is not current income differences and actual differences in unemployment rates that drive migration, but expected income and employment gaps. In migration decisions, the future stream of income is compared with the costs; the present value of the additional income in future periods net of migration costs must be positive. Therefore expectations on future income play an important role. If people expect that the income gap will level out over time, they will tend to stay at home. In a model with uncertainty, for instance with a Brownian motion on future income, the option value of waiting is a relevant variable. If the option value of waiting is positive, and if it is sufficiently strong, people will stay at home. Of course, we know from many empirical studies that convergence takes a long time; nevertheless, the expectation of convergence implies a positive option value.

Moreover, looking at the German experience with immigrants from the Mediterranean countries, immigration surprisingly occurred in the late 1960s and early 1970s, way before the enlargement of the Community took place in the 1980s. Immigration from Greece, Spain, and Portugal reached its maximum in 1970 at two persons per thousand of the German population. As a matter of fact, there was negative emigration from these countries in the period after southern enlargement. Of course, it can be argued that southern enlargement is not a relevant analog, because historically people have not migrated from the south to the north (except for the tribes of the Angles and the Saxons from northern Germany to British Isles), whereas migration from East to West has been more the norm. But if there was a strong urge to migrate from the East to the West, it is surprising that net immigration to Germany from the seven major central and eastern European countries (Bulgaria, the Czech Republic, Hungary, Poland, Romania, Slovakia, and Slovenia) has been less than 20 000 per year since 1995; this is about one person per four thousand of the German population. In 1993, a year after the recession, net immigration from these countries was negative, and in 1994 it remained slightly negative. Admittedly, a free movement of people did not exist during that period, but determined people are likely to devise cunning ways of overcoming legal hurdles. In all these arguments, the official numbers have to be regarded with some caution. It is estimated that the number of illegal and seasonal workers from central and eastern European countries in

Germany is several times the official figures. Empirical evidence shows that, especially on building sites, in agriculture, and in catering, there are a lot of illicit workers.

From these analytical considerations and past empirical experience, the tentative conclusion is that we will not see a major wave of immigration from the new EU members except in the event of a political shock, for instance if a major political risk arose from Russia. Moreover, there is an interim period of up to seven years in which the free movement of people for the new EU members will not apply. Finally, the very low-income countries like Romania and Bulgaria, from which migration is most likely, will be admitted to the EU only at a later stage, probably in 2007.

Since 2000 there has been a new nationality law in Germany. Foreigners with eight years' legal residence will be granted the right to citizenship, on the condition that they can support themselves financially and have no criminal record. Furthermore, conditions for foreign spouses of Germans have been eased. Children who are born in Germany of foreign parents will receive German nationality automatically if at least one parent was born in Germany, has had legal residence in Germany for at least eight years, or has an unlimited residence permit. This introduces the *ius soli* into the German nationality law, which so far was based on the *ius sanguis*.

Future Immigration Policy

For four years, Germany has struggled to develop its first immigration law. As of mid-June 2004, a compromise on the new law has been reached by a committee of the government and the Christian Democrats. At the time of writing, it is almost certain that the new immigration law, passed by the Bundestag in March 2003, will now be accepted by the second chamber, the Bundesrat.The strength of emotions on this issue is shown by the fact that the voting procedure in the Bundesrat in March 2003 had to be examined by the Supreme Court, which ruled the procedure as unconstitutional. The country seems split on the issue of how much integration from non-EU countries it wants to have in the future. So far there has been no consensus on the benefits and costs of immigration—or, to put it differently, on what weights to assign to immigration and integration. Nor was it clear what role asylum policy should play in relation to immigration policy. Thus, Germany, itself an immigration country, has not yet managed to define its interest in such matters. This means that the type of immigration, the methods of implementing immigration policy, and the total numbers to be admitted remained open to question.

Several interdependent aspects are relevant here. One is the aspect of helping poorer people from other countries by letting them immigrate.

Some see immigration simply in these terms. They are prepared to take in not only political asylum seekers but also people who are persecuted in their home countries for other reasons (e.g., religious, sexual). The churches in particular tend to see immigration as a way of helping others and are inclined to be more generous towards immigrants from poor countries and asylum seekers, neglecting the fact that such immigrants can cause a serious drain in their home countries, or that Germany's capacity for absorption of such people is limited. Others stress the much needed contribution that immigrants make to German economic activity; for them, the interest of the immigration country plays a larger role. This would imply drawing up an explicit immigration policy aimed at talented and productive immigrants. Yet another aspect is integration. Some are prepared to accept a more multicultural society; they consider immigration an enrichment of Germany's life by different ethnic backgrounds, and for that reason are prepared to take in not only political but also other asylum seekers. Others stress the need for the foreigners to integrate into German life, to learn the German language and accept the basic values of their new country, for instance those of the Constitution.

I start from the premise that asylum policy and immigration policy have to be considered as intellectually separate issues, even if it proves difficult to disentangle the two aspects in practice. In both areas, the total number of immigrants and the methods used to determine who can enter have to be chosen.

With respect to *asylum*, the right of asylum, i.e., of accepting people who are prosecuted in their home countries, is one of the basic elements of the German Constitution, as a result of German history. Asylum policy has to specify the conditions under which asylum seekers and refugees from countries at war will be allowed to enter Germany. These conditions will then help to determine the number of refugees granted immigrant status. Even with the best of intentions, no country can accept every persecuted person in the world. Some rules and restrictions must be laid down; and a method must be found by which welfare migrants can be separated from asylum seekers. This is an issue that traditional immigration countries in the nineteenth century did not have to solve; it is also not a problem today in countries like the United States, where immigrants, e.g., the illegal immigrants from Mexico, have to support themselves through the labor market.

With respect to economic immigrants, it seems acceptable for a country to define its own interest. A minimal condition for granting residence should be that the immigrants will not create economic problems. They should have a high labor productivity, or be capable of developing it, and they should not carry a greater risk of being unemployed than the native population. A more far-reaching approach is to impose an immigration policy with the explicit goal of attracting the most highly qualified workers, in order to enhance the country's human capital, effort, and entrepreneurial spirit. Such a policy would be aimed at the upper segments of the international labor supply curve. If the highly qualified are attracted, labor productivity would be raised and economic growth stimulated. Such an immigration policy would not be hindered too much by the non-functioning lower segment of the German labor market because it would be aimed at the qualified (the low segment nevertheless remaining important as a safety valve when too-high expectations of the migrant do not materialize). By this approach the economic interest is given priority; humanitarian aspects are much less important, and would have to be covered by asylum policy.

Germany cannot set out its requirements from immigrants unilaterally. The interests of the immigration country and the those of the would-be migrants must be brought together. Therefore it is necessary that the policy be attractive to foreigners, especially highly qualified ones. It must be remembered that many countries will be competing for the talents of the world. Signs of xenophobia, regulations involving a long waiting time, difficulties for the entry of family members, or inhuman bureaucratic conditions, e.g., for scientists, will all be counter-productive. In addition, Germany has to make sure that its own talents do not leave. An important condition is to have a competitive and attractive university system, to ensure the prevention of a brain drain.

In such an approach, a credit point system for selecting migrants, as is used in the immigration policies of Australia and Canada, is an appropriate method. The credit points relate to such criteria as productivity, human capital, and knowledge of the language. This procedure considers at least some of the properties behind the demand curve for immigration. There is, however, the risk that in such a bureaucratic approach social criteria will be introduced under the German setting, and that the administrative courts will assume a large role. Therefore, economists favor the auctioning off of immigration rights, thus moving along the demand curve of the immigrants. Part of the expected immigration gain has to be left to the migrant, but part of it represents revenue for the immigration country. Minimal requirements in terms of productivity and training can be used in order to prevent money alone from buying the immigration ticket.

These considerations do not yet specify how many immigrants should be accepted per year, how immigration would fit with policies for an ageing society, the extent to which immigration should depend on the labor market situation and the business cycle, or what concept of integration should be applied to those already in Germany and to those to come. With respect to the total number, the green card arrangement set a limit of 20 000. But the green card was seen as only a temporary solution, which was to be replaced by a comprehensive reform within a couple of years. The Immigration Commission has discussed the number of 20 000 workers, which, together with their families, would amount to 50 000 persons per year. This would be 0.5 person per thousand of the population. It seems to me that this figure is too low, taking into account the prospect of an ageing society and the experience of immigration over the last five decades. Germany had a net immigration of 10 per thousand of the population in the peak year of 1970 during the second immigration wave, 5 in 1980 in the third wave, and 16 in 1989 and 1990 in the fourth wave. Since the mid-1990s it has stood at 2.5 per thousand. The average for the period 1965–2002 is 3.9 per thousand.

In contrast to these ideas, the new immigration law uses a purely administrative procedure. The Labor Office decides whether an immigrant can come. The immigration stop of 1973 remains in force except for specialists earning more than €84 000 per year and foreign students who got their degree in Germany.

Immigration policy has to be integrated into a European dimension. Since immigrants into the EU member states also have the freedom of movement, the size of Germany's foreign population will depend on the immigration policy of other EU countries. If the requirement of unanimity that has existed so far for the movement of people from third countries and for asylum seekers were exchanged for a qualified majority, an independent immigration policy would no longer be possible.

With the attacks of September 11, 2001, in New York and March 11, 2004, in Madrid, terrorism has added a new dimension to immigration policy. A foreigner can immigrate with the aim of executing a terrorist attack, taking advantage of the institutional arrangements of an open society. He may remain unnoticed as a potential terrorist (being a "sleeper") until the attack is carried out, as the attack in Madrid, especially, has shown. The new task for immigration policy is to sort out potential terrorists before they become active. This requires instruments that have not previously been necessary, including the option of not accepting a specific immigrant or sending him home. This means changing the legal procedures that apply to immigration, for instance the three-step appeal procedure in the German administrative courts. The new law allows centralization of the administrative decision of eviction at the federal level, with a legal examination of this decision only by the highest administrative court. Clearly, these instruments put a limit on liberal immigration policy.

APPENDIX

Table 7A-1 lists immigration statistics for 1965–2002.

TABLE 7A-1
Immigration, emigration and net immigration, 1965–2002 (000)[a]

	Emigra-tion	Immigra-tion	Net immigra-ation	Total popula-tion	Net immigration/ population (%)
1965	496	840	344	58619	0.59
1966	614	746	132	59148	0.22
1967	609	432	−177	59286	−0.30
1968	408	686	278	59500	0.47
1969	440	1012	572	60067	0.95
1970	498	1072	574	60651	0.95
1971	557	988	431	61280	0.70
1972	572	903	331	61697	0.54
1973	584	968	384	61987	0.62
1974	639	630	−9	62071	−0.01
1975	655	456	−199	61847	−0.32
1976	571	499	−72	61574	−0.12
1977	507	540	33	61419	0.05
1978	461	576	115	61350	0.19
1979	421	667	246	61382	0.40
1980	441	753	312	61538	0.51
1981	473	625	152	61663	0.25
1982	496	421	−75	61596	−0.12
1983	489	372	−117	61383	−0.19
1984	608	457	−151	61126	−0.25
1985	429	512	83	60975	0.14
1986	410	598	188	61010	0.31
1987	401	615	214	61077	0.35
1988	422	904	482	61450	0.78
1989	545	1522	977	62063	1.57
1990	632	1661	1029	63254	1.63
1991	596	1199	603	79984	0.75
1992	720	1502	782	80595	0.97
1993	815	1277	462	80930	0.57
1994	768	1083	315	81422	0.39
1995	698	1096	398	81661	0.49
1996	677	960	283	81896	0.35
1997	747	841	94	82053	0.11
1998	755	802	47	82030	0.06
1999	672	874	202	82087	0.25
2000	674	841	167	82260	0.20
2001	606	879	273	82441	0.33
2002	623	843	220	82537	0.27

[a] Until 1990, West Germany only; from 1991, unified Germany.

CHAPTER EIGHT

Regulation of Product Markets

The regulation of markets is an important aspect of German economic policy. We have already seen how it affects the labor market, including the considerable impact that the social security system and social welfare have on unemployment. The institutional setup of other important factor markets, the market for financial and physical capital, and the market for human capital, are still to be discussed. Environmental policy, the topic of the next chapter, is another relevant aspect of regulation, one that is somewhat idiosyncratic to Germany. In this chapter we consider the regulation of the product market. This relates to product market restraints that firms have to take into account and to the impact of these regulations on the economy. It also relates to the interdependence of product and factor market regulation. Establishing restraints for producers is one form of government intervention in product markets; the other—quite opposite—government activity is opening up markets and keeping them open. The latter aspect deals with the privatization of public monopolies and the establishment of new property rights for the network industries and competition policy. Here, as in state aid, the European Union plays a major part in defining the framework of the product markets.[1]

ATTITUDES TOWARDS REGULATION

Germany has a history of regulation. Traditionally, the government has played a strong role in setting the institutional rules and implementing them. Administrative law, police law, and business law with respect to licensing of products, machines, and buildings have developed their own systematic philosophy, from which it has followed more or less naturally to extend such a frame of reference into additional regulations. Things have to be orderly. In spite of the devastating experience of central planning and of utmost regulation in eastern Germany, with a loss of

[1] I appreciate critical comments on this chapter from Juergen B. Donges, Henning Klodt, Matthias Knoll, and Klaus-Werner Schatz.

economic and personal freedom, quite a few Germans, probably a good majority of them, have a paternalistic view of the state as overseer and solver of problems. This is in stark contrast to the basic assumption that the cornerstone of the institutional setup of a democratic society is individual liberty, which should be restrained only if the freedom of one individual hurts the freedom of another. When these attitudes prevail, and when the state is seen as being paternalistic, looking after its citizens like a *pater familias*, regulations are likely to prevail.

An often cited example of the attitude of Germans towards governmental regulation are the closing hours of shops. Whereas you can buy a bottle of mineral water in the rue Mouffetard in Paris at night if you are thirsty, or buy an orange in the small shops still open there, one will find stores closed in Germany late in the evening. Instead of leaving it to the individual shop-owner to decide for himself whether he can attract business after 8 pm on weekdays, this is *verboten* (forbidden) in Germany. The 1956 law regulated that shops were allowed to open only between 7.30 am and 6.30 pm on Monday through Friday and until 2 pm on Saturday. This persisted for a long time, but in 1989 an "innovation", in the eyes of Germans a tremendous one, was introduced when stores were allowed to be open on Thursday evenings until 8.30 pm. Too overwhelming was the evidence from other European countries that the world would not collapse if shops opened a little longer. In 1996 closing time was extended to 8 pm on all weekdays except Saturdays when it had to be 4 pm. A more recent success of German deregulation of 2003 was that shops could be open until 8 pm on Saturdays as well. Quite a number of opponents of the longer opening times were surprised that consumers actually enjoyed shopping in the inner cities on Saturday afternoons and evenings, thus making the cities more lively. For a long time the coalition of small shop-owners, fearing competition from larger chains and from potential newcomers as well as the trade unions' representing the sales personnel, resisted any changes to the closing hours. Amazingly, Germans had to drive to gas stations, railway stations, or airports to buy some essential foodstuffs, at distinctively higher prices, after 8 pm or on Sundays, when not even bakeries were allowed to open in the morning for a long time.

The Germans did not revolt as the government limited their options for shopping; it seemed as if they had no concept of their own independent choice but were willing to accept what the government had degreed. The majority of Germans do not even, or cannot, distinguish between a constraint and a norm; they tend to think that if 8 pm is established in law as a limit, all stores actually have to be open until that time. With this state of mind, there is still a long way to go before the average German citizen demands that his government actually justify why the closing of stores cannot be left to the individual shop-owners to decide. And it is an equally long time to wait until the average German thinks in terms of individual freedom and choice as the original frame of reference, from which the regulation must be conceived as deviating.[2]

AREAS AND INTENSITY OF REGULATION

Regulations take many different forms. They relate to permits for new products, to product requirements (absence of toxic substances in products, health hazards), permits for production processes and technologies (safety, health, and environmental considerations), especially time-consuming permits for new production facilities, permits for buildings (safety considerations, zoning laws, environmental constraints), permits to open up a business (market entry), time constraints such as shop opening hours or working times (per day, per week, minimum days of leave), regulations of prices and rules for property. Regulations may not relate directly to specific products but nevertheless affect the production conditions for products. An example are permits for infrastructure projects, which are the precondition for transportation services, e.g., airports. Part of the regulatory system consists not in constraints but in personal entitlements vis-à-vis the state, such as the right to enter a university if one has successfully passed the high school diploma. These entitlements then necessitate new regulations, such as allocating scarce student places through a national agency.

Licenses or permits have the specific characteristics in Germany that, once granted, they usually cannot be revoked. This sort of a legal guarantee provides some certainty for investors, but it means that granting the permit is a cumbersome and time-consuming administration process. This is one reason why permits tend to take a long time in Germany.

Traditionally, the regulation of economic activities has occurred in many sectors of the German economy, for instance agriculture, coal mining, the public and semi-public banks, the banking industry and insurance, housing, the university system, and—via product norms and licensing permits—industry. Through permits granted for opening up a business, regulations extend to many service activities, including the crafts and the so-called "free" professions such as lawyers and architects

---

[2] Another important example, not from the product market, is the regulation of retirement, whereby the rule is that retirement has to be taken at the age of 65. A decision of the US Supreme Court that compulsory retirement at a predetermined age represents a discrimination for the elderly, and thus is unconstitutional, is inconceivable in Germany. Germans lack the imagination to realize that chaos does not have to break out without a compulsory retirement age and that things can sort out themselves by decentralized individual decisions.

(see below). Strict regulations used to hold for transportation and communications, the postal service, public electricity, gas and water utilities (see below).

Regulations affect some markets more than others. For instance, the licensing of new products has a strong impact on biotechnology and the pharmaceutical industry. As a matter of fact, it is seen as a major reason why German pharmaceutical firms tend to have their research labs abroad instead of in Germany. The closure plan for nuclear power stations will finish this line of new technology in which Germany had a leading position. Together with the institutional arrangements for the university sector, another important factor market regulation, all this makes for a less innovative environment. Thus, product market regulations tend to affect new sectors negatively. In contrast, older and declining sectors are protected not so much by specific product market regulations, as by trade policies and subsidies. In the agricultural sector, production is heavily subsidized at the European and national levels; in addition, it is protected against international competition. The coal sector receives subsidies as well (see chapter 12). This leads to a bias in favor of old and declining sectors.

The housing sector in Germany is strongly regulated, with a price cap on rents and with rules that protect the tenant against a notice of the landlord; at the same time, the government provides funds to build apartments for low-income groups—which are, incidentally, occupied in part by higher-income earners, owing to a lack of sufficient control and misplaced incentives. Moreover, the government gives grants to families to build their own homes; there is a housing allowance for low-income groups; and the municipalities pay the rents for social welfare recipients, which is a good and very safe business for landlords. Whereas investment in apartment houses was a traditional vehicle to save for old age for people from the Mittelstand such as doctors and lawyers, it no longer is. Investment of that type has also been discontinued by the life insurance companies.

Another heavily regulated industry in Germany is television. Frequencies are licensed by the government. Furthermore, there are public TV stations, which control roughly 40 percent of the market; as for the remaining 60 percent, the RTL group has 25 percent, and the Sat1-Pro7 group, which used to belong to Leo Kirch but was bought in 2003 by the American media tycoon Haim Saban, controls 22 percent; the rest is under the control of other TV channels that are of rather marginal size and cover special interests, such as sports or music. The content and the source of the programs are regulated, and there are industry-specific ceilings regarding the market share beyond which special competition provisions apply. One reason for the heavy regulations in TV is the important role of the media with regard to opinion building and therefore the political process. The freedom of the press and the freedom of reporting by broadcasting and film are protected by the German Constitution (Article 5).

A special regulation is that of craftsmen, a sector with a total employment of 5.4 million persons, including the self-employed, and a gross value added of more than 10 percent of the total value added. Here the license to do business, i.e., market entry, is limited to those who have passed their "master" exam or who have an equivalent qualification in form of a formal degree. Such craftsmen are also entitled to have apprentices. This entry constraint, from the regulation of (94 different) crafts which was in force from 1953 until 2003, was motivated by the desire to ensure quality of service for the consumer. Even taking into account that the craftsmen train a large number of young people during their apprenticeship years (who later on go to work in industry), such a regulation erected unnecessary barriers to market entry. Besides, it is not consistent with the single EU market because it hinders the free movement of people. Together with the ruling on closing hours for shops, this regulation can be seen as one reason for the underdeveloped state of the service sector in Germany.

A new law of the Schröder government on craftsmen got a positive vote in the Bundestag, but was not passed by the Bundesrat in December 2003 in its original form. The Red-Green government had intended to liberalize the sector and keep a somewhat loosened entry restraint in only 29 crafts involving potential health/safety risks, e.g., electricians. The Christian Democrats and even the Liberal Democrats opposed this liberalization and defended the regulation of the craft sector. The compromise upholds for 41 crafts the entry constraint of having to have passed the exam of master. However, journeymen with six years of professional experience, four of which in a managing position, can open up a business on their own. Only in six crafts—those in direct relation to human health such as opticians, hearing aid specialists, and dental technicians—is the old permit system to be retained.

Another specific aspect of the German labor market concerns the regulation of the professionals (*freie Berufe*), i.e., physicians, veterinarians, lawyers, architects, engineers, auditors, and others.[3] They are subject to regulations setting out in detail the maximum fees they can charge for a certain service. Furthermore, some groups are not allowed to advertise, apart from announcing that their office is closed for holidays or that a new partner will be joining the practice. These regulations emerged a long time ago, when they were created in order to reduce price increases and

---

[3] The total number of people working in this group amounted 761 000 in 2002, every fifth self-employed belongs to this group.

protect the consumer. It is highly questionable whether such motivations are still valid today. Actually there is a discussion going on in the EU Commission about whether these regulations—similar regulations exist in most other countries of the EU—are in line with the articles on competition in the EU treaty, especially with Article 81, concerning the freedom of competition. The Schroeder government intends to suspend these regulations. Like the regulations of the crafts, this move has met the opposition of the Christian Democrats and the Liberal Democrats.

In addition to these professional activities, the regulation of the education and university sector, although strictly not a product market regulation, has to be mentioned as a severe form of government intervention (see chapter 11).

Regarding the total dimension of regulation, an earlier estimate came to the conclusion that, measured in terms of value added, roughly 50 percent of the German economy is heavily regulated (Donges and Schatz 1986: 26). An actual indication of the government's influence on the product market is the index of government regulated prices that is calculated by the German Council of Economic Advisers (2003: table D1). This index includes not only prices that are actually fixed by the government, such as fees, but also prices affected by regulation with respect to product quality and product safety. It does not include the prices of intermediate goods for production or of investment goods, but only the prices of consumption goods. Products whose prices are affected by the value added tax, which means nearly all consumer goods, are not included in the index since it would then approach 100 percent and become meaningless. Social security payments are also left out. It is surprising that, according to this index, the prices of 30 percent of consumer goods are affected by government regulation.

In an international comparison, the intensity of product market regulation in Germany is higher than in the Anglo-Saxon countries whereas it may be possibly lower than in France and Italy (Nicoletti, Scarpetta, and Boyland 1999). For instance, Germany has been rather slow in deregulating the network industries and privatizing the telephone service, the postal service, and the railroads; without a push from the EU, it would have been even slower. There is long tradition of regulation in specific areas like craftsmen. Moreover, Germans have been, and are, very environmentally conscious (see chapter 9). And it is fair to say that they have been more risk-averse with respect to new technologies such as biotechnology or nuclear energy than other countries. Regulation for building permits, for instance for large projects, is another case in point. It is definitely more difficult to built new railroad tracks in Germany than in France. It took thirty years to build the Munich airport from its initial conception. A reason for this may be the density of population in

Germany, which means that productive activities and the living space for people are close to each other.

BENEFITS AND COSTS OF REGULATION

All these regulation define how things are to be done in a society. They specify the way of doing business, of producing, innovating, acquiring labor, locating premises—i.e., of all economic decisions. Of course, there are reasons for government activity in product markets. There are benefits of regulations, and there are costs. The benefits depend on the policy goals. Thus, one would not question that the government has to intervene in the case of Mad Cow Disease in order to protect the health of its citizens, or that it has to regulate to prevent toxic material from turning up in foodstuffs. However, some of the regulations had arisen historically and are no longer justified, because the original reason for the regulation has disappeared; others have been the result of political manipulation by interest groups and were not justified to start with. In the other cases, one has to weigh the benefits and the costs. The costs entail the fact that the regulations take time and put restraints on the market participants. They restrict the production space of an economy. They also limit the options available to consumers. Here the assumption for lawmaking is that the politicians know better than the consumers what is good for them. Politicians deeply mistrust consumer sovereignty. Furthermore, regulations affect incentives. Moreover, owing to the interdependency of the economic system, one regulation may require another one because market participants will seek to find ways around the first one. Finally, regulations have to be administrated; they are subject to a legal process in the administrative courts, and they involve legal quarrels on who has the right to go to court over the administrative decisions and which procedures have to be established.

A promising approach to the weighing of benefits and costs is the test of market failure: if markets fail, then there is a reason for government regulation. In this context "market failure" refers to allocation, but in practice many regulations are motivated by equity considerations. The test of market failure, however, applies only under the additional condition that government intervention does not cause higher damages than the ones it intends to correct. This approach has been followed by the Deregulation Commission (Deregulierungskommission 1991).

It is apparent that the tendency of product market regulation is in conflict with an open economy that needs flexibility in order to be competitive, and needs to be able to adjust to developments in the world. But a large part of product market regulations relate to non-tradable goods, for instance retail trade, where competitiveness is not directly affected. Indirect links are often not noticeable to the public.

Since regulations often define entry and exit conditions, either explicitly or implicitly, it becomes profitable for sclerotic firms to devote resources to lobbying in favor of regulation and insider protection. The entrepreneur then gives up his classical function as a Schumpeterian innovator who introduces new combinations of productive factors. Instead, he operates in the political market to secure a protective level of regulation for his firm. As a side product, the resulting confusion of private and public interest erodes people's belief in justice and fairness. The higher the level of regulation, the more rent-seeking is induced so that a vicious circle begins. One way to reduce rent-seeking is to lower the level of regulation in the economy.

Thus, regulations tend to bring about a lower rate of investment,[4] less innovation, a less dynamic economy, and weaker growth. Germany as a location becomes less attractive for an international investor, and it loses out in the eyes of a German investor relative to other countries. Often, the effects are not readily visible.[5] A regulation-growth linkage shows up in empirical studies for the OECD countries; economy-wide indicators of lower regulation coupled with higher privatization and industry-level indicators of entry liberalization are found to exhibit a positive impact on multifactor productivity. (Nicoletti and Scarpetta 2003).

INTERDEPENDENCE OF PRODUCT AND FACTOR MARKET REGULATION

The regulation of product markets and that of other markets are interdependent. An important aspect of this interdependence is the two-sided relationship between the regulation of the product markets and that of the labor market. It is not only that labor market regulations—for instance general time constraints affecting the working time of researchers in research labs in the same way as that of normal employees—have a negative effect on the competitiveness of firms and of a country in product markets. There is also a link in the other direction. The regulation of product markets determines the intensity of competition and market

---

[4] There are now cases in which permits have been received quickly, especially in eastern Germany.

[5] For instance, the previously strict German regulation on trucking increased the comparative advantage of Dutch truckers and has shifted locational advantage away from the north German ports. Moreover, regulation of trucking, e.g., forbidding market entry to the trucking division of producing firms or sabotage rules for foreign truckers, generated excess traffic, which is not consistent with transport efficiency, energy conservation, or environmental protection. Some of that regulation has now been changed.

entry, and thus determines the size of rents that firms have. Labor market regulations, however, determine the power of trade unions and insiders; these insiders then influence how the rents are distributed to the different groups. When entry to the product market is limited, generating monopolistic profits or rents, this is an inducement for interest groups to organize themselves in order to capture the rents. Once organized, they will defend the product market regulations because these regulations are at the root of their power.

Thus, trade unions traditionally boasted a high degree of organization in public monopolies and government-owned firms where rents were large and could be dissipated to the union members. This applied, for instance, to the government-owned postal service in its old form, including telecommunications, and to the railroads. The same phenomenon could be observed with respect to shipyards, which were under a strong government influence, both because of public ownership in the past and because of subsidies. It also held for the energy companies, which were natural monopolies because they owned the transmission lines. It is still true of quite a few municipal utilities and a large part of the savings banks. Trade unions were, and still are, interested in early closing hours for stores in order to defend the interest of their members. If closing hours are lifted and if many self-employed, especially immigrants open up small shops like in France and Italy, the rents of the existing stores might by reduced, and trade unions would lose members and power. Therefore trade unions fought and continue to fight strongly against liberalization in these areas. Because of the link between product market and labor market regulation, the deregulation of specific product markets can be seen as instrumental in contributing to bring about at least a partial reform of the labor market.

Privatization of Public Monopolies and New Property Rights

Traditionally, public monopolies, mostly owned by the government, have existed in many sectors in Germany. This relates to the postal service, including telecommunications, to the railroads, to harbors and airports, to the national airline, in part to electricity in terms of generation, transmission, and distribution, and to public enterprises of municipalities such as local transportation, water supply, electricity distribution, and garbage collection. As monopolies, these activities were not exposed to competition; also, they were largely exempted from the control of competition policy for a long time. The reason for this was a public interest in these domains, an important aspect being the *Daseinsvorsorge*, the services of general interest, i.e., the notion that it is up to the government to provide these presumably public or semi-public goods and services.

In a way, public ownership and the special status of public utilities can be interpreted as a form of product market regulation. The government as owner supposedly looks after the common interest. Of course, the intensity of competition was low in these sectors, so rents were high. Trade union membership was strong in these government-dominated areas, the high rents resulting from product market regulation being an incentive for a strong organization. Together with the regulation of the German labor market protecting the insiders and excluding the outsiders, unions could use their power to distribute the high rents to their members. Moreover, public utilities provided attractive positions for politicians, who could either earn an additional income or find employment after they had lost out in the political arena. Thus, there was a strong coalition supporting the public monopolies. The flip side of the coin was that until the late 1980s, for instance, the installation of a new telephone was an official activity of the government, for which the citizen as a potential customer had to formally apply, filling out an application form. He was seen not as a customer to be wooed, but more nearly as a beggar to whom graciously a favor was granted. In addition, there were efficiency losses in terms of higher prices and a much lower rate of innovation. Thus, Siemens was sort of the official provider of the German postal service and of its telecommunications branch with telephone equipment; apparently, there was only a weak incentive for innovation under these conditions.

Several developments led to a different view on these issues and eventually to a change of policy. Privatization took place in other countries, so that there were examples of how things could be organized differently, with better service and lower costs for the consumer. Innovation, for instance in the telecommunication sector, was taking place abroad, but not in Germany; this was hurting Germany's export position. Moreover, there were technological developments that allowed competition like satellite connections or the mobile phone. Finally, economic thinking changed; a natural or a public monopoly rooted in a network (of telephone lines, electricity lines, gas pipelines or railroad tracks) disappeared intellectually when new property rights for the transmission or network use could be clearly defined, so that the use of the network could be priced. Thus, pressure built up to change the regulation. The government installed a Deregulation Commission (Deregulierungskommission 1991) in 1987. Nevertheless, change was difficult, because many jobs existed in these sectors; at the same time, trade unions were strongly represented in these public monopolies where the rents were high. Besides this, some public monopolies such as the municipal energy distributors partly guaranteed high and constant revenues for the government, which would diminish in an open market with competition.

But reforms did come about. They relate to three different aspects: to the formal privatization of public or semi-public utilities, so that these activities became private incorporations and were eliminated from the governmental budgets; to an effective privatization, in the sense that private ownership was established with an initial public offering; and to new regulatory rules for previous public monopolies, for instance for the network industries. It must be admitted that, from the German perspective, the European Union was the most important driving force in these liberalizations, overcoming strong opposition from the interest groups in Germany with the concept of a single market and pushing the process ahead with its directives. Among these were the EU directives on public broadcasting (1989), telecommunication (1988, 1990 and 1995), the railroads (1991 and 1995), the postal service (1997), electricity (1997), and gas (1998). These measures had their impact; institutional changes in the member states took place not only after the regulations became effective, but before (table 8.1).

The German airline Lufthansa had been run as an independent company for a long time although originally it had been publicly owned. The government reduced its involvement by not participating in the capital increases that took place in 1987—afterwards its share in the total stock was still 65 percent—and also in 1988 and 1994. In 1997 the government sold its last shares in Lufthansa, after having transferred them to the Kreditanstalt für Wiederaufbau, the government's bank, a year earlier.

The airports have already been separate legal entities for a long time and are run like private companies. They were in the joint ownership of the federal government, the state in which the airport is located, the neighboring state, and the city of the airport. The public owners are now selling their shares. For instance, the airport in Frankfurt and the connected services (Fraport) were privatized and the shares partly brought to the stock market.

The biggest privatization process[6] in Germany started in 1989 with the separation of the former federal postal service, with its then 576 000 employees, into the three units of postal service, telecommunications, and postal bank. In 1994 both the Deutsche Telekom and the Deutsche Post, the remaining postal service per se, were transformed into a stock company, and Postbank was acquired by the postal service. The European Union had initiated the process in 1988 by appealing to the member states to abolish the monopolies and privatize their telecommu-

---

[6] There were incentives for small investors, with the goal to make the Telekom stock a new *Volksaktie* (stock for everybody). The big media coverage and public discussion helped to foster a new "stock-culture" in Germany, as for many people it was the first stock they ever bought.

TABLE 8.1
Major changes in public monopolies

Area	Legal incorporation as a private company	Sale of public equity of stock	Major regulatory change
Lufthansa Airline		1997: the government sold its last shares in Lufthansa	
Airports (e.g., Frankfurt Airport)	Since 1954	2001: initial public offering, 71% still in public ownership	
Railroads	1994	Initial public offering planned in this decade	1994: Separation of tracks and operation
Telecommunications	1995	1996: initial public offering, 42.8% still in public ownership	1998: Market opening for long-distance-calls, in 2003 also for local calls; regulatory authority established in 1998
Postal service	1995	2000: initial public offering, 62.6% still in public ownership	Market for parcels is liberalized; monopoly for letters of 100 g or less upheld; from 2006 on the monopoly limit will be reduced to 50 g or less; regulatory authority established in 1998
Power generation, transmission, and distribution		The state reduced its shares in the big power companies in several steps; currently only Bavaria holds a small stake in e.on. There are numerous small power distribution companies, mostly owned by the municipalities	1998: third-party access to transmission lines, voluntary agreement of sector associations on the property rights

Gas	Some of the municipal utilities are transformed into private companies	Most of the non-local gas companies are owned by the big electricity companies, many distributors belong to the local municipalities	2000: third-party access, voluntary agreement of sector associations on the property rights, but effectively no market opening up to now; a new EU directive urges free choice of supplier for businesses until 2004 and for households until 2007
Water distribution, waste water	Some of the municipal utilities are transformed into private companies	Most of the water distributors and waste water companies belong to the local municipalities, some of them partly belong to private companies. Quite a few municipalities have auctioned off garbage collection, some also local parts of transportation.	Not decided yet
Local garbage collection and transportation			
Additional sectors			
Airline traffic			Barring of bilateral traffic agreements, free access for airlines
Insurance			Institutional competition through the home rule, dismantling of mandatory public insurance for buildings

TABLE 8.2
Public ownership, June 2004 (% of equity)

	%
Deutsche Telekom	
Federal Republic	26.1
Kreditanstalt für Wiederaufbau	16.7
Deutsche Post	
Federal Republic	20.0
Kreditanstalt für Wiederaufbau	42.6
e.on	
Bavaria	4.86
Volkswagen	
Niedersachsen	18.2
Fraport	
Hessen	32.1
Frankfurt	20.5
Federal Republic	18.4

nications companies. In a later directive the EU required member states to liberalize and completely open the market for telecommunications services for competition until 1998. The Telekom's initial public offering took place in 1996. It was the biggest initial public offering in Germany ever, accompanied by a massive advertisement campaign.

The postal service itself was privatized in 1995, its initial public offering taking place in 2000. The postal service is far from being liberalized. Its opening had been requested by an EU directive in 1990, but requested less vigorously than for telecommunications. Whereas the market for parcels is liberalized, the monopoly for letters weighing 100 grams or less is upheld. Since most letters fall into this category, the degree of market openness is 10–20 percent only. From 2006 on, the monopoly limit will be reduced to 50 grams, thus opening between 20 and 30 percent of the market.

A decisive share of stocks of both the Telekom and the postal service are still in the possession of the government (26.1 percent of the Telekom, 20.01 percent of the postal service), but these will be sold on the market in the future. (See table 8.2, which lists the most important government ownership in firms of the production sector, excluding municipalities and banks.) The government sold part of its shares to the Kreditanstalt für Wiederaufbau, a government-owned bank (16.7 percent of the Telekom, 42.6 percent of the postal service), in order to receive the revenue when it needed to reduce the budget deficit. This is rather a legal trick. Before the initial public offering the government promised to sell its stocks slowly and in small quantities, in order not the flood the market with its shares. Selling the stocks to the Kreditanstalt enabled the government to create revenue and at the same time keep its promise to the capital market. Furthermore, the government is hoping that it will participate in a higher share price when the shares are eventually sold in a better market.

The legal status of the railroads was changed into a stock company in 1994 as a holding for five different units into which the railroads were split up; one of these units is the track system. An EU directive of 1991 had required the separation of the railroad infrastructure and operation. Owing to high deficits, huge pension commitments, and needed investments, the railroads are not yet competitive. Its shares are not listed on the stock market, but an initial public offering is planned before 2010. An EU directive of 1995 has stipulated how the allocation of use of the infrastructure is to be done and how the fees for using it have to be calculated.

A major difficulty in the privatization of the postal service and the railroads is that a large part of the employees in these sectors were government officials so that their status had to remain untouched while they changed to working for a privatized company. In addition, since their pensions as government officials are financed from taxes (unlike from the employee's retirement system), the government has had to take over these pension loads; they enter the public budget.

In power generation, transmission, and distribution, an EU directive of 1997 requires the opening of the electricity market. The general idea is that buyers can get into direct contact with suppliers instead of having to rely on an energy distributor. This means defining new property rights for the transmission lines and changing the traditional vertical structure of the electricity market with its three parts of energy production, transmission, and distribution. The hierarchical organization is altered and substituted by markets, thus bringing competitive pressure to the electricity sector. In the gas sector an EU directive of 1998 has attempted to initiate liberalization, but deregulation has not yet taken roots in this sector.

Quite a few municipalities have started to auction off some of their services like buses or garbage collection for a period of, say, ten years; but others have kept these services under their ownership, albeit as legally separate entities, continuing to subsidize the bus service though the energy prices of the municipal energy distributors. Some of the municipalities have privatized and partially or totally sold their municipal utilities for electricity, gas, and water distribution. One such municipality is Berlin. As early as 1997 it sold its electricity company BEWAG to Vattenfall, a Swedish electricity company; in 1998 its gas supplier GASAG was sold to a consortium of different companies, and 50 percent of its water supplier was privatized in 1999.

A New Regulatory Regime

In addition to privatization, another major development was a change in the regulatory regime. In part, this became necessary because of new technological developments such as cellphones, including satellite and other forms of transmission, so that the presumed natural monopolies ceased to exist for technical reasons. In part, new property rights for networks were introduced following a new line of thinking in economics. The important intellectual innovation was the distinction between the ownership of the common carrier and the right to use it (for instance power lines, gas pipe lines, and railroad tracks).

Four important new problems had to be solved in the new regulatory framework: (i) defining entry conditions for new suppliers with new technologies, (ii) allocating the use of the capacity of an existing network to different and competing users, (iii) setting the fees for using the common carrier, and (iv) defining interfaces between different suppliers of the same product, for instance between different railroad operators and between stationary and cellphones, or between long-distance lines and the last mile to the final consumer. This required a new form of regulation with a new regulatory authority. Fee-setting can be used to solve the static allocation problem. But fees should be not only scarcity prices, determining users' willingness to pay and solving the allocation of a given capacity: they should also be a price signal to increase the network's capacity when demand rises; and they should represent a scarcity price for network capacity; an increase in the fee should represent an incentive to invest in the network capacity.[7] As we know from network breakdowns in the electricity sector, for instance in New York and the northeastern United States in 2003, California in 2001, the United Kingdom in 2003, and Italy in 2003, this is an important aspect of the regulatory framework. This also applies to the quality of the network, as the British railroad system tells us.

In the deregulation of natural monopolies, a major problem is the way in which markets could be made contestable in light of the fact that the incumbent in the industry, i.e., the previously publicly owned natural monopolist, continues to have a dominant market position. The three alternatives are (i) an ex post control of the abuse of market power by the German cartel office, (ii) voluntary agreements of sector associations, or (iii) the ex ante regulation by a new regulatory authority. The advantage of a new agency is that it can better control the breaking up of a public monopoly by using ex ante instruments such as price caps for interfaces with new suppliers, whereas the cartel office can control the

---

[7] This raises complicated issues how the fees should be set if the regulatory agency decides that the infrastructure of an incumbent can be used by the newcomers.

misuse of market power only ex post.[8] Indeed, the decision was taken in favor of a new regulatory agency. Such an agency has considerable power in influencing costs and revenues of companies; regulatory capture therefore will be an issue.

For telecommunications and the postal service, a new regulatory agency was founded in 1998 with the task of controlling the market power of the still dominating suppliers and defining the conditions of business.[9] This includes specifying the conditions for interfaces of different suppliers, especially regulating prices for certain services, for instance how much the Deutsche Telekom, who owns the last mile to the customers in the stationary system, is allowed to charge other service suppliers. The agency also defines a price cap for the monthly fees, or influences the relationship between the monthly fee and prices for individual calls, as well as between local and long-distance calls. Quite a few of the regulations relate to market entry conditions. For example, the agency auctioned off the licenses for the Universal Mobile Telecommunication Systems (UMTS) in 2000. These specific issues could not be dealt with by the Federal Cartel Office, which continues to be in charge of competition policy, especially of merger control.

As an alternative to a new regulatory agency, voluntary agreements of sector associations have been used for electricity and gas transmission. They represent a voluntary agreement of the industry, defining the use of transmission lines including the fees to be charged for it. In part, these agreements came about because there was the threat that the government would otherwise establish a regulatory agency. However, these agreements have failed; they did not provide a sufficiently free market access, maybe because of the influence of the large energy producers who own the transmission lines and are distributors as well. From 2004 on, the regulatory agency for telecommunications and the postal service will also regulate the electricity and gas sectors.

In the telecommunications sector, five new EU directives—on access and interconnection, on authorization of electronic communications networks, on a common regulatory framework, on universal service, and on users' rights and the protection of privacy[10]—enforce a change in German regulation. These directives define conditions for the telecommunications industry, for instance that a new supplier has an automatic right of entry without having to apply for a license, that an ex ante regulation should not apply when market power exists, that in the defini-

---

[8] It can be argued that once the newcomers are established relative to the incumbent, traditional ex post control of the abuse of market power becomes more relevant again as a policy approach.

[9] Regulierungsbehörde für Telkommunikation und Post.

[10] Directives 19, 20, 21, 22 and 58, all 2002.

tion of market power the EU norms of competition policy are to be applied (and not the national norms), and that the regulatory authority has the power to order access and the interconnection of networks (Klodt 2003: 198). In contrast, the intended German law favors control of the abuse of market power. This is likely to give a preference effectively to the incumbent German Telekom, and to keep the market relatively closed for the newcomers to the industry.

In the case of the railroads, a mixed system is used. The existing operators, including the new entrants, negotiate the conditions of access and the fees with the unit of the railroad holding that is in charge of the track system. An already existing governmental agency, the *Eisenbahn-Bundesamt*, has the ultimate decision if an agreement cannot be reached.

In airline traffic, more competition has been introduced. The bilateral air traffic arrangements between governments were inconsistent with a single market and were driven out by principally free access for airlines. As a consequence of EU regulation 2407/92, business licenses for air lines are granted under the same conditions in the European Union. Even the bilateral traffic agreements between individual EU member states and non-EU countries, most prominently the United States, have been barred by a decision of the European Court of Justice in 2002. There is still a limited access due to the grandfather slots at airports, but changes are likely to occur in the future.

Finally, the regulatory system for the insurance industry, which was long under government influence, both with respect to the institutional setup and public ownership, changed as a result of initiatives at the European level. Several major directives harmonized important aspects of the supervisory regime, among them the directive 73/239/EEC, which establishes the appropriate legal framework for exercising freedom of establishment in the Community in respect of direct non-life insurance, and a coordinating directive for the insurance sector in 1979. However, while these directives set the theoretical framework for a free market, it was the third coordinating directive for the insurance sector in 1992 that gave rise to the free market in practice, with the "home rule". Like the home rule in the second banking directive, this rule makes the home country, i.e., the country in which the insurer has its seat, responsible for supervision. This opens the door to institutional competition in the spirit of the 1979 Cassis de Dijon ruling of the European Court of Justice. In addition, some of the states in Germany had a mandatory insurance for buildings (mostly against fire); the third EU directive on direct on-life insurance ended the government monopoly. Some of these insurance schemes are still government owned, but they are now operating in a free market.

These institutional changes overwhelmingly came about through the European Union. The concept of the single market proved to be a power-

ful approach that has been used to open up markets that were characterized by public monopolies

The Impact of Deregulation

By means of the developments described above, competition has been
introduced into German markets. In telecommunications new firms
have entered the market; it is now possible even to choose the supplier
individually for every telephone call. Prices for telecommunications
services have dropped considerably. Suppliers other than the German
railroads are offering rail services, especially in a regional setting,
where the federal states auction off railroad connections, paying a subsidy
to ensure that a service is provided. In electricity, the prices for the industrial buyers have fallen in the EU by about 20 percent since 1992. Households now can choose their electricity supplier; even if not many
households have switched to a new supplier up to now, the old monopo-
lists like the municipal agencies have come under pressure and have had
to bring their prices down.

It is difficult to estimate empirically the total impact of these changes on
the German economy. But important infrastructure sectors have been
affected. Employment in the previously public companies has fallen, for
instance in Telekom from 197 000 in West Germany in 1989 to 175 000
in united Germany in 2003. In the postal service the number of employees
was reduced from 259 000 in 1989, again in West Germany, to 219 000
in 2003 in united Germany. But new companies have been born, generating new employment outside the previously publicly owned utilities.
Consumers and users in the business sector have benefited from lower
prices. Moreover, the environment can be expected to be more conducive
to technological innovation. It is difficult to find a measure of this change,
such as the share of these sectors in GDP. As an indication, we may add
up the annual turnovers of the German Telekom (€53 billion in 2002), the
postal service Post (€39 billion), and the German railroads (€19 billion)—
the three biggest privatizations. This gives a sum of €111 billion amounting to roughly 3 percent of the gross value of German production. Privatization definitely has affected the German economy.

Competition Policy

Whereas regulation can be viewed as an ex ante attempt to open up
markets, for instance of public utilities, and thus can be regarded as a
substitute for competition policy, it must be remembered that under the

more traditional relationship between these two policy areas the regulated sectors were exempt from competition policy. From that viewpoint, regulation imposes constraints on firms, limiting their behavior for instance in defining market entry conditions. Regulation, then, can be regarded as the antagonist of competition policy. This relationship becomes apparent when we examine the German law on competition policy (the antitrust law) that was introduced in 1958 by Erhard to enhance competition and free markets after it was passed by parliament in 1957 under heavy fire from industry and in long battles. This law in its original form exempted quite a few sectors, including agriculture, coal and steel, banking and insurance, airports and harbors, transportation, communications, the postal service, public electricity, and the gas and water utilities, from competition policy. These were the heavily regulated sectors. Since then the institutional arrangement has changed with European integration; for one the competence has shifted to the European level, which has most of the policy instruments for agriculture in its hands. Moreover when some of these exempted sectors were later exposed to competition in the European Union, their legal status as exempted sectors had to be changed in amendments of the competition law. Thus, in the fifth amendment in 1990 the postal service and the railroads lost their status as exempted sectors. In the sixth amendment in 1999 electricity, gas, and water as well as transport were no longer listed as exempted sectors, whereas the banking and insurance and the sports sector are still exempted.

Competition policy is one of the areas in which national policy has substantially lost importance. The European Commission has been entrusted by member states with the power to deal with competition matters at the EU level. While there still is a Federal Cartel Office in Germany, it now is in charge of cases that are of relevance to Germany alone. German merger control sets in if one of the merging firms has its residence in Germany, if the revenue is at least €25 million in Germany, and if the worldwide revenue is at least €500 million. But mergers with a revenue of at least €250 million in the European Union and €5 billion worldwide are dealt with by the European Commission. Thus, much of the competition policy that is relevant to Germany is now under the jurisdiction of the European Commission. The basis for competition policy follows from one of the Union's principles that member states must adopt an economic policy "conducted in accordance with the principle of an open market economy with free competition."

According to Articles 81 to 90 of the EU Treaty and other rules, among them the "Merger Regulation" of 1989, the Commission has a far-reaching competence in matters of competition policy. It can investigate suspected abuses of competition law and issue injunctions against, and impose fines on firms found guilty of anti-competitive conduct. The amount of these fines varies according to the gravity and duration of the anti-competitive activities; it may be as much as 10 percent of the firm's worldwide turnover. The Commission can prohibit mergers if the new company has a market-dominating position. It can forbid firms to fix prices or to divide up the single market or parts of it in a cartel, and it has set fines in quite a few cartel cases. It can also prevent the misuse of market power by a firm controlling a large part of the market. This relates to horizontal as well as vertical constraints on competition. Thus, the Commission forbade car manufactures to fix the sales prices for their sellers, to restrict their sales area, and to oblige them to sell only cars of a specific manufacturer. The enterprises affected may lodge an appeal against a Commission decision with the Court of First Instance or the European Court of Justice. The Court of Justice has annulled some decisions of the Commission.

The power of the EU Commission to forbid mergers applies even to mergers in the United States. The most prominent cases have been the mergers of Kimberley Clark and Scott Paper (1996), of Boeing and McDonnell Douglas in 1997, and the intended merger of General Electric and Honeywell; while the US Department of Justice allowed the latter merger, the EU Commission forbade it in 2001, because of the dominant market position of the merged companies. The EU Commission applies the criterion of market dominance; the United States looks at the reduction in competition, of which market dominance is one possible aspect. Under the new EU regulation on mergers that is in the making, this criterion applied may be changed to some extent to bring it more into line with the American approach.

The shift of responsibility for competition policy from the national authority to the European Commission not only means an institutional reorganization, it also implies a new and different orientation in substance. Competition policy now applies to the single market of the European Union, even to the world market—and no longer to the national market. This means that openness of the economy and of markets gets more weight per se. This evaluation, however, would not hold if competition policy became subject to the national political interests of the member states, or if it were sacrificed to European industrial policy. The consequence is that the sectoral exemptions from the German law of competition have had to be removed from that law because of pressure from the deregulations of the European Union already described.

The changed responsibility also relates to procedural aspects. One very important case relates to the fact that in the German system firms wanting to merge have to apply and get a license for merger from the Federal Cartel Office. While the same procedure had been adopted by the EU Commission, from May 2004 this procedure will be changed in the

European Union: in future mergers will be legally accepted if they satisfy certain conditions (EU Treaty, Article 81, Sec. 3); it will then be up to the EU Commission to prove the negative impact of the merger within a given period. This and other changes in the new regulation require alterations in the German law on competition policy in a seventh amendment.

To sum up, competition policy is one of the areas where the national policy instruments have lost nearly all their significance. In this area national sovereignty has been nearly completely delegated to the European level.

Subsidy Control

The openness of markets may be affected not only by product market regulations and actions of firms reducing the intensity of competition, but also by subsidies. If in a single market the member states use national subsidies to reduce the costs of their firms, and if these subsidies differ in the sectors favored or in size, this is a hindrance to the single market. It is therefore only natural that the Commission should have the power to control national subsidies and to require that illegally granted aid be repaid by recipients to the public authorities that granted it. The Commission has used this power in several cases and has gained respect in this domain. Thus, Volkswagen had to pay back €123 million of the €399 million it received in subsidies from the state of Saxony and the German government for its location in Mosel and Chemnitz in eastern Germany. Part of the subsidies were to compensate for present disadvantages arising from German unification. Nevertheless, there are still areas where, owing to compromises in the European Council, national subsidies prevail, e.g., in coal mining and the shipyards (see chapter 12). Moreover, the Commission looks predominantly at border-crossing distortions in the single market. National subsidies, or subsidies in the sector of non-tradables, are not in its focus. Nor is it interested in international distortions; subsidies that have the blessing of the EU, e.g., in agriculture, industrial policy, research policy, and regional policy, are not the subject of the Commission's subsidy control. Finally, the Commission concentrates on explicit state aid rather than on tax privileges; it has, however, included state guarantees as for the German savings banks.

CHAPTER NINE

Environmental Protection: a German Topic

In the last four and a half decades, since the 1960s, environmental quality has been a specific concern in Germany. In 1970 the first Ministry for the Environment, then still coupled with agriculture, was introduced in Bavaria. The immediate stimulus for taking up environmental policy was a visible deterioration of the environment, with air polluted and fish dying in the rivers. New property rights for using the environment as a receptacle of waste were defined, and environmental quality improved.[1]

However, the opportunity costs of improving the environment cannot be neglected, especially if Germany as an open economy follows the first-mover strategy in its environmental approach. Not only will this affect comparative advantage, but the leakage effect may partly undo the positive environmental effect in the case of a policy for global environmental media (e.g., the ozone layer). The opportunity costs also signify that environmental policy has to derive its legitimacy from protecting the environment, and not from attempting thereby to create jobs.

Integrating the Environment into the Market Economy

When pollution became a problem, the conceptual issue was that the environment did not formally constitute a part of economic thinking. It had to be recognized that the environment is a good that can be used for different purposes: both as a means of consumption, for instance the air we breathe, and as a receptacle of waste, for instance emissions from the smoke-stacks (Siebert 1973, 2004). While as a means of consumption the environment is a public good, from whose use no one can be excluded, in its role as a receptacle of emissions it has the property of a private good. These functions compete with one another, since emissions determine environmental quality, i.e., the ambient pollutants in the environment. The competing use implies scarcity. As long as there was free access to both functions of the environment—i.e., as long as the environment was treated as a commons—it was overused. Accordingly, environmental quality was low. Moreover, private costs and social costs diverged. Polluters did not have to pay for

---

[1] I appreciate critical comments on this chapter by Gernot Klepper and Matthias Knoll.

the environmental damages they caused. This implied an allocation distortion in the economy in favor of intensively pollution-producing activities. Their price was too low from the cost side, too many such goods were produced, and they used a too high resource input in their production.

With a growing awareness of environmental scarcity, it came to be accepted that a correction of this situation was necessary, requiring a definition of new property rights relating to the use of the environment as a receptacle of waste. First, however, the political process was going to have to decide on the *quality* of environment that society wanted. Environmental scarcity then had to be introduced into the decisions of the subunits of the economy. This was a shock to the system—not exogenous, as in the oil crisis, but endogenous; not abrupt, but gradual.

STOPPING ENVIRONMENTAL DEGRADATION AND IMPROVING THE
ENVIRONMENT

Major laws were introduced in the 1970s for improving air quality, water quality, waste management, and noise pollution, to mention the most important areas. These included the gas-lead law (Benzin-Blei-Gesetz 1971), the waste law (Abfallgesetz 1972), the air quality law (Bundes-Immissionsschutzgesetz 1974) and its regulations, as well as the water management law (Wasserhaushaltsgesetz), the water effluent fee law (Abwasserabgabengesetz), the nature protection law (Bundesnaturschutzgesetz) and the nuclear energy law (all 1976). Except for the law on effluent water fees, these laws predominantly used the regulatory (licensing) approach to reducing environmental degradation. This gave rise to a long-lasting and still ongoing debate on institutional arrangements for environmental incentives that would use market instruments such as taxes or prices for emission rights instead of administrative measures.

These initial laws were changed and intensified later. For instance, Germany has developed its own system of waste collection, whereby households and firms separate their waste for collection into different bins, which in some communities are now subject to the control of the local "waste police" who check to ensure that the correct type of waste has been put into the appropriate bin. Separating waste collection allows recycling. The majority of landfills are now closed and waste is burnt in incinerators after pre-treatment.

The issues dealt with by environmental policy have changed, so that several waves of environmental policy can be distinguished. Whereas in the 1970s the concern was to stop environmental degradation of air, water, and land and to improve their quality—all questions that could be tackled nationally in a first attempt—the focus of environmental policy then shifted to cross-border questions such as the acid rain. Thus, the

1980s were characterized by focus on a new phenomenon, the dying of forests, with a new German word finding entry into other languages, e.g., *le waldsterben* in French. This damage to forests was the result of long-range trans-boundary air pollution. Reductions in sulfur dioxide became the overwhelming target. In the 1990s the issues of global warming and biodiversity came to the foreground, and the reduction of carbon dioxide became the dominating issue.

The European Union plays an important role in defining new property rights for the use of the environment. It has introduced minimum standards for the permissible level of air pollution, water pollution, and waste management. In the 1990s, after the principle of sustainable development was enshrined in the Treaty of Amsterdam (1997) as one of the goals of environmental policy, the EU established a more comprehensive approach to the environment. Through its framework legislation, a number of directives were adopted by member states in the 1980s and the 1990s on water quality, e.g., on drinking water and bathing water quality. The EU also developed standards on ambient air quality assessment, for instance in the Council directive 96/62/EC.

Looking at the goals of environmental policy in more detail, it can be seen that they range from preserving the earth's climate, stopping the depletion of the ozone layer, lowering acidification of rain, and preserving nature and biodiversity, to reducing the "eutrophication" of rivers and lakes, improving water quality, preserving forests, restoring soil quality, improving the urban environment, and decreasing material waste (Kirkpatrick, Klepper, and Price 2001: table 1). "Sustainable development" has become the key term describing most of these aspects.

In the political arena, the subject of the environment has been incorporated into the programs of German political parties since the 1970s. In 1977 the first Green lists appeared in the federal states; in 1983 the Greens were elected to the Bundestag, the national parliament. In 1986, six weeks after the Chernobyl nuclear accident, a federal ministry for the environment, the Protection of Nature and Reactor Security, was established. In 1994 environmental protection was introduced as an official goal of the state in Article 20a of the German Constitution. One of the reasons why environmental concerns are so prominent in Germany is that the country is densely populated and production, housing, and recreation facilities are physically close to each other; consequently, a policy of spatial separation, by which a distance is established between pollution-generation and normal human activities such as housing and recreation, cannot be imposed.

Environmental quality has improved. While problems remain, for instance damage to forests (albeit on a reduced level), the emission of air pollutants has fallen considerably (table 9.1). Most of this reduction is due to the shutting down of firms in East Germany, which were not only

TABLE 9.1
Air pollutant emissions (million tons)

	1975	1980	1985	1990	1995	2000
Sulfur dioxide	7.6 [3.5][a]	7.7 [3.3]	7.9 [2.5]	5.3 [1.0]	1.9	0.6
Nitrogen oxide[b]	3.2 [2.7]	3.6 [3.1]	3.7 [3.1	3.2 [2.6]	2.0	1.6
Carbon dioxide	1.0 [0.7]	1.1 [0.8]	1.1 [0.7]	1.0 [0.7]	0.9	0.9

Source: Federal Statistical Office.
[a] Values in brackets, West Germany only.
[b] Measured as NO_2.

inefficient in terms of production, but also wasteful with respect to the environment. But West Germany too managed to bring down the quantity of emissions. Thus, sulfur dioxide, the pollutant responsible for forest damage, was reduced from 3.5 million tons in 1975 to 1 million in 1990 in West Germany. Surface water quality has improved considerably: quality class II water, i.e., water suitable for drinking purposes, now prevails in most rivers (Kirkpatrick, Klepper, and Price 2001: 9).

OPPORTUNITY COSTS OF ENVIRONMENTAL POLICY

These improvements were not attained without costs. The permissible level of pollution—or the desired level of environmental quality—is determined by the net marginal benefit from abating or preventing pollutants becoming zero; this means that the total net benefit cannot be further improved. It is not worth reducing pollution beyond that level. Thus, there are opportunity costs.[2] The tradeoff can be visualized by a three-dimensional concave transformation space with two traditional goods on the horizontal axes and environmental quality on the vertical axis (Siebert 2004). From this transformation space we can see that to improve the environment it will be necessary to renounce some forms of traditional output, and the jobs that go with them. The intensively pollution-producing sectors will be required to decrease their production and also to scale down employment. The output of environment-friendly sectors will be able to increase. But an important input into the production process will be made more costly, so it would be naïve to believe that environmental improvement is a free lunch. Only if technological progress occurs can the conflict in goals be resolved. However, caution is recommended when empirical studies show that environmental policy creates more jobs in an economy than it drives

[2] There are also opportunity costs within environmental policy. Thus, diesel cars reduce CO_2 emissions but can increase the emissions of carcinogenic substances.

out. Environmental policy derives its legitimacy not from additional employment, but from an improvement of the environment.

A new motivation for implementing environmental policy has been the concept of a double dividend. The idea is to tax activities harming the environment and to use the tax receipts to finance pensions, thereby lowering compulsory contributions and reducing the tax on labor. In this way, it is claimed, labor demand will be increased and unemployment reduced. This double dividend is supposed to stem first from reducing the distortion that results from not pricing the use of the environment, and second from reducing the tax wedge on labor arising from compulsory contributions to social security. In this way one policy instrument would solve two problems.

In the formation of ecological policy, these arguments have been used to garner support for halting global warming. In Germany such an ecological tax was introduced in April 1999 by the Red-Geen government. The "eco tax" entails raising the tax on petrol, diesel, fuel oil, and natural gas and introducing a tax on electricity. These taxes have been raised in several steps; for instance for petrol and diesel in five steps over 1999–2003, each consisting of 6 pfennig in Deutschmark currency and 3 cents in euro currency and amounting to 15.2 cents per liter (2003). The new tax on electricity is 2.05 cents per kilowatt-hour. This tax revenue amounted to €17.4 billion in 2003. Nearly all the tax revenue was used for transfers from the federal budget to the pension system, allowing a reduction in the contribution rate by 1.7 percentage points.

While the averted increase in the gross wage had a positive effect, in the sense that unemployment was not increased, when one considers that the elasticity of wage demand is an absolute value in the range of 0.5 to 1, the postulated double dividend cannot be seen to have materialized in practice. The contribution rate did not come down by 1.7 percentage points. Taking 1998 as the year of comparison, it was reduced by a mere 0.1 percentage point (see table 5.4), and compared with 1996 it actually increased, by 1.0 percentage point. Moreover, the tax affects productivity negatively and hurts the competitiveness of pollution-intensive industries if it is applied unilaterally. Consequently, some exemptions were made for very pollution-intensive activities. Furthermore, what is called an ecological tax is merely an increase in the oil tax and a new tax on electricity: it shifts demand away from these types of energy and thus indirectly reduces CO_2; but it is not a tax on CO_2 emissions, which would stimulate all possible production processes to reduce CO_2, including those that are still unknown. Thus, the instrument is rather coarse and its link to the environmental problem rather weak. Additionally, looking somewhat more closely at the approach, it is even inconsistent. A ton of CO_2 is taxed quite differently depending on

TABLE 9.2
Implicit tax per ton of CO_2

	Tax/ quantity unit	Energy intensity	Emission factor	€/ton on CO_2
	(€/ton)	(MJ/l)	(kg CO_2/MJ)	
Petrol	669	34.2	0.072	271
Diesel	486	38.6	0.074	170
Fuel oil	61.35	40.8	0.074	20
	(€/Mwh)		(tons CO_2/Mwh)	
Natural gas	5.5		0.202	27
Electricity	20.5		0.560	37

Source: Own calculations; see German Council of Economic Advisers (1998: table 81).

the energy source it comes from. Thus, the tax on a ton of CO_2 stemming from gas for cars is ten times as high as CO_2 from natural gas (table 9.2).[3] On the other hand, a kilowatt-hour of electricity is taxed the same, irrespective of whether the electricity is produced by coal (with a high CO_2 content), natural gas (with a low CO_2 content), or nuclear power (with a zero CO_2 content). This is clearly inefficient.

Finally, it is questionable whether it is advisable for a country to link the financing of its pension system with receipts from taxes on a factor input that has to be imported. How will such an institutional arrangement perform in a future oil crisis? All in all, it does not seem to be a prudent way to solve the pension crisis by making energy more expensive ("fuel up for the pensions"). An ecological tax should seek its legitimacy in its capacity to improve the environment.

Some Basic Issues

A number of basic issues are raised in the subject of German environmental policy. One of these is the presumed first-mover advantage. A first mover has the advantage that its own industry and other pollution-intensive processes adjust early on to the new environmental scarcity created by its activities, and that abatement and less intensive pollution-producing technologies are implemented earlier on, rather than at a later stage. The new technologies represent an export base. But the other side of the coin is that the first mover in environmental policy increases the costs of production for its traditional sectors, including the export sectors, and thus reduces its international competitiveness. A separate ecological first

[3] Calculations have been applied to the total tax and not to the additional eco tax. For a more detailed analysis, see German Council of Economic Advisers (1998: table 81; Kirkpatrick, Klepper and Price 2001: table 10).

mover therefore has its shortcomings. National environmental policy becomes easier if other countries follow suit. If environmental disruption is a purely national problem, then, the environment being a national good, other countries have no reason to apply similar standards to those of the first mover, unless they are part of an economic union. Thus, preventing distortions arising from national environmental policies is an issue for the European Union. If environmental disruption is a global problem, as in global warming, the problem of leakage arises. The first mover may reduce its emissions, but firms can move to other countries with less strict environmental regimes, thus contributing even more emissions to the global problem than were prevented in the first-mover country.

Another issue is the European Union's new emission trading system for CO_2, to be applied to larger emission sources in industry and power production from 2005 on. The European Commission leaves it to the member states to allocate emission rights to the different sources and offers three different approaches to allocate the rights: the historic approach with emissions of a base year, the forecasting approach, and the least-cost approach (Klepper and Peterson 2004). In Germany's national allocation plan, the emission rights will be allocated to the individual sources according to past emissions—according to a grandfather clause, so to speak, using the period 2000–2002 as a base. In a compromise solution between the economics and environmental ministers at the end of March 2004, the reduction was set at 503 million tons in 2007 (from 505 in 2003) and 495 million tons until 2012. The steel and glass industries, heavy power users, were exempted. New power plants will receive emission rights as if they were coal power plants. Nuclear power plants, which do not generate CO_2, received emission rights for 1.5 million tons because they have to close down and shift production to alternative energy sources. The emission rights do not cover all sources; they exclude for instance the emissions of households, transportation, and waste incineration.

The various national reduction obligations in the context of the EU's program to satisfy the Kyoto protocol will be integrated into this system. Here Germany has committed itself to reduce the CO_2 emissions of 1990 by 21 percent by the period 2008–12. Since the emission reduction of industry and power production accounts for only part of Germany's emission reduction, what is not reduced by industry and power production has to be reduced by the other sectors. It is heavily debated to what extent voluntary reductions that German industry has implemented in the past have been taken into account adequately. It is also an issue whether the cost for electricity, an important input for Germany's export industry, will be severely affected, i.e., whether the EU approach will have a negative asymmetric effect for Germany, compared with countries that are not specialized in that activity. Finally, the competitiveness of coal relative to other energy sources was at stake.

Germany has used voluntary agreements with industry to reduce environmental degradation, especially in the areas of air pollution and waste management. In about a hundred agreements negotiated between government and industry associations, abatement targets (mostly for air quality management) and implementation-oriented specific measures (in waste management) have been specified (Kirkpatrick, Klepper, and Price 2001: 20). These agreements represent self-obligations of industry: they are not legally binding, but the government can threaten to make them so if no compliance is observed. In the new area of environmental policy, the advantage of these agreements—a form of Germany's method of consensus—is that a voluntary informal solution can be found instead of a mandatory one. Such an approach may be appropriate for uncharted waters, when the government has only scarce information on what can be done. However, the approach also has its shortcomings. The agreements reflect the interest of the incumbents, which of course do not want to alter their position any more than necessary. Thus, they tend to have only a limited environmental effectiveness. Moreover, agreements may impose identical reduction targets for firms with the goal of equal treatment; this, however, does not mean minimizing costs for society as whole. Finally, the agreements may lead to a cartel-like behavior in other areas.

The political decision to exit from nuclear energy, which at present provides about 30 percent of electricity in Germany, is another topic that is much discussed. In 2001 the Schröder government concluded an agreement with the nuclear industry, establishing specific closing plans for all nuclear plants in Germany. Thus, Germany is giving up a line of technology that had established a high level of competence, especially with respect to safety. Surprisingly, the Red-Green government has put the issue of final storage of atomic waste in caverns onto the back burner. Equally surprisingly, atomic waste is now stored for a longer interim period near the nuclear plants, which often are not too far from populated areas.

It remains to be seen whether this exit decision has been a wise one. If electricity has to be imported in the future, Germany is likely to pay a higher price. Moreover, the single EU market for power will not allow Germany to discriminate against imports produced by nuclear energy elsewhere. The exit from nuclear energy has increased the comparative advantage, not to mention the advantage of energy-intensive industrial or other activities, of power producers in other countries. The ultimate test will come when a future energy crisis considerably increases the price of electricity, and when Germany as an important industrial producer finds itself without a backstop technology. Since alternative energy sources depend on weather conditions, which are not available with the same reliability as other energy sources, they hardly represent a full backstop technology.

To promote the production of alternative energy, for instance through windmills and bio mass, heavy subsidies are being used in power generation. Electricity distributors are required to accept alternatively produced energy at a relatively high price prescribed by law (Erneuerbare Energie Gesetz). The price differs with respect to the technology used to produce the alternative energy, the type of alternative energy, and other factors. Whereas it costs 2.5 cents to produce a kilowatt-hour by traditional means, the official prices for alternative energy range from 6 to 10 cents. This is a heavy subsidy, amounting to €1.5 billion in 2001. Moreover it is a hidden subsidy, not shown in the budget. The electricity distributors shift the higher price to their customers. About 6 percent of total electricity supply is now provided by alternative energy. The production of bio-ethanol from plants as a gasoline substitute is also heavily subsidized; financial support is estimated at €1 billion annually.

Besides renewable energy sources, the cogeneration of heat and power is heavily subsidized in Germany. According to a law from 2002, electricity producers that also generate heat receive the preferential electricity prices accorded to windmills. They also obtain investment subsidies.

Germany's environmental policy has been characterized by some inconsistencies. The first is the large difference in emission taxes per ton of CO_2 for different energy sources. A second one, but related to this, is that an implicit tax is put on CO_2 emissions—but at the same time the production of coal, a rich source of CO_2, is heavily subsidized. A third inconsistency stems from the phenomenon of leakage. Increasing the costs of environmental pollution in Germany makes locations in other countries more competitive and leads to more emissions elsewhere, thus not contributing to the global solution. A similar effect happens when Germany subsidizes alternative energy sources at home: this reduces the price of CO_2 emission rights elsewhere and leads to a higher energy use (and more CO_2 emissions) globally. Thus, subsidies for renewable energy de facto subsidize the CO_2 emissions in Europe outside German power generation. Moreover, the German subsidies are inefficient because the Kyoto mechanisms of Joint Implementation and "Clean Development" allow cheaper ways of reducing CO_2, for instance in the developing countries. (Wissenschaftlicher Beirat des Bundesministeriums für Wirtschaft und Arbeit 2004). These inconsistencies imply that current German environmental policy is inefficient.

A major issue is whether the four instruments now being used in air quality management are inconsistent with one another: the new emission trading system at the European level, the eco tax, subsidizing renewable energy resources, and subsidizing the cogeneration of heat and power. These instruments all address the same problem. The issue is to what extent any one of these instruments only duplicates what another instrument is already doing. This would imply unnecessary costs, and at least one of the instruments should be scaled down or eliminated.

The Capital Market and Corporate Governance

Germany's bank-based financial system relies on bank-intermediated products and only to a lesser extent on capital market processes. Moreover, one of the pillars in the three-pillar system (see below), the savings banks, is publicly controlled, and a second one, the cooperative banks, has a special statute. Neither of these pillars risks coming under the control of the capital market through the usual possibility of a change in ownership. As for the financing of firms, bank credits are far more important relative to market products, i.e., equity and bonds, than in the United States and the United Kingdom. Moreover, banks so far have occupied a dominant position in corporate control through their holdings and their votes on the supervisory board in Germany's two-tier system of corporate governance. This system, also characterized by block holdings, rivals the Anglo-Saxon model of corporate governance. With the banks themselves under pressure from changed international conditions, however, it has yet to prove its viability.[1]

A BANK-INTERMEDIATED FINANCIAL SYSTEM

The German financial system is bank-dominated. Banks play a leading role in mobilizing savings, allocating capital, overseeing investment decisions of corporate managers, and providing risk management vehicles. They act as intermediaries between households and firms, collecting deposits from households and extending credits to firms. Households contribute financial assets to the other sectors that require external funding, i.e., to the non-financial corporations and the government. Banks, denoted "monetary financial institutions" in the official language, are the go-betweens in this net lending and net borrowing process, amounting to a volume of roughly 3.5 percent of GDP annually. Moreover, banks have

[1] I appreciate critical comments on this chapter from Martin Albrecht, Claudia Buch, Günter Franke, Christine Hübner, Terhi Jokipii, Christian Pierdzioch, Bennedikt Wahler, Ingo Walter, and Jens Weidmann.

TABLE 10.1
Intermediated and non-intermediated financial assets and liabilities (% of GDP)[a]

	Financial assets		Liabilities	
	Inter-mediated	Non-inter-mediated	Inter-mediated	Non-inter-mediated
Resident non-financial sectors	148.1	110.6	156.6	123.4
Non-residents	48.4	65.0	23.3	71.5
Total	196.5 [162.0]	175.7 [169.1]	180.1 [132.4]	194.9 [217.7]

Source: European Central Bank (2002a: table 1).
[a] End of 2000; in brackets, EU values for comparison.

increasingly financed themselves through the issue of bonds. The German banks are in close contact with firms and have been called "house banks" (*Hausbanken*). They play an important role in the German approach of corporate governance by exercising control over the firms through representation on the supervisory boards and in giving them credit through "relationship banking". This intimate approach, grounded in a reliance on personal information and personal contacts, stands in contrast to the market-oriented Anglo-Saxon system, where the allocation between savings and investment is performed predominantly by market instruments via a more anonymous market process (European Central Bank 2002a). Whereas part of this difference can be explained by the structure of the enterprise sector, with the small firms prevailing in Germany relying on credits from banks and larger firms, e.g., as in the United States, favoring market products, this does not fully explain the difference between the two approaches.

Evidence of bank-based intermediation instead of market allocation becomes apparent when we analyze the structure of financial assets and liabilities (table 10.1). The resident non-financial sector, i.e., households, non-financial corporations, and the government, have provided financial assets to the intermediary sector to the order of 150 percent of GDP in the intermediated form of deposits, money market funds, and mutual funds shares,[2] whereas the market attracted non-intermediated funds of only 110 percent of GDP in 2000. A similar picture emerges if we study the liabilities side. This preference for intermediated products is due to the behavior of households. Non-financial firms prefer non-intermediated products both for their financial investments and for their borrowing.

---

[2] Money market funds and mutual funds take an intermediate position: they are not "intermediated," in that they do not run through the balance sheet. They represent "fiduciary" or professionally managed third-party assets; the fiduciaries may or may not be banks.

The dominance of intermediated products in Germany is in contrast to the euro area as a whole, where the funds received from the markets amounted to 220 percent of GDP and those from intermediated products to 130 percent (European Central Bank 2002a: 68). Non-residents of Germany prefer market products. Market products are also more important in the EU, with non-intermediated liabilities amounting to 217.7 percent of GDP (table 10.1). The relative importance of intermediation implies that the stock markets as well as shares are relatively less relevant in Germany than in most other countries. German stock market capitalization of 40 percent of GDP (May 2003) is indeed low compared with other countries.

The dominating players among the German intermediaries are the *banks*, whose assets account for 300 percent of GDP while the assets of other financial institutions and insurance companies make up only 41 and 64 percent, respectively (table 10.2). Banks in Germany have a virtual monopoly on retail distribution, although not in the production of intermediation services. So the non-bank intermediaries' market share is trivial compared with that in the United States. In the European Union monetary financial institutions play a smaller role, whereas other financial institutions are more important. At the end of 2000, bank loans amounted to €3 trillion, and €2.2 trillion worth of debt securities were in circulation, meaning that loans by banks accounted for most of the finance raised by the economy as a whole. Of those debt securities, around €1.4 trillion were issued by banks, which used this as a principal instrument to refinance their lending business.

The German financial system differs from the Anglo-Saxon model in that generally banks or credit institutions operate as "universal banks," with the exception of mortgage banks and other banks with special functions (e.g., government-owned banks providing subsidized lending).[3] As a rule, there is no distinction between commercial and investment banks, and hence the term "banks" in Germany typically refers to financial institutions, which are allowed to participate in a broad range of activities, including investment banking, mortgage banking, insurance services (through subsidiaries), security brokering and dealing, payments services (in Germany these require a banking license), and commercial banking activities. The core of the banking business, however, still rests with the granting of credits to resident non-monetary financial institutions with the main activity being based on the differential in interest rates.

Besides banks, *money market funds*, often spin-offs of banks, are another element of monetary financial institutions. Money market

---

[3] Part of the difference is related to the dominance of the Mittelstand in the German structure, i.e., companies that even in the United States would rely mainly on bank finance.

TABLE 10.2
Structure of the German banking system

Importance of intermediaries, assets in per cent of GDP[a]

Monetary financial institutions	Other financial institutions	Insurance companies
300.4 [255][b]	40.1 [50][b]	64.0 [58][b]

Number of monetary financial institutions[a]

Private commercial banks	Cooperative enterprises	Savings banks	Foreign branches and subsidiaries	Other credit institutions	Money market funds	Total
148	1 796	575	146	75	40	2780

Share of banking gropups of the balance sheet total in per cent[c]

Commercial banks	Savings banks and federal state banks	Cooperative banks	Mortgage banks	Banks with specific functions	Building societies
28	36.1	11.5	13.4	8.4	2.6

Source: European Central Bank (2002a): tables 3.2, 3.4, 3.5 and 3.6, p. 72-7; for balance sheet total, Bundesbank Monthly Report, September 2003, p.24f.

[a] At the end of 2000.
[b] In brackets, euro area values for comparison.
[c] In July 2003.

funds were introduced in 1994 and by May 2002 had a total market share of around 10 percent of the monetary financial institutions balance sheet total, a relatively large portion when compared with only 2–3 percent of the euro area balance sheet total. Such funds invest mainly in high-quality, liquid, short-term government and corporation obligations that can be sold at or close to par value. They stand ready to pay out the deposits immediately; deposits in them are like money and therefore are included in the money stock M3. On the liability side of banks' balance sheets, traditional deposits have lost importance relative to money market funds, which yield higher interest.

Other financial intermediaries, essentially comprising *investment funds*, play a modest role, accounting for 11 percent of households' financial assets (in 2000: European Central Bank 2002a: 75). Investment funds in the euro area constituted around 40 percent of total assets in 2000. Special funds, accounting for about two-thirds of investment fund assets, are issued to institutional investors, e.g., insurance companies; like the investment funds that are open to the public, which account for the other one-third of the assets, they are security-based. The idea of open-ended investment funds is to collect and manage assets on behalf of small investors with specific objectives regarding the risk, return, and maturity of the involved claims. They enable investors from all classes of society to participate in and benefit from profits of productive capital as well as real estate. In open-ended funds, also referred to as "mutual funds" or "unit trusts," the number of certificates is changing constantly. Investment funds stand ready to redeem certificates on the investor's demand, as well as to sell new certificates to them without limit; the certificates can be bought and sold at net asset value. The investment fund industry has experienced rapid growth in Germany over the last decade. Since 1995, a key driver of this substantial growth has been the huge increase in special funds.

The German insurance sector includes *insurance corporations and pension funds*. These play an important part in the financial industry, as the issuance of insurance policies generates substantial investable funds. Like investment funds, they collect and manage assets, but with the difference that insurance contracts are typically designed with certain guarantees, meaning that the insurance company acts as a risk bearer, while the investment funds usually operate strictly on an individual net asset value basis and do not take on any risk.[4] With respect to gross premium written in 1999, the German insurance industry is the fourth largest insurance market in the world after the United States, Japan, and

---

[4] If however investment companies offer their investment products within tax-supported individual pension accounts, then they must by law give a so-called "money back" guarantee owing to regulatory solvency requirements.

the United Kingdom. Approximately 6 percent of the world's premium volume was collected in Germany (Maurer 2003).

Total liabilities of German insurance companies and pension funds amount to 64 percent of GDP. Most of the liabilities are technical insurance reserves for claims held by households; these reserves can be interpreted as precautionary savings for old age. Households can invest in life insurance policies that receive favorable tax treatment. The German Retirement Savings Act of May 2001 created a new system of supplementary pensions in addition to the public pay-as-you-go system. These include pensions, agreed upon by the social partners, whereby employees can convert part of their salary into contributions to such pensions, exempting that part of the salary from income tax and from social security contributions. Households also have claims against pension funds; employers as well as employees make contributions to these pension funds. Moreover, households have direct claims against firms from company pension commitments amounting to 8 percent of GDP in 2000; these claims are carried on firms' balance sheets as pension provisions.

Most German insurance companies are organized as stock corporations. Only around 15 percent are listed on the stock exchange, usually the mother company, as subsidiaries do not tend to be listed. This is due to the fact that the current regulations require obligatory specialization, prohibiting life insurance companies from providing insurance coverage in other lines of business. With more than €850 billion of assets under management in 2000, the German insurance companies can be considered the most important institutional investors within Germany.

THE SEGMENTED THREE-PILLARS APPROACH

A distinct feature of the German banking system is that the private commercial banks have only a very small share of the total market, when measured in terms of the balance sheet total. It may come as a surprise to international readers, and to many Germans as well, that Deutsche Bank, the internationally known largest German bank and a major global player, has a market share of only 5.4 percent in Germany (2003). The top four private banks—Deutsche Bank, Bayerische Hypo-Vereinsbank, Commerzbank, and Dresdner Bank—account for only 16 percent of the market.[5] All the commercial banks together, which do a

[5] In terms of pure numbers, commercial banks, among them the five largest commercial banks, account for 5.5 percent of the total number of 2780 banks, savings banks for 21 percent, and cooperative banks for 65 percent (as of 2000: European Central Bank 2002a: 72).

considerable amount of the more complex type of banking activities such as security and asset management, account for only 28 percent of the market. Apart from the four big banks, they include the regional commercial banks and the Postbank,[6] which account for 10.3 percent of the market, and subsidiaries of foreign banks, which have a market share of 1.7 percent.

The German banking industry is characterized by a large presence of publicly owned or government-influenced institutions. Publicly controlled savings banks, including their central institutions, the state banks (*Landesbanken*), make up 36.1 percent of the market; here important changes in the public guarantees can be expected from 2005 on (see below). Cooperative banks, including their central institution, account for 11.5 percent; the mortgage banks for 13.4 percent, while banks with specific functions, among them government-owned banks for public credits such as the Kreditanstalt für Wiederaufbau, account for 8.4 percent (table 10.2). Savings banks and their central institutions represent a two-tier system where the central institutions, the Landesbanken, are true universal banks, performing significant investment banking and wholesale banking functions including liquidity provision and risk transformation. The savings banks and co-operative banks are legally allowed to operate as universal banks. However, the majority clearly focus on retail banking and on keeping in touch with their local customers, especially the small and medium-sized firms, owing to their local orientation. The same holds for the two-tier system of the cooperatives.

The German banking sector is rather fragmented. The Herfindahl index of market concentration is very low. This could be taken to indicate a high degree of competition between banks in their product markets. If this were the case, Germany could be presumed to have an efficient banking system. However, this, is not a true representation of the situation. For one thing, there is a fair bit of regional segmentation among banks; also, they have tried to establish their own market segments on the product side, where they would be somewhat protected against competition. To this end, they have used different strategies. The commercial banks shifted resources out of retail banking in the late 1990s, but have lately rediscovered it as commission incomes and profits on proprietary trading declined in the wake of the stock market collapse. The savings banks and cooperatives have stressed their local bias, including access to liquidity from their local customers. In addition, competition from foreign banks is low: just 214 branches and subsidiaries of foreign banks (131 foreign banks and 83 subsidiaries) were operating in

---

[6] The semi-privatized Postbank with 27 000 employees is used for personal financial transactions such as paying monthly bills in preference to bank accounts. Almost one in three Germans has an account in the Postbank.

Germany in April 2003.[7] Thus, there is still a great deal of segmentation of the German banking sector.

What is more important, when looking at competition among banks in a wider concept than just the numbers of banks and their market share, and when corporate governance of the banking sector and competition in terms of ownership control are taken into account, a very different assessment on the German banking system can be made. The banking industry is segmented into three pillars: the commercial banks, the savings banks (including the state banks), and the cooperatives. (There is even a (slightly) smaller fourth pillar, namely the government-owned specialty banks.)

With respect to the first pillar, the savings banks were founded in the nineteenth century when the municipalities gave guarantees for the deposits of the customers in order to protect, for instance, workers' savings against loss from bank failure. The savings banks were also supposed to extend credits to local craftsmen and small businesses that would otherwise have limited or no access to credit. The savings banks, which are in the legal form of public corporations, are obliged to serve the public interest; they then have other then purely economic goals in terms of societal, social, and cultural responsibilities according to their statutes. Profit is not their first priority. They are organized regionally, i.e., one bank for a region, and they have accumulated their capital from retained earnings. Profits that arise are regularly used to augment reserves or to be distributed to the public owners. Mayors and other local dignitaries are represented on the supervisory boards of these banks, and it is common for savings banks to support local initiatives in different walks of life such as sports and culture, which, of course, is very welcome to the local politicians. Through this financial support, local politicians have a shadow budget at their disposal.

Legally, the counties and municipalities are not the owners of the savings banks, although they can demand the distribution of profits. They are merely the guarantors, meaning that the public entity is liable without restriction in the event of a default, and hence provides a guarantee for third-party lenders. Historically, governmental entities did not put up equity for these banks. Savings banks and their central institutions receive two types of public guarantee. Maintenance obligation (*Anstaltslast*) characterizes the commitment to equip the institution under public law with the necessary means to fulfill its public mission; it is a general concept of German administration that is applied and guaranteed to all public bodies. Guarantee or bail-out obligation (*Gewährsträgerhaftung*)

---

[7] Most keep to a few specialized fields of banking, e.g., trade finance, investment banking, or asset management. German banks have 323 branches and 407 subsidiaries abroad, most of them in the European Union (as of 2002).

describes the unlimited responsibility of a public corporate body for the liabilities of its public institutions, to protect creditors. There are seven private savings banks, e.g., in Hamburg and Frankfurt, which prove that regional and local savings banks are able to compete in the German market without the two public guarantees.

The central institutions of the savings banks, the Landesbanken, are stock companies and are owned by the savings banks and the federal state in which they are located. For instance, the West LB, Germany's fifth largest bank, is owned by the State of North Rhine-Westphalia (42 percent), by the Rhenish and Westphalian savings banks (17 percent each group), and by regional authorities. The federal state takes over the maintenance and bail-out obligations in a fashion similar to that of the municipalities in the case of the savings banks, even for the business the West LB does in London. This has in recent years become highly controversial, as did another state-supported bank, Crédit Lyonnais in France, a decade earlier. Public guarantees will change in 2005 (see below).

When a savings bank gets into financial distress, the municipality has to step in and use tax money to consolidate the bank. This happened for instance in 1998, when the municipality of Mannheim had to come up with the equivalent of €25.6 million to bail out its savings bank; in 2000 it guaranteed another €76.7 million. Similarly, when a federal state bank becomes illiquid, the Land has to bail it out. For instance, in 2002 the Bankgesellschaft Berlin, with its subunits of Berliner Sparkasse, Berliner Bank, and the Berlin Hypothekenbank, had to be rescued from insolvency, mainly as a result of a miscalculation of real estate risks in the mortgage business leading to high losses. The state of Berlin had to inject new capital of €1.7 billion and cover potential risks up to €21.6 billion in order to attract a private equity holder; Berlin still holds 81 percent of the equity. All this happened in a federal state that is itself in financial distress. The taxpayer has to cover the failure of a bank that is under strong political influence regarding its credit and in hiring policies.

Savings banks are protected against takeover by the legal proviso that they serve the public interest, so that they are immune against a takeover bid by commercial banks or cooperatives. They are not for sale, and thus are protected in their ownership structure. In fact, savings banks are so well protected that, while they can merge within a state, it is not possible for savings banks of neighboring federal states to merge even if they serve a common economic area. The reason is that the regional principle applies to them, delineating their market area, and the public interest is defined according the law of the individual Land. For instance, it is impossible for a banking district to cut across the boundaries of two Länder. This is a logical outcome of the definition of the public interest, as usually defined for a state,[8] and of the guarantee structure: why would taxpayers of one Land agree to bail out loans to clients in a different Land? In a similar way, savings banks cannot take over a cooperative or a commercial bank, because they would then lose the attribute of serving the public interest; nor can they be taken over by a cooperative or a commercial bank. This may change; some municipalities are now attempting to sell their savings banks, albeit meeting strong opposition from the association of savings banks and from the states in which they are located and which have some supervisory functions. So far, the first pillar is completely closed off against competition, and a market for corporate control does not exist. Clearly, such a stipulation does not fit into an institutional environment where the EU is attempting to reduce institutional barriers between the member states.

With respect to the second pillar, the cooperatives, which provide mainly retail banking services to their local market, are typically owned by their depositors or their borrower-clients. Usually a broad ownership is required and ownership shares cannot be sold. Like the savings banks, cooperatives are organized regionally. Again, the cooperatives are not for sale and, thus, are not subject to a market of corporate control. Profits are distributed as dividends to the mutual owners. As with the federal state banks, the central institution of the cooperative banking group, the DZ-Bank, provides a wide array of services for its primary institutions. Besides the regionally organized cooperatives, there are also a number of nationally active "special banks," such as banks of the churches, of government officials, and of physicians and pharmacists.

The commercial banks, the third pillar, are fully open to competition. Deutsche Bank, HypoVereinsbank, Commerzbank, and Dresdner Bank, a subsidiary of Allianz, offer the full range of banking services, in that their retail and corporate banking businesses are complemented by investment banking activities, although only partly in high-level investment banking relating to mergers and acquisitions. They form the core of Germany's private commercial banking group. However, as noted, the private banks in this third pillar have a market share of less than one-third of the total banking business in Germany. Looking at the banking sector somewhat differently, commercial banks and mortgage banks account for only 42 percent of the market volume; the publicly supported banks, the savings banks, the Landesbanken, and the government-owned "special banks" make up 44 percent of the market, not counting the cooperatives, performing such specialized services as agricultural, craft, or mortgage lending. Together with the cooperatives and the building societies, the publicly influenced part of the banking industry is nearly 60 percent.

[8] This does not apply to the state banks.

Surprisingly, this means that Germany, known as a market economy, has a banking system that is strongly influenced by the public sector.

It must be questioned whether this three-pillar banking system is efficient. Benchmarking shows that German banks perform below international standards when profitability is considered. Profitability is defined as the net interest margins, i.e., the banks' revenues from lending minus the remuneration of deposits minus expenses and loan losses, relative to average assets. This figure for Germany, 1.12 percent in 2001, a record low, is below the EU-11 average; it is about half that of the United States.[9] The return on assets, i.e., the ratio of pre-tax profits to average assets, the return on equity, and earning power all are much lower than for the United States, and except for the return on assets are also lower than in the EU-11[10] In 2002, the German banking sector's profitability was down to 0.1 percent of assets (IMF 2003: 31). Low domestic lending margins, high operating costs, significant loan write-offs and the large market share enjoyed by publicly owned and cooperative banks have had the combined effect of keeping the profitability of most private German banks among the lowest in Europe. And bank profitability has continued to deteriorate drastically, not just since the stock market bubble burst. According to the association of private-sector banks (Bundesverband Deutscher Banken), German banks' average net profit as a percentage of total assets has nearly halved in the period 1993–2003.

Competition in the German banking sector is severely distorted. Savings banks and Landesbanken can compete with the commercial banks under privileged conditions, thereby driving down the rates of return. If these semi-public institutions fail, the municipalities and the Länder will pick up the bill. At the same time, they are protected against competition in the market for corporate control since they are not for sale. This means that, in an international comparison, German banks are not efficient. Coupled with the country's distorted competition in the banking industry, Germany is considered "over-banked," in spite of recent consolidation. Thus, the low Herfindahl index mentioned above may be an expression of inefficiency, rather than an indication of competition-induced efficiency through market discipline. All this may be one reason why the big German banks, whose stock market value is a bit on the low side, have not been taken over by foreigners.

An advantage of the German system seems to be that customers enjoy lower banking fees and lower interest rates for credits than in other countries, possibly also higher rates for deposits. But this comes at a price. The allocation of the factors of production is distorted, in that

[9] The figures for 1998 were: 1.2 percent in Germany, 1.5 percent in the EU-11, and 2.1 percent in the United States (Belaisch et al. 2001: table 12).
[10] Ibid.

there is a bias in favor of capital relative to labor which is reinforced by wage policy. In addition, lower lending rates are made possible only by an implicit subsidy of the government in the form of guarantees, which involve public funds, if the risks materialize. Moreover, the system itself is exposed to a systemic risk because the interest rate differential between deposit and lending rates is not sufficient to cover the expected losses emanating from credit risks. The ultimate costs of the system would become apparent if the government were no longer to finance the subsidies, so that financial institutions would have to ration credits independently of Basel II. It seems that in 2001 and 2002 we were not too far from this scenario. In a recent publication, the Bundesbank (2004) surprisingly found that German incorporated firms actually paid higher interest rates than in the euro area in the year 2003, according to newly harmonized ECB statistics. For instance, new credits of one to five years had an interest rate that was 0.25 percentage point higher then the average of the euro area. This partly reflects a variety of factors: lower competition because of the housebank system, housebanks solving the adverse selection problem by a higher risk premium, and a bias toward longer-term credits in Germany; this applies even in spite of the harmonized date because each credit class has such a bias. Nevertheless, the higher rate also may signal the actual pressure on the German banking industry.

RECENT FINANCIAL MARKET DEVELOPMENTS

During the past decade, significant institutional, political, and technological advancements have occurred around the globe, collectively resulting in a breakdown of the traditional way in which banks, and financial institutions generally, do business both in Germany and in many other industrialized countries. Structural shifts in the financial system and on financial markets have been caused mainly by the removal or loosening of regulations within the financial sector. While deregulation and globalization have led to both product and geographical expansions within the banking system, the implementation of new technologies has accelerated that process. Banks are facing increased competition, both from within the immediate industry and from the non-bank providers of financial institutions. Disintermediation, i.e., a greater reliance on market processes instead of the active matching role of banks, has been occurring as more and more non-banks and on-line banks are now providing the more traditional banking products. These changes have resulted in a fundamental shift in the cost structure of the distribution of financial services. As a result, the way in which banking business is conducted, both at an individual firm level and for the industry as a whole, has

changed significantly. Moreover, some additional trends of disintermediation have been observed recently. Large-scale public enterprises have
been privatized, so that the stock market plays a larger role. Neuer
Markt, a stock market segment for technology-oriented, fast growing
firms, was established in March 1997; with the ending of financial
exuberance, it was closed in June 2003. Maybe it was premature and
investors were not yet ready to accept major losses; the US Nasdaq
bounced back despite similar market pressures.

Until the early 1990s, the German savings and commercial banks could
rely on cheap funding through their depositors. That is why Deutsche
Bank once was called Germany's biggest savings bank. Customers were
interested mainly in the safety of their deposits and did not have too many
alternative short-term options. This changed when money market funds
and other market instruments became available and when depositors
became interested in returns as well as security. Bank customers have
switched to money market funds, so the liability side of the balance
sheet structure of banks has changed, with deposits losing some of their
importance relative to market products. The new market products have
absorbed the commercial banks' cheap funding sources. Further, the
enlarged currency area and financial liberalization resulting from a set
of EU directives have created a broad, liquid financial market offering
many different types of investment without any exchange rate risk.[11]
Thus, the second EU banking directive of 1989 introduced the principle
of mutual recognition. Member states must recognize financial institutions licensed in another country. This created a single "license" or "pass-
port," eliminating the need for EU banks to obtain a local banking charter
from the host country for branches and bank products. Banks can offer
banking services freely across the EU; according to the principle of home
country control, the supervisory function is allocated to the home country.[12] Another principle in the second banking directive was the concept
of harmonization. This aimed to create uniform safety and soundness
standards and a comparative competitive environment across the EU. It
means that banks operating in countries within the EU face regulation
through a set of harmonized rules rather than a variety of different standards and requirements.

Eight more directives were adopted between 1986 and 1992 which
required that banks be examined annually at the fully consolidated banking institution level for risk exposure and risk management; furthermore,

[11] The Directives 86/566/EEC and 88/361/EEC were instruments for the full liberalization
of the capital markets.

[12] The home country rule replaced the host country rule, for which the first banking
directive of 1977 had set the criteria of expansion across national boundaries within the
European Community.

minimum capital and solvency standards were required in order to limit an institution's exposure to large borrowers, plus standards for reporting financial and accounting data. Adoption of all of these directives by each of the member states was crucial to the long-run integration of the EC banking market. Although segmentation still exists as a result of national regulation, for instance of the insurance industry, borrowers and lenders can take advantage of the broader market. Customers too are internationalizing, for instance with the greater mobility of enterprises and an increasing cross-border migration of people, e.g., students to universities and the elderly to residences abroad.

The larger commercial banks, which stressed the role of investment banks in their strategy throughout the years of financial exuberance and now seem to be looking for the right balance between internationalization and home business, need to obtain internationally comparable results in their profits and in their evaluation by the equity market. If they do not succeed in reducing inefficiencies, they run the risk of being taken over. Admittedly, this threat is reduced by the institutional setting under which they operate in Germany, including the low interest rate differential between deposit and lending rates. This threat for a takeover may become more real when the remaining institutional segmentations are weakened. The removal of capital gain taxation on divested cross-holdings is expected to further affect the restructuring of the German industry.

The banks have responded to the changed environment with mergers and acquisitions. The banking sector has consolidated significantly, recently reducing the overall number of banks dramatically from 4719 in 1990 to 2592 in 2002. This intense consolidation has been driven by the need to solve cost-related profitability problems arising from the combination of its dense network of branches and its high employment costs relative to other European banks. In addition investment funds and insurance companies have started to compete more fiercely for the financial assets of households. Among the banking and insurance sectors, in 2001 Allianz, the insurer, took over Dresdner, the fourth largest German bank, to reap the expected (and so far disappointing) synergy effects from the sale of insurance contracts. This acquisition still lays heavy on Allianz, which has lost over half its market value and was forced to raise new equity capital. At the same time, the HypoVereinsbank agreed on a strategic partnership with the re-insurer Münchner Rück. The smaller savings and loan associations and cooperatives are also consolidating within the limits allowed by law; for instance, two central institutions of the cooperative banking group, the DG bank and GZ bank, merged to form the DZ bank in 2001.

Several years of weak growth, along with a sharp downturn in the stock market, overambitious expansion strategies, and low profitability, have put substantial strains on the German banking system. As a result, in 2002 and 2003 speculation increased about a possible banking crisis. Major consolidation measures have brought about a significant improvement; problems still exist, however, placing additional pressure on the need for even more consolidation within the sector.

Starting in 2005, the savings banks and Landesbanken will face a new regulatory regime with respect to their public guarantees. Their cozy position will be dismantled. In the negotiations with the European Commission, the German authorities have agreed to redraft their legal provisions. The two public guarantees will no longer apply in German law. The maintenance obligation (*Anstaltslast*) will be replaced by a normal ownership structure between the owner and the public-sector savings banks. The bail-out obligation (*Gewährsträgerhaftung*) will be completely abolished for all state banks and public-sector savings banks. Losing these state guarantees, which underpin the AAA ratings and cheap capital market funding of state wholesale banks, these banks will have to cut costs, refocus operations, and become more profit-oriented. The decision by Westdeutsche Landesbank, Germany's largest public-sector bank, to split itself into a public-sector holding company and a private commercial bank, does not however address the heart of the problem, because the private unit will still be 100 percent publicly owned. Interestingly, an attempt by Standard & Poor's to suggest indicative state bank debt ratings without the guarantees triggered massive political pressure against the firm in 2003. Standard & Poor delayed publication of the ratings, suffering in the process a serious blow to the firm's independence.

Basel II will also have its implications for Germany. The inclusion of the exposure maturity under the preliminary document for the rules to be implemented under Basel II has come as a great surprise to the German banking industry. This means that a long-term exposure will require up to six times more capital than a one-year exposure. The established corporate structures in Germany entail a significantly higher percentage of long-term involvement of the banking industry than in the United States or even the United Kingdom. Such capital "add-ons" will significantly affect the competitiveness of the German banking industry compared with other structures and will increase borrowing rates to a level that may not be justified by the risk they are taking on.

STOCK AND BOND MARKETS

The stock market is generally less important in Germany than in many other countries. It also plays a smaller role than the bond market.

The Stock Market

Measuring the size of the stock market by the relative market capitalization, i.e., the ratio of the value of all shares of firms listed on a national exchange and the host country's gross domestic product, Germany's market capitalization of 40 percent of GDP (in May 2003) is low by international standards.[13] It is about the same as in Italy (48 percent), but lower than in France (106 percent), the United Kingdom (128 percent), and the United States (140 percent). Despite the stock market boom in the period 1998–2000, investment in securities other than shares was higher than investment in shares. In contrast to the flow data, holdings of shares are higher. However, while shareholdings of households increased from 15 percent of GDP in the 1990s to 30 percent in 2000, the ratio remains much lower than that of the euro area, at 55 percent. Shares are more important for firms than for households, accounting for more than 50 percent of the asset side in the balance sheet of firms (in 2000) again, significantly lower than in the euro area (71 percent).

For households, Germany seems to have developed a somewhat broader culture in equities following the privatization of the telecommunications company Deutsche Telekom in 1996 and the establishment of the Neuer Markt in 1997. The number of shareholders rose from 3.2 million at the end of the 1980s to 6.2 million in 2002, but has fallen since then owing to the slump in the stock market. Like other European countries, Germany has witnessed a strong growth in its market capitalization ratio, from 12 to 67 percent between 1975 and 2000; but other countries such as France, having started from about the same ratio, have seen a much stronger increase in stock market capitalization. German investors still seem to see equities as "savings" vehicles rather than as true risk capital.

On the German stock exchanges, 973 domestic companies and 9737 foreign companies were listed in January 2004. In addition, shares of 9677 non-listed public companies were being traded. The 42 largest companies (constituting 5 percent of all listed stocks) accounted for 74 percent of total market capitalization in 2000; electronic trading accounted for 44 percent of the volume traded in that year. In the primary market, the annual issue of shares (issued by residents) was 11.9 percent of GDP in 1998–2000. Initial public offerings totaled €25.6 billion, or 1.3 percent of GDP, in 2000. The stock segment Neuer Markt was introduced as a special market for growth stock

---

[13] Source for data: Capitalization, Statistical Abstract of the United States, World Federation of Exchanges (FCSM). The values for 2000 were 67 percent for Germany, 70 percent for Italy, 110 percent for France, 179 percent for the UK, and 149 percent for the USA.

companies that were mostly internationally oriented and committed to high international transparency standards. It was terminated in 2003 following the collapse of the international information and communications technology sector and the ensuing correction of the international stock markets, leaving its market capitalization at around a thirtieth of its peak.

The Bond Market

The German bond market is dominated by the banks, with a volume of funds allocated from savers to borrowers second only to intermediated credits. Almost two-thirds of the outstanding debts—110 percent of GDP—were issued by banks. Government bonds account for 40 percent of GDP. The volume of German government bonds is second in Europe only to Italian bonds. The ten-year German government bond, known as the Bund, enjoys benchmark status. The Bund future has become the most important hedging instrument for long-term interest rate risk in the euro area.

The German bond market is a long-term market where 80 percent of debt securities are issued with an original maturity of over four years. Specialties of the German capital markets are the mortgage-backed bonds and municipal bonds known as *Pfandbriefe*. Both are a kind of asset-backed security, overwhelmingly communal, bond, providing security independent of the individual debtor via real estate collateral or a collateral pool of public-sector loans.

The European Monetary Union has boosted the trend towards securities by opening up a larger market for bonds in a common currency. In addition, many institutional investors who until the end of 1998 had spread their portfolio risks among government bonds issued by various EMU member countries began to look for alternatives once the exchange rate risk disappeared. The euro eliminated the currency-matching requirements for certain investors, such as insurance companies and pension funds, opening up the whole euro zone to German asset allocation. Bonds issued by German banks have proved an attractive alternative for such investors. Accordingly, they launched a jumbo issue of *Pfandbriefe* with an issue volume of over €500 million, providing security independently of the individual debtor through a public-sector body guarantee or the existence of real estate lien. With this issue came the introduction of book-building as a method of issue and the assignment of an external rating. For the German *Pfandbriefe* issuers this rating is commonly AAA. *Pfandbriefe* have consequently evolved from a German specialty to an international investment vehicle.

FINANCING THE ENTERPRISE SECTOR

In the financing of German enterprises, equity financing is relatively low in importance compared with borrowed funds. For all enterprises in the producing sector, in trade, and in transportation (apart from communications), equity accounts for 8.1 percent of the enterprises' balance sheet total in 2001. All own funds, including (besides equity) retained earnings, reserves, and capital surplus, comprise 17.6 percent.[14] Provisions represent 19.9 percent, with provisions for pensions accounting for 8.4 percent. Provisions excluding those for pensions (11.5 percent) may be viewed partly as equity. This means that equity financing in a broad interpretation constitutes only 29.1 percent of the total liabilities. The overwhelming part of the balance sheet total is financed via borrowed funds (61.9 percent). Among the credits, 20.4 percent of all liabilities are from credit institutions, for short-term (9.8 percent) or long-term credit (10.6 percent). The role of bond financing (*Anleiheverbindllichkeiten*) is very low, making up 0.2 percent of the liabilities. The data for 2000 are of a similar pattern.

The financing structure varies notably with the legal form of enterprises, as the more detailed data for 2000 indicate (table 10.3). Corporations have a higher share of equity financing, both from own funds of 23.3 percent in 2000 and from provisions (excluding those for pensions) of 13.7 percent. In contrast, partnerships and sole proprietorships have significantly lower internal financing capability. Small and medium-sized companies rely heavily on financing via bank loans (Sauve and Scheuer 1999). In the case of sole proprietorships, internal financing is even negative, which seems to imply that owners on average were withdrawing not only the current cash flow, but the substance of the firms' assets (although the distinction between firm and personal assets in these cases is often very vague).

Credit institutions are of particular importance in providing long-term financing: they provide 67.4 percent of long-term credits for the average firm, 62.3 percent for corporations, and an overwhelming 87.9 percent for sole proprietorships. The lower ratio for partnerships may be due to the role that credits are given by one or more of the owner-partners in those cases. As for short-term credit, the non-institutionalized forms of this, such as trade credit by deferred payment, decrease the respective percentages of bank loans. Notwithstanding these forms of credit, sole proprietorships depend on banks for more than half of all their borrowed funds. This dependence, and their low or non-exis-

---

[14] Data provided by the Bundesbank.

TABLE 10.3
Financing of German firms

	All legal forms	Corporations	Partnerships	Sole proprietorships
Liabilities (% of the balance sheet liabilities)				
Own funds[a]	17.21	23.27	11.87	−10.14
Creditors	62.67	51.68	74.74	105.90
Provisions	19.67	24.41	13.20	4.25
for pensions	8.33	10.77	5.03	0.47
Borrowed funds (% of the sum of borrowed funds)[b]				
Short term by credit institutions	11.61	8.19	14.90	20.56
Long term by credit institutions	13.19	8.38	14.69	32.55
Total by credit institutions	24.80	16.57	29.59	53.10
Share of long-term borrowing coming from credit institutions	67.39	62.28	58.87	87.86
Short-term funds from trade creditors	15.54	13.55	16.52	22.91
Pension provisions	10.11	14.15	5.72	0.43
Non-pension provisions	13.79	17.92	9.29	3.43

Source: Deutsche Bundesbank, Monthly Report, April 2003: 60.
[a] Own funds (Eigenmittel): equity, retained earnings, reserves, capital surplus.
[b] Sum total of liabilities less own funds.

TABLE 10.4

Sources of corporate credit bank loans versus capital market financing: an international comparison [a]

Country	1996	1997	1998	1999	2000	2001	2002
Germany	94.41	95.10	95.59	96.11	96.02	95.54	na
France	81.93	81.61	80.03	80.45	79.78	77.84	na
Italy	68.86	68.85	74.84	73.32	71.58	71.35	na
Euro area[b]	Na	88.73	88.41	88.57	88.72	87.93	87.07
Japan	69.31	68.48	69.62	67.22	67.50	66.29	63.80
UK[b]	70.42	70.73	67.86	64.40	63.70	62.96	62.59
USA[b,c]	47.37	47.27	46.39	46.11	45.12	44.57	41.65

Source: Bank for International Settlements. 73rd Annual Report 2003: graph VII.12, p. 131; http://www.bis.org/publ/arpdf/ar2003e.pdf.

[a] Bank loans to corporations as a percentage of the sum total of bank loans plus short- and long-term securities issued by corporations (% for annual averages).

[b] First quarter averages.

[c] Excluding mortgage credit.

tent own funds in the firm, make them particularly vulnerable to changes in the credit policies of banks.[15]

To put the financing side of German non-financial enterprises into an international perspective, the low market capitalization is evidence of the relative insignificance of equity finance in Germany. While this information does not stem from an internationally consistent data set on the financing structure of the enterprise sector, internationally consistent data show that in Germany bank loans play a much larger role than market instruments of financing (table 10.4). Thus, the ratio of bank loans to the sum of all bank loans plus short- and long-term securities issued by corporations was about 95.5 percent in 2001. This is an unusually high rate, even for continental European countries that have traditionally relied more on a bank-based system; the shares in France and Italy, of 78 and 71 percent respectively, were much lower. The frontrunners of financial market access of corporations—Japan, the United

[15] However, there are means of financing such as leasing that (depending on the stipulations of the underlying contract) often do not show up on balance sheets but only in the notes of a company's Annual Report and as current costs in its profit and loss accounting. Were they fully included with their present value as liabilities on the balance sheet, the above mentioned ratios would then shift even more to external, longer-term financing, but somewhat to the cost of the importance of bank loans. Sale-and-leaseback arrangements have become increasingly popular in recent years, particularly for firms in financial distress, using the initial cash flow of the sale of assets to reduce some debt. Even major German banks have recently undertaken such moves, liquidating some of their real estate holdings to counterbalance credit write-offs. Estimates put the share of leasing in financing investments of German firms at around 17 percent.

Kingdom, and the United States—come much closer to equality between bank loans and bond issues in corporate finance.

The pattern of German corporate financing, in which loans from domestic banks, along with trade credit, has traditionally dominated, has been changing of late. Enterprises today obtain more capital in the marketplace than they used to. A main reason for this is that the European Monetary Union has made bond issues more important as a source of corporate financing. The extended market has increased the potential for placing bonds issued by private non-banks. Moreover, there is a growing tendency on the part of German enterprises since the mid-1990s to obtain funds through affiliates abroad. Between the end of 1995 and the end of 2001, the debt of domestic enterprises with foreign affiliates increased by around €270 billion. During the same period, domestic banks' total lending to domestic enterprises grew by €245 billion. The reason for this drift is that financing within groups is handled centrally and that, given the growing number of international mergers, a sharp increase in intra-group flows of funds is the result. The financing and tax advantages that an individual group can enjoy within a certain market are exploited. Around 35 percent of domestic enterprises' total debt with foreign affiliates is accounted for by offshore-affiliates in another European country (e.g., the Netherlands Antilles).

There is a fear that the implementation of the Basel II accord as it stands will pose a great threat to the survivability of small and medium-sized enterprises. The proposed internal and external ratings put a greater emphasis on financial ratios than on the soft facts that are very decisive factors particularly for small and medium-sized enterprises. Consequences could range from worsening ratings to a rise in credit costs. Moreover, the proposal for Basel II is based more on Anglo-American economic and financial structures, where credit financing is much less important than in Germany. A rise in the costs of financing will therefore have a significant impact on the competitiveness of German small and medium-sized enterprises, which in turn could have detrimental effects on many of the banking institutions in Germany.

Corporate Governance

Another distinguishing feature of the German banking industry is that commercial banks generally hold equity in firms and thus have capital locked into industrial holdings. They play a vital role in corporate governance.

Bank Ownership of Firms

Banks owned 13.5 percent of the shares of the enterprise sector in the late 1990s; this share increased in the 1990s (table 10.5). Moreover, there are cross-holdings between the three different groups of intermediaries, i.e., banks (monetary financial institutions), other financial institutions, and insurance companies. Banks and insurance companies together own 22.5 percent, nearly a quarter, of the shares of the enterprise sector (table 10.5). While it is not too surprising that insurance companies hold part of their portfolio in stocks, for banks it is more unusual—after all, banks are in the business of debt financial intermediation rather than equity investment. Stock held by banks is used by them as a lever in "relationship banking," generating a large amount of loan business. As predominant providers of capital, it is the banks' interest to be represented on the supervisory boards of firms, giving them permanent contact with their credit customers and enabling them to collect the information necessary to extend credit and to take an active part in the corporate governance of firms, thereby indirectly controlling their credit risk.

TABLE 10.5
Ownership structures of shares in Germany and the United States (1990s)

	Germany		USA	
	Beginning	*End*	*Beginning*	*End*
Non-financial sector:	62.1	47.8	50.8	41.9
Companies	41.6	29.3	– [a]	– [a]
Individuals	16.9	17.5	50.8	41.9
Public authorities	3.6	1.0	0.0	
Financial sector:	25.8	36.1	41.7	49.6
Banks	10.3	13.5	5.4	3.4
Insurance companies	11.2	9.0	5.0	6.0
Pension funds			24.2	24.0
Investment funds	4.3	13.6	7.1	16.3
Foreign	12.1	18.5	6.9	7.3
Other			0.7	1.1

Source: Van der Elst (2001).

[a] For the USA, share ownership is included under the heading 'Other'. Therefore the total of the non-financial sector is incomplete. Given the small amount, this is probably not an important incorrectness.

A Two-tier Structure of Control and Management

German corporate governance is characterized by relatively little reliance on capital markets and outside investors and greater reliance on large domestic investors and financial institutions to achieve efficiency within the corporate sector. Unlike the Anglo- Saxon model of a board of directors, which directs the company, manages the business, and represents the firm, the German two-tier system of corporate control, which dates back to the late 1800s, distinguishes between the supervisory board (*Aufsichts-rat*) and the management board (*Vorstand*). The supervisory board is the controlling body of a company. It controls the management board, which is the operating arm of a stock company, and elects its members. The supervisory board has an insight into all accounts and can exercise a veto where its consent is necessary. The management board has to inform the supervisory board of ongoing and planned businesses. Furthermore, the supervisory board has the competence to set the by-laws unless the statutes are defined by the shareholders' meeting.

The management board is the administration organ of the company. Its function is to manage the firm's business, especially its day-to-day business, in the best interests of the company and to represent the company in its business dealings and legal affairs. In a sense, the management board directs the company and takes responsibility for its actions.

The shareholders exercise the ultimate rights of control via the shareholders' meeting. There they can change the charter, decide on dividends, and approve the actions of both boards ex post by a vote of confidence. Additionally, the shareholders' meeting elects a part of the supervisory board, i.e., the representatives of the capital side (on the labor side, see chapter 14). In this election, the management's board proposal is usually followed.

This system of corporate governance is an insider control system. The supervisory board members are generally well informed of what is happening within the company and are able to influence the management board, partly by virtue of their membership of the supervisory board and partly by other means. They must therefore be "insiders." In practice, the members of the supervisory board end up with many board mandates and usually a major day job as well, often resulting in a lax "duty of care" and conflicts of interest in the "duty of loyalty," the essence of board responsibility.

German banks exercise control in the supervisory board of companies, where they are represented on the capital side of the supervisory board, whereas labor fills the other side (see chapter 14). To have a seat on the supervisory board, a bank does not necessarily have to hold a proportional equity of a company. Bankers tend to be elected to the supervisory board because of their comprehensive information on other firms, corporate trends, the political scene, and international developments. For example, Deutsche Bank, Dresdner Bank, and Commerzbank hold around 16 percent of about 231 positions reserved for stockholders on the supervisory boards of the 24 non-financial companies comprising the German stock market index DAX30. Banks therefore have a substantial influence over the exercise of voting rights in publicly held stock corporations. Moreover, they have additional voting power in the shareholders' meeting via proxy voting, whereby they vote on behalf of their bank customers in cases where voting instructions are often not specified by the customer. Banks have conflicts of interest in their role as equity holders, creditors, advisers, underwriters, and fiduciaries, all at the same time. Furthermore, they have a strong influence on non-incorporated firms if these firms use the bank as their house-bank for credits.

Cross-holdings

Equity held by banks and insurance companies creates a network of cross-holdings between the financial and non-financial sectors. Like spiders, the larger banks and insurance companies are sitting in a delicate and complex cobweb of holdings, so that firms of the industrial and service sectors are intertwined with those in the financial sector. These interdependencies are even further intensified because in Germany other financial institutions, e.g., investment funds, are interrelated with banks or insurance companies as well (figure 10.1). In the 1990s these cross-holdings between the three different groups of intermediaries increased, so that the different groups of financial institutions have become progressively interlinked, as a result of mergers and acquisitions and the spinning off of subsidiaries to form jointly owned operations. In the first decade of the twenty-first century, equity holdings of banks are coming down, with banks actively reducing their holdings in non-financial firms.

In addition, it has been customary for major German corporations in the past to own large blocks of each other's shares. Within the non-financial sector, German corporations held about 30 percent of the shares of other corporations at the end of the 1990s (table 10.5). Many of these cases are either in subsidiaries of multinationals separately incorporated in Germany (such as Ford, Alcatel, Nestlé, or Pirelli) or other acquisitions in the process of formation of industrial groups that have not led to full mergers (e.g., VW's Audi), or the inverse case of establishing new business lines that are independently incorporated, such as the do-it-yourself chain Praktiker of retail giant Metro, or Siemens' Infineon spin-off. Note that most of these do not represent cross-holdings in the strict sense, but are

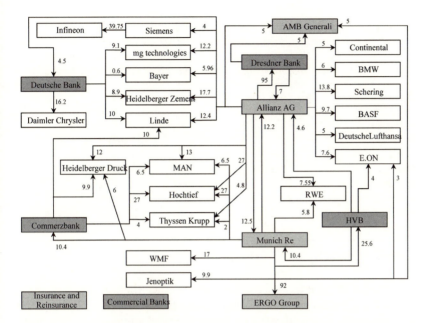

Figure 10.1 Important cross-holdings in Germany, 2002 (% of equity), End of 2002; HBV: HypoVereinsbank. *Source*: Germany's Top 500 Edition 2003. A Handbook of Germany's Largest Corporations, published by F.A.Z.-Institut für Management-, Markt- und Medieninformationen GmbH, November 2002; Bloomberg Information Service, Querries N200 Equity DES and dgp Equity PHDC as of November 8, 2003; and Die Deutschland AG, Wirtschaftswoche, 19/2002: 48

hierarchical holdings. Explicit cross-holdings can be found on the level of medium-size enterprises, where cross-ownership refers to ownership titles not listed on the stock exchange; they also refer to joint family ownership. On a more personal level, it is common practice for German industrialists to be on the supervisory board of a number of other non-competing corporations. These cross-holdings generate a picture of Germany Inc., where important decisions are supposed to be informally coordinated. It must be noted, however, that the ratio of cross-holdings without the financial sector fell considerably during the 1990s, from 41.6 to 29.3 percent. As a result, current figures of cross-holdings such as shown in figure 10.1 differ considerably from those of the early 1990s.[16] It should also be noted that corporations trade their blocks of shares among themselves; this is a substitute for the market, but of course is not an open market.

[16] Compare, e.g., the year 1993 (Story and Walter 1997: 184).

TABLE 10.6
Majority control and blocking majority, 2000

	% of listed companies under majority control	% of listed companies with a blocking majority of at least 25%
Austria	68	86
Belgium	65.7	93.6
Germany	64.2	82.5
Italy	56.1	65.8
Netherlands	39.4	80.4
Spain	32.6	67.1
Sweden	26.3	64.2
UK	2.4	15.9
Nasdaq	2	5.2
NYSE	1.7	7.6

Source: Country chapters in Barca and Becht (2001).

Cross-holdings effectively reduce still further the already low stock market capitalization that applies to market participants other than cross-holders. When adjusted for the substantial amounts of cross-holdings, the free stock market capitalization in Germany, open to the market participants, is only 14 percent of GDP instead of 67 percent, much lower than the 48 percent in the United and States and the 81 percent in the United Kingdom (Boehmer 1999).

Block-holdings

Cross-holdings of banks, other financial institutions, insurance companies, and corporations imply a high concentration of ownership in large firms. Together with a substantial deviation from the 1 share-1 vote paradigm by way of preferred stock,[17] block-holders, commanding many votes, tend to dominate or control companies where a block-holder appointed board is in control. In the majority of listed companies in Germany there is a single voting block commanding more than 50 percent of the votes; in more than 80 percent there is a single voting block with a blocking majority, i.e., more than 25 percent of the votes (table 10.6). Large block-holders, often heirs to the founding industrialists, and banks control a substantial portion of exchange listed firms, while the role of smaller shareholders in influencing corporate governance is negligible.

[17] Preferred stock allowing multiple votes is a pertinent feature of the legal environment in Germany. The stock corporation law does not permit the issue of such shares today, but firms that have issued them in the past have not been forced to convert them into ordinary shares. Shares of preferred voting stock are not traded on the stock exchange.

The Issue of Control

The German system gives power to the block-holders and the managers. Thus, large block-holders have incentives to maximize the value of their shares. Whether this involves maximizing firm value depends on the extent to which they can extract transfers from small shareholders. German law (*Aktiengesetz*) allows sizable transfers to block-holders once a coalition controls at least 75 percent of the votes. Another issue, and an open question, is whether managers are sufficiently controlled, as they can form an implicit coalition with large block-holders. Last but not least, cross-holdings represent political power. Supervision of the banking sector may be harder, and it may be more difficult for the government to instigate structural adjustment of the economy, if cross-holdings represent an implicit organization of vested interest. To control the political power of that system by introducing another vested interest, i.e., the trade unions, into the supervisory board is to stray further from the market process (see chapter 14).

The German versus the Anglo-Saxon System

Similar two-tier systems of corporate governance to those in Germany are in place in Austria and Italy and, for large stock corporations, also in the Netherlands and France. In contrast, the unitary board system is internationally the most applied structure. Besides in the United States and the United Kingdom, it can be observed in Canada, Belgium, Denmark, Greece, Japan, Sweden, and Spain—and for small stock corporations also in the Netherlands. In this system, the board of directors directs and represents the company while simultaneously managing the business. It draws up the goals and strategies of the company and elects and controls the officers. It also decides on the appropriation of profits and informs the shareholders. Additionally, the board of directors has the right to set and change the by-laws. Moreover, it has a trustee function in the interests of the shareholders. In fact, it has to control itself. To a large extent, decisions are made autonomously by the board of directors. The board consists of inside directors and outside directors. The shareholders' meeting elects the members of the board of directors from board nominations, and sets and changes the charter of the company. In extraordinary situations, such as a merger or the dissolution of the company, the meeting is in charge of decisions to be made. As control of the shareholders' meeting is limited, there is a strong focus of power on the board as a whole. Within the board of directors, power is concentrated with the inside directors directing the information flow to the outside directors, and proposing the outside directors for election to the shareholders' meeting. Additionally, the committee consists mostly of inside directors.

It is heavily debated in the economics literature whether the Anglo-Saxon system, with its strong reliance on the equity market, or the German model of corporate control, with banks, block-holders, and personal contacts, is more efficient (Holmstrom 1999; Hopt 1998; Mayer 1998).[18] Leaving aside the question of workers' participation, which will be discussed in chapter 14, the issues are how strongly management is controlled, and how responsive the system is to changed economic conditions.

The Anglo-Saxon system concentrates power in a small group of people and has a low potential for conflict, enabling decisions and their implementation to be made quickly. This ability to adapt quickly to changing conditions strengthens the competitiveness of a company and the professionalism of the members of the board of directors, provided they remain alert—unlike the dog that didn't bark in the night, to quote Sherlock Holmes. At the same time, the board has relatively little explicit institutional control of the management, relying on the potential threat of the capital market—i.e., that inefficiently managed companies can be taken over—as a decisive mechanism of control.

The German system of control has been called a passive form, in the sense that unfavorable developments can be prevented. As a form of corporate governance, this may allow a longer-run orientation of firms, which some view as necessary, and may therefore have its advantages. One of the shortcomings of the German system, however, is that it is geared to the incumbent firms and not to the uncertain terrain of new firms. It is amazing that Germany has managed to solve its structural adjustment mainly through existing firms in the country and not by new firms, as was pointed out in chapter 3. Indeed, there are only a very few examples of new firms that have gained eminence in the German economy.

The German approach to corporate governance may be good at initiating marginal improvements, but it is deficient in leapfrogging to new approaches and new products. Incremental technological improvements along established lines, mainly in the export-oriented automobile, machine building, chemical industry, and electro-technical industries, are therefore typical in Germany. In contrast, there has been a more remarkable restructuring in the corporate sector of the United States, where the equity markets have forced management to restructure (Holm-

---

[18] For the view that the relative merit of the two systems is undecided, see Becht, Bolton, and Röell (2002: 112).

strom 1999; Mayer 1988). In Germany, as on the Continent generally, management has less freedom to restructure. The block-holder model is not good in Schumpeterian innovations, i.e., in major technological breakthroughs. The contention that the Anglo-Saxon system is oriented to the short term, lacking a long-run orientation, is not backed by the literature.

Another disadvantage of the German approach is that new market solutions such as a venture capital market have greater difficulty getting established in an environment that is characterized by intermediated products and personal informal relationships.[19] This has negative implications for the financing of new, innovative—but risky—technologies. Moreover, the commercial banks, savings banks, and cooperatives tend to shy away from financing large risks. They are more comfortable with incremental changes. R&D funding of the private sector typically comes from retained earnings, which is a means more readily available to established firms with relatively constant cash flows. In Germany, it has been decried as a destructive short-termism of Anglo-Saxon provenance that firms should be oriented to creating "shareholder value." What has been given little attention, however, are the severe incentive problems that arise when creditors are given an eminent role in corporate governance and are invited to overlook the interests of the company's owners and judge investment decisions mainly according to the firm's ability to sustain interest payments. This problem is compounded by German accounting standards, which have traditionally espoused a creditor bias. Accordingly, principles of utmost caution and lowest considerable value apply, rather than the "true and fair view" that Anglo-Saxon accounting standards take as a guiding line. It is on these principles that huge asset under-valuations and low market capitalizations flourish. In addition, their dual role of shareholder and creditor creates a major problem for the German banks themselves. It is likely to expose them to the accumulated risk that makes them more prone to adverse economic developments that affect the value of both their credit and their stock portfolios. This constellation may actually help to explain the severe *baisse* of German financial stocks in 2002 and 2003.

An important prerequisite of administering a governance system for the enterprise sector through the capital market has come to light in the context of the US Enron scandal in 2001 and similar cases in the United States in 2001.[20] Using the capital market as an instrument of control presupposes that the information processed by the market on the firm's assets and liabilities is reliable. When assets are overvalued and liabilities

[19] The venture capital market has improved.
[20] Compare also the Parmalat case in Italy in 2003.

underreported, i.e., when fraud is possible, the capital market cannot fulfill its controlling function. The supervision of the financial market, guaranteeing transparency and accuracy of financial accounting of publicly traded companies, as intended by the Sarbanes-Oxley Act of 2002 in the United States, is therefore an important prerequisite of the governance of firms.

The German system is changing. The close relations brought about through cross-holdings previously enabled the country to keep foreign competition at bay. As financial markets have grown together, national markets are no longer isolated. A better stock market culture is developing; households have more options for their savings. Quoted companies can raise finance internationally, and German stock corporations are in direct competition with demands for capital worldwide. The shareholder structure is becoming more international; several major German companies are now listed at the New York Stock Exchange (e.g., Deutsche Bank, DaimlerChrysler) and have to satisfy the transparency demands that listing entails. A recent law has allowed major listed companies to move to International Accounting Standards for their annual reports, reducing the creation of balance sheet reserves and creditor bias. The influence and expectations of foreign institutional investors is growing. The internationalization of share ownership will eventually change the German blockholder model. New regulations of the European Union referring to the takeover of enterprises will also push back preferential arrangements that favor block-holders, albeit with quite a few safeguards in the final agreed text of the takeover directive (see chapter 14). Moreover, block-holding seems to dominate in Germany because share owner representatives are more powerful in bargaining with employee representatives on the supervisory board than if they had dispersed votes. Thus, changes in codetermination may reduce the incentive to have block-building. Under conditions of increased globalization, the large financial concerns have come increasingly to regard the permanence of the German structure as a straitjacket. The tax reform that became effective in 2002 relieves the seller of any capital gains taxes on the sale of these cross-holdings. This reform removed the implicit incentive for banks, insurance companies, and corporations to have holdings and to keep their balance sheet reserves under seal. For this reason, larger banks and insurance companies have been selling off some of their holdings and reinvesting the proceeds in their core businesses. Moreover, the central institutions of the savings banks and the savings banks themselves will lose their public guarantees.[21]

---

[21] Krahnen and Schmidt (2004: 497) do not find any clear evidence that the German system has changed into a market-based system.

More importantly, the trend is toward international competition.[22] The German model relies on the banks as controlling agents. However, the banks themselves are under international pressure to change; and, given their comparatively low market valuation, they also face a serious threat of being taken over. The way in which they deal with this challenge will also play a deciding factor in the future of the German model. There is the further issue of the extent to which the German nature of codetermination can survive under global conditions (see chapter 14). In the end, only the market process will be able to determine which model is viable.

[22] On these issues, see European Commission (2002), and Becht, Bolton, and Röell (2002). On an interesting taxonomy with respect to the superiority of one of the institutional approaches for the banking industry, albeit without the question of codetermination, see Krahnen and Schmidt (2004: 498).

CHAPTER ELEVEN

Human Capital and Technology Policy

Technological advances and human capital ultimately determine a country's competitiveness. Germany's system of human capital formation, however, though having an asset in its vocational training programs and in a highly and broadly qualified workforce, has come under severe criticism. Its university system is not competitive internationally. Its school system is wanting. The orientation of politics in this sector, so important for the dynamics of an economy, has led the government not to challenge students to strive for excellence, and not to exploit to the full all talent available in the country, but instead to produce graduates with relatively similar sets of acceptable qualifications. Instead of aiming for distinction, Germany has chosen a uniformity of outcome.[1]

HUMAN CAPITAL AS A GROWTH DETERMINANT

As already discussed in chapter 3, human capital can be viewed as a decisive factor in economic growth, particularly in a country like Germany, which lacks significant natural resources. The estimated production elasticity for a combined input of human and physical capital in the range of 0.6–0.7, against 0.4–0.3 for traditional labor in older studies, suggests that in the information and knowledge economy qualification and ideas play a more important part than the other factors of production, e.g., physical capital and land. Whereas these econometric estimates have to wrangle with the difficulty of measuring the input of human capital, and whereas the estimated high value of the production elasticity reflects the difference in the delineation of inputs from previous studies of growth determinants, there are some arguments that make the relevance of human capital plausible.

Over a longer time horizon, the relative weight of factors of production has changed considerably. Land and traditional labor used to be the dominant factors of production in an agricultural society, where a large

---

[1] I appreciate critical comments on this chapter from Daniel Hobohm and Bennedikt Wahler.

part of the population lived outside the towns. Capital in the form of machines, again together with traditional labor, constituted the most important determinant of growth in the age of manufacturing and the industrial society, implying a geographical concentration of activities in the cities in order to make use of economies of scale. Capital and labor in a different mix were then required in the service economy, where for some activities capital is needed together with qualified labor as an instrument to produce services, for instance in transportation, banking, and insurance; and in other activities, e.g., tourism or nursing care, a more traditional type of labor is necessary. A quite different mix of capital and labor is in demand in the information and knowledge society, where highly qualified labor is needed to use the rather complex physical capital. This applies to the information technology sector itself, for instance for the production of IT products, but also to those sectors using the IT products, including manufacturing. This historic change in the use of factors of production is mirrored in the trends in the proportions of value added or employment of the respective sectors over time, with the service sector now accounting for 70 percent of GDP (see chapter 1).

Human capital, or knowledge capital, is instrumental in shifting the production frontier outward—by adding new products to the product set of the economy, by introducing new production processes, and by making possible new organizational solutions. Improved human capital means an increase in welfare, a greater product choice for consumers, higher labor productivity, an improved competitiveness of firms, and a higher probability of employment. Human capital leads to geographic clustering of economic activities, influences the attractiveness of a country for investment, and represents an important factor in international locational competition. It thus is the key to a higher growth path, especially for a country such as Germany that has virtually no natural resources. Consequently, the organization of the production of human knowledge is of utmost importance, both in the context of growth and policy and in the fight against unemployment.

At the root of human capital formation is the investment decision of the individual, who has to compare future expected benefits with the costs of his education. The government can influence the institutional framework of the system and the taxation of future gross returns. But in essence, a country depends on the willingness of its citizens to invest in their human capital in order to reap its benefits in the future. It is therefore paramount that policy respects the decisions of the individual and takes them as the core of any approach to human capital formation.

GERMANY'S SYSTEM OF HUMAN CAPITAL FORMATION

While succeeding in generating a qualified workforce, Germany's system of education and training has serious shortcomings regarding the formal education of its children.

The Three-tier System

Germany's human capital is formed via a three-tier system. Pupils in the *first tier* start primary school at the age of 6 and complete it after nine or ten years, then go into a practical job at the age of 16. They have few qualifications. Some of them can take up an apprenticeship in the dual system, but prerequisites for getting apprenticeships have increased considerably over time. In the *second tier*, after grade 4 pupils move from primary school either to middle school (*Realschule*), where they work towards a certificate, or to a high school (*Gymnasium*), where they work towards their diploma (*Abitur* or baccalaureate). After completing these different stages at the middle or high school level, they may then move into a practical occupation, for instance a crafts apprenticeship. Pupils in the *third tier* continue to university level after obtaining their *Abitur*.

Thus, after grade 4 the German system establishes a decisive selection process along three different tracks, one leading usually to university training, one leading to less academic professions such as managerial or production positions in companies, and the third leading to a rather basic education for practical jobs. This early selection can be corrected to some extent, because cross-mobility between the tiers has increased since the 1960s. Later in working life, training on the job and formal training programs by the firms are an important factor in forming human capital.

Expenditure

Overall public expenditure on education in Germany represented 4.3 percent of GDP in 1999; this is similar to the proportions for other EU countries (Netherlands 4.3 percent, Italy and Spain 4.4 percent, United Kingdom 4.5 percent, France 4.8 percent); the United States spends 4.9 percent. However, Germany ranks fifth in terms of private expenditure on education, with its sizable sector of professional education after primary and secondary school the among the industrial countries, so another 1.2 percent of GDP needs to be added to arrive at society's total yearly monetary investment in education. Taking both public and private funds into account, German expenditures are well placed among the upper-middle sector of OECD countries (OECD 2002: 170). With respect to the structure of expenditures, Germany spends over-proportionally only on the upper secondary level of schooling, while its expenditures on both primary and lower secondary schools are nearly 20 percent below OECD averages (OECD 2002: 171).

Germany thus has chosen to give relatively less weight to laying a sound, broad basis for fostering talents at an early age and helping those who lag behind catch up while it is still possible. This is not really a policy that can be subsumed under the heading "equality of opportunity." At the same time, while the salaries of German teachers at both primary and secondary levels is high on the list of OECD countries, exceeded only by Switzerland and Japan (OECD 2002: 339), teacher-student ratios in Germany are less favorable than in comparable countries owing to funding restrictions. In any case, vast expenditures and good salaries are not a guarantee of high-quality output.

Performance of Schools

German schools were rated poorly for the performance of their students in international comparisons in the PISA (Deutsches Pisa-Konsortium 2001) and TIMMS (Baumert et al. 2000) studies. With respect to reading, writing, and mathematics, they showed below-average capabilities, although there are significant differences among the German states. Econometric analysis suggests that these results are due to the institutional setting and to the orientation of school policy toward producing uniform, i.e., non-differentiated, qualifications instead of aiming to provide equal starting conditions and then allowing a differentiation of results (Wößmann 2002). Thus, even in the educational sector, where it is important for the country to exploit all the talents it has and where the system should permit talent-focused education, the goal of equity has taken efficiency out of the German system.

Owing to the branched educational system and the limited requirements for the lowest degree (*Hauptschulabschluss*), Germany has a level of dropouts that is low by international comparison. Among those without German citizenship, however, the dropout rate is a worrisome 20 percent, signaling the failure of the educational system to function as an effective means of integration. As the social stigma of having not achieved even this lowest-level certificate is accordingly high, the job prospects for those without any certificate are poor. Given Germany's effective eradication of the low-wage sector, these youngsters are institutionally condemned to depending on social assistance from an early age. In effect, Germany is choosing to simply neglect this part of its labor force. The German reform discussion after the PISA and TIMSS studies has been dominated by the repackaging of the traditional, ideological concepts.

However, cross-country analysis suggests that more expenditure would not be a panacea: what is needed is a profound reform, realigning incentives in the institutional setup of public education and fostering creative competition among schools and states to establish a quasi-market.

The German school system contains a bias in favor of the humanities and against technological fields. The special composition of subjects in the *Gymnasium*, which relates to the entry-level requirements for university, is likely to be a disincentive for those with more pronounced interests in technological fields. Together with the provision that an alternative way into university requires additional schooling after having finished an apprenticeship, this places a considerable restraint on those from modest family backgrounds and with preferences and skills outside the humanities.

Vocational Training

The institutional arrangement of the dual system of apprenticeship and vocational schools represents an asset. This system is considered one of the best in the world, providing excellent facilities for the creation of human capital. It equips young men and women with both firm-specific and general skills and combines learning on the job with formal education. It also is an important mechanism for the socialization of young people and for integrating them into the labor market.

Apprenticeships have traditionally held an important role in Germany's system of education and until very recently were the main recruitment pool of technological intelligence, middle management, and even upper management in Mittelstand firms, in addition to providing a source of entrepreneurs.[2] Stemming from the guilds, the concept of the apprentice partly financing his education by receiving lower pay remains an important incentive for firms to accept trainees and allows for smoother labor market entry of the young and relatively unskilled, resulting in an internationally low unemployment rate among German young people.

Problems arise, however, in that the system adjusts only slowly to incorporate new profiles of occupation into it, e.g., in the IT sector.[3] Moreover, trends in recent years have caused an apprenticeship crunch: many apprenticeship candidates from the *Realschule* are being replaced by graduates from the *Gymnasium* (particularly among banking and

---

[2] In addition, the apprenticeship system allows young people to work toward acquiring an additional degree at the tertiary level (*Fachabitur*), and thus provides the universities with technical students who have already got a good grounding of practical skills and experience.

[3] In recent years several highly successful new apprenticeship programs have been introduced, among them several computer-related courses and one in "Mechatronics," to equip young machine builders with ever more relevant electronics skills.

insurance apprenticeships)—at a time when many positions in industry and trade that were formerly assigned to those with an apprenticeship background are now going to university graduates. This raises the apprenticeship prerequisites and the average age of labor market entry of apprentices, and makes it more likely that they will feel de-motivated and will be unable to utilize their skills to the full extent. If these apprentices then decide to go on to university—after all, they have their *Abitur*—as is not now uncommon for students in business administration, they will graduate at the age of, say, 27 or 28, by which time a *Realschule*-graduate could have completed his apprenticeship and worked for about eight years, advancing in his career and paying into Germany's social security system.

Training on the Job

Most German employers are strongly involved in continuing job-relevant education, with many large corporations having their own educational department as part of the human resources department or an outsourced institution. Training is focused on firm- or even job-specific technological knowledge but also includes general skills training. German employers seem to have not yet embraced the concept of lifelong learning, as the significantly lower spending on the training of those over 45 bears witness to. They have become only vaguely aware of the implications of an ageing population on future labor supply. Moreover, a branch of institutionalized, private or public, continuous education exists to provide longer-term training to advance employees' qualifications and career prospects (e.g., *Fachakademien*). These are financed mainly by the employee himself through fees, while the employer often adds some financial support and the government picks up the infrastructure.

THE DEFICIENCY OF THE GERMAN UNIVERSITY SYSTEM

Universities play a crucial link in the development of technologies; they produce human capital and are involved in essential research. The German universities, including the more practice-oriented universities of applied sciences (*Fachhochschulen*),[4] had an annual budget of €28.6 billion in 2001 and educated 1.94 million students during the winter semester of 2002/03 (Federal Statistical Office 2003a). It is administered and financed by the states, which have the lawmaking competence in cultural affairs including education except for the framework

---

[4] These universities are not to be confounded with the technical universities.

competence of the federal level; this limits the maneuvering space of the Länder, most importantly the framework law for universities (*Hochschulrahmengesetz*). Moreover, formal agreements among the federal states regulate specific aspects, such as not allowing universities to take fees from their students.[5] Joint funding by each state and the federal government on a 50/50 basis applies to investment, for instance university buildings, according to the constitutional arrangement of joint tasks with co-financing. In an international comparison, the performance of this system is not satisfactory.[6]

Long Duration of Studies

The German educational system is characterized by a rather long period of studies leading up to the first university degree, the diploma. Owing to their relatively late entry into the school system, and then 13 years in primary school and the *Gymnasium* and a long period of study at university, it is not uncommon for German students to receive their university diploma at the age of 27. (Admittedly, this includes the required year of military or civil service for men.) The average age at which a student graduates from university in Germany is 25–26. At that age, a student with a British university degree who joins a German research institute will have obtained his Ph.D. Since German students are competing in the international labor market, they often find themselves at a disadvantage with students from other countries.

Unexploited Student Potential

While the reforms of the 1960s opened university education to a broader stratum of society, this development has effectively come to a stand-still. The proportion of pupils fulfilling the entry requirements for tertiary education (i.e., *Abitur* or *Fachabitur*) in a cohort nearly doubled in each of the two decades from 1960 to 1980, from 6 to 21.7 percent. The rate of increase slowed during the 1980s and 1990s, reaching 31.4 percent in 1990, and then leveled off at around 36–37 percent in the first decade of the twenty-first century (Egeln et al. 2003: 10). Key to this rising trend has been the increase in young women attending university; among them, the proportion gaining *Abitur* has risen from 8.5 percent in 1970 to over 40 percent today, and they now account for more than half of all young Germans entering university. However, this growing participation of young women in higher education does not apply to the engineering sciences, where their share of graduates

---

[5] Several states have now announced that they will terminate this agreement.

[6] For an evaluation of the system, cf. German Council of Economic Advisers (1998: 240).

stood at 6.3 percent in 1999, much lower than the 14–20 percent in most other advanced OECD countries.

Germany has a lower percentage of university graduates than other countries. Of those *Gymnasium* graduates of a cohort taking up tertiary education (about one sixth of them do not go to the university or drop out), Germany is in last place among comparable OECD countries in 2000: 30 percent versus 37 percent in France, 43 percent in the United States, and 71 percent in Finland (Egeln et al. 2003: 20). The problem lies not only in the relatively lower percentages of those meeting university entry-level requirements, but also in the high percentage of them choosing not to exercise their option to continue studies at university or *Fachhochschule*. Furthermore, there has been a trend of late away from the natural and engineering sciences, with a dramatic fall in the number of enrollments and graduations in these subjects (except for computing and biology), which is already showing up in supply-side shortages for firms seeking graduates with such technological qualifications.

Unattractiveness to International Students

The German university system of the nineteenth century used to attract many foreign students and researchers, for instance the economist Alfred Marshall, who studied under members of the German historical school in Dresden (1869) and in Berlin (1870–71). Today, the future elite of the world is educated in the United States. Admittedly, Germany does attract a sizable number of foreign students, making it the third most education-exporting country in the world (behind the United States and the United Kingdom).[7] But the students' regional origins are mainly China and eastern Europe, so that it is fair to say that, by and large, Germany is now focusing on the diffusion of technology to countries catching up, rather than on the education of students from comparable economic or technological levels. Moreover, the foreign students coming to study in Germany may be a result of a process of adverse selection, because there are no tuition fees or because studies represent an alternative to immigration.

Exodus of German Talents to Study Abroad

An indicator of the unattractiveness of the German system is the exodus of highly talented young Germans to study at Anglo-Saxon universities,

[7] The internationalization of German universities has made some progress in recent years. Several bilingual or all-English study programs as well as some cross-country programs have been established. Foreign language requirements have been integrated into many programs. The level of German students abroad with academic experience is competitive in an European context.

thus voting with their feet against the German system: 12–14 percent of German post-docs go to the United States after completing their dissertation, concentrating in those areas of science and research in which US institutes occupy an unchallenged top position (Federal Ministry of Education and Research and Center for Research on Innovation and Society 2001: 3). Moreover, it has become common for bright and adventurous Germans to study in Anglo-Saxon countries after having received the German *Abitur*. The high percentage of German students abroad would not represent a problem if a similar percentage of foreign students wanted to study in Germany. Nor would it be a problem if the German talents came back upon the completion of their studies. But quite a few tend to stay, so that their human capital is lost to Germany. Also, the recruitment of professors for German universities is restrained.

Equality of Qualification versus Excellence

The implicit objective of the German education system is to aim for a broad qualification of graduates. Excellence is not the institutional target; it is thought that this can be achieved by the intrinsic motivation of individuals and groups of individuals, for instance by single departments and institutes. Rather, the political goal for the university system has been a relative uniformity of quality, i.e., qualifications that are not too greatly differentiated. For many politicians, tertiary educational policy is a social policy wherein university attendance is open to all groups of society and where a uniformity of results is as important as in school policy; for them, it is not enough to provide equal starting conditions. Such an implicit objective drives efficiency out of the educational system. For other people—those in politics in the federal states with a larger territory—university policy is also regional policy, and thus an instrument with which to spread economic activity spatially and to aid the development of all regions of a state. With such targets, the international competitiveness of universities does not play a role. Whereas some of the German states, among them Baden-Württemberg and Bavaria, explicitly attempt to make their universities more competitive, many politicians define universities as a policy instrument in a rather broad concept of economic and social policy. Only in January 2004, for the first time in his two terms of office, did Chancellor Schröder address the issue of modernizing the university system, using the catch-phrase "Elite-Universitäten," i.e., a "university for the highly qualified."

The intended uniformity of outcome has a serious feedback in this system. Professors are only as good as their students are. If you as a professor are challenged by the expectations and the intellectuality of your students, it makes your mind tick. Students are a challenge for teachers and researchers. They are the addressees of the professors' production function, but they are also an important input into it. Having worked on both sides of the Atlantic, it seems to me that this is one of the basic reasons why German professors simply cannot perform better than they do.

An Inequitable System

Politicians place great weight on social justice with respect to the German university system. In reality, however, the goal of an equitable system has not been attained. The university system has not been opened up to the lower-income groups of society. German higher education today is more closely related to relatively high social backgrounds than in any other advanced country. This is particularly detrimental as students of the natural and engineering sciences are recruited mainly from those with more modest family backgrounds. Germany is effectively restricting its competitiveness and growth perspectives by restricting the access to higher education of pupils interested in technological subjects. Moreover, those from lower social strata are more likely to leave their *Abitur* unused—despite tuition-free universities and public grants. All this works to make German public education a down-to-up redistributive machine, thereby restraining economic growth opportunities.

But the issue is not only that children from the lower strata of society do not de facto enjoy adequate access to the universities. Since a large part of tax revenue comes from income taxes, these lower strata contribute proportionately more toward the financing of the universities. Thus, workers contribute a much larger share toward university provision than the share of their children in universities: in 1996 only 14 percent of all new students were from workers' households, whereas such households comprised 33 percent of all households working as dependently employed and self-employed (German Council of Economic Advisers 1998: 252). Although these percentages are not identical to the proportionate contribution to income tax revenue, the working class is nevertheless helping to finance the education of upper-middle-class children—an extremely unjust arrangement.

No Tuition

It is a sacred cow of German university policy not to introduce student fees. Politicians, especially the Social Democrats, justify this on the grounds of social justice—an argument that is completely false, as has been shown above. The equity goal is already being violated, and severely so. Opening the university system to competition would not violate it further, but would improve it, as would an open system of entry. Of course, such a system should favor neither income nor inheritance and should provide grants and scholarships for talented people unable to afford the fees. As is the practice in most excellent American universities, anyone who passes the university entrance examination should receive funds enabling them to attend. Incidentally, I would like to see a survey of the sons and daughters of those politicians defending the German system, especially of the Social Democrats, to ascertain how many of them are now studying abroad.

Students consider free access to a university as an entitlement that they do not want to give up, and politicians fear that students would be revolting in the streets if this right were revoked. Consequently, bureaucratic mechanisms of allocation have to be used (see below). Germany has also renounced the option to charge foreign students for the university tuition that they receive. Thus, it is not feasible for a German university to finance a new department building by borrowing and using future student fees as collateral, as can be done in the United Kingdom.

Compression of the Wage Structure: A Reduced Incentive

Compared with other countries, Germany has a compressed structure of wages. This is due only in part to the fact that an informal minimum wage pushes up the lower wages. In addition, higher wages are met with public opposition; and net wages are compressed from above because distribution takes place within the labor income, i.e., from high wage earners to lower wage earners. A compressed wage structure reduces incentives to accumulate human capital. Moreover, empirical studies show that the rate of return on human capital in Germany is lower than in the United States and some other European countries (Wößmann 2003).[8] Whereas in the United States the trend during the 1980s and early 1990s showed an increase in rates of return to education, these rates actually fell in West Germany.

A Central Planning Approach

German universities are administered by the respective ministries of the states. Traditionally, the ministry approves the curricula and the requirements for the degrees; it also selects each new professor from a list of three candidates proposed by the university (as is the custom of choosing a new bishop for a vacant diocese by the Roman authority in the Catholic Church). It negotiates the professor's salary, and also determines the

---

[8] Returns are, however, higher than e.g., in France, Italy, and the Scandinavian countries.

maximum number of students a university department has to take in and sets the department's capacity accordingly. Standards specify the teaching capacity of an institution and the number of students it can take. Thus, the approach to this important segment of the economy is a governmental administrative planning approach, making use of capacity norms, standards influenced by past experience, and bureaucratic allocation procedures. It is a Gosplan-type approach, as in former central planning. In areas where capacity is lower than the number of students seeking admittance, a central governmental agency allocates the scarce places to students in a nationwide bureaucratic process in which criteria other than quality also play a role. As in the labor market, Germans believe in *Behörden*, in governmental agencies. As in the labor market, they find it difficult to understand that competition can and must be the approach adopted for the university system.

Target Contracts

A new approach that is becoming fashionable concerns target contracts, in which the respective ministry of culture and education of a German Land and the university agree on a contract (*Zielvereinbarungen*) defining the targets of the university; at the same time, the government guarantees to finance the university for some years. In a way this is a principal-agent contract, in which the principle, the ministry, attempts to steer the behavior of the agent, the university. Owing to the dire fiscal situation in the last five years, the government in question often has not been able to keep to its promises, so these contracts have proved disappointing for the universities. Moreover, such contracts are extremely difficult to draw up, because the ministry must fully anticipate the behavior of the universities. Since the agents have better information, these contracts run into similar informational disincentive problems as those that arise in traditional central planning between the planner and the firms.

The pay of university professors, who are lifetime government officials, is regulated by law. As public servants, all are included in the annual pay increases, regardless of performance. In addition, the pay scale is in several stages; a professor attains a higher scale when he gets an offer from another university. All these conditions mean that, if a university is doing a good job, it is due not to the institutional incentive structure, but to the intrinsic motivation of some of its members.

Universities also operate according to the rules of codetermination, as specified in the university laws of the Länder. These decisions, which differ from state to state, are taken in faculty councils and the university senate with the participation of groups of professors, assistants, students, and administrative staff. Some decisions, e.g., choice of candidates for a professorship, require the assent of a majority of the professors. In addition, the rules of the personnel council and the equal opportunity conditions have to be respected. For instance, the hiring of personnel (including assistants, but not professors) is subject to the approval of the personnel council in most of the federal states. All exams, however, are exempt from the rules of codetermination; they remain at the discretion of the professor. As in firms, these institutional arrangements have been devised with the goal of reaching consensus. They are the result of attempts in the 1970s to introduce explicit participation into the German institutional setup.

Favoring the Incumbents

The German educational system is not geared to change. It is characterized by path dependency. Known trajectories often are comfortable—and this in spite of the fact that universities represent a walk of life where innovation is the key word. As in other areas already discussed, incumbents are favored. Inside the system, those who are well established have an edge in defending their position, for instance with respect to the allocation of funds within a university. The system hands them the tools to ensure their prevalence. If excellence is not there, it is hard to produce it. It is difficult to change a mediocre situation. The system also favors existing universities in Germany since they are financed by the government irrespective of their performance. For the newly founded private universities, there is no fair market access. In raising funds for their endowment or operation in order to enter the market, they must overcome a sizable threshold. All this impedes innovative changes and couples the system to the status quo.

CONCLUSION: NO EXCELLENCE, NO EQUALITY

The German approach to the university system, and to education in general, is a mixture of an administrative approach and a social policy. It forgoes the target of quality, but fails to achieve the target of equality.

Competition as the Solution

Many proposals have been made to improve the German university system. These include shortening the duration of studies by introducing a Bachelor's Degree (now being widely implemented), distinguishing better professional and academic tracks, changing the legal status of the universities which are statuary public corporations, granting universities more institutional independence, opening new channels of funding including tuition fees, and organizing an official ranking system of universities. The main point, however, is the need to use competition as the central mechanism for organizing the tertiary educational system. Universities should compete for the best students and the best professors, and students should compete for the best universities. Student fees are a part of this approach, but they must be accompanied by a system of scholarships or other ways of financing that will guarantee that everyone who passes the entrance exam will be able to study. Student fees will not be sufficient to finance the university system entirely. The funding of universities must therefore be linked to the number of students a university is able to attract.[9] Funding for basic research should be provided by the government. Universities that are not viable should be closed. University policy should not be dominated by regional policy of the state. Competition would stimulate the imagination for new solutions and represent a discovery process, and should apply to all universities. The proposal made by Chancellor Schröder in January 2004, to organize a contest to determine the five best universities and then award them some prize money, is insufficient and even misleading; it is rooted in the administrative governmental philosophy and does not remove the obstacles to excellence that characterize the German system.

Technology and Industrial Policy

In a market economy, the division of labor between the government and the private sector stems from the distinction between public and private goods. This also applies to technology policy. The results of basic research represent a public good that can be used by all. *Basic research* lays the groundwork for innovations; it is an input into private invention and new technological applications. *Applied research* and specific inventions represent private goods for which property rights can be defined through patents and copyrights. Although the delineation of the two types of technological knowledge is difficult to draw, the division of labor between the state and the private sector goes along the following lines: it is the state's role to define the conditions for basic research, to organize it, and to finance it; whereas it is the function of the private sector to search for knowledge that can be applied in new products and new production processes. In implementing innovations, the private investor has to evaluate the risks and the returns of specific innovation—if he succeeds he can reap the profit; if he fails he has to bear the costs.

[9] This can be done with a voucher system.

In organizing basic research, the expected, broadly defined, benefits and costs should be compared; research lines with the most promising net benefit should then be pursued, led by market forces. This procedure should be organized by means of competition. New knowledge by definition is not known ex ante: it requires research. Government itself, politicians, parliamentarians, and bureaucrats in a ministry—none have a priori information on what the knowledge frontier will be ten years from now. There is also the risk of political capture and rent-seeking by interest groups, including those from industry and academia, who want to see research lines financed so as to yield specific benefits to themselves. The government therefore should be cautious in deciding which research lines should be followed. This also applies, of course, to the European Union.

Germany has organized its basic research in five major institutions. The *Herman von Helmholtz Association of National Research Centers* represents the largest of the natural science research institutions with 24 000 employees, 10 000 of whom are researchers. It has a financial volume of €2.1 billion in 2003. The *Max Planck Institutes*, with 12 000 employees, 3500 researchers, and a financial volume of €1.24 billion (again in 2003), are active mostly in the natural sciences, but also in the social sciences. The *Wissenschaftsgemeinschaft Gottfried Wilhelm Leibnitz*, with 12 400 employees, 5 300 researchers, and a financial volume of €0.95 billion, encompasses institutes of different disciplines, including Germany's economic research institutes and quite a few institutes in East Germany. The *German Research Association (Deutsche Forschungsgemeinschaft)*, with €1.26 billion, funds research of individual researchers and research groups. The research organization with respect to applied research is the *Fraunhofer Gesellschaft*, with 13 000 employees and a financial volume of €1.0 billion (Siebert and Stolpe 2002). In all these organizations, competition is used as a method of allocating funds and of controlling expenditures.

Applied technology has received a stark focus in German technology policy. A first aspect of this is the weight given to the diffusion of new knowledge and the application of new technological knowledge (Ergas 1997, Siebert and Stolpe 2002). A second is that German research aims to adapt to mature technologies and to incrementally improve them. Although Germany's technological sophistication and productivity per hour are high, it has to wait for technological breakthroughs from abroad and then pay for them to be adopted domestically. Essentially, as the period of catch-up has ended, Germany is finding it hard to generate economic growth endogenously by developing its own technologies.

A third aspect concerns the specific, government-picked, future technologies that received large subsidies in the past. These include the fast breeder SNR 300, the high-temperature reactor, the Siemens large-capacity computer, and the Transrapid. They all failed. These examples do not suggest that a US mission-type technology policy would be successful under the German conditions. Only the Airbus, a cooperative effort with other European nations, can be considered a positive example, if one neglects the heavy subsidies that were paid for it. The concept of private-public partnership also proved to be unsuccessful, as witnessed by the failure to introduce a modern, satellite-based Toll-Collect system on the German highways by 2004.

There are quite a few reasons why an activist governmental technology policy of picking technological winners is likely to fail. Technological breakthroughs usually require an environment with many complementary positive technological developments. It is often impossible to force innovations when these conditions are not in place (Klodt 2004). The government simply does not have the a priori information about which technology will succeed. The risk that it will become the victim of political capture and rent-seeking of firms and sectors is high. The costs of applied technologies are likely to be picked up by the government, especially when they fail. Moreover, the technological orientation of government is likely to change over time, for instance when governments change after elections. Thus, in the 1960s and 1970s nuclear energy was heavily subsidized; now an exit plan from nuclear energy is to be implemented.

Technological policy is a tempting field for an interventionist politician. With specific technological projects, he can show the electorate in a media-influenced democracy that he is active. Technological symbols make nice pictures on television. Thus, the politician derives legitimacy from technological policy. Whether, five or ten years later, the dreams have materialized does not count. This type of policy is likely to lead to "ad-hockery," to inefficiency and the wasting of resources, and to inconsistency over time (chapter 14). This also applies to the German-Franco-British idea, formulated in early 2004, of installing a EU commissioner in charge of technology policy and giving him special recognition by making him the vice president of the European Union.

As a corollary, a number of conditions must be met for technology policy to be successful. One is that the university system must be internationally competitive: only then will it be able to provide sufficient stimuli for basic and applied research. Second, it will have to supply the qualified researchers that high-tech firms need. Third, product market regulations should not prevent or impair either basic or applied research; and economic conditions in terms of taxation, contributions to social securities, and entrepreneurial freedom influence where the actual investment will take place. Today, if an invention occurs in one country, that is not a sufficient reason for the innovation to occur in the same country; the new knowledge may very well be applied in another country.

In addition to all of this, German industrial policy is biased toward old and declining sectors such as coal and shipbuilding, which have always been heavily subsidized. This is an aspect of social protection, but it means that the government is favoring old technologies that are no longer competitive. Germany's strategy to play it safe and let others take the risk has come full circle and is now putting Germany in a very difficult position. In eastern Germany the approach has been to subsidize new capital. This may imply a modern technology, but it can also mean over-capitalization and excess supply.

CHAPTER TWELVE

The Fiscal Policy Stance

Germany's fiscal policy condition has deteriorated since 2001. From 2002 to 2004, the budget deficit exceeded the Maastricht limit of 3 percent of GDP in all three years. Tax revenue remains way below expectations, the strategy of budget consolidation has been abandoned, and the public's confidence in the government's fiscal policy is in jeopardy. As in other policy areas, major reforms are required to effectively institute the structural features needed to redress the situation. The high debt-GDP ratio limits the maneuvering space of government, the revenue-sharing mechanism prevents a competitive federalism, and the finance minister has to pick up the deficits that social policy leaves behind. These factors not only weaken the prospects for reform, but also make a steady fiscal policy nearly impossible and even put its sustainability into question. The already high annual transfers to the social security system and its implicit debt will preoccupy German economic policy for the next two decades.[1]

GOVERNMENT SPENDING

In Germany the public sector absorbs half of GDP. The state's share in GDP amounted to 49.2 percent in 2003, and 48.5 percent was forecast for 2004. This includes the federal level of government, the Länder, the municipalities, and the social security system. The share has increased by nearly twenty percentage points since 1950, when it was 31.6 percent (table A12.1 in the appendix). It was 32.9 percent in 1960 and rose by six percentage points in the 1960s; in the 1970s it then grew from 39.1 percent by nine percentage points. In the recessions of 1975 and 1982 it stood at 49.9 and 48.9 percent, respectively. After having been reduced to 44.0 percent in 1989, it rose to a maximum of 50.3 percent in 1996.

In the consolidated budget of the state, i.e., of the public sector, consisting of the three layers of government and the social security system,

[1] I appreciate critical comments from Alfred Boss, Eduard Herda, David Moore, Rolf Peffekoven, and Joachim Scheide.

24.5 percent is spent on wages and intermediate goods, 3.3 percent on investment, 6.3 percent on interest, 3.0 percent on subsidies, and 55.7 percent on social benefits and social purposes (according to the macroeconomic accounts of 2002[2]). The expenditure on social benefits and social purposes are predominantly expenditures of the social security system.

Germany is a federal state. Federalism entails assigning tasks to those layers of government that are best fit to solve them. Accordingly, issues of a local nature are handled at the local level, where relevant information is most likely to be available and local preferences can be voiced. Thus, municipalities are involved in shaping local public goods and addressing local problems. This means, for instance, that they are responsible for the local infrastructure and for administering social welfare. Issues with a larger, but intermediate, dimension are allocated to the federal states, the Länder; and problems where the benefits or costs affect the country as a whole are dealt with at the national level. Note that the spatial dimension of public goods is also discussed under the matter of the spatial extent of technological externalities or spillover effects. The method of first assigning tasks to the lowest level of government, and then assigning those tasks that cannot be solved at that level to the next higher level of government is referred to as the Subsidiarity Principle in continental European tradition. This principle is at the heart of federalism. The assignment of public goods of different spatial dimensions to different levels of government provides the guideline for the allocation of expenditures and revenues to the different levels ("fiscal equivalence": Olson 1969).

The expenditures of government, i.e., of the three organizational layers of the state—the federal level, the Länder, and the municipalities—excluding the social security system, account for about three-fifths of the state's spending. The social security system takes up the remainder. The federal layer comprises about 40 percent of government spending (table 12.1). There are many cross-flows between the different layers; therefore the sum of the gross expenditures is not identical to consolidated spending of either the federal government or the state governments.[3] For instance, the federal government provides transfers to the Länder, and the Länder allocate funds to the municipalities. Moreover, the social security systems receive transfers from the federal level.

As was argued in chapter 3, Germany's high share of government spending in GDP can be expected to have a negative impact on the economy, especially on the growth rate. With the German government

---

[2] Data bank of the Bundesbank, A-Staatsausgaben. The data are different in the financial statistics.

TABLE 12.1
Structure of the state's budget, 2002 (€bn)[a,b]

	Expenditures	Revenues	Balance
Government	645	577	−68
Federal	302	268	−34
Federal states	289	258	−31
Municipalities	155	152	−3
Social insurance	465	459	−6[b]
State	1024	950	−74

Source: Federal Statistical Office, Macroeconomic Accounts.
[a] Unconsolidated flows, therefore not addable vertically.
[b] Figure rounded downward.

controlling aggregate spending amounting to nearly half of GDP, it is likely that Germany is on the right-hand slope of a bell-shaped curve representing growth rate versus share of governmental spending. A reduction in the government's expenditures would free up resources and create more maneuvering space for the private sector, would stimulate new initiatives by firms, and would entice the efforts of market participants. This prescription applies particularly to the overwhelming part of government expenditures on consumption; governmental expenditures on investment stood only at 1.6 percent of GDP in 2002, having fallen to one third of its 1970 level. The task of German economic policy must be to determine the optimal size of governmental activity and to rethink and reduce the role of government spending in the market economy.

THE TAX SYSTEM

The two taxes raising the highest revenue are the income tax and the value added tax (table 12.2). The income tax has as its tax base both individual income and the income of corporations. It includes seven income categories, among them the wage income of employees, the income of the self-employed (assessed income tax), and income from capital. The corporate tax, a tax on the income of incorporated firms, normally provides a revenue of around €20 billion per year; however, it raised revenues of

---

[3] Not all transfers are calculated identically. Thus, at the federal level supplementary transfers to the Länder are netted with tax receipts so that they appear as a lowering of tax revenue, whereas financial transfers represent expenditures and are itemized on the expenditure side.

TABLE 12.2
Tax revenue, 2003 (€bn)[a,b]

Income tax (wage income plus assessed income)	138.0
Corporate income tax	7.5
Other income taxes[b]	28.4
Value added tax	137.0
Petroleum tax	43.1
Local business tax	24.2
Other taxes	92.9
Total revenue	442.2

Source: German Council of Economic Advisers (2003: 266).
[a] Preliminary data.
[b] Tax on interest income, solidarity payment.

only €7.5 billion in 2003, €2.9 billion in 2002, and even a negative revenue of −€0.4 billion in 2001 owing to the tax reform of 2000. The value added tax is paid on the value generated at each stage of production. (This is passed on to the final domestic consumption price.) Investment and exports are exempt from it. Another tax that raises a significant amount of revenue is the petroleum tax, on gas for cars and on heating oil; the local business tax is yet another important source of revenue for the municipalities.

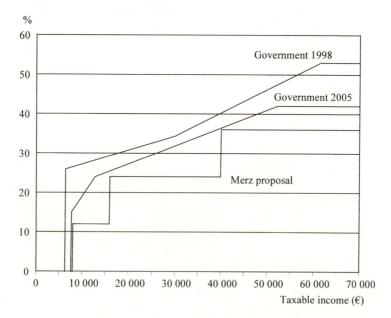

Figure 12.1   Marginal income tax rates.

The distribution of tax revenue also reflects the federal structure. Thus, returns from the two taxes with the highest revenues are split between the federal, state, and municipal levels of government. The federal level and the Länder each receive broadly 42.5 percent of the wage and assessed income tax revenue, with the remaining 15 percent going to the municipalities. The corporate income tax is split half and half between the federal government and the Länder. The revenue of the value added tax is divided between the federal government, the Länder, and the municipalities in the proportions of 51.4, 46.5, and 2.1 percent, respectively. While the petroleum tax is purely a federal tax, the tax on property (real estate) is purely a local tax. At present, a wealth tax is not levied.

From 2005, the income tax will be imposed at a taxable income base of €7 665 per year for single individuals at a tax rate of 15 percent. Income below that threshold will not be taxed. The tax rate then increases in stages to a maximum of 42 percent for incomes of €52 152 and over. These rates represent the marginal rate. In the income bracket up to €12 755, the marginal rate increases steeply to 25.97 percent; it then rises more slowly up to €52 151. For a married couple, total income is split in half and each half is then taxed separately (known as "splitting"). For each child, €5 808 can be deducted per year from the taxable income. Families that do not earn enough to benefit from this arrangement receive a child allowance (*Kindergeld*) amounting to €154 for each of the first three children and €179 for each child thereafter.

Value added tax is paid on the additional value generated at each stage of production, where "value generated" means income paid to factors of production plus pure profits at each stage. The tax base is defined as sales minus costs for intermediate products bought from other suppliers minus investment expenditures. Each firm pays tax on its revenue and subtracts the value added tax paid by the previous suppliers in the vertical chain of production. There is no value added tax for exports, including exports to the other EU countries. Exporting firms can deduct the value added tax paid by the previous suppliers. Imports are taxed with the value added tax. This means that in the European Union the country where the product is finally consumed carries the burden of the value added tax (the so-called Principle of Destination). Investment goods also are exempt from value added tax. Thus, the value added tax is de facto a tax on consumption. Unlike a cumulative sales tax, it avoids accumulating the amount of tax over the vertical chain of production. The rate of the value added tax in Germany is 16 percent; however, a reduced rate of 7 percent applies to foodstuff, media products, and some other goods. There is no value added tax on housing rents for private persons.

In addition to some changes introduced in 1998–2001, the tax reform passed in parliament in 2000 reduces the tax load in several consecutive steps over 2001–2005 (table 12.3). Regarding income tax for individuals, the threshold of taxable income has been raised; moreover, the initial income tax rate has been brought down, so that people with lower incomes pay less in taxes. The maximum income tax rate also has been lowered considerably, down to 42 percent from 53.0 percent in 1998. However, the threshold from which the maximum income tax rate applies has also been brought down, so that the maximum rate now applies to lower incomes. The revenue elasticity of the reformed income tax scheme is even higher than the elasticity for the 1998 tax, according to a simulation, owing to the steeper rise in the marginal tax rate over some income ranges (Boss and Elendner 2003).

For firms, the rate of the corporate income tax has been reduced from 45.0 percent in 1998 to 25.0 percent. This rate applies independently of whether earnings are retained or are paid out as dividends. Additionally, all firms must pay the local business tax, so that the combined tax rate is estimated at 39 percent for incorporated businesses, i.e., stock companies and limited liability companies. The owners of small firms can deduct part of the local business tax from their peronsal income tax. The tax load for firms is still high compared with other countries. Thus, for incorporated firms the marginal tax rate is estimated to be 40.7 percent in 2003, with an effective marginal rate of 31.1 percent, and an effective average rate of 37.2 percent. This is higher than in France (apart from the effective marginal rate),[4] Italy, Ireland, the Netherlands, and Sweden (Council of Economic Advisers 2003: table 58).

For the owner of capital, who supplies his savings, the tax rate is different from that of the firms because he must pay personal income tax on his dividends or interest income. There is no capital gains tax outside the speculation period.[5] However, only half of his dividend income is subject to the personal income tax rate, the argument being that the income was already taxed at the firm level (the "half-income approach," or *Halbeinkünfteverfahren*). Prior to the tax reform, the capital owner could deduct the corporate income tax already paid by the firm from his income tax liability (the "credit approach," or *Anrechnungsverfahren*). Therefore the reduction in the tax rate of firms does not mean a similar reduction for the capital owner. The smaller and medium-sized firms complain that the tax reform favors the larger, incorporated companies. As long as the firms keep their profits as retained earnings, the earnings effectively have a lower tax rate than dividends for the suppliers of capital. Indeed, the tax is not neutral

[4] For France, the rates are 35.4 percent, 34.9 percent, and 34.1 percent; for Italy 38.3 percent, 32.4 percent, and 21.4 percent; and for Sweden 28.0 percent, 23.3 percent, and 17.0 percent.

[5] One year for shares, ten years for houses.

TABLE 12.3
Tax base and tax rates of the income tax, 1998–2005[c]

Year	Income tax threshold (€)	Taxable income at which the maximum rate applies (€)	Initial income tax rate (%)	Maximum income tax rate (%)	Corporate income tax rate for retained earnings (%)
1998	6365	61042	25.9	53.0[a]	45.0
1999	7067	61042	23.9	53.0[a]	40.0
2000	7499	58696	22.9	51.0[a]	40.0
2001	7093	55568	19.9	48.5	25.0[b]
2002	7235	55008	19.9	48.5	25.0[b]
2003	7235	55008	19.9	48.5	26.5[b]
2004	7426	52293	17.0	47.0	25.0[b]
2005	7664	52152	15.0	42.0	25.0[b]

Source: Federal Ministry of Finance, Boss and Elendner 2003.
[a] A different rate applied to commercial income; maximal tax rate 47, 45 and 43 percent, respectively.
[b] Applies also to the distribution of dividends.

with respect to the legal forms of enterprise. However, the person who provides capital is taxed at about the same effective rate, independently of whether he invests in his own firm or in a publicly traded company and a limited liability company.

The application of different tax rates to enterprises and to persons, as is the case in Germany now, requires a clear separation of the tax base for the enterprise sector from that of individuals. In the case of sole proprietorships, many details in the taxation laws have to be specified to delineate the two areas. In the case of incorporated firms, the more favorable tax rate for them requires some type of additional taxation when ownership titles are sold. This would mean that a capital gains tax would become necessary in such a system, at least when the equity titles are sold.

On a more fundamental aspect, there are two different concepts of an income tax system (German Council of Economic Advisers 2003). According to the concept of a synthetic income tax, all types of income are subject to the same tax rate. This avoids delineation issues. Admittedly, the German system has become inconsistent because of the many exemptions. One line of reform therefore is a simplified tax system where exemptions are abolished and tax rates come down. This was highlighted in 2003 by the Merz proposal of the Christian Democrats; similar proposals have been made by the Council of Economic Advisers in its Annual Reports of the 1990s, the Bareis Commission, the previous constitutional court judge Kirchhoff (2004), the Petersberger Beschlüsse of the Christian Democrats, and the Liberal Democrats.

According to an alternative approach, a distinction should be made between taxing capital income (the enterprise sector, dividends, and interest) and other income, i.e., income from labor. (This is the "dual income tax approach.") Since capital is mobile internationally, a lower tax rate should be applied to capital income, as in the Scandinavian approach. This concept, for which the German Council of Economic Advisers has expressed consideration in its Annual Report 2003/04, has to solve the delineation issue for the multitude of firms falling between the enterprise sector and the individual area. It is likely to entail bureaucratic decisions. This is a specific problem with respect to the Mittelstand.

This approach may lend itself to a more active and interventionist role of government, defining income taxation from the aspect of functionality instead of from the premise that the state's infringement on the individual's maneuvering space and liberty should be limited.

Subsidies

Governmental financial support to firms and households plays an important role in the German economy. Subsidies can be explicit transfer payments or can come in the form of tax breaks. Under the narrow interpretation used in macroeconomic accounting, subsidies are transfers to producers. This delineation would exclude transfers to households and to targeted groups of society, which constitute an important element of governmental transfers in a social market economy. It would also exclude transfers to semi-public service suppliers or tax breaks for them, such as the supply of community heating by municipal suppliers or the operation of museums. I therefore apply the wider definition as used by the Kiel Institute for World Economics, which includes these aspects (Boss and Rosenschon 2002). Subsidies then are defined as financial support or tax breaks, which affect the allocation of resources. They account for €156 billion per year in 2001—equal to 7.5 percent of GDP or 35 percent of total tax revenue.

Subsidies include sector-specific subsidies (€86 billion) for agriculture, coal mining, transportation (especially for the public transport system), housing and subsidies to firms in general, such as in regional and structural policy, and employment policy (table 12.4). Subsides also include transfers to specific groups, e.g., housing allowances for low-income groups, but they do not include funds spent for the general functioning of the state, such as for poverty relief, or on schools, universities, and

TABLE 12.4
Subsidies, 2001 €bn

By kind and source		By target	
Financial support	116	Sector-specific subsidies to firms	86
		of which	
Federal level	−30	Agriculture	−13
Federal states and municipalities	−71	Coal mining	−5
European Union	−6	Transportation	−24
Federal Labor Office	−9	Housing	−22
Tax breaks	40	Non-sector-specific subsidies to firms	25
		of which	
		Regional and structural policy	−6
		Employment policy	−11
		Subsidies to semi-public services	45
Total subsidies	156	Total subsidies	156

Source: Boss and Rosenschon (2002: tables 5 and 6).

research organizations like the Max Planck institutes. Subsidies can come from any of the three layers of government, the Federal Labor Office, or the European Union.

The political compromise between the government and the Bundesrat in December 2003 that enabled part of the tax reduction to be moved forward by one year also saw the reduction of two subsidies: the financial assistance to families for building a house, and the tax allowance for commuters to work—which, incidentally, had been expanded only in 1990 by the Red–Green government. Subsidies to the coal industry were set to end in 2005; in November 2003, however, the Chancellor promised a continuation of these subsidies until 2012, amounting in total to €16 billion for the whole period. In principle, this violates the EU's code on state aid. But, in a compromise with the European partners, Germany secured the votes of some EU countries and obtained the permission of the EU Council to continue the coal subsidies. In return, it agreed that these countries could continue their preferential treatment of their trucking industries. Thus, together with German taxpayers, German truckers are paying for the coal subsidies.

This identification of subsidies does not include all types of state aid. This is because the calculations are simply too difficult. For instance, the bail-out obligation of municipalities and the federal states vis-à-vis the savings banks and the federal states' banks are not factored in. Another aspect ignored is that the electricity distributors are forced to purchase electricity produced from windmills and facilities cogenerating heat at an artificially high price.

Subsidies create large opportunity costs. These costs stem from the heavier tax burden, which reduces the efforts of workers and entrepreneurs and negatively affects labor supply and demand as well as investment. Traditionally, the inefficient or less productive sectors receive state aid, so that overall productivity is reduced. As a result, new sectors are hurt, and allocation is distorted. Firms engage in rent-seeking in an attempt to receive favorable treatment, instead of competing in the marketplace. Once an economy gets used to subsidies, it is difficult for a politician to say "no" when a firm, a sector, or a whole region finds itself in trouble. Moreover, subsidies are one reason for a high government share of GDP, which has a negative impact on growth once a certain threshold is surpassed. Germany from time to time has considered cutting subsidies, either in a "lawnmower approach," reducing all subsidies by an equal percentage, or by getting rid of specific subsidies. At the same time, new subsidies, e.g., for windmills or for the cogeneration of electric power and heat, are introduced.

TABLE 12.5
Income distribution before and after taxation, Gini coefficients, 2000

	West Germany	New Länder	Germany
Market income before taxation	0.4459	0.4758	0.4549
Income after taxation and transfers	0.2843	0.2253	0.2777

Source: German Council of Economic Advisers (2002: 350).

DISTRIBUTIONAL ELEMENTS IN THE BUDGET

Besides its function of allocation, i.e., of providing public goods, Germany's fiscal policy traditionally has a distributive role. A large part of government expenditure is for social purposes. Analyzing governmental expenditures by function, 42 percent of the expenditures of the federal government (€102 billion out of €243 billion in 2001) are for social purposes, according to the government's official classification. This includes transfers to the social security system—one-fifth of the expenditures of the social security systems comes from tax revenue (see below)—unemployment benefits of type II, social policy for farmers, education allowances (*Erziehungsgeld*), maternity benefits (*Mutterschutz*), and payments for war victims and their widows (see chapter 5). There are additional expenditures that are not included in the social expenditures but do have a social dimension, such as for education (€0.7 billion), housing benefit (€1.8 billion), and subsidies for the coal industry (€3.6 billion).

The effect of the government's activity on the distribution of income can be seen by comparing the Gini coefficients for income distribution before and after taxation and government transfers. For the households surveyed in the Socio-economic Panel (Council of Economic Advisers 2003: 349), this coefficient is reduced considerably when comparing the market income distribution with the distribution after government activity (table 12.5): it is 39 percent lower for the united Germany. This means that taxes and transfers have made income distribution more equal. For East Germany, the coefficient fell by 53 percent, showing the more redistributive nature of government activity there.[6]

[6] The average income per month in the sample is lowered from €3908 to €3058 for Germany. Note that the average here is weighted in the sense that the head of the family receives a different weight from other family members.

The Impact of German Unification

To effect the transformation of the previously centrally planned economy in eastern Germany into a market economy, quite sizable transfers were needed. The precise magnitude of these transfers, however, is difficult to calculate. The last official estimate of the transfers was undertaken by the German Council of Economic Advisers (1995: table 40).[7] The Council distinguished between gross or unconsolidated transfers from the different layers of the state, and net transfers. The net transfers were defined by consolidating the transfers of the different layers, i.e., eliminating double counting, and by taking into account government revenue such as tax revenue in the new (eastern) states. For 1995 the gross transfers, including interest payments and repayment of debt directly associated with unification, were estimated at €108 billion; net transfers amounted to €82 billion or, neglecting interest and repayment of debt, to €64 billion. This was 4.6 percent[8] (unconsolidated between the different layers of government) or 3.6 percent of the German GDP (consolidated, i.e., without doubling counting), respectively. Of the two, the consolidated figure is the relevant one.

Of the gross transfers of €108 billion, 28 percent went to the public sector, i.e., to the budgets of the new Länder, 22 percent was provided by the public budgets to private households, and 26 percent went to households through the social security system. Of the transfers to households, €14.6 billion flowed to East German households via the pension system; €12 billion was transmitted via unemployment insurance. Unfortunately, only a small part of all the transfers, about a quarter, was used for investment, while the overwhelming part represented, and still represents, transfers for consumption purposes, including government consumption. This holds true not only for transfers within the social security systems, but also (largely) for transfers between the layers of government, for instance for paying for the over-manned administration in East Germany.

Transfers are still being made to eastern Germany, but for a variety of reasons we do not have sufficient data on their magnitude. First, we no longer have a separate macroeconomic accounting for the expenditure side of East German GDP; the last separate status was for the year 1994. Such accounts would make it possible to calculate a balance of payments with the current account deficit for East Germany and thus to determine the real resource flow. Second, one cannot simply interpret government spending at the federal level in eastern Germany as transfers, e.g., to the

---

[7] For other estimates see Deutsche Bundesbank (1996) and Boss and Rosenschon (1996).

[8] The original figure is 4.7 percent; GDP was revised downward.

transportation infrastructure or the army, because the federal government makes expenditures for the same purpose in western Germany as well; therefore, one would need a norm from which to calculate spending above the norm. Third, the mobility of people, including commuters, makes it more difficult to calculate financial flows to eastern Germany. For instance, commuters pay contributions to the social security system in western Germany, and people do their shopping and pay the value added tax in both eastern and western parts. Fourth, the regional delineation is complex. With respect to Berlin, only East Berlin belonged to the former German Democratic Republic; but, of course, we do not have separate data for East Berlin. What is more important, it makes little sense, in a problem-solving approach, to look at the East German region without Berlin. Also, there was little interest among the political elites in emphasizing the transfer concept, for fear that East Germans would feel that they were not getting enough and West Germans would believe they were paying too much to finance the transfer. Such a debate would be a source of friction instead of harmony between the two parts of the country.

One can argue that the size of transfers has decreased since 1995. There has been economic growth in eastern Germany, and the tax base has been enlarged. With a higher personal income, more contributions are being paid into the social security system. Unemployment, though still high, has receded. Governmental programs for the unemployed have been scaled down considerably. Specific investment subsidies for the private sector have been discontinued so that the same regional support scheme applies as in western Germany, albeit with higher flows to the East because of the lower level of GDP per capita there.

Nevertheless, transfers still flow to eastern Germany. These include transfers from government to the enterprise sector, from the federal government to the public budgets of the federal states in eastern Germany (vertical revenue-sharing), within the revenue-sharing among the federal states (horizontal revenue-sharing), and within the social security system. There are two major types of investment aid to firms: a tax subsidy (*Investionszuschuss*), with a volume of €2.3 billion in 2002, and an investment support in the context of regional policy, with a volume of €1.9 billion in 2002 (*Gemeinschaftsaufgabe regionale Wirtschaftsförderung*). Whereas an investor in the producing sector or the production-related service sector is entitled to a tax subsidy of 12.5 percent of the investment outlay (25 percent for small and medium-sized firms) according to federal law, the investment support, which can reach 50 percent of the investment for small firms in structurally weak areas, is granted upon a filed application and is subject to the financial means available. It is administered by the Länder. The tax subsidy was supposed to stop at the end of 2004 but has now been extended to 2006. The investment support is a normal policy instrument in regional policy and therefore will continue. With respect to the flows within the governmental system, the federal layer provides supplementary transfer payments (*Bundeser-gänzungszuweisungen*) in a vertical revenue-sharing. In addition, a scheme which is to be effective until 2019 has been agreed upon for the flows between the federal layer of government and the eastern German Länder (*Solidarpakt Ost*). These flows, with an annual volume of €3.4 billion, are intended to finance infrastructure projects (*Sonderbe-darfs-Bundesergänzungszwuuweisungen*). Together, these vertical flows to the five states in eastern Germany amounted to €10.2 billion in 2002. Adding the federal supplementary transfer payments to the horizontal flows from the other Länder, the eastern German federal states received a total of €13.4 billion in 2002 (see table 12.6 on page 280). The horizontal transfers between the Länder are indicative of the institutional setup of Germany's revenue-sharing (see below). With respect to the flows within the social budget, the West-East transfers are estimated €27.9 billion for 2001 (Federal Ministry of Health and Social Security 2002: table 43). This is the upper bound for flows within the social security system for which there are no official data. The sum amounts to about €45 billion, which is about 2 percent of GDP.

It is apparent that these transfers have affected Germany's fiscal position negatively. Transfers were financed partly by higher taxes, though admittedly only to a minor extent. Nevertheless, taxes had to be raised; they could not be reduced as in other countries. A larger part of the transfers was financed through credit, leading to a doubling of government debt from €0.46 trillion (1989) or 42 percent of GDP to €1.35 trillion in 2003 (64.2 percent of GDP); a debt of €1.42 trillion is forecast for 2004. Transfers and debt have repercussions on the maneuvering space of government in many ways. In the first place, the interest load is high, with 15.2 percent of the tax revenue being spent on servicing the public debt. Another consequence is that the option to reduce taxes is severely limited by the interest load for new debt. Thus, even after the 2000 tax reform, the final stage of which will be implemented in 2005, the effective tax rates for German firms are high relative to the other EU countries. All of this has had a negative impact on growth; to put it differently, a potential stimulus for economic growth was not available.

There are additional consequences for Germany's economic position. Transfers were organized within the social security system. The share of contributions to social security increased from 15.0 percent of GDP in 1990 in West Germany to 17.5 percent in 2001.[9] It is not clear to what extent this increase can be traced exclusively to transfers within the system

---

[9] German Council of Economic Advisers, *Annual Report 2002/03*, table 34*

and to what extent it reflects a general expansion of the welfare state. As an example, compulsory nursing care insurance was introduced in 1995, requiring additional contributions amounting to 1.7 percent of the gross wage or 0.8 percent of GDP. But even if only part of the higher contributions within the social systems is due to unification, it means that the tax on labor has been raised in western Germany, with a negative impact on employment there. Another effect of the consumption transfers is that domestic demand increased, leading to a real appreciation of the Deutschmark which affected Germany's competitive position until 1995. It seems that western Germany has been partly inhibited by financing the transfers, but it also seems that it was not able to come through with sufficient economic dynamics to effect a strong carry-over to eastern Germany.

The political demand for transfers can be considered the Achilles heel of German fiscal policy. This demand would be reduced if the catch-up process picked up in eastern Germany; GDP per capita of the population for this region stood at 66.2 percent of the western German figure, including Berlin, in 2002, or 71.2 percent of the overall German level. Unfortunately, the convergence process has come to a halt since 1997. An important prerequisite for strong regional growth is initiative and an optimistic mood, as the rare examples of successful regional restructuring and of a successful quick convergence process in Ireland and, at the municipal level, Pittsburgh show. I hesitate to mention the coastal regions of mainland China as another example. Whereas the majority of people in eastern Germany seem to have a somewhat optimistic outlook, the PDS (Party of Democratic Socialism, the political successor of the previous communist SED) appeals to people's feelings of deprivation and still collects up to 20 percent of the votes in the regional elections. In such an environment, optimism is constrained.

The demand for transfers would also weaken if eastern Germans were prepared to give up their mentality that 100 percent of the west German level must be attained on all accounts in the East and accept the fact that the same conditions cannot prevail everywhere in the federal republic, that the same income per capita cannot be reached in every locality of the country, and that the same public infrastructure cannot be provided everywhere. The policy issue for Germany, then, is to inject more economic dynamics into eastern Germany.

THE DOUBLING OF DEBT

Tax revenue in Germany has not been sufficient to finance the expenditures of the state. Since 1990, the deficit of the state budget has been 3.0 percent on average per year. It seems to have become normal business practice to finance government expenditures on credit. Only in the years leading up to the establishment of the European Monetary Union, with its entry criteria on the budget deficit and the debt levels, was there some restraint on deficit financing. When we look at the 1990s in more detail, the only annual positive balance in the state's budget, in the year 2000, is due to the special circumstance of auctioning the licenses for the Universal Telecommunications Systems; without these receipts there would have been a deficit in that year as well, in the magnitude of 1.2 percent. The peak in the deficit in 1995 was caused by integrating the debt from the shadow budget of the East German privatization agency (Treuhandanstalt).

Germany has seen quite an increase in debt relative to GDP (figure 12.2; table 12A-1). This ratio has more than doubled from 1970 to 1990, from 18.6 percent in 1970 to 41.8 percent in 1989. Since then it rose again by twenty percentage points to 64.2 percent in 2003. The absolute amount of debt doubled in the 1990s. Only in the 1980s was the budget deficit reduced, and debt increased more slowly in this period. The 1970s and the 1990s were decades in which debt was on a stark rise. Germany violated the maximum 3 percent debt to GDP criterion of the Stability Pact for the European Monetary Union in the years 2002, 2003, and 2004. The deficit of 2.8 percent of GDP in 2001 hardly upheld the spirit of the treaty either. Apparently, an international treaty on the important issue of a common European currency does not represent a sufficient constraint for German government spending.

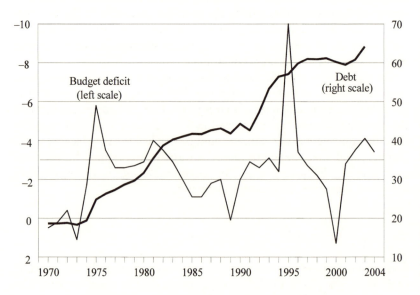

Figure 12.2   Budget deficits and debt, 1970–2004.

Nor have national institutional arrangements succeeded in restraining the increase in public debt. Thus, Article 115 of Germany's Constitution limits the issuing of new debt to the amount of public investment. This requirement has been violated quite often in the last twenty years, because there is a clause in Article 115 specifying that, if the macroeconomic equilibrium is disturbed, the government may incur new debt—i.e., finance expenditures out of credits or reduce taxes—if such expenditures would turn the economy back toward an equilibrium. It has become almost a routine that the government simply proclaims a macroeconomic disturbance once its budget shows a deficit. Governments have not been very choosy in explaining and defining the type of disturbance. For instance, they have regularly pointed to the high rate of unemployment. But this is a phenomenon that has existed for more than two decades, and was well known when budgets were passed in parliament. The government also does not make an effort to prove, as required by the Constitution, that the measures taken will be appropriate to restore equilibrium. The political process, the public, and the media have all become accustomed to not taking this constitutional constraint seriously. Those in charge of the budget violate well established practices and well founded norms. Another institutional feature—that the finance minister has a right of veto against expenditures—has not succeeded in restraining debt, either. The consequence of using the veto would be credible only if in the end the minister were willing to resign, and ministers are reluctant to do that. This instrument has been used only twice, by the Social Democratic ministers Alex Möller in 1971 and Karl Schiller in 1972. Moreover, the inclination of the chancellor to dismiss the minister is simply too strong, so that finance ministers are disinclined to use the veto.

A specific concern is the implicit debt of the public insurance systems. This amount equals the sums of deficits that will arise in the social security system over the next decades, discounted to its present value. In these calculations it is assumed that the benefits continue to be paid according to the actual legal stipulations and that contribution rates remain at their actual level. The ageing of the population is also taken into account. Assuming a GDP growth rate of 1.5 percent and calculating the present value with an interest rate of 3 percent, the German Council of Economic Advisers (2003: 420) estimates the implicit value of debt of the social security system (including the pension system for government officials and deficits of the government) of the period 2002–50 at 270 percent of the GDP of 2002. This figure indicates the size of the adjustment that needs to be made if such a debt is to be prevented. According to previous OECD studies, Italy and France have markedly higher implicit debt than Germany (OECD 1997: table 2).

DISTRIBUTIVE FEDERALISM

A specific feature of Germany's fiscal policy is its federal structure. Fiscal federalism is rooted in German history, where for centuries people lived in a number of independent principalities. Unification occurred only in 1871; however the regional states continued to play an important role in economic decisions. With this historical background, and with the experience of a centralized state under the Nazis, a federal structure was attractive when the new constitution was developed, first to guarantee that regions could voice their preferences, and second as a check on excessive power.

As already discussed, according to fiscal federalism and fiscal equivalence, the federal government level should be in charge of those public goods having a spatial dimension extending over the whole political area, and lower levels should be responsible for those public goods that are spatially less extended. Fiscal equivalence, the subsidiarity principle, and fiscal federalism are concepts relating to allocation. They define organizational layers of governments that are consistent with a hierarchy of public goods in their spatial dimension. These concepts thus belong to Musgrave's (Musgrave and Musgrave 1989) allocation branch. Germany has supplemented this allocation concept by equity considerations, i.e., with the distributive branch. Article 72 of the German Constitution expressly cites the target of achieving similar living conditions throughout the Federal Republic.

The term "living conditions" is vague. Looking at economic conditions in terms of productive capacity, measured by GDP per capita of the population, there *are* differences among the German states. Of course, these are especially great between states in western and eastern Germany. In the new Länder (except Berlin) GDP per capita was 66.2 percent of the overall German level in 2002; it was a little bit higher in Saxony (data for 2002; see table 12A-2). Berlin including East Berlin reached 89.0 percent, while eastern Germany including Berlin was 71.2 percent; western Germany at 107.5 percent was above the German average. Even without the strong differences between eastern and western Germany, it is perfectly normal to have a variance in the economic situation among the Länder. Some of the larger Länder in the West are below the average GDP per capita. For example, Lower Saxony and the Rhineland Palatinate stand at 84 percent of the average western German level, with Schleswig-Holstein and the Saarland one or two percentage points higher. In contrast, the city-states of Hamburg, with 170.4 percent, and Bremen, with 136.0 percent, are above average, as are Hessen

(123.2 percent), Bavaria (116.8 percent), and Baden-Württemberg (113.1 percent).[10]

The reference to similar living conditions does not, however, concern GDP per capita. Indeed, it could not, since GDP per capita is the result of market processes. The requirement of similar living conditions relates to aspects that are under government control, such as the transportation infrastructure and the school and educational system. Not all of these goods are public goods in the strict sense, as defined in economics. Some are *merit goods*, goods judged to be so meritorious that most people want them—kindergartens or schools, for example; of course, the supply of these goods depends on the government's capacity to generate tax revenue. Since this capacity varies among the Lander, a revenue-sharing mechanism was established to provide additional income to those states with a lower tax revenue. This system was in place long before German unification, and applies within western Germany as well.

In horizontal revenue-sharing, the Länder with a relatively high tax revenue transfer part of their takings to the poorer states. Thus, Bavaria gave up €2 billion of its tax receipts in 2002, amounting to 8 percent of its total tax revenue in 2002 (6 percent if the tax revenue of the Bavarian municipalities are also included), whereas Lower Saxony was in receipt of €0.5 billion and Berlin, €2.7 billion (table 12A-2). Total horizontal flows amounted to €7.4 billion. Note that the criterion used in apportioning revenue-sharing, i.e., the power to generate tax revenue, apparently deviates considerably from GDP per capita. Thus, North Rhine-Westphalia, with its GDP per capita at about the German average, makes considerable contributions, whereas Bremen, with a GDP per capita of 136 percent is a major recipient. In vertical revenue-sharing, the federal layer transfers funds to the Länder (*Bundesergänzungszuweisungen*); these flows of €16 billion are in addition to the distribution of revenues from income tax, corporate income tax, and value added tax. Furthermore, other transfers occur in the form of mixed financing (see below).

The formula for revenue-sharing is complex. As a separate aspect, before the revenue of the value added tax is distributed among the federal states according to the population, the weaker Länder receive part of that revenue ("VAT in advance compensation," or *Umsatzsteuer-vorwegausgleich*). When this has been done, and when the capacity to raise revenue for the federal states has been determined, then, beginning in 2005, the marginal fill-up rate for the receiving states will be 75 percent of the difference from the average; this applies to those states whose capacity to generate taxes is less than 80 percent of the Länder

---

[10] There was quite a change in the regional structure in the last thirty years in western Germany. The southern states caught up and overtook the northern states, implying that the northern states fell behind.

TABLE 12.6
Revenue-sharing, 2002 (€bn)

	Revenue-sharing between the Länder	Federal supplementary transfer payments	Total
Paying Länder			
Bavaria	−2.0	–	−2.0
Hessen	−1.9	–	−1.9
Baden–Wurttemburg	−1.6	–	−1.6
Hamburg	−0.2	–	−0.2
North Rhine–Westphalia	−1.6	–	−1.6
Total payments	−7.4	–	−7.4
Receiving Länder			
Berlin	2.7	2.6	5.2
Saxony	1.0	3.2	4.2
Saxony–Anhalt	0.6	2.0	2.6
Thuringia	0.6	1.8	2.4
Brandenburg	0.5	1.8	2.4
Mecklenburg–W. Pomerania	0.4	1.4	1.8
Lower Saxony	0.5	0.8	1.3
Bremen	0.4	0.8	1.2
Rhineland–Palatinate	0.4	0.6	1.0
Saarland	0.1	0.6	0.7
Schleswig–Holstein	0.1	0.3	0.4
Total receipts	7.4	15.9	23.2

Source: Federal Statistical Office [http://www.destatis.de/basis/d/fist/fist023.htm].

average. It then falls to 70 percent until a capacity of 93 percent is reached. For the remaining difference in capacity, the fill-up rate falls to 44 percent. The skim-off rate for the paying states is symmetrical. It starts at 44 percent for the paying states when their capacity to generate tax revenue is just above 100 percent of the average; it goes up to 70 percent when the capacity is 107 percent, and then rises to 75 percent at 120 percent or more of the average capacity (German Council of Economic Advisers 2001: 134). The previous arrangement was declared unconstitutional by the Constitutional Court in 1999 and a change was required by the court, in 2005 at the latest (Figure 12.3).[11] There are

[11] Prior to 2005, the fill-up and skim-off rates were step-wise. For instance, the fill-up rate was 100 percent for a capacity to generate tax revenue of up to 92 percent below the average. This represented an even greater distortion. The fill-up rate then fell to 37.5 percent, which was more incentive-compatible than the new solution. Together with the supplementary vertical transfers by the federal level, it even reversed the ranking of the states in terms of their capacity to raise taxes.

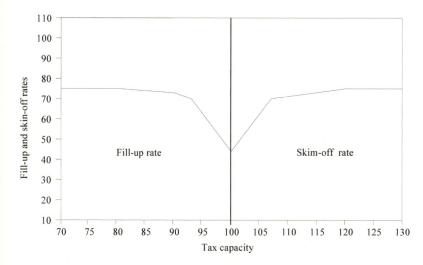

Figure 12.3 Marginal fill-up and skim-off rates in horizontal revenue-sharing.

additional provisions defining the expenditure needs of states; for instance, the population of city-states is weighted by 135 percent on the assumption that they have higher expenditures per capita. Moreover, the average skim-off rate is capped at 72.5 percent; 12 percent of an over-proportional increase in tax revenue relative to the last year is not factored into the revenue of the state paying in.

This system sets the wrong incentives. Federal states that succeed in enlarging their tax base and generating additional tax revenue have to give up part of their additional tax revenue to other federal states. This reduces their incentives to attract firms and economic activities in order to enlarge their tax base, it also weakens incentives of individual states to build up a long-run growth strategy. It helps to cover up political mistakes and does not assign the responsibility for failure to those who cause the failure. Moreover, it prevents an institutional arrangement in which the federal states would be given greater tax autonomy while at the same time taking over more responsibility for the result of their policies. The incidence of the given setup of revenue-sharing would be less severe if the fill-up rate were lowered much more when the states approach the average of the other states. Then the poorer states would be helped, whereas those closer to the average would have to rely on their own initiatives. But such an approach is hard to conceive, given the current political orientation in Germany.[12] It is fair to say that German fiscal federalism is a distributive federalism, not a competitive one.

In addition to this formal mechanism of revenue-sharing, both the federal government and the Länder must provide aid if any one of the federal states becomes insolvent. This is required by the Principle of Cooperation and Support, the Bündisches Prinzip, which is one of the many principles that pertain in German public finance. Thus, according to a decision of the Constitutional Court, both the federal government and the Länder had to step in to help when Bremen and the Saarland fell into financial distress (*Haushaltsnotlage*) in 1992. In the actual solution, only the federal government provided funds for the period 1994–2004; it can be expected that the obligation will be continued after that period. In 2003, in view of its financial distress, Berlin asked the Constitutional Court for similar help. This trend shows that states in financial distress can count on being bailed out. It also implies that the financial markets can serve as a controlling mechanism only in a very limited way.

It should be noted that the German system of fiscal federalism also widely uses the instrument of mixed financing, whereby the federal government and the Länder finance projects together, as a general rule, on a 50/50 basis. For example, Article 91a of the German Constitution designates mixed financing to support the specific joint projects (*Gemeinschaftsaufgaben*) of renovation and expansion in university construction, improvement in regional economic structure, and improvement in agricultural structure and coastal protection. A total of €3.0 billion was dedicated to such projects in 2002. Other collaborations of the federal layer and the Länder that come under mixed financing include the promotion of research and development (€3.2 billion), social housing construction (€0.7 billion), regional transportation improvements (€1.5 billion), and city construction and development (€0.4 billion). Although mixed financing has intensified in the last three decades, it is now common opinion that this type of financing should be reduced to make way for a clearer assignment of responsibilities. In addition, the institutional setup for the voting procedure in many areas, where both the Bundestag and the Bundesrat have to agree, has also been called into question (see chapter 14).

Moreover, it should be noted that flows between the regions also occur in the social security systems. Thus, labor market districts with high unemployment receive funds to pay unemployment benefits from areas in which the unemployment rate is low, but where higher contributions to the insurance are paid. Similarly, in the other branches of the pay-as-you-go systems of social security, the regions with a strong economic activity pay funds out whereas the regions with a lower performance receive funds. Unfortunately, there is not sufficient information on these flows.

---

[12] Cf. the proposal of the German Council of Economic Advisers (2001: 132 passim).

FISCAL POLICY STRATEGY: DEMAND SIDE VERSUS SUPPLY SIDE

Regarding Germany's fiscal policy, the debate between demand-side versus supply-side approaches tends to pop up quite regularly. This discussion has several aspects relating to the business cycle, to growth, and to the philosophical position with respect to the relevance of the demand side versus the supply side for economic policy.

Recessions are characterized by a lack of aggregate demand. It is now common opinion that one should let the automatic stabilizers operate and should accept that thereby a budget deficit may arise or increase. But in the European Monetary Union there is a cap placed on the budget deficit by the Stability Pact, motivated by a desire to defend the stability of money (see next chapter). Those who favor aggregate demand as an important policy variable do not accept this restraint; they are not so concerned with the impact of debt on the stability of money. Quite a few, among them the trade unions, would like the government explicitly to expand aggregate demand in addition to letting the automatic stabilizers operate. They put great weight on the demand stimulus, directly associated with government spending. This group is a minority among German economists, including the Deutsche Institut für Wirtschaftsforschung in Berlin with its strong leaning toward demand policy. The majority of German economists, among them the Kiel Institute for World Economics and the Council of Economic Advisers, points to the long-run and short-run effects of such a demand stimulus. First, it increases debt, because the political process has not been able to balance the budget over the cycle. Institutional restraints simply are not sufficient to control the increase in debt. Thus, the demand stimulus comes at a high cost, and it threatens the sustainability of public finances. Second, it is doubtful whether aggregate demand actually would be stimulated. Government demand accounts for only 20 percent of aggregate demand. If consumers anticipate the long-run effects on debt and expect taxes to be raised in the future, for instance if they see unemployment rising, they would feel uncertain about the future and therefore might tend to increase their savings, which in turn would reduce the most important part of aggregate demand: consumption. Likewise, entrepreneurs might become more cautious with their investment demands. These psychological effects become especially relevant when market participants lose confidence, for instance when a government uses budget deficits over and over again, and when it is clear that politicians are using deficits as a way out of their political malaise.

From the point of view of growth policy, a short-term demand stimulus is an even more questionable concept, since growth policy needs a long-run orientation. Whereas it is true that the growth process requires sufficient aggregate demand, and that a weakness of demand would curtail the growth rate, the growth itself must come from the supply side, i. e. from an increase in the labor force, from capital accumulation, and from technological innovations and institutional improvements. Moreover, in the long run the issue of sustainability becomes more important.

German fiscal policy has had some experience with demand stimulation. For example, the high growth rates of 1990 and 1991 were the result of a Keynesian demand stimulus, initiated by government transfers to eastern Germany, most of them consumption transfers. Distortions in the construction sector and the recession of 1993 were the consequences. Then finance minister Lafontaine, after some government restraint with respect to expenditures since 1992, used the policy of demand stimulus to expand the federal government expenditures in 1999 by about 4 percent in an approach similar to the first two years of the Mitterand presidency in France. He failed after six months because the negative impact quickly became apparent.

EROSION OF CONFIDENCE

It seems to be an ironclad law that during their terms in office finance ministers experience a tarnishing of their reputation with a resulting loss of public confidence. Most of them start out with a strict consolidation plan and a clear determination to keep their budget in balance so that debt does not increase. Only a few can live up to the promise. Among them were Schäffer, who accumulated public funds in the 1950s (it is said in preparation for being able to pay for the Bundeswehr when it was established), and Stoltenberg, who reduced the budget deficit in the 1980s. For most of the others, new and unexpected political problems arose requiring additional financing, for example a recession, or the need for the government to win an important election and therefore to increase spending, or a change in their chancellor's line of politics. More recently, fiscal policy has had to step in when the social security systems ran out of money (see below).

When Eichel took over the position of finance minister from Lafontaine in the spring of 1999 he announced a strategy of consolidation. Instead of Lafontaine's philosophy of aggregate spending, Eichel promised to consolidate the budget. According to his consolidation plan, the federal budget was to be balanced by 2004; this then was shifted to 2006 and eventually given up. Surprisingly, it was after the election in the fall of 2002 that the dire situation of the budget became known to the public. Eichel at first had introduced a new principle into fiscal policy: that of sustainability, a concept stressed by the German Council of Economic Advisers in its

Annual Reports in the 1990s. According to this concept, popular from environmental economics, the long-run effects of fiscal policy, i.e., the opportunity costs for future generations, must be taken into account. Most importantly, this relates to the long-run effects of increased government debt. However, Germany's budget deficit increased from 1.5 percent to GDP in 1999 and 1.2 percent in 2000 (if one excludes the receipts from the sale of licenses for the Universal Mobile Telecommunication Systems (UMTS)) to 3.5 percent in 2002 and 3.9 percent in 2003. These figures apply to the federal state in total, including the social security system and all three layers of government. It is the unpleasant job of the finance minister to assume responsibility not only for the federal government's actions, but also for the expenditures and revenues of the country as a whole. This accountability relates not only to the social security systems, where the federal layer (together with the Länder) has the authority to set the laws, but also to the Länder and municipalities, over whose budgets the federal minister has no direct control. Nevertheless, expenditure by the Bund creates the overwhelming part of the budget deficit, i.e., roughly two-thirds, though varying through the years. Moreover, the federal government is responsible for defining the institutional setting for fiscal policy, including the taxation system.

The increased budget deficit is only one of the indicators of Germany's disappointing fiscal policy situation. Thus, it now has become almost customary that a budget that has been passed in parliament will not survive the year. The budget does not cover all the unexpected expenditures that arise, and it is too optimistic about expected revenue, so that a revised budget, with a much higher deficit, becomes necessary in autumn to correct the formal financing for the year's expenditures.

It is fair to say that the budget deficits are not caused by spending sprees. Expenditures at the federal level increased by 2.3 percent per year from 1999 to 2003 in nominal value, and those of all three layers of government together rose by 2.1 percent. A major factor in the budget deficits is the poor showing of tax revenue. Total tax revenue declined by €22 billion from 2000 to 2001, i.e., by 4.4 percent. It remained at about that lower level in 2002 and increased slightly in 2003—by 1.1 percent, according to the taxation forecast of the German Council of Economic Advisers. Previous recessions of 1975, 1982, and 1992 had not led to a reduction of tax revenue, although in 1975 it more or less stagnated. Thus, one must look for one-off causes or structural factors to explain the recent decline. One possible explanation is that the fall in revenue in 2001 is simply the effect of the tax reform. Thus, firms were allowed to apply (unused) depreciation allowances of periods prior to the tax reform, and the revenue from corporate income tax fell by 20 percent. But other taxes also brought in lower revenues, namely the income tax, and as part of it the tax on wage income, value added tax, and the local business tax. It remains to be seen whether structural issues are behind the fall in tax revenue. If so, this would have long-run implications for Germany's fiscal policy position.

A specific issue, also showing the actual strains of Germany's fiscal policy stance, is the reduction in total revenue of the municipalities since the mid-1990s relative to nominal GPD by about one percentage point. One aspect is that the revenue of the local business tax has fallen from 2 to 1 percent of nominal GDP in the last three decades. Another is that the revenue of municipalities relies to a large extent on transfers (more than one-third); only one-third of the revenue comes from taxes. The problem is that municipalities do not have their own tax base, and a reform is needed in which they will receive more taxation autonomy. This, however, can be achieved only by a major restructuring of Germany's fiscal federalism.

The Libero of Social Policy

A major problem of German fiscal policy is that it has to step into the breach when the social security system creates a deficit. Fiscal policy thus is like the libero in soccer, representing the last resort. The finance minister has to help out when the rising expenditures of the social security system can no longer be financed from contributions. It is remarkable that the elasticity of transfers with respect to nominal gross domestic product is so high. In the period 1998–2002 it amounted to 4; an increase of nominal GDP in the whole period of 9 percent was accompanied by an increase in transfers of 39 percent. Indeed, transfers to the social security systems have risen considerably in that period (table 12.7). In addition, the social security system has developed a sizable deficit, amounting to €6.6 billion or 1.4 percent of its expendi-

TABLE 12.7
Received transfers of the social security systems (€bn)

	Transfers	Budget surplus or deficit
1998	61.3	2.7
1999	70.9	5.4
2000	72.5	0.3
2001	78.3	−3.3
2002	86.2	−6.6
2003	90.9	−6.4[a]

Source: Federal Statistical Office, Macroeconomic Accounts.

tures. Part of this high elasticity can be explained by the automatic stabilizers operating when nominal economic growth was low, at around 2 percent. That is not disturbing, because in periods of higher nominal, and of course more importantly of higher real, growth, transfers would increase less. However, the fact that a large part of the increase is structural, so that the higher elasticity expresses a new long-run relationship, i.e., an increased absorption of transfers by the social security system, is a different story. Unfortunately, with the expansion of the welfare state, the calculation of elasticities of previous periods as points of orientation is not too helpful, because the structural relationship has changed. Thus, transfers from the federal budget to the social security system account for 25 percent of federal expenditures. This proportion has doubled since the 1980s; it was 15 percent in 1995 (German Council of Economic Advisers 2003: 257).

As we have seen in chapter 5, over the last thirty years politics has done away with some of the buffers that existed between the deficit of the social security system and fiscal policy. Thus, the precautionary mechanisms of the pay-as-you-go system, such as maintaining reserves of one year's expenditures in the pension system, were given up. More recently, the Schröder government even reduced the required reserve of the pension system from one month's expenditure to 0.8 month, then to 0.5 month and now to 0.2 month, in order to gain a tiny short-term source of finance. This implies that fiscal policy has to take over the deficit of the social security system as it arises, making governmental expenditures more volatile. Another repercussion is that the responsibility for welfare recipients capable of working will have to be transferred from the municipalities to the federal level. This means that a decentralized institutional buffer between social policy and fiscal policy will be abolished.

Given the future ageing of the population, the converse development would have been preferable: namely, to introduce additional buffers between the two areas of policy so that fiscal policy can follow a steady course and declining revenue in the social security systems in a recession is cushioned by sufficient reserves in these systems. Moreover, such a buffer is needed for protection when the implicit debt of the social security system becomes explicit. Thus, the simple concept of the elasticity of transfers to the social security system from tax revenue in relation to nominal growth can be used to illustrate the conundrum of policy issues facing Germany today. At the same time, it shows how important reform of the social welfare systems is if fiscal policy is to become credible again.

NEW INTERNATIONAL CONSTRAINTS

Although stepping into the breach as a financier of last resort for the different branches of the social security system is one of the new job requirements for a finance minister, fiscal policy also faces a new international environment.

One international restraint for German fiscal policy arises in the context of the Stability Pact in the European Monetary Union (see next chapter). If this pact were taken seriously, which does not seem likely at the moment, Germany would still have to allocate responsibility among its three layers of government. The federal layer should be responsible for controlling the deficit of the social security systems, but it cannot directly influence the expenditures and the budget of the Länder with their municipalities. So far, there exists only an agreement that the layers of government *take into account the implications* of their behavior with respect to deficits in their medium-term financial planning.

The solution must be set into a binding agreement between the federal layer and the Länder whereby they take joint responsibility for preventing excessive deficits. In such an internal stability pact, the obligations of the European Monetary Union's stability pact would have to be broken down for the three layers of government, while taking into account such factors as sensitivity of expenditure at these levels with respect to the business cycle and, of course, the structure of the expenditure. Thus, the permissible deficit of 3 percent could be allocated in accordance with the proportions of the expenditures at the federal level and the Länder level if one excluded the municipalities. This would be a 50/50 split.

A much more important change in the international environment is that most factors of production, capital, technology, and also highly qualified labor, as well as portfolio capital, have become more mobile. These factors of production have an exit option: i.e., they can avoid national taxation if they simply move to a location abroad or into the shadow economy at home. According to the concept of locational competition, the maneuvering space of national governments and fiscal policy is reduced (Siebert 2000). Consequently, it becomes harder to tax these mobile factors of production. In the future this change will also apply, at least to some extent, to the choice of residence of pensioners in Europe and especially in the euro area. Of equal importance is the fact that national policy has to react to tax reductions in other countries. This will not make it easier for German fiscal policy to solve the structural issues it faces, including high debt, large transfers to the social security systems, a sizable implicit debt, and a distributive federalism.

The attempts to restrain this tendency of locational competition by international macroeconomic cooperation have not been too promising, even within the European Union. Some of the EU member states are not prepared to cede their national sovereignty in these matters; they are not willing to renounce their own options in this competitive game in order to make it easier for the finance minister of another country. Thus, it can be expected that the European Union will not go beyond some agreements of minimum standards in taxation, as has already been done for minimum rates for the value added tax. For instance, some of the distortionary business taxes representing strong location incentives for production or holding companies may be prevented in the future. Macroeconomic coordination in this area beyond the European Union is a fruitless attempt, anyhow. Fiscal policy will have to live with the exit option of the mobile factors of production.

Appendix

Tables 12A-1 and 12A-2 present the structure of national budget and tax revenues.

Table 12A-1
Different Shares of the state (% of GDP)[a]

Year[b]	Expenditures	Taxes and contributions	Taxes	Budget	Gross debt[c]	Interest[d]
1950[e]	31.6	30.3	21.3	0.6	19.3	n.a.
1960	32.9	33.6	23.5	3.0	18.7	n.a.
1970	39.1	34.9	23.8	0.5	18.6	4.5
1971	40.6	35.9	24.3	0.2	18.6	4.5
1972	41.6	36.2	24.0	−0.4	18.8	4.5
1973	42.1	38.2	25.2	1.1	18.3	4.7
1974	45.6	38.5	25.1	−1.7	19.4	5.3
1975	49.9	38.5	24.1	−5.8	24.8	6.1
1976	49.1	39.9	24.9	−3.5	26.3	6.8
1977	48.7	40.8	25.9	−2.6	27.3	7.0
1978	47.5	40.1	25.4	−2.6	28.7	6.9
1979	47.2	40.0	25.3	−2.7	29.7	7.3
1980	47.9	40.3	25.3	−2.9	31.7	8.1
1981	48.8	40.1	24.5	−4.0	35.4	9.9
1982	48.9	40.1	24.2	−3.5	38.7	11.9
1983	47.7	39.6	24.2	−2.9	40.2	13.0
1984	46.9	39.8	24.3	−2.0	41.0	12.9
1985	46.3	40.0	24.4	−1.1	41.7	12.8
1986	45.4	39.5	23.9	−1.1	41.6	12.8
1987	45.8	39.6	24.0	−1.8	42.6	12.5

TABLE 12A-1 (*continued*)

Year[b]	Expenditures	Taxes and contributions	Taxes	Budget	Gross debt[c]	Interest[d]
1988	45.3	39.3	23.8	−2.0	43.1	12.4
1989	44.0	39.7	24.4	+0.1	41.8	11.4
1990	44.5	38.1	23.1	−2.0	44.3	12.2
1991	47.1	39.8	23.5	−2.9	42.6	13.1
1992	48.1	40.5	23.9	−2.6	47.4	14.9
1993	49.3	41.1	23.9	−3.1	53.3	15.0
1994	49.0	41.5	23.9	−2.4	56.4	15.8
1995	49.4	41.3	23.5	−10.0	57.1	15.9
1996	50.3	42.1	23.8	−3.4	59.8	16.4[f]
1997	49.3	42.1	23.5	−2.7	61.0	16.6
1998	48.8	42.1	23.9	−2.2	60.9	16.1
1999	48.7	42.8	24.9	−1.5	61.2	15.5
2000	45.7	42.9	25.4	+1.3[g]	60.2	14.5
2001	48.3	41.2	23.7	−2.8	59.5	15.2
2002	48.5	40.6	23.2	−3.5	60.8[i]	14.7
2003[h]	49.2[i]	40.8[i]	23.2[i]	−3.9	64.2[i]	15.2
2004[h]	48.5[i]	40.7[i]	n.a.	−3.4[i]	65.7	15.9

Source: Federal Statistical Office, Kiel Institute of World Economics, own calculations.

[a] All shares in current prices according to the Macroeconomic Accounts, European System of Macroeconomic Accounting, basis 1995.

[b] Until 1990, West Germany; since 1991, Germany.

[c] For West Germany until 1989 according to ESMA 1979.

[d] Interest payments for public debt in relation to tax revenue.

[e] Excluding the Saar and West Berlin.

[f] Tax revenue is reduced since 1996 by the child allowances, which are considered a negative tax and are netted out.

[g] Including the revenue from auctioning the licenses for the Universal Mobile Telecommunication Systems (UMTS), amounting to 2.5 percent of GDP.

[h] Forecast of the Kiel Institute.

[i] Council of Economic Advisers Annual Report 2003/04.

TABLE 12A-2
Regional GDP per capita, 2002[a]

State	Relative to the German average	Relative to the West German average
Baden–Württemberg	113.1	105.2
Bavaria	116.8	108.6
Berlin	89.0	82.8
Brandenburg	66.7	62.1
Bremen	136.0	126.5
Hamburg	170.4	158.5
Hessen	123.2	114.6
Mecklenburg–Pomerania	66.1	61.5
Lower Saxony	89.9	83.6
North Rhine–Westphalia	100.5	93.5
Rhineland–Palatinate	90.1	83.8
Saarland	93.4	86.9
Saxonia	67.9	63.2
Sachsen–Anhalt	66.1	61.4
Schleswig–Holstein	91.4	85.0
Thüringen	66.2	61.6
Germany	100.0	93.0
Western Germany	107.5	100.0
Eastern Germany[b]	71.2	66.2

Source: Arbeitskreis Volkswirtschaftliche Gesamtrechnungen der Länder (internet).
[a] Per inhabitant, in current prices.
[b] Including Berlin.

CHAPTER THIRTEEN

Germany in the European Union:
Economic Policy under Ceded Sovereignty

Like the other member states of the European Union, Germany has given up sovereignty in a number of policy areas and subjected itself to joint decision-making at the European level. This means that many policy instruments are no longer available nationally. From a historical perspective, the number of such instruments that are no longer at the disposal of German politicians and policy-makers in other EU countries as a result of ceding national sovereignty to the EU level is quite impressive. This trend is manifest in many policy areas, including monetary policy, trade policy, the more important part of competition policy, subsidy control, and a large number of the regulations in the product market, the environmental arena, and the capital market. The maneuvering space for national economic policy-makers has been considerably reduced. More and more, the efficiency of policy instruments is coming to be judged in the European context. In quite a few areas in which decisions are taken with a qualified majority, the member countries can be outvoted and have to accept the decisions taken by others.[1]

TRADING NATIONAL SOVEREIGNTY FOR THE BENEFITS OF INTEGRATION

The most prominent policy area that has recently been assigned to the European level is monetary policy, but many other policy instruments, of no lesser importance, in quite a few policy areas have been shifted to the European level. Because the notion of a common market lies at the core of the economic union, a wide range of barriers for the free movement across borders needed to be abolished by harmonizing important aspects of the institutional framework of the national economies, or simply by mutually honoring each member state's internal rules and regulations, for instance in licensing products.

The basic economic motivation for giving up national sovereignty derives from the benefit-cost analysis that every country carries out: the advantage of European integration for the individual member country substantially exceeds the lost opportunity of its being able to make independent decisions on economic policy issues. More specifically, the advantage consists in sharing a larger market for sales of products, allowing more options for consumers with respect to a wider variety of products, enjoying efficiency and specialization gains for the member states, and reducing trans-frontier externalities between national decisions. European integration, however, goes beyond these more or less functional economic reasons for establishing a common market in the strict sense. The ultimate motivation for beginning and sustaining European integration has been, and remains, the possibility to solve problems within a common institutional framework instead of going to war over them. Economic integration is thus used as a vehicle for political integration.

European integration has been a continuous process with many consecutive steps with respect to both the countries involved (widening) and the areas or intensity of integration (deepening). The EU started with the European Coal and Steel Community in 1951 and the European Economic Community (Belgium, France, Germany, Italy, Luxembourg, and the Netherlands) in the treaty of Rome in 1957. The United Kingdom and the Scandinavian countries put up an alternative model, the European Free Trade Association (EFTA), in 1960; however, this eventually lost ground to the EEC. European integration continued with the northern enlargement in 1973 (Denmark, Ireland, and the United Kingdom), taking in the most important EFTA counties, and the southern enlargement in the 1980s (Greece in 1981, Spain and Portugal in 1986) and the entry of the so-called neutral states in 1995 (Austria, Finland, and Sweden). In May 2004 the European Union of 15 was enlarged to a union of 25, including eight central and eastern European countries. The EU-25 will have a GDP of €9.2 trillion, nearly as much as the United States. It represents 455 million people.

Over the last five decades, then, European integration has proved to be quite attractive for nations outside the European Union. Soon, probably in 2007, Bulgaria and Romania will join to form the EU-27. The successor states of the former Yugoslavia and Albania are likely to become members at some point in the future. For Russia, Belarussia, and the Ukraine too some form of association will probably be found. Entry negotiations with Turkey may be opened up within the next several years. This, however, raises the question of where Europe sees its boundaries, and whether Turkey as a member may not imply such an overstretch of the European Union that it will either break up or require a much more intense integration of the core, thus again running the risk of a breakup. Of the European countries, only Switzerland, Norway, and Iceland look set to remain outside the EU.

With respect to the areas of integration and the process of deepening, the core cell was the European Coal and Steel Community of the Six in 1951, which then was extended to the common market of the six for all products. This consisted of a customs union without any tariffs between the member states, a common external tariff, realized in 1968, and a common trade policy; a common agricultural market with the common agricultural policy was introduced in 1962. Over time, the product market segmentations were reduced or even abolished, for instance by not attempting to harmonize all aspects of life but instead accepting the legal setting of the other member countries according to the country-of-origin rule or the principle of mutual recognition. The Cassis de Dijon ruling of the European Court of Justice meant that different legal settings could coexist and compete with each other (see below). Except for the northern and southern widening of membership, the Community did not make much progress in the 1970s and the early 1980s with respect to the areas of integration.

Then in 1985 the Delors Commission came up with a White Paper; this permitted the 12 members to sign the Single Act, which became effective in 1987, containing a blueprint of about 270 measures to create a single market and do away with national segmentations. At the end of the 1980s controls on border-crossing capital flows, which were still in effect in some major countries such as France at that time, were abolished as a necessary preparation for the proper functioning of the monetary union. The late 1980s were also characterized by the deregulation of the network industries, including telecommunications, the postal service, and power transmission. The Maastricht Treaty of 1993 brought about the establishment of the European Union, replacing the former European Community. Its main aim was to establish the monetary union, but it also introduced political and social aspects of integration, including European citizenship, a common foreign and security policy, and internal security. Applying the review clause in the Maastricht Treaty, the Amsterdam Treaty (1997) strengthened the Union's powers in judicial cooperation, the free movement of persons, foreign policy, and public health. Finally, on January 1, 1999, the euro was introduced as a legal tender for book transactions in 11 member states; the member countries' exchange rates were irrevocably frozen. Monetary authority was transferred from the national central banks to the European System of Central Banks (ECB) in Frankfurt. The euro emerged as currency in 2002.

REPLACING THE DEUTSCHMARK WITH THE EURO

Germany has been an ardent promoter of European integration. Economic and political integration into the institutional framework of the Western nations not only paved the way for the country to become a fully fledged member of the international community, and acted as a shield of protection in the days of the cold war: it was also seen as an anchor, giving stability to the values and the orientation of German society and the political process. Giving up national sovereignty to the European level was not a problem for postwar Germans, for whom nationalism had lost its attractiveness and national pride was not, as in other European countries, a central value. Only in one area in the monetary domain did the delegating of decisions to EU level prove hard for the Germans: in giving up the Deutschmark.

To Germans the DM was a stable currency. Although its purchasing power of 1948 had been reduced to a quarter by 1998, the last year of the DM era, it had still lost less than other currencies in Europe and less than the US dollar, which had fallen to 15 cents over the same period. Germans had confidence in the Bundesbank and found part of their identity in the Deutschmark. The Bundesbank was the guarantor of a stable money, and a stable money was an important value for the Germans who had two major inflations in their collective memory: the hyperinflation of 1923 and the currency reform of 1948. In the hyperinflation of 1923 the Reichsmark was devalued at a tremendous speed. As fathers and grandfathers would tell their children and grandchildren, money was devalued at such a rapid pace that wage-earners had to spend their wages immediately after they were paid, because within half a day their real value would have halved. When the inflation was finally stopped by the introduction of the Rentenmark on November 16, 1923, the exchange rate was 4.2 trillion marks to the US dollar—i.e., 4,200,000,000,000 marks. Savings were destroyed, pensions devalued, lives ruined. In the currency reform of June 20, 1948, it was made explicit that the suppressed inflation since 1936, using price and wage controls to finance military and other expenditures, had produced such a money overhang that the existing money had to be declared invalid. Each German received 40 marks of the new currency in June and another 20 marks in August. Private deposits and private credits (or liabilities) were exchanged at a ratio of 10 Reichsmarks to one Deutschmark, and were partly blocked; they were effectively exchanged at the rate of 6.5 to 1. Credits of the state and of banks became extinct. Wages, housing rents, and the new pensions were changed at a ratio of one to one. Thus, the average person lost nearly all his savings again, and hence his savings for old age, for the second time within 25 years. It is because of this experience that stable money ranks high in the scale of priorities for the average German, and that there was quite a reluctance to give up a monetary arrangement that had succeeded in providing the monetary stability desired so desperately.

The acceptance of the euro as a common European currency has brought many advantages. For the average citizen, it is possible to travel in Europe now without the nuisance of changing currencies—and Germans like to travel during their ample vacation time. For consumers it has become easier to buy abroad. For the German export industry, a common currency has meant that it can enjoy an export area covering the main part of Europe without any disturbing exchange rate changes. Transaction costs in the capital market have been reduced. Moreover, politicians like Kohl are convinced that the euro is an important symbol of the bringing together of Europeans from all the member countries.

However, there are also disadvantages. Monetary policy instruments such as setting the interest rate for short-term money, providing liquidity to the economy, and steering the money supply have been shifted up to European level. These decisions are now made within the Governing Council of the European Central Bank, where a simple majority is required. Germany and all other members of the euro area have just one vote each. Moreover, neither members of the Executive Board nor governors of the 12 national central banks of the euro area, i.e., the members of the Governing Council, can consider themselves as representatives of their country. German monetary policy with its rich tradition of the Bundesbank has ceased to exist. The only comfort that Germans have is that the European Central Bank was modeled along the lines of the Bundesbank, thus transferring the credibility and reputation it had especially among the German population to the new institution. Although Germany is the largest economy in the euro area, producing a third of the area's GDP, and thus has some impact on the economic variables of the common currency area, the ECB cannot possibly differentiate its policy instruments to the specific economic situation in Germany. This became apparent in the years of stagnation 2001–2003, when both the GDP growth rate and the increase in the price level were lower in Germany than in the other countries of the euro area. The ECB has to orient its policy to the common consumer price index of the euro area as a whole, the harmonized index of consumer prices (HICP).

The nominal exchange rate, which may have been used as an instrument of adjustment in extraordinary circumstances, such as asymmetric shocks, is no longer available. Adjustment now must come about by a change in the real exchange rate, i.e., in the relative price between exportables and importables or between tradables and non-tradables. This requires institutional changes that make the economy more flexible. This loss of sovereignty shows up in the substitution of real exchange rate changes for nominal exchange rate variations. Looking at the nominal exchange rate, the issue of a loss of a policy instrument may be more an academic rather than a public policy question, anyway. First, a central bank cannot determine the price level and the nominal exchange rate simultaneously. If the price level is specified, the exchange rate will follow in the long run according to purchasing power parity. Whereas smaller countries may take the monetary policy of another country as an anchor and peg their exchange rate to it, larger countries or regions of the world such as Europe would not be inclined to follow someone else as a monetary leader. Second, it is highly questionable in the post-Bretton Woods era whether a larger country can consider the nominal exchange rate as a policy variable anyway. The exchange rate is influenced by the markets, i.e., by trade flows, capital movements, and expectations. Capital flows and expectations make the exchange rate volatile, so it is fair to state that a central bank cannot determine the nominal exchange rate: it is constrained by interest rate parity. The most it can do is to lean temporarily against the wind.[2]

But the concern of Germans with the new common currency was not only that the monetary policy instruments were migrating to the European level. An equally strong fear, if not a greater one, was that the other member states of the euro area would not attach the same importance to price level stability as Germans had in the past and as most of them still do today, and that the "Club Med" countries, with a supposedly less strict preference for monetary stability, would push for an easy money policy and take a much softer stand on price level stability. Germans feared that, in the struggle between a stable money and softer financial constraints for the state, or in the presumed conflict between a stable money and less unemployment (if you believe in the Phillips curve), other member states would give preference to other targets, e.g., for fighting unemployment by expanding the money supply, rather than to the stability of money. It was feared that the European Central Bank would have a different reaction function from the Bundesbank and that its institutional environment would be prone to a laxer monetary policy.

With these concerns in mind, the European Central Bank was conceived as independent. Article 105 of the EU Treaty defines the main objective of the European System of Central Banks (ESCB) as follows: "The primary objective of the ESCB shall be to maintain price level stability." Other target, such as supporting employment, are only secondary and conditional with respect to the target of price level stability. "Without prejudice to the objective of price level stability, the ESCB shall support the general economic policies in the Community with a view to contributing to the achievement of the objectives of the community as laid down in Article 2" (Article 105). Article 2 defines the task of the Community in general:

---

[2] The central bank can, of course, depreciate a currency by an excessive supply of money.

to promote ...a harmonious and balanced development of economic activities, a high level of employment and of social protection, equality between men and women, sustainable and non-inflationary growth, a high degree of competitiveness and convergence of economic performance, a high level of protection and improvement of the quality of the environment, the raising of the standard of living and quality of life, and economic and social cohesion and solidarity among Member States.

Although members of the Executive Board are all appointed by common accord of the heads of state, and the national governors by the national governments, they tend to internalize the ECB's mission as their guideline. Reappointment of members of the Executive Board is not possible. It must be acknowledged that the ECB succeeded in delivering a stable money for the euro members in its first five years. Inflation expectations, as measured by survey data or financial market indicators, have remained consistent with the ECB's definition of price stability. This becomes all the more remarkable if we take into account that the ECB had no track record of formulating monetary policy at the beginning, when it was faced with a euro area economy that was being hit by repeated upward price shocks. As a result of all these shocks, HICP inflation has been above—and sometimes significantly above—2 percent for quite some time. But inflation has always bounced back following these shocks.

Nevertheless, not everyone in the European Union was convinced by the monetary union. The Swedes voted in 2003 to stay out of the monetary union; it may take a decade for a new referendum to be put to its citizens. In Denmark, too, a referendum in 2000 brought a "no." And it remains uncertain whether and when the United Kingdom will join. Some of the new EU members seem interested or even eager to join early, in order to participate in the euro's credibility and enjoy low interest rates. But they may need the exchange rate as a buffer for longer time.

The Germans welcomed the euro when it was finally introduced in 2002. In January 2002, 67 percent responded that they were personally happy or very happy that the euro had become their currency, whereas only 23 percent said they were unhappy (and 10 percent were undecided), according to the Flash Eurobarometer of the EU Commission. This percentage, however, has declined; it was only 44–47 percent (with 9 percent undecided) in November 2003. Thus, the ECB and EU politicians cannot take it for granted that the euro will be widely supported by the population; efforts will have to continue to convince the public of its merit.

THE STABILITY PACT: RESTRAINT ON NATIONAL BUDGET POLICY

The ECB's success in the euro's first years is no guarantee of a stable money in the future. This will depend on the behavior of the central bank, the stability culture, and the institutional setup. A common European currency is not without potential conflict. One of the points of contention is the dichotomy between the Europeanized money and national political decision-making, the other is the possible confrontation between monetary stability and fiscal laxity.

The common monetary policy has been shifted to the union level and must be oriented toward price level stability in the monetary union as a whole. Consequently, it cannot take into consideration specific national conditions. In a monetary union, the monetary "suit" is no longer custom-tailored for each nation: one size must fit all. But political decision-making, for instance in budget policy, remains with the nation states. This is a major characteristics of monetary policy in an economic union, unlike the relationship of a central bank to the political authority in an individual country. This condition can be a source of conflict that may cause problems to the European Monetary Union in the future. Some consider it a massive potential conflict, one that may even break up the currency union (Feldstein 1992, 1997). Even if countries are in a different stage of the business cycle, with one in a boom and another in a recession, if they experience an asymmetric shock and get stuck in a self-inflicted crisis, they must cope with the same monetary policy. But monetary policy is still judged in national political decision-making processes, since a political union does not come into existence simultaneously with a monetary union.

Thus, a potential for conflict, additional to and different from the situation in an individual country, inevitably arises in a monetary union between a common monetary policy and national economic interests. One may argue that the interest of one of the member countries can be neutralized by the other countries, but one also can take the view that the common monetary policy must find acceptance in all countries as long as political decision-making processes are national. To put it differently, in a monetary union quite a bit of political discipline is required from a member country in crisis to accept a monetary policy that is oriented toward European price level stability, but, by necessity, not to the specific economic situation in the individual country. If, however, the country in crisis were allowed to have its way and getting an easy monetary policy adopted, inflation throughout Europe would result.

In addition to this potential conflict between the Europeanized currency and the national interest, there is a possible confrontation between a stable money and distress in the public finances. By entrusting an independent European central bank with the authority to steer the money supply, i.e., to set the interest rates and determine other monetary policy instruments, the process of money creation in the euro area is not in the hands of politicians: it is depoliticized, as it was during the time of the Bundesbank. But even if it is conceived as being politically independent, a central bank tends to be exposed to political pressure. Such pressure may originate from countries facing severe economic problems. Member states of the monetary union with high government debt will be interested in low interest rates, a lax monetary policy, and a slightly higher inflation rate than that anticipated by financial markets, because such a scenario would ease their budgetary situations, especially because debts would melt away in real terms. Political pressure will be exerted on the European Central Bank if the economy of a highly indebted state is hit by recession and faces severe financial difficulties. The issue is not that a country will deliberately follow a policy of excessive deficits in order to force the European Central Bank eventually to step in as lender of last resort; it is that a long-run process of debt accumulation may occur as a result of political weakness, so that eventually the European Central Bank will have no other option than to adopt a soft monetary policy.

Historically, it has not been possible to maintain a stable currency when the finances of the state are in disarray. High government debt tends to lead to financial disorder. In a monetary union an important controlling mechanism of fiscal policy is no longer available: the national currency can no longer be devalued when a country runs a high balance of payment equilibrium, often together with a budget deficit. For example, Portugal had an unusually high currency account deficit of 10.4 percent in 2000. Before monetary union this would have required a devaluation of the escudo. The EMU countries, however, can have higher current account deficits. They benefit from increased capital mobility as long as there are surpluses elsewhere and the Union's current account position does not degenerate.[3] They can take the free-rider position with respect to price level stability, for instance with high public debt.

Admittedly, the treaty has a no-bail-out clause in Article 103, according to which a member state cannot expect to receive financial support from other member states or the European Union if it is in financial distress. If this bailout rule is credible, financial markets will punish the country lacking fiscal solidity by imposing higher interest rates. This threat represents an incentive to keep the public finances in order. To some extent this mechanism is indeed operating. However, Article 100, allowing financial assistance in the case of economic crisis and natural

---

[3] Jones (2003) shows that the variance in the country's current account positions has increased with the monetary union.

disasters, may be interpreted as a type of stand-by. If transfers have to be made after all—in spite of liability being excluded—then the donor of transfers, as well as the recipient, may develop an interest in keeping these transfers as low as possible, replacing them by a rather lax monetary policy. As national safeguards against governmental financial distress either do not exist in all member states or are not sufficient to shield the European Central Bank from political pressure in a situation of unsound public finances, the requirement of sustainability of the government's finances is a major issue in a currency union. This is the role of the Stability and Growth Pact (Article 104). Its overriding objective is that governments remain solvent. Usually, this is interpreted as requiring stationarity of a tolerable level of debt: the debt/GDP ratio has to remain constant. In the protocol of the Maastricht Treaty, this limit has been set at 60 percent of GDP. This target was chosen at a time when the debt level of most of the potential euro members was below that threshold and when 60 percent appeared as a limit that would not become relevant so quickly. The restraint for a debt level of 60 percent implies a limit for an excessive deficit of 3 percent of GDP if nominal GDP growth is 5 percent and real growth at 3 percent.[4]

The excessive deficit procedure itself is specified in Article 104 in general terms. Several consecutive disciplinary steps will be taken if a country runs an excessive deficit. The most important ones are: a report by the Commission; a decision of the Council (with qualified majority) concerning whether an excessive deficit exists; recommendations to the member state; a warning to the member state if it fails to put into practice the recommendations of the Council; and the request of additional information for the Council; then the request of a non-interest-bearing deposit; and eventually the imposition of a fine.[5] Taking into account the guidelines in the Resolution of the Council on the Stability and Growth Pact of 1997 and the Council Regulation on the Implementation of the Excessive Deficit Procedure of 1997, the following rules apply to situations in which a budget deficit surpasses 3 percent of GDP. (i) A real decrease of GDP on a yearly basis of at least 2 percent is viewed without any further argument as an exception; the 3 percent limit then is not binding. (ii) In the case of a fall of GDP in the intermediate range of 0.75–2 percent, a set of discre-

---

[4] This follows from

$$\frac{D_{t+1}}{Y_{t+1}^N} = \frac{(D_t + \dot{D}_t)}{Y_t^N} \frac{Y_t^N}{Y_{t+1}^N}$$

Solving for $\dot{D}_t/Y_t^N$ and setting D/Y^N for both periods equal to 0.6, we get 0.03 for the budget deficit in relation to GDP. D_t denotes debt in period t, $\dot{D}_t$ the change in debt, and Y^N nominal GDP.

[5] The non-interest-bearing deposit will be converted into a fine after two years if the budget deficit remains excessive.

tionary decisions of the European Council has to be made. The situation may be regarded as exceptional if the country can demonstrate that its recession is exceptional in terms of its abruptness. (iii) If GDP falls by less than 0.75 percent, an exception cannot be claimed.[6]

It was not possible for the Council to agree upon an automatic excessive deficit procedure when the common currency was established. Now, the excessive deficit procedure contains many discretionary steps. The determination of an excessive budget deficit remains uncertain if a member state, after being forced to delay restorative measures by a formal resolution, does then take appropriate measures. Whether the measures taken are appropriate is also decided by the European Council. These discretionary steps raise the question of whether the Stability Pact will be effective. Moreover, there is a conflict of roles, since those who are responsible for the excessive budgetary deficit will also be the ones to define it and to vote on the fines. The pupils write their own grades. Reading through some of the documents, for instance the guidelines of the Stability Pact of 1977, where, for instance, the member states "commit themselves to respect the medium-term budgetary objective of close to balance or in surplus…," one cannot but have the impression that some of the documents have been produced to ease the anxiety of the German population prior to the founding of the European Monetary Union.

It is embarrassing that Germany was one of the countries violating the Stability Pact in 2004, for the third year in a row. Germany had pushed for the Stability Pact to be adopted by euro member countries to make sure that excessive deficits would be avoided by those countries. All EU countries accepted the basic idea of the pact, and Germany's membership was to some extent dependent upon such a pact, as Germany's Constitutional Court had given the green light for membership in the monetary union only under the condition of a clear and long-term commitment to low inflation rates and stability.

Many statements were made in 2002 and 2003 by the German and French finance ministers, the German chancellor, the French president, and also the president of the EU Commission, shedding doubt on the wisdom of the Stability Pact. All these statements can be interpreted as attempts to soften the restraint of the Stability Pact. In fact, in November 2003 the finance ministers decided in the Econfin Council not to follow the proposal of the EU Commission to initiate the excessive deficit procedure against France and Germany, in spite of the fact that the two countries had a budget deficit higher than 3 percent of GDP for three

---

[6] The rule of the third case apparently was not applied by the Council when the excessive deficit procedure was not opened against Germany and France in November 2003.

consecutive years and were not in recession. This not only called into question the preconditon of the two fiscal criteria of 3 percent for the deficit and 60 percent for the new EU member countries, but also was an invitation to all euro area members to adopt loose fiscal policies. Moreover, it is difficult to explain to new EU members that want to join the monetary union that entry criteria have to be satisfied. Once the financial markets become aware that the restraint of fiscal soundness in Europe is being abandoned, and that a situation is likely to develop that is unsustainable (and taking into consideration the implicit debt of the social security systems in the three largest continental countries), the external value of the euro may very well be at risk. As is well known, the mood of financial markets can change quickly. Thus, there is a definite risk that the stability of the new common money may be endangered by the decisions of politicians, in spite of the independence of the European Central Bank. The year 2003 may go down in history as the year when politicians redefined the conditions of the European Monetary Union in their favor, thereby weakening the ECB (see below on the Convention).

THE EXPECTED IMPACT OF THE COMMON MONEY

A common money will change the prevailing economic conditions in the member countries of the euro area both in the product and factor markets and in the institutional setup of these markets. Thus, the euro will stimulate the processes that will reduce market segmentation in the capital market, leading to a deeper market that can be more competitive internationally. The business cycle will become more synchronized for the simple reason that an important policy instrument will affect the countries symmetrically, except for the remaining differences in the monetary transmission channels. However, the properties of the business cycle depend on many factors, such as the structure of the economy in terms of locational specialization and trade linkages within Europe or with non-European countries. These factors may offset, and even overcompensate for, the synchronizing effect of the euro.

High hopes were placed on the euro for straightening out some of the rigidities of the labor market in the large continental European countries. The argument is that prices and costs are more directly comparable in a currency union, and that therefore price and cost competition will be enhanced. Owing to the increased mobility of capital, firms have the option to respond to an inflexible national labor market by moving elsewhere. This will put pressure on the political process to redefine the institutional setup of the labor market and to make it less rigid. In a way, the euro, once established, should improve ex post the optimality conditions that are, in theory, required as necessary conditions ex ante for the start of the currency area. To what extent this is likely to become true will depend on many factors, one of which is whether the forces aiming for a more centralized and more social democratic labor market will win the upper hand. There is no question that a currency union needs a flexible labor market, but there is no guarantee that this will come about in the major continental European countries.

It can even be argued that German trade unions have gained an additional degree of freedom in their wage policy because they no longer have to take into account the direct reaction of the Bundesbank to their wage policy. The ECB is unlikely to respond to the wage policy in a single member state of the euro area. Accordingly, Hancké and Soskice (2003) claim that some smaller countries are now able to use tripartite wage policy to undercut Germany, while the wage-controlling role of the Bundesbank against German unions has been lost with the passage of power to the ECB. As an implication, the authors recommend a type of central bargaining in the euro area that would take the form of an agreement on inflation coordination in the major economies of the euro area.

This argument, however, overestimates the role of the Bundesbank. It is true that the Bundesbank did not accommodate the nominal wage increases by ordering an increase in the money supply, as was the case in Sweden, for instance, before the 1992 crisis—leading to a depreciation in the krona which undid the nominal wage increase in real terms: people had a wage illusion. The Bundesbank aimed for a stable price level; it stabilized inflationary expectations, keeping nominal wage increases low by international comparison and preventing a steeper rise of the price level resulting from the wage increase. But the Bundesbank was not able to prevent wage overshooting in real terms and a stepwise increase in unemployment, as discussed in chapter 4. It is too simple to base economic policy on the macroeconomic Phillips curve, which cannot be taken as a given relationship that remains constant over time. If the argument is presented in terms of unit labor costs, i.e., that some countries now will have a lower increase in their unit labor costs, it must be noted that unit labor costs are not an appropriate measure of wage policy if unemployment is increasing because this raises labor productivity artificially. Besides, unit labor costs on a national currency basis rose much more in Germany in the 1990s during Bundesbank times than in most other countries.[7]

What is more important, trade unions are under a more effective constraint than that of the currency union: namely, the fact that the

---

[7] The rate of change of unit labor cost in Germany was 3.1 for 1990–95 and 0.7 for 1995–2000, in contrast to 0.2 and −0.5 for the United States (US Department of Labor 2003: table B).

mobility of capital, technology, and highly qualified labor has increased considerably worldwide. Firms have an exit option that implies domestic job losses, and this restrains the wage demands of the unions. At the same time, governments no longer are able support unemployment schemes to the same extent as in the past. It seems that up to now, trade unions in the euro area have tended to demand higher wage increases in real terms in line with productivity growth. As we have seen in chapter 4, this strategy is not appropriate for the reduction of unemployment; but at the same time, if applied, it does not aggravate the existing unemployment. Indeed, it is cost neutral, as long as the trade unions do not succeed in inducing the government to raise its expenditures on unemployment programs.[8]

Another issue that comes to the forefront is whether the common currency requires the coordination of macroeconomic policy of all euro area member countries. This question is deemed relevant since monetary policy has now been Europeanized, whereas the other areas of macroeconomic policy remain at the national level. One approach is to limit negative spillovers between the different macroeconomic policy areas, as in the Stability Pact. Thus, the Stability Pact can be viewed as a specific form of coordination, i.e., coordination by constraint. Other attempts at coordination represent a form of atmospheric coordination including mutual information. This means that national policy-makers are informed about what is intended elsewhere and start from a common frame of reference. In part, coordination will have to rely on moral suasion, for instance if a country with high growth rates benefits from the low interest rates of the ECB and is not willing to reduce its governmental absorption. Some groups, especially in France and among socialists, voice strong support for an economic government as a counterweight to the ECB. However, most of the coordination philosophy is based on extremely simple and naive Keynesian ideas of controlling and fine-tuning aggregate demand over the cycle; inside and outside lags are neglected. The political process in the member states seems unable to smooth government expenditures over the cycle. While additional spending in a recession is seized wholeheartedly by the political process, reducing demand in a boom is unlikely to take place. Thus, I am skeptical about more intense macroeconomic coordination at the European level.

ASSIGNING THE TASKS: WHICH COMPETENCE TO WHICH LEVEL?

More straightforward and basic to the European integration process than the introduction of a common currency is the integration of product and

---

[8] On the argument that a still-independent Bundesbank would have given Germany lower interest rates than the ECB has delivered, see chapter 3.

factor markets, because this refers to the real side of the economy. Here, in the ceding of sovereignty, three important issues have to be decided: (i) Which decisions should be taken at which level? (ii) Which body should decide? And (iii) which decision rule, e.g., qualified majority or unanimity, should be applied?

The Four Freedoms

The core of European integration is the single market and its four freedoms: the free movement of goods, people, services, and capital. This gives a first answer to the assignment issue of which decision in an economic union should go to which level. According to the principle of the free movement of goods, all obstacles to the common market are to be dismantled. Member states no longer have the option to erect barriers to trade, barriers including not only tariffs and quantitative restrictions, but also national regulations representing barriers to border-crossing flows of goods. Only in cases where products are hazardous and damaging to health, to safety, or to the environment does this principle not apply (Article 30 of the EU Treaty).

The principle of the free movement of people specifies that EU citizens have the right to move and reside freely within the territory of the member states in order to work, study, seek employment, start a business, or live, for instance as a pensioner. They should receive the same treatment in all member states; i.e., it is not permissible to discriminate against EU citizens on account of their nationality. Today this right has been implemented in all member states. Free movement also means that border checks on individuals are to be abolished; this has been achieved in the Schengen countries (named after the town where the agreement was signed) to which Austria, Belgium, Denmark, Finland, France, Germany, Greece, Italy, Luxembourg, the Netherlands, Portugal, Spain, and Sweden belong (as of 2003).

According to the principle of the free movement of services, services offered in one member country can also be supplied in the other member countries. The free movement of services is especially linked to the right of establishment; individuals have the right to establish businesses anywhere in the European Union.

Finally, the free movement of capital implies that all segmentations of the capital market that hinder border-crossing capital flows can no longer be justified.

From these four freedoms, and from the concept of the internal market, it follows that all national decisions and the corresponding policy instruments that can erect barriers to the free border-crossing flows must be given up. What is essential for a single market, i.e., for all border-crossing activities, has to be addressed in some form of a common institutional setup.

Federalism and Subsidiarity

But European integration goes beyond the concept of a single market aiming at an economic and political union. The additional issue concerns which competences have to be shifted to the European level in addition to the very essentials of guaranteeing the free flow of goods, people, services, and capital in a single market. The economist's answer to this question of the optimal degree of decentralization or centralization is the concept of fiscal federalism, which was explained in chapter 10. As this concept suggests, an economic activity should be assigned to those organizational levels of government that can best deal with it. In this assignment of tasks, one should start with the lowest level. This is what the subsidiarity principle requires. The reasoning behind this principle is that a more decentralized unit has better information on preferences and on the structure of problems. The lower level can deal better with local or regional issues; it can also respond more flexibly. Higher levels of organization tend to have less information on local matters; and distortions in collecting information are more likely to occur. In the spirit of this approach, regional problems should come under the responsibility of the regional authorities, problems with a national dimension should be decided at the national level, and economic problems of a European dimension such as trade policy should be assigned to the European level.[9]

Policy Areas at the European Level

Following the requirements of the single market and the subsidiarity principle of the economic union, a number of policy decisions have to be centralized in the European Union, among them trade policy, competition policy, and subsidy control. Trade policy is carried out at the European level, since the European Union is also a customs union with a common external tariff, which incidentally is now 3.5 percent for all trade in industrial products. Other trade policy instruments like antidumping are applied uniformly at the EU level as well. The European Union has a Common Commercial Policy vis-à-vis third countries and the World Trade Organization (WTO). Competition policy, which has to make sure that market processes in a single market are not distorted by

---

[9] In the assignment of tasks, one has to make sure that the lower levels cannot free-ride on the higher levels, for instance through a no-bailout clause or through limits on the level of permissible debt. Compare, for instance, the experience with the provinces in Argentina prior to the breakdown of the currency board.

the market power of firms, must be directed to the single market as a whole. Thus, the abuse of market power in the EU and the creation of new dominating positions (monopolies) by mergers have to be controlled at the European level. Cases affecting only an individual member state are left to the national authorities. Subsidy control has a similar task, i.e., to prevent competition in the single market from being distorted by state aids of the member countries. The Commission controls national subsidies and has established a respected power in this domain.

The Common Agricultural Policy (CAP) owes its existence only indirectly to the single market. Assuming that there were national agricultural policies in the traditional form, i.e., where different levels of national subsidies applied to the production of agricultural goods in different countries, then, in order to prevent distortions between agricultural production in the various countries, one would need to have separate border controls for these products. But it is not practical to have separate border controls in a single market for specific products: that would require determining at each border which trucks were carrying agricultural products. Therefore, to prevent such border controls, the union would need to have a single agricultural market. But since this sector might not be strong enough to survive exposure to international competition, recourse has been taken to external protection. The Common Agricultural Policy, undertaken at the European level, defines reference prices for agricultural products and accordingly pays subsidies to farmers. It uses quantity restrictions for production, for instance milk quotas. It also pays subsidies for exports and uses a variable import levy to bring the price of imported products up to the European level.[10] Agricultural policy absorbs nearly half of the EU budget. In recent years, direct price supports have been partly substituted by income transfers. It has been widely debated to what extent subsidies and agricultural policy can be nationalized. This option would require a switch from direct subsidies to income transfers for farmers. The nationalization of agricultural policies would also be feasible, if minimum requirements for state aid could limit the potential distortions between member states.

Other areas in which decisions have to be centralized are those where severe distortions of competition or in the allocation of resources would arise. For instance, large differences in indirect taxation would imply arbitrage on the goods markets by consumers and firms. For this reasons, in indirect taxation in the single market countries a minimum rate for the value added tax has been set that applies to most commodities. Even though the destination country principle holds for value-added tax, whereby the tax is paid by the final consumer, a minimum rate reduces

---

[10] With rising world market prices, this instrument has lost importance.

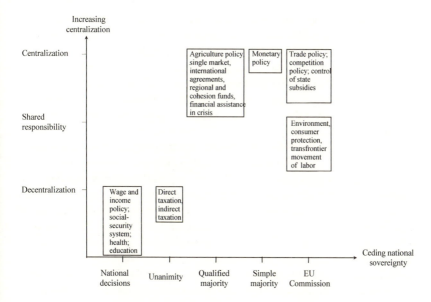

Figure 13.1 Degree of centralization.

distortions that may arise from the exemption for direct mailing.

In contrast to these centralized areas, the other policy areas are allo-cated to the national level. These include taxation; wage policy in those countries where wages are not determined by the markets, i.e., where they are negotiated by the social partners; the organization of the health, education, and culture sectors; and the social security systems, including pensions, health, and unemployment insurance (figure 13.1).

Tendencies of Centralization

The two criteria of the single market and subsidiarity set general guide-lines for addressing policy problems in an economic union. These criteria, however, may be interpreted quite differently by the political process depending upon the specific issue in question. Thus, the criterion of a public good with a spatial dimension the geographic size of the European Union is a precise concept to apply, for instance, to the issue of global warming, where Europe has to be considered a major player. But in practice, politicians may interpret all sorts of externalities broadly, not least to initiate programs involving expenditures and financing at the European level. Moreover, other goods will be considered so meritor-ious—the so-called "merit goods"—that they will be put on the European agenda. They open up new sources of financing at the European level and correspond to the preference function of politicians. An example of these merit goods are roads or railway lines which, according to the subsidiarity principle, should be dealt with nationally, once the points of intersection are properly defined. Last but not least, distributional considerations at the EU level are introduced under the heading of social coherence. It is for this reason that, in the observed assignment of issues, some areas take an intermediate position between central and national competence—transport, energy, the environment, and consumer protection, for instance.

In addition to the above mentioned points of contention, there is an ongoing debate about how intensive the regulation by the Commission, e.g., through its directives (some 270 so far), and how detailed the decisions of the European Court of Justice, should be. From a practical point of view, it has proved to be impossible to harmonize all legal rules of all the different member countries. Therefore, in the Cassis de Dijon case of 1979, the European Court of Justice established the country-of-origin principle, or the principle of mutual recognition. The Cassis de Dijon, a fruit liqueur, is widely used in France to prepare Kir Royale, Kir Archeveque, and Kir Bourgeois. However it was not permitted to be marketed in Germany. By German regulation, the monopoly law on spirits (Branntweinmonopolgesetz) of 1922 required fruit liqueurs to have an alcohol content of at least 32 percent, and thus the alcoholic content of 17 percent in the Cassis de Dijon meant that it was *verboten* (prohibited) to sell this product as a fruit liqueur in Germany. (The logic behind such a law is another matter.) The European Court of Justice ruled that a product legally sold at market in one country of the European Union has to be accepted by other countries for sale. This ruling thus permitted the export of Belgian beer, which is not brewed in accordance with the German beer purity regulations of 1516, to Germany; and it allowed the export of pasta not made from Italian buckwheat flour (durum) to Italy. According to this country-of-origin principle, the different regulations must be mutually recognized and allowed to coexist. The Cassis de Dijon verdict of the European Court of Justice not only holds for goods, but also applies to services, for instance banking and insurance. In the same way, a bank product sold in the United Kingdom can be marketed in Germany under UK laws. This principle has proved to be a proverbial can of worms regarding national regulations.

Be that as it may, the European Commission, endowed with the power to regulate, is tempted to use its power and to over-regulate. For instance, in Regulation 1677/88 from June 15, 1988, the Commission defines the quality norms for cucumbers, specifying even their required curvature in quality classes I, II, and III (requiring for instance that the curvature does not surpass 10 mm for a length of 10 cm in quality class I (Siebert 2003). As another example, the European Court of Justice decided in September

2003 that the practice in Germany of not counting the "on-call" time of doctors in hospitals (during which they have to be available in a hospital, but can sleep if not needed) as working hours violated the EU directive on working time. Germany was therefore obliged to change its laws. It is hard to see why all these details have to be uniform, from Feira in Portugal to Rantasippi in Finland.

Ex Ante Harmonization versus Institutional Competition

In the assignment of competences, two opposing strategies have been followed: institutional competition, and prior harmonization. Institutional competition means that different national institutional arrangements can exist simultaneously in a single market, and that the rules of the country of origin (for a product or a service) are mutually recognized. The implication of institutional competition is the arbitrage of consumers and firms. Consumers vote with their purses and their feet, and firms take advantage of differentials in national regulations. Countries compete for the mobile factors of production, and the emerging institutional setting is the result of an open-ended process. The most important impact of institutional competition will be to open up markets that have so far been closed because of national regulations.

The conflict between the strategies of institutional competition and prior harmonization is an expression of a deeper conflict of orientation: on a constitutional level, it is the conflict of federalism and centralization. On a philosophical level, it is the conflict between liberalism in the classical or British sense and a more planning-oriented approach. Here we have diverging views on such issues as confidence in the functioning of markets or any type of interventionism; the sovereignty of the consumer or need for his "protection"; the role and the size of the government versus the spontaneity of autonomous decision-making; and decentralized processes versus constructivism, or the English case law versus the logic of the Roman law. Europe is in search of its institutions, and the showdown between the British and the French concept of Europe is still to come.

SHARING THE DECISIONS: WHICH BODY AND WHICH MAJORITY?

Besides the question of which issue should be centralized and which should remain at the national level when looking at the characteristics of the issue, the other two important questions of decision-making are which body can take which decision, and which decision-making rule, for instance qualified majority or unanimity, applies to which body and to which issues. The answer that the European Union has found to these questions has led to a system of multi-level governance. Decisions are taken in a complex web of decision-making bodies with complex decision rules.

The Council of the European Union

The Council of the European Union is the central decision-making body. It is made up of the member states and meets in more than twenty different forms, for instance as heads of states (the Council) or as ministers for a specific portfolio (Council of Ministers; e.g., Foreign Affairs, Economy and Finance (the Ecofin), Agriculture, Transport, etc.). The Council in its different forms is the decision-making body in such fundamental questions as changing the treaty subject to ratification in the member states, taxation, and all other issues where unanimity applies. It is also the decision-making body in the many fields where a qualified majority is needed.

For decisions of the Council, there are three different types of majority according to Article 205.

- If not stated otherwise, a *simple majority* of votes of the member states is needed. This is 13 out of 25 in the enlarged Union; it was 8 out of 15 member states in the EU-15 up to May 2004. Simple majority, however, is practically never used.[11]

- For a *qualified majority* in the enlarged EU-25, as of January 2005, 232 out of 321 votes (72.3 percent) will be required.[12] Votes are then assigned to the member states according to the weighting specified in the Treaty of Nice; these new weights have been defined in light of the expected enlargement (table 13.1). The qualified majority is required in such areas as agricultural policy, trade policy in a narrow sense (on the operative level, i.e., commercial policy except e.g., trade in cultural and audio-visual services), technical and financial cooperation with third countries, the free movement of citizens within the European Union, and technical and anti-discrimination measures. This type of qualified majority is needed for decisions that are taken by the European Council with respect to proposals of the European Commission. In all other cases, it is additionally required that the 232 votes represent the approval of at least two-thirds of the member states, i.e., 17 members (Article 205). A member state has the right to request verification that the member states constituting the qualified

---

[11] It applies, for instance, in the Governing Council of the European Central Bank.

[12] Council of the European Union, November 26, 2002, Document 14702/02 EN. In the interim period between the date of accession and December 2004, the old weighting of votes applies, with the weights for the new members defined accordingly.

TABLE 13.1
Allocation of votes in the EU-27

	Population[a] (m)	Votes (pre-Nice)	Votes (post-Nice)
Germany	82.2	10	29
UK	59.6	10	29
France	59.2	10	29
Italy	57.7	10	29
Spain	39.4	8	27
Netherlands	15.9	5	13
Greece	10.5	5	12
Belgium	10.2	5	12
Portugal	10.0	5	12
Sweden	8.9	4	10
Austria	8.1	4	10
Denmark	5.3	3	7
Finland	5.2	3	7
Ireland	3.8	3	7
Luxembourg	0.4	2	4
Poland	38.6		27
Romania	22.5		14
Czech Republic	10.3[b]		12
Hungary	10.1		12
Bulgaria	8.2		10
Slovak Republic	5.4		7
Lithuania	3.7		7
Latvia	2.4		4
Slovenia	2.0		4
Estonia	1.4		4
Cyprus	0.7		4
Malta	0.4		3
Total votes	482.1	87	345

[a] December 2000.
[b] July 1999.

majority represent at least 62 percent of the total population of the Union. The blocking minority is 90 votes in the EU-25.[13] In the EU-15 up to May 2004, these figures were 62 out of 87 votes for qualified majority (71.26 percent); the blocking minority was 26 votes. In the case where the majority of member states was also needed, the approval of at least 10 members was required. This

[13] When not all the candidate countries listed in the Declaration on the enlargement of the Union will have joined, as now is the case, the threshold for a qualified majority will move, according to the pace of accession, up from the actual percentage of 71.26 percent to 73.9 percent. The blocking minority will change accordingly.

voting scheme with the pre-Nice weights has been adjusted for
enlargement in 2004 until the new weights become effective in
2005. From 2007 on, when Bulgaria and Romania join, 258 of
345 votes (73.8 percent) will be needed for the EU-27. The blocking minority then will be 88 votes and 18 members.

- *Unanimity* is required in the most important policy areas. In addition, in the case of qualified majority there has been a consensus so
  far, whenever a vital interest of a member state is involved, not to
  take votes and to continue negotiation.

Basic decisions require unanimity (table 13.2). The most important
areas where unanimity is needed are: admitting new members (Article
49), indirect taxation (Article 93), direct taxation (Article 95,), the budget
of the European Union (Article 269), and fundamental rules (Articles 94,
95). Unanimity is also required in international treaties in trade policy
(Article 133), cultural policy (Article 151), industrial policy (Article 157),
social cohesion policy (Articles 157, 161), i.e., the regional funds,
research and development policy (Article 166), and environmental
protection (Article 175). Asylum policy, while respecting international
agreements, is under national authority and requires unanimity. This
also holds for immigration. From 2004, the procedure of co-decision
with qualified majority applies to certain aspects of asylum and immigration policy (Article 67). Of course, the unanimity principle in the area of
taxation is at the heart of the question of national sovereignty and political union.

TABLE 13.2
Required majorities

Required majority	Policy area
Simple majority	European Central Bank Council
Qualified majority	Agriculture
	Internal market
	Environment
	Transport
	Trade policy in the narrow sense
	International agreements including trade policy
	in the wider sense (except for some areas)
	Regional and cohesion funds[a]
Unanimity	Harmonizing the legal framework
	Indirect taxation
	Direct taxation
	Admittance of new members
	Culture

[a] After the next funding round (post-2007).

According to the Treaty of Nice, qualified majority voting will apply in some areas where up to now unanimity has been required. This includes among others legislation on the free movement of EU citizens (except measures concerning passports, identity cards, social protection, and social security); rules on antidiscrimination at the workplace; common commercial policy, where qualified majority will now also apply to most agreements on trade in services and commercial aspects of intellectual property (except trade in cultural and audio-visual services, educational services, social and human health services, and treaties in international taxation); economic and social cohesion actions outside the structural funds; and some formal procedures such as the appointment of the secretary-general of the Council and the approval of the Rules of Procedure of the European Court of Justice. After the next funding round to be decided in 2007, i.e., around 2014, decisions and codecisions on the structural and cohesion funds will be taken by a qualified majority and the co-decision of Parliament. Financial assistance to a member state threatened by a serious economic crisis or natural disaster (Article 100) will henceforth be decided by qualified majority. This may very well become relevant in the euro zone when a country gets into financial distress. It softens the no-bail-out clause (Article 103) or can even be in contradiction to it. Together with the weakening or effective abandonment of the Stability Pact, this may change the incentive mechanism to prevent high debt.

A special majority of four-fifths of the member states is needed for determining a serious breach of fundamental rights by a member state.

The European Parliament

The European Parliament participates in the different forms of approval, co-decision, and hearing. The approval of Parliament is needed in declarations of fundamental violations of the treaty. The proceedings of joint decisions according to Article 251 apply to proposals of the Commission to which Parliament submits a statement. On the basis of this statement, the proposals of the European Commission are enacted by the Council. If Parliament alters the Commission's proposals in joint decisions, rules specify how to proceed. The European Parliament does not have the right of initiative.

The European Commission

The Commission is the operating arm of the European Union; it implements policies, creates secondary law, and, together with the European Court of Justice, is the guardian of the treaty. Primary Community law can be established by the Council—or in the case of the co-decision procedure by Parliament and Council—only in those areas that have been defined for joint decisions; where unanimity is required, the power to legislate still rests with the individual member state. The Commission establishes secondary law in the form of regulations, directives, and decisions. Regulations are directly applied; they form part of the legal system and there is no need for national measures to implement them. Directives bind member states with respect to the objectives to be achieved. It is up to the national authorities to choose the appropriate means to implement the directives. Decisions are addressed to a specific member state or to all member states and are binding. Informal procedures and rules of the game play an important role in the decision making of the European Union.

The European Court of Justice

The European Court of Justice is concerned with the interpretation of EU law. The Court also provides the judicial safeguards necessary to ensure that the law is respected. The types of action include actions brought before the Court by a member state against a member state and by the Commission against a member state.

The Binding Character of Legal EU Rules

All these different layers of law are binding for the member states, i.e., for the governments and the citizens of the member states. European law takes precedence over the law of the member states. European law also binds the courts of the member states; in developing law further and in interpreting it, they have to take into account European law. This is an important aspect of ceding national sovereignty. The European Court of Justice with its 15 judges is the ultimate guardian of European law; it also understands itself as the promoter of European law.

Even the constitutions of member states are affected. Thus, Germany had to change its Constitution in order to allow female soldiers to use weapons in the army. Apparently, conflicts between the European Law and the national constitution, or between the European Court of Justice and the German Constitutional Court, cannot be ruled out. The German Constitutional Court has the role of examining the constitutionality of laws, having declared quite a few laws unconstitutional and forced Parliament to change existing laws substantially in the past. The Constitutional Court wants to retain the right to examine the constitutionality of European law as well. In that function, it may indeed clash with the European Court of Justice. So far, the German Constitutional Court speaks of a relationship of cooperation with the European Court of

Justice. It is quite possible that, in an atmosphere of cooperation, severe clashes can be prevented. After all, over time all agents will become accustomed to European law. A potential solution to major clashes between European law and the constitutional law of member states would be a competence court, which would decide on where the competence for decisions lies.

THE BUDGET OF THE EUROPEAN UNION

Besides establishing a system of institutional rules at the European level, the political will of Europe finds its expression in the budget. Actually, the EU budget is restricted to a limit of 1.27 percent of the GDP of all member states. EU expenditure amounted to €98.6 billion in 2002. Of this, 45.2 percent was spent on agricultural policy, and 34.5 percent on the structural and regional funds.

The budget of the European Union is financed by agricultural levies (1.3 percent),[14] import duties (8.3 percent), and contributions of the member states (72 percent).[15] Contributions by member states consist partly of the value added tax resource (23.5 percent for 2002); 1 percent of the national revenues of the value added tax is transferred to the EU budget. The other EU revenue is the gross national income (GNI) (48.5 percent), calculated as a proportion of national GNIs. The GNI includes income earned abroad, whereas GDP denotes income produced in a country, irrespective of whether foreign-owned factors have to be paid. The intention is to shift EU financing more toward the GNI resource in the future. The percentage of the value added tax has been reduced from 1.4 to 1.0 percent in 1999. The tax base of the value added tax to be taken into account is capped at 50 percent of GNI instead of 55 percent as previously. Therefore, contributions are de facto related to GNI. The EU has no right to tax or to incur debt.

Germany has been a net payer to the budget of the European Union. It contributed 22.8 percent of the EU budget in 2002 and received 15.8 percent. It was the largest contributor and the third largest recipient. Its net contribution was €5 billion, or 0.24 percent of its national income. This is a relatively low figure. The transfer is more than compensated by the advantages that Germany enjoys from the European Union, especially having the common market as an export area for its industry. Italy pays nearly the same percentage of its national income, other countries even more (the Netherlands pays 0.5 percent, Sweden 0.3 percent). The main

---

[14] There is also a fixed duty on sugar and glucose produced within the EU, transferred directly from the sugar manufacturers.

[15] The rest of the EU revenue is miscellaneous income.

recipients were Spain (1.29 percent), Ireland (1.50 percent), Portugal (2.14 percent), and Greece (2.39 percent).

The Impact of the EU on the German Economy

The question of how European integration has impacted on the German economy is a contrafactual question; we simply do not know how Germany would have developed if the EU had not come into existence. There is no doubt that Germany's integration into Europe has brought economic benefits from trade and specialization. Moreover, it can be seen as a foundation on which German unification was achieved.

As described above, the process of ceding national sovereignty has gone a long way. Besides monetary policy, all policy areas essential to the single market—such as trade policy, competition policy, the control of state aid—have been shifted to the European level. Decisions at the European level have changed national policy considerably, for instance, through a set of EU directives, the new institutional arrangements for the former natural monopolies. Among these directives are those on public broadcasting (1989), telecommunications (1988, 1990, and 1995), the railroads (1991 and 1995), the postal service (1997), electricity (1997), and gas (1998). In air traffic, business licenses for airlines are granted under the same conditions in the European Union (1992), although grandfather slots at airports still are prevalent. Bilateral traffic agreements between individual EU members and non-EU countries are no longer permitted following a 2002 decision of the European Court of Justice. In the liberalized financial markets, the home rule is applied in banking (1989) and insurance (1992), according to which the home country where the bank or the insurer has its seat is responsible for supervision. This allows institutional competition. In consumer and environmental protection, standards were established including for bathing water (1976), drinking water quality (1980, 1998), and ambient air quality (1996) that have to be respected by all member states.

The legal framework of the EU dominates the national laws. All these developments have redefined the conditions under which German economic policy has to operate. The most obvious change is that policy instruments simply are no longer available to the German policy-maker; he has to utilize a different instrument set. In quite a few areas, decisions are no longer taken nationally. Germany and the other EU countries each have just one vote by which to influence the outcome. At the same time, the European approach takes precedence over national findings. Moreover, the reaction of the European partners to the policy instruments chosen comes to play. Thus, some targets may get a different weighting when European conditions are taken into account.

The German public is not aware of the size of the institutional change that has occurred. For instance, according to a survey of Allensbach, only 42 percent of the German population knew about a proposal of the Convention for a European Constitution in December 2003 which the European Council failed to push through.[16] There is a gap between the power already vested in the European Union and the public perception of the EU's role. Again according to the Allensbach survey, only 21 percent of the population thinks that the EU has a large responsibility for European economic development in the future, against 74 percent who believe that the decisions of the German federal government are still of great relevance. This is not consistent with reality. Moreover, the national government is held politically liable, whereas the European level can act without being held responsible by the voters.

THE ROAD TO A EUROPEAN CONSTITUTION

With EU institutional setup dominating the German legal rules, the further development of European-level institutions will have a further influence on Germany's economic future. In this context, a constitution for Europe is a major issue.[17]

The EU treaty is a multilateral arrangement by which sovereign member states give up some sovereignty in favor of joint decision-making at the European level. This treaty is not a constitution. If the EU had a constitution—assuming that it would be a democratic one—the fundamental decisions would be made not by the Council but by the sovereign, that is, by the people or by a parliament representing the people. It is fairly realistic to state that at this time in history the European Union lacks even one of the decisive elements of a constitution, i.e., the European people as a sovereign, since a European citizen with a clear identification to Europe does not (yet) exist. Nor, therefore, is the EU a state. Neither is it a confederation with an intra-state pattern of rules, or an association of completely sovereign nation states. European integration relies on the method of intergovernmental cooperation where most of the decisions are taken in the European Council, reaching agreements between the heads of state or the ministers of specific portfolios (Siebert 2002c). It takes its democratic legitimacy from the inhabitants of the member states by having the decisions of the various bodies of the European Union coupled to the national parliaments, as the German Constitutional Court stated in a major decision in 1993, in which Germa-

[16] See Frankfurter Allgemeine Zeitung, December 17, 2003.
[17] Besides these constitutional questions, the EU also faces the problem of how it can move to a higher growth path (Sapir et al. 2003; Siebert 2001).

ny's membership in the Monetary Union was called into question by the plaintiff.

The European Union has been empowered by the individual member states through a treaty that has developed in several stages, beginning with the Treaty of Rome (1956), and encompassing the Single Act (1981) and the Treaties of Maastricht (1992), Amsterdam (1997), and Nice (2000). The EU has the power to establish primary and secondary laws. New laws can be enacted only in the context of the Treaty and according to the stipulations of the treaty. The Treaty can be changed only in the same way that it was originally concluded: namely by negotiation and ratification by the individual member states. Thus, the member states are the masters of the Treaty.

The enlarged European Union of 25 faces two basic issues, one practical and one fundamental; both are interrelated. From a practical point of view, the enlarged Union can no longer be governed by the existing procedure of intergovernmental decision-making. Given the requirement of unanimity in a wide area of decisions, including even such aspects as the regional and cohesion funds in the next round of funding which will start in 2007,[18] and the possibilities of a varying set of coalitions for a blocking minority when qualified majority applies, it is hard to see how decisions can be reached. The risk of an institutional deadlock is real, unless recourse is sought in a variable geometry with different speeds. The European Union's development nearly stalled in the 1970s and the first half of the 1980s because of the members' veto and the Luxembourg Compromise. Introduced in 1966, the compromise stipulated that member states could claim a vital national interest so that the qualified majority rule was then not applied. Thus, members were able effectively to block unwelcome decisions. From a fundamental point of view, the EU has a democratic deficit. Many decisions are taken at European level by the Commission and the Council that directly affect the lives of Europeans, and these Europeans have only a very indirect and remote means of expressing their preferences and influencing these decisions. They do not have the option to vote someone out of government if they dislike a specific policy. After all, their national governments will put the blame on other countries if the public does not accept decisions. Thus, the argument of the German Constitutional Court that the EU takes its democratic legitimacy from the people of the member states by having the decisions of the bodies of the European Union coupled to the national parliaments may be practical, but it is rather weak. Europe lacks the democratic responsibility of those who take decisions; it lacks democratic legitimacy.

---

[18] Qualified majority will apply thereafter.

The Constitution, agreed upon by the European Council at the Brussels meeting in June 2004, is an attempt to break that impasse. The Constitution still has to be ratified by the member states; several states including the United Kingdom will hold a referendum. If this process goes smoothly, the Constitution will become effective in 2007 at the earliest, except for provisions where specific dates have been set.

According to the new institutional arrangement, some decisions will be moved from unanimity to qualified majority. Thus, the powers of the EU are increased in areas such as asylum and immigration, energy, and space research, and to some extent in economic coordination, here with a newly created majority. The co-decision process, whereby the European Parliament has to agree on measures shaping policy, is to become the general rule between Parliament and Council. By and large however, not too many areas are designed to be moved to qualified majority. As a rule of thumb, about 65 percent of the decisions will be taken under qualified majority rule instead of 60 percent. The core decisions remain under the unanimity requirement. Member states retain the right to set national entry levels for third-country nationals. Social policy, taxation policy, foreign and security policy also require unanimity and thus remain national. This means that the constitution represents only a small change toward a more intensified form of integration. In any case, moving unanimity items to a qualified majority will not reduce the democratic deficit, because the power to decide rests with the Council irrespective of the increased importance of the co-decision procedure.

The main point of contention why the first attempt to find a consensus in December 2003 failed was the new decision rule for qualified majority, a dual majority—that is, to require the majority of the member states and the majority of the people, defined as 60 percent of the population. This 50–60 voting rule was to replace the voting procedure as defined by the Treaty of Nice, in which votes were assigned to the member states (see table 13.2). In this treaty, however, the votes were not really allocated proportionally to the population. The small and medium-sized countries (from Slovenia to Romania) have been designated a more than proportional share of the votes relative to the larger countries. And Spain and Poland had only marginally less votes than Germany with double the population size. (In the case of Germany, there was also a distortion relative to the three other large countries). Poland and Spain (under Aznar) insisted on the weighting as agreed upon in the Treaty of Nice. As a way out, qualified majority was redefined in the new Constitution with 55 percent of the member states comprising at least 15 of them and 65 percent of the population (Article I-24). Thus, it is made more difficult for larger countries to organize a majority. It also needs four members to block a majority. Moroever, a new type of qualified majority has been introduced: 72 percent of the members plus 65 percent of the population are needed, when the Council is not acting on a proposal from the Commission or from the Union Minister for Foreign Affairs. This new majority also applies to enhanced cooperation for the Eurozone where not all members are allowed to vote.

Other planned changes involve the organization of administrative decision making and attempt to enhance efficiency. A president of the European Council will be elected for 2.5 years. A post of foreign minister is to be established to represent the EU on external matters. The position of the president of the European Commission is strengthened. He lays down guidelines within which the Commission carries out its tasks. The members of the Commission shall resign if the president requests. From 2014, the Commission has to consist of only two-thirds of the member states, with rotation among the members.

Member countries may be given the right to opt out. This opting-out exception is a dangerous strategy for the Union because it can be used as a threat to get one's way and introduce a greater heterogeneity in institutional arrangements. The EU is a single undertaking, and the net benefits come in a package. Only in areas where the policy of two speeds applies should an opting out clause be granted.

For the European Central Bank, the Constitution contains some major changes. Whereas in contrast to the original plan the target of price stability is now included as one of the economic policy goals of the European Union (Article I-3 Sect.3), the ECB no longer is an institution *sui generis*, which it was according to its special mention in Article 8 in the Treaty of Amsterdam. It is now named an organ and is mentioned before the European Court of Auditors within the section "Other Institutions and Bodies". Usually, an organ has the duty of a loyal cooperation with the other organs of the union. This may sound relatively unimportant at first glance, but it can be detrimental to the independence of the ECB in the longer run. Furthermore, the national central banks that form the European System of Central Banks (of which the ECB is a part) no longer have their independence guaranteed. Finally, but most important, the European Council may amend all or parts of the provisions of Titel III of Part III which contains the institutional arrangement of the ECB. Whereas such a decision requires unanimity and consultation with the ECB, a new treaty is not necessary. Neither the national parliaments nor the people in a referendum will be asked to agree to a change in this important area. Together with the attempts to soften the stability pact, this is a rather worrisome development. The EU citizens and the financial markets may get the impression that politicians can now rearrange the contract of monetary union to strengthen the arm of politics and weaken the monetary authority. People in Germany may indeed feel that they have been misled, because monetary union was sold to them as something different. As a matter of fact, the concept of monetary union as a community of stability was the basis of the German law with respect to the entry into the monetary union, as the German Constitutional Court stated in its major decision of 1993 in which it asserted the constitutionality of giving up the Deutschmark.

There is a declaration to prepare the conditions for fiscal stability in the good years of the business cycle, but this is not binding. The hand of the Commission in the deficit procedure has not been strengthened, it can only make recommendations to the Council, except for the proposal that an excessive deficit exists. This proposal can only be rejected with unanimity.

The Constitution lays out the basic goals of the European Union, putting some weight on social coherence and social protection. The Commission can start initiatives in social policy, including conditions of the labor market, health and industrial and research policy. It seems that to a certain extent Europe finds its identity in the idea of reducing differences in income and endowment with public goods. Although only a minor part of GDP is actually spent on these purposes, one can get the impression that the proposal can be interpreted in the sense of distributive federalism, where integration is seen as bringing people together via the vehicle of redistribution. In that sense, one can say that the Constitution is a welfare state and social democratic document, not a liberal one in the European sense. It does not cultivate the spirit of competitive federalism. Looking ahead, the interpretation of social cohesion and of social protection by the European Court of Justice Europe may rely more on the equity element than on the competition element in the future. In any case, the Constitution can be seen as moving the center of gravity away from the market mechanism.

The Constitution will still have to be ratified in the member states, in quite a few by a referendum. Blair's decision in April 2004 to hold a referendum on the constitution in the UK has added fresh uncertainty about whether the new framework will be accepted in the end. Belgium, the Czech Republic, Denmark, Ireland, Luxemburg, Poland, Portugal and Spain will hold a referendum as well. Until the uncertainty on the acceptance of the Constitution has been dissolved, the Treaty of Nice (with the weighting of votes) will remain the relevant legal setting. Then it is likely to become more difficult to make decisions in an enlarged European Union, because the veto power that each country holds as a result of the principle of unanimity will become a powerful hindrance.

Looking into the very distant future, one can imagine how far away the European Union is from an intensive form of integration if one envisions a scenario with an improved democratic legitimacy of the European level as follows. More decision power is given to the European Parliament. This implies that national parliaments must cede some of their competences. The European Parliament itself can be conceived as a two-chamber system. Representatives for the first chamber would be elected, for instance by a majority rule for each election district; a second chamber would represent the member states. The electoral districts for the election of the members of the first chamber should be delineated such that each district represents a similar percentage of the population. The second chamber should represent the member states, ideally by electing the representatives of the member states directly (as in the US Senate). The Commission represents the European government. A constitution-like system of rules would define the competences of the European Parliament, its two chambers, the Commission, the member states, and the regional levels of member states.

Describing the future road in this way exposes all the problems that an enlarged Europe faces. From historical experience, we know that the principle of "no taxation without representation" is the basis of democracy. It seems realistic that the European population will not be prepared to cede national sovereignty, shifting the power to tax, the power to spend, and the power of the budget to the European level. This would mean that a European institution such as the European Parliament would be authorized to decide which type of tax to levy, the tax base, and the tax rate for the individual taxpayer; it would also be able to decide whether or not a tax collected in country A could be spent in Country B, either explicitly or implicitly.

The European Treaty allows member states to form special clubs that intensify their cooperation in specific areas such as border controls (Schengen countries) or monetary union. Countries may move at different speeds of integration. According to this approach, the dynamics of integration may be determined by a subset of the member countries, for instance by military cooperation. Different speeds and a variable geometry cannot, however, relate to the very essentials of a union. They must refer to additional steps that one may consider as desirable but not strictly necessary. Nor can a variable geometry solve the core issue of a democratic void; it is simply not conceivable that a European Club as a subset of member countries will develop a separated constitutional arrangement diverging from the other members, including for instance parliamentary voting and taxation. Moreover, a variable geometry would discriminate between members and entail the risk of splitting up the EU. Thus, the strategy of multiple speeds can be applied in the context of intergovernmental decision-making. It is less suitable for a more intense form of integration. Variable geometry or separate speeds can only be part of an intermediate step of integration.

CHAPTER FOURTEEN

The System of Governance in Germany's Social Market Economy

Germany has developed a system of governance in which, besides markets, non-market mechanisms play an important role in finding a consensus and solving economic issues. Markets are used as a coordination and allocation device, but they are replaced in part by the decision-making of social groups and by informal personal relationships. This approach to governance includes the social partners, that is the trade unions and employers' associations, in wage formation; it involves banks, workers, and trade unions in the governance of firms through codetermination, where in addition block-holders have strong positions; and it brings the workers' councils into the operation of firms. The approach also involves informal personal relationships, as in the bank-based capital market with intermediated products. But it applies to other areas as well, for example the regional associations of statuary health insurance physicians in the public health system, and to the administration of the university system by codetermination and through a governmental planning approach. Moreover, market outcomes are corrected or influenced by a set of policy instruments. Germans look for consensus and seem to have some preference for non-market solutions. In addition, the mechanisms of consensus are an important feature in the governance of government and its federal structure.[1]

THE ROLE OF MARKETS

In the product markets, Germany relies on the market mechanism to coordinate the decisions of households and firms, to stimulate technological innovations, and to introduce new solutions to problems in a decentralized way. As the country is an open economy, and as openness has been a basic principle of German economic policy that was never really called into question, firms are free to compete. The need to produce

---

[1] I appreciate critical comments on this chapter from Terhi Jokipii, David Moore, Eduard Herda, Eirik Jones, and Bennedikt Wahler.

internationally competitive export goods in terms of quality and price, and the necessity for domestically produced goods—the import substitutes—to stand up to the imported products of other suppliers in the global market, are important reasons why government intervention in the product markets of tradables is kept to a minimum. In addition to this aspect of openness, competition policy has a long tradition in German economic policy, to ensure that large firms cannot dominate the market process, that market power is not misused, and that mergers leading to monopoly-like constellations are prohibited.

Since the late 1980s, privatization has taken place in the areas of telecommunications, the postal service, and the railroads. Municipalities have sold part of their equity holdings in regional public utilities (electricity and water supply); also, local transportation and garbage collection have been auctioned off (outsourced) for an operating period. The federal government and some of the Länder have also sold or are selling their equity, in telecommunications and power transmission firms, for example. Moreover, former stiffly regulated markets have been liberalized and new property rights have been defined for the network industries, including telecommunications, power transmission, and gas. All this, together with a new regulatory regime, has meant that the old "natural" monopolies in the above-mentioned sectors have been abolished.

Other product markets, however, are still characterized by strong government intervention; the market is restrained by government. Modern sectors like biotechnology and pharmaceuticals are regulated by a licensing procedure of new products, requiring time and thus engendering costs that do not arise in other countries. An exit program from the field of atomic energy, with a timetable for the closure of individual nuclear power plants, has been set up; this was done in agreement with the atomic industry, which in exchange was guaranteed that the plants would run up to the agreed closing dates. Other regulations relate to operating permits for plants and building permits. Generally, it can be said that in Germany economic activities in most areas are regulated in minute detail; extensive permits have to be obtained in advance of actual investment, and regulations have to be satisfied. Store closing hours in Germany are strictly limited, which obviously constrains consumer freedom and entrepreneurial options.

In yet other product markets such as housing and apartment rents, prices are controlled; the regulations specify the permitted increase in rents and define the entitlements of the tenant, such as his protection against a notice to quit. This, however, does not apply to office space. Since housing belongs to the sector of non-tradables, this type of regulation does not have direct international repercussions. However, the regulation reduces incentives to supply apartment space and to invest in the housing sector. The decline of the West German construction industry since the 1990s is likely to have been caused partly by this regulation. A measure of the intensity of regulation is the index of prices administered and influenced by government: 30 percent of the prices in the consumer price index are regulated in some way. This indicates the significant government influence on the private sector in the product markets. Moreover, some of the goods markets are heavily affected by subsidies. This applies to agriculture, coal production, shipbuilding, and nowadays also for alternative energy such as windmills and the cogeneration of power and heat. To a large extent, the subsidies in agriculture are taking place within the context of an EU framework.

Factor markets are more intensively regulated than goods markets. The bank-based capital market is segmented into the three-pillar system (see chapter 10) whereby the savings banks, together with their head institutions and the cooperatives, one of the other pillars, are protected against takeover by other banks. Under these circumstances, corporate control cannot function. In addition, there are public banks completely owned by government. Only the commercial banks, which have a market share of just 28 percent, are exposed to full competition. No wonder that competition in the banking industry is distorted and that the rate of return in the industry is low compared with other countries.

The most intensively regulated market is the labor market. Many regulations influence the supply of labor by workers, the demand for labor by firms, and the equilibrating mechanism of the labor market. These regulations constrain firms' demand for new labor, as managers are afraid of not being able to lay workers off during a recession. They are also responsible for the existence of an informal minimum wage, determined by social security benefits; this prevents the emergence of a market-clearing wage and dries up the lower segment of the labor market. It also compresses the wage structure. The relatively small degree of market orientation in the German labor market is evident from the fact that, among the reforms on unemployment compensation of type II, the Schröder government considered introducing a formal minimum wage (agreed upon by the social partners) for social welfare recipients capable of working: only if this wage were offered would the job-seeker have to a accept a job offer. And, of course, labor market regulation gives the social partners the right to set wages without having to accept responsibility for the resulting employment and unemployment in the labor market. This is the most obvious deviation from the market process.

It is naïve from the point of view of basic economics to expect a market-clearing equilibrium under such circumstances. If one sets a price in a market, demand and supply will react to that price. The social partners, naturally guided by their self-interest, are unlikely to settle on the market-clearing equilibrium price that would bring full employment for the economy. In addition, labor market institutions, which protect the insiders and their wage contracts, including the wage rate, restrict market access for the outsiders, thus raising the rents of insiders and creating unemployment for outsiders. Moreover, the trade unions will be tempted to rely on governmental schemes to reduce unemployment, i.e., to be bailed out from their responsibility by a third party—the state and the taxpayer. In essence, labor market rules can be seen to protect the wage cartel and secure the power of the trade unions.

CODETERMINATION IN CORPORATE GOVERNANCE

In several respects, Germany has chosen a distinct approach to the control and the management of firms, commonly referred to as *corporate governance*. Important differences exist relative to other countries in the entire range of mechanisms and arrangements that shape the way in which key decisions are taken within German companies. First, a special feature of German corporate law is the separation of a supervisory board (*Aufsichtsrat*) and a management board (*Vorstand*) in stock companies, as discussed in chapter 10. Second, banks play a vital role in the controlling of firms owing to the dominance of intermediated products and the banks' position on the supervisory boards. As indicated by the term "housebanks," informal or personal relationships are relevant factors, because of the lack of alternatives to these mechanisms of allocation, namely market products. Third, in contrast to the system in operation in the more stock market based economies of the United States or the United Kingdom, block-holder representation in the supervisory boards is much more pervasive within the German system. Fourth, employees and the trade unions represent half of the votes in the supervisory board of incorporated companies with more than 2000 employees, and one-third of the votes in smaller incorporated companies with over 500 employees. Fifth, according to the law on the constitution of firms, the formal agreement of the workers' council is required in a number of important management decisions.

Rules of Codetermination

Under the law of codetermination, introduced in 1976, employees are legally allocated control rights over all corporate decisions in the form of seats in the supervisory board. They have the same right as an owner of equity. The general idea is that the suppliers of capital and the suppliers of labor steer the firm "cooperatively." Depending on the size of the firm, workers and trade unions constitute either half or a third of the votes in the supervisory board of firms. In incorporated firms, i.e., stock companies and limited liability companies (GmbHs) with more than 2000 employees, half of the seats are allocated to the capital owners, the other half to the employees. In firms with less than 10 000 employees there are six seats for each side: one of the seats on the employees' side is earmarked for a managerial employee, and two seats on the employees' side are reserved for trade union representatives, who do not have to be employees at the firm in question. This regulation gives trade unions a foothold in the governance of firms entirely independent of the degree of organization (or lack thereof) among the company's employees. The number of seats increases with the size of the firm. In firms with more than 20 000 employees, with ten seats for each side, the unions have three seats. The board members representing the equity holders are elected at the shareholders' meeting, while members of the board on the employees' side are elected at a conference of employee delegates or by direct ballot.[2] The employee representatives have to be employees of the company, with the exception of the trade union representatives. Trade unions have the right of nomination for their positions. Employee board members can be recalled if a motion supported by three-quarters of employees finds a three-quarters majority among the delegates. The members of the supervisory board elect its chairman and the deputy chairman with a two-thirds majority. If this majority is not attained, the representatives of the shareholders elect the chairman, and the representatives of the employees his deputy. At a parity of votes in decisions of the supervisory board, the chairman has two votes. In incorporated companies with more than 500 and fewer than 2000 employees, workers must make up a third of the member of the board according to Business Constitution Act (Figure 14.1).

A specific law of codetermination applies to the coal and steel industry (the Codetermination Law of 1951, Montanmitbestimmungsgesetz) and calls for a stricter form of participation. The threshold is lower than in the general law on codetermination; applying to companies with more than

---

[2] In companies with up to 8000 employees, the law prescribes the ballot, but employees may, by a majority vote, opt to be represented by delegates. In the case of enterprises with a workforce of over 8000, the law prescribes elections through delegates. The employees may, however, reverse this procedure; in other words, they can choose by a majority vote to have a direct ballot. If the board members from the employees' side are chosen by delegates, there is a two-phase electoral process. In a first, universal, vote delegates (in general, 1 per 90 employees) are elected from among candidates that were backed by at least one-tenth or 100 employees; these delegates in turn elect the employee and executive representatives on the supervisory board out of a list of candidates that were proposed by either one-fifth or 100 employees.

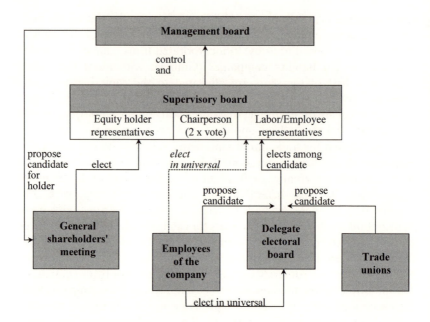

Figure 14.1   Codetermination in German firms.

1000 employees. The supervisory board consists of an equal number of shareholder and labor representatives along with a "neutral" member; it has 11 members (which in larger companies may be increased to 15 or 21). In the case of a supervisory board consisting of 11 members, five must be appointed by shareholders and five by employees. Two of the five seats for labor must actually be employees proposed by the workers' councils and two must be proposed for election by the national organizations of trade unions represented in the company. The fifth member is also proposed by the unions but must neither be an employee nor a representative of the trade unions or employers' associations; nor can he have any economic interests in the company (a "neutral man" on the side of labor). But even with respect to employee members elected by the workers' councils, the trade unions have the right to disapprove of any nominee who is unlikely to cooperate to the best interests of the company and the economy—a rather vague concept indeed. All labor representatives are first elected by the workers' council and proposed for election at the shareholders' meeting. The election is only a formality since the meeting cannot reject the nominees.

Thus, the supervisory board is free to choose only the five members on the capital side, among them one "neutral" person. In the supervisory board of this industry, the chairman does not have two votes, but there

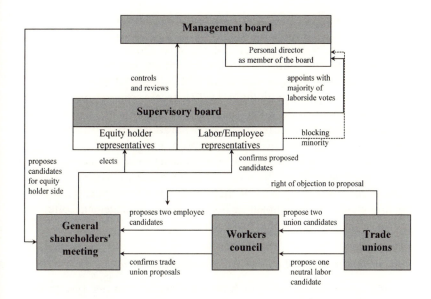

Figure 14.2 Codetermination in the coal and steel industry.

is a third "neutral" member, in addition to the neutral man on the side of capital and labor, who is elected at the shareholders' meeting with the consent of both sides. In the event of a stalemate, this member of the supervisory board is the tie-breaker. The members of the management board are appointed and dismissed by the supervisory board. One of the members must be a personnel or labor director who cannot be appointed or dismissed against the wishes of the majority of the workers' representatives on the supervisory board, who have a blocking minority. In a way, the labor directors are the exponents of codetermination at the management level. Trade unions thus choose the person who is ultimately responsible for employment planning, layoffs, and wage negotiations (Figure 14.2).

Limited liability companies (GmbHs), which are not generally required by law to have a supervisory board, are obliged to establish such a board in order to introduce codetermination. For them, the same thresholds and majorities of codetermination apply; i.e., half of the seats for companies with more than 2000 employees and one-third of the seats for companies with 500-2000 employees go to employees. In Germany there is a formal division of corporations into stock corporations (*Aktiengesellschaften* or AGs) and private limited liability companies (*Gesellschaften mit beschränkter Haftung* or GmbHs). Both types of corporation are governed by different acts of German law, namely the Aktiengesetz

(Stock Corporation Act) and the GmbH-Gesetz (Limited Liability Companies Act). This distinction has nothing to do with size, but rather refers to the ability of the shares of the company to be listed on the stock exchange. Only the shares of stock corporations can be floated on the exchange. In 2003 there were around 700 000 limited liability (GmbH) companies, compared with only 15 271 stock corporations.[3] Of the latter, only about 1000 domestic companies were listed on the stock exchange,[4] meaning that most stock corporations are privately held. If it were not for the rules of codetermination, limited liability companies would be free to set out in the partners' contracts whether they wanted to have a supervisory board. If they chose to have one, the same rules would apply as for stock companies. If they chose not to have one, the owners' meeting would be the controlling body to which management, often one or two of the owners, would have to report.

Codetermination and the Firm as an Implicit Contract

In addition to the question of how the German two-tier system fares relative to the Anglo-Saxon system of corporate governance (see chapter 10), there is much debate in Germany about how codetermination affects the decisions of firms and their performance in an international comparison.

It can be argued that the advantage of this system of codetermination is that cooperation is engendered between different groups of a company, so that the interests of the employees, of the shareholders, and of the firm are all considered when important decisions are made. It is a kind of "stakeholder value" concept, which attempts to lessen conflict potential by institutionalizing consultation and cooperative decision-making. This, along with the participation of the workers' council, is expected to secure the employees' positive motivation, which is seen as beneficial for a company's performance. Of course, people dislike hierarchies, and in the American approach the aspirations and fears of a company's employees tend to be anticipated by management in a less formal way. After all, the reputation of a company is important in attracting qualified employees, and consequently its market value in the financial community hinges on the motivation of its employees.

A firm can be understood to represent an implicit contract between the factors of production, defining which factor carries which risk and which factor receives which expected remuneration in unknown states of the world. Traditionally, this contract is understood to guarantee a secure

---

[3] 3780 in 1995, 7375 in 1999: data from Bundesbank, *Monthly Report*, January 2004.
[4] *Deutsche Börse* for December 2002.

income for labor, an important input to the firm, with capital taking the income risk. Income to labor is guaranteed only under the assumption that the firm continues to be economically viable, so that labor too carries a risk, albeit one reduced by the legal setting; capital, on the other hand, carries the risk of bankruptcy. With codetermination, employees can influence how this implicit contract is written de facto and how income is distributed among the factors within the firm. If codetermination suffi-ciently empowers employees, and if stockholders' rights cannot be contractually protected, then employees are able to change the risk allo-cation, redistributing the firm's surplus toward themselves and thereby increasing the ex ante uncertainty for capital owners. In this way they can alter the nature of the firm. In addition, if employer interests are not contractually protected, employees are able to choose a different objec-tive function for the firm, including a higher reward for labor and more job guarantees. Thus, codetermination is about the allocation of risk and the very nature of the capitalist firm. It is also about the allocation of power over the distribution of income and employment opportunities under unknown states of the firm's environment, and it determines the weight of shareholders versus that of stakeholders in these basic issues. Both sides are likely to have different preferences on these points, espe-cially with respect to securing jobs.

It is argued by some that, under the existing rules of codetermination, final decisions always lie in the hands of the shareholders, and that conse-quently codetermination does not make too much of a difference for the decisions of a company. This is not correct. In such an institutional setup one normally likes to have the consensus of all the groups involved. Thus, if the employees' representatives choose not to vote for the candidate proposed by the management board as chairman, the management side is likely to withdraw that candidate, or the candidate himself may with-draw his candidature; this happened in the election of the last chairman of BMW in 1999. Decisions thus tend to be politicized. There is no question that this institutional setup significantly influences corporate decisions.

In the context of motivation and the allocation of power, a distinction should be made between the employees and the trade unions. Viewing codetermination as an instrument for improving the relationship between management and its employees, the question can be raised of whether this is an appropriate approach, especially in the presence of outside trade unionists. Furthermore, it is actually in the self-interest of management and shareholders to take into account the interests of the firm's employ-ees. Nevertheless, there clearly are cases when the views of shareholders and employees diverge, for instance when a plant is to be closed.

For trade unions, codetermination is an important source of power; it increases their political leverage and also provides board seats for their

members, especially their leaders. Consequently, they have a strong interest in preserving codetermination. However, there is a clear conflict of
interest between their role as a trade union leader and as a member of the
supervisory board. For a member of the board, the obligation is to
promote and to protect the interest of the firm, whereas for a trade
union leader, the aim is to promote the interest of the union. The possibility of having to call a strike against the firm arises in this case; in
principle, the firm would have the option of locking workers out. This
conflict became apparent in early 2003, when Birske, the leader of the
service sector union Verdi, along with a member of the supervisory board
of Lufthansa and its vice chairman, called a strike against this very firm.
This conflict of interest exists independently of whether the trade union
members of the board pass on their remuneration largely to the trade
unions' foundation.

WORKERS' COUNCILS

The workers' council has a set of decision-making rights by which its
consent is mandatory according to the Business Constitution Act
(Betriebsverfassungsgesetz). These rights of codetermination (*Mitbestimmung*) effectively limit management's directive powers, demanding
either the approval of the workers' council or successful mediation for
decisions to become effective. In addition, the law establishes the right of
collaboration in decision-making (*Mitwirkung*), requiring that the workers' council must be heard on the relevant issues—failure to do so may
result in the invalidity of a decision taken by management. Furthermore,
there are informative and consultative rights and the right of autonomous administration of all workers' council affairs (Niedenhoff 2000).

The rights of codetermination apply to decisions of special interest to
employees, especially concerning the conditions of work and the workplace. This includes the organization of the work process, for instance
group work, the number of working hours per day in a plant, the length
and layout of work shifts, the scheduling of working time on weekends,
and overtime, unless specified by a collective contract with the unions.
Codetermination also applies to vacation plans, ergonomic standards,
special company benefits such as housing or day care, remuneration
schemes, means of measuring and supervising the efficiency and performance of employees (e.g., agreements with superiors on individual
annual objectives, performance-based remuneration schemes, and
process performance measurement such as activity-based costing), and
team-based arrangements of work flows. Agreement is needed on
measures to be taken when employees lose their qualifications as a

result of the introduction of new production processes. The workers' council also approves the hiring of new personnel, staff planning pertaining to the assignment of new responsibilities, and within-company transfers. Thus, the workers' council can effectively block the promotion of an employee if it believes, say, that the accompanying pay rise favors this employee unfairly over others. Its consent is required for layoffs and for social closing plans which are mandatory in case of larger layoffs. In the case of regular layoffs, the workers' council can disapprove of a decision to lay workers off on the basis of certain criteria (the employer did not screen for social repercussions in selecting which employee to lay off; or continued employment would be possible given certain adjustments); this disapproval by the council gives the employee the right to sue for continued employment, delaying his dismissal until a final court ruling.

The general brief of the workers' council extends to supervising compliance with collective bargaining results and legal obligations falling on the company, among them workplace safety and environmental regulations, promoting equal rights among the workforce, and helping to improve employment conditions. On all these issues, management and the workers' council, which meet at least once a month, are required by law to cooperate, and to seek solutions in the best interests of the company and its employees; accordingly, the workers' council as an institution may not take part in the hostile activities of collective action. The agreement of the workers' council is not explicitly required for strictly entrepreneurial decisions, such as investment and financing, product development, marketing, and public relations.

Decisions of the workers' councils are binding for all employees.[5] In joining a firm, an employee automatically renounces some of his individual rights and takes on those defined by the workers' council. Workers' council members are elected; they are not necessarily representatives of the trade unions, although the unions play a dominant role. By law, employees have the right to establish a workers' council for each business in a firm and for the firm as a whole, where "business" refers to the organizational unit, i.e., the *Betrieb*, which is not identical to the legal unit of the firm or to the technical unit of a plant. The right to establish a workers' council applies to businesses with at least five regular employees. A council is established by election of its members through the firm's employees. Where employees choose not to vote, firms will go without a workers' council. As a matter of fact, many smaller firms do not have workers' councils. According to a survey of small and medium-sized

---

[5] Unless they represent recommendations for the individual labor contract (*Regelungsabreden*).

German enterprises, only 4 percent of firms with 5–20 employees had a workers' council in 1999; in firms with 21–50 employees it was 16 percent, and in firms with 51–500 employees, 67 percent. In contrast, nearly all firms with more than 1000 employees had workers' councils (Wassermann 2002: 165). According to information from the trade unions, the average voter turnout in firms having a worker's council was about 72 percent in 1998.

The size of a workers' council varies with the number of employees. For instance, in firms with 51–100 employees the workers' council has to have five members.[6] Council members are given time off work to fulfill their responsibilities to the council while continuing to receive their regular pay; in addition, they are entitled to three weeks' educational leave per year. In firms with at least 200 employees, some council members (usually starting with the chairperson) must be relieved entirely of their regular work tasks to dedicate their full working time to the workers' council; in organizations with 10 001 employees or more, the number of full-leave council representatives is 12, and it rises by one for every additional 2000 employees. During their time in office, and for an additional year after leaving the workers' council, members enjoy far-ranging protection against layoff. If the workers' council has nine or more members (i.e., in firms with at least 201 employees), it elects an executive committee to handle its daily business. For firms with over 100 employees, a business committee of three to seven members must be selected at company level; only one of these members has to be on the workers' council. This committee has far-ranging rights to be informed and consulted once a month by the company's management concerning current business matters such as investment projects, sales numbers, or rationalization efforts.

As the various layers of the company's organizational structure give rise to different issues, the individual workers' councils in an organization usually send representatives to form a council at company level and, if applicable, at the group or holding levels (*Gesamtbetriebsrat* and *Konzernbetriebsrat*). Among those different layers of council, the principle of subsidiarity prevails, rather than a hierarchical structure. For firms with at least five employees below 18 years of age or with five or more apprentices below 25 years of age, a separate youth and apprentices' council is elected to advise the workers' council on issues pertaining to such employees. The law also calls for the gender that is in the minority among the company's personnel to be represented on the council in a number at least proportional to its share among employees. It goes without saying that all costs of the workers' council are borne by the firm.

[6] The council consists of one representative for businesses with 5–20 employees. For firms with more than 9000 employees, two additional representatives are added for every additional 3000 employees until a maximum number of 35 is reached.

Similar rights hold for the personnel council in the public sector, including the universities and research institutes.

The workers' council represents an institution that helps to standardize rules in firms and allows for the discussion of conflicts and the resolution of problems. At the same time, the institutional setup assigns decision-making rights and thus power to an elected body, taking it away from individual employees and from the management and owners of a firm. It allows the participation of employees and trade unions, but put restraints on the management of firms. If things go smoothly, this institutional arrangement reduces transaction costs; however, if issues flare and the relationship between the two sides hardens, transaction costs may actually be increased. For instance, the workers' council may use its power to refuse to consent to a management proposal unless it gets one of its own projects through in return. This deal-making may lead to economically inefficient solutions. The whole procedure is time-consuming. More importantly, a workers' council requires the input of a good deal of attention and effort. In larger firms, in which the personnel director maintains the ongoing relationship with the workers' council, this normally does not represent a problem. In smaller and medium-sized firms, however, which crucially depend on the energy of the owner-entrepreneur, the attention required by the workers' council eats into part of his available entrepreneurial energy, which then is no longer available for innovation, marketing, and strategic activities of the firm.

The Red–Green government extended the Business Constitution Act in several ways in 2001, following trade union pressure. The threshold at which the chairman of the workers' council is released from his normal work was reduced from 300 to 200 employees. Additional procedures were introduced to establish councils in smaller firms. This means an extension of codetermination to such firms, where the role of the owner-entrepreneur or family management tends to be prevalent. As no quorum is set for electing the workers' council, well organized groups may hijack the council for special interest purposes. The law has also been changed to give workers' councils more rights, one of them being the obligation that the proposals and opinions of the workers' council have to be considered by management, and during the time of consideration no decisions can be taken on these matters. In addition, the new law contains further requirements pertaining to environmental protection in the firms, equal opportunities for women, and the discrimination of foreigners. However, one of the major articles of the law, para. 77, sec. III, preventing a deviation from the collective contract even if there is agreement in the firm, was not changed. To sum up, the law has made decision-making processes more complicated and inflexible, and has strengthened the position of the trade unions in an economic situation in which the German economy has sunk into stagnation and requires more flexibility rather than less.

The Future of Codetermination?

Impact on the Decision-Making within Firms

With codetermination defining the weights of the shareholders and the employees, and with workers' councils additionally voicing the interests of employees, it is held within the economics literature that the German system, particularly when also taking into account the role of banks and block-holders, has proved less able than the Anglo-Saxon system to make decisions quickly (Holmstrom 1999; Hopt et al. 1998; Mayer 1988). It is fair to say that, in the end, structural change and plant closings were not prohibited by Germany's institutional approach.[7] If people had to be laid off, it was accomplished predominantly via a combination of social closing plans and governmental programs of early retirement, thereby solving labor market issues at the cost of the pension system. Given the rigidity of wages, however, the adjustment of the German industry has not led to the creation of any new jobs. As far as structural change is concerned, codetermination can be viewed as a defensive instrument. Looked at from a long-run point of view, it protects the insiders, at least temporarily—to the disadvantage, of course, of the outsiders.

Next, there is the question of the effect of codetermination on innovation. It can be said that codetermination and the workers' councils seem an appropriate means of arriving at a consensus along the firm's *established* technological trajectories, marginally improving the existing production technology and modernizing established products. These approaches are, however, less suitable in an environment where a new technology has to be applied, where new products have to be developed, and where leapfrogging to a new technology is the key objective. These more radical changes, often viewed with suspicion as job-killers, conflict with the structurally conservative mindset epitomized by the institutions of codetermination.

Both forms of employee participation, therefore, negatively influence the attractiveness of Germany as a location for investors from abroad. They also affect the locational advantage seen by domestic investors comparing options in other countries with those at home. This argument demands increasing credence with the escalating international mobility of

---

[7] For instance, when Krupp had to close its steel plant in Rheinhausen under severe public and workers' protest in 1993, it was able to do so with the vote of the "neutral man" in the supervisory board.

capital and technology. A smaller capital inflow, or even a capital outflow, in consequence of these forms of participation means that less capital will be accumulated in Germany and fewer new technologies may be attracted, so that the German employee will be equipped less generously with capital, reducing his productivity and his wage-earning potential. In addition, codetermination as practiced in Germany leads to a lower international evaluation of companies incorporated as joint stock companies. This means that Germany is becoming increasingly unattractive to holding companies.

Historically, raising such issues of codetermination in public has been virtually unthinkable, with chairmen of boards usually stressing that such institutional approaches are a good thing, and that they personally are getting along very well with their partners in the supervisory boards and the workers' council. Meanwhile, one hears comments questioning the concept of codetermination, especially in light of the growing need to respond swiftly to a changed economic environment and to reach decisions quickly. It is now recognized that, in addition to endowing trade unions with power, codetermination serves to develop the coherence of the firm, allowing the implicit contract between the factors of production within the firm to be self-enforcing and sustainable, but at the same time delaying decisions, slowing down innovations by focusing interest on the marginal improvements of a given trajectory, and making Germany less attractive as a location for international investment. In a way, we again come face to face with the basic conflict of the German approach: the dichotomy between coherence, social considerations, and equity on the one hand and dynamics and efficiency on the other.

A Changing International Environment

I have already discussed the advantages and disadvantages of the two-tier board system versus the unitary board system in chapter 10, where I suggested that the market will tell us which of the two systems will prove viable in the future. One important aspect to this answer is that the international conditions in which the German system of governance, including codetermination, is embedded, and by which it is affected, are changing. In the banking industry, market products are developing as a result of internationalization, disintermediation, and growing pressure on banks by their clients to facilitate access to capital markets. The shareholder structure is becoming more international because of globalization and the diversification of large, institutional and actively managed portfolios, making block-holding less likely. "Shareholder activism," exercised increasingly by institutional investors, should work toward more profitability-oriented and value-oriented corporate policies. The establishment of investor relations departments in most German exchange-listed companies is evidence of this trend. Block-holding will also be discouraged by new regulations of the European Union referring to the takeover of enterprises. Banks, insurance companies, and corporations no longer have an implicit incentive to maintain holdings, since they can sell their shares without paying any capital gains taxes on the profits from such sales. All in all, these international developments in the market for corporate control will leave their mark on Germany, and are likely to have an impact on the role of codetermination in German corporate control.

In addition, the German system of codetermination is becoming incongruous with the internationalization of German firms (Baums 2003). Foreign employees of German firms do not participate in the election of the workers' representatives in the supervisory board, nor are their trade unions represented. Since larger German firms meanwhile often have half of their employees abroad, the legal stipulations of the codetermination law of the 1970s now appear as an attempt to secure the representation and voting power of German employees alone, i.e., as an institutional arrangement in favor of a specific group of insiders. As mentioned in chapter 8, such arrangements are an instrument for guaranteeing income and even rents to those employed and to members of the unions. This inconsistency between the desire to secure the position of German employees and the reality of worldwide employment in German firms cannot be overcome by a worldwide approach to codetermination along German lines. On the contrary, the issue is that the actual system does not seem to be tenable under conditions of globalization.

Moreover, in the European Union the principle of non-discrimination of EU citizens prevents the continuation of the current German arrangement. Any attempt to extend the German approach of codetermination to other member states, for instance via EU-wide regulations, would rightly be met with opposition from the other EU members, which have different institutional practices based on their own historic experience, and which also have their own preferences. Moreover, the concept of institutional competition and the EU's principle of mutual recognition of national institutional setups prevent such a harmonization. In this spirit, the European Court of Justice has allowed firms from other EU countries with different forms of incorporation, and without codetermination, to operate in Germany. This ruling, from November 2002, has generated interest among German companies in the idea of moving their legal headquarters into a neighboring country, thereby evading codetermination, while continuing their operations in Germany. Codetermination thus joins tax optimization as an important rationale for corporate relocation. Aventis's selection of Strasbourg as new headquarters reflects this just as well as EADS's decision to take its legal seat in the Netherlands.

Rules for Takeover

Along with all other aspects serving to make a company attractive or otherwise to an international investor, e.g., taxation, the rules regarding codetermination, and the workers' councils, explicit conditions for mergers and acquisitions are an important aspect of corporate control. While takeover activity has increased in the 1990s and more recently, Germany continues to experience a relatively low level of takeover proceedings. Thus, only 2 percent of the transaction volume of announced hostile corporate takeovers worldwide in the period 1990–98 involved German companies as targets, in contrast to 89 percent for Anglo-Saxon companies, 6.4 percent for French and 1.3 percent for Scandinavian firms.[8] As a matter of fact, takeover activity and hostile bids have been so rare that Germany has no law for takeovers, but merely a voluntary takeover code that very few listed companies have submitted to. It was only in 2002 that Germany introduced its first takeover code, setting ground rules for companies and investors alike. The new law regulates all public offers to acquire certain market-traded equity securities of German domestic companies, whether for stock, cash, or a combination thereof, with additional provisions applying where the acquisition or holdings exceed a defined threshold. When the new German Takeover Act replaced the voluntary Takeover Code, the "squeeze-out" of minority shareholders in a stock corporation, at the request of a majority shareholder (holding at least 95 percent of the issued shares), was permitted. Since the expulsion of minority shareholders can now be accomplished in a relatively straightforward process instead of via a risky multi-step transaction, many investors view the new rules as the single most important improvement in German corporate laws in recent years. This new law also sets out the reporting requirements, the criteria for the offer-bid, the duration of the offer period, and the conditions under which the takeover law applies to all public offers where the target is a German-based stock corporation or limited partnership by shares (*Kommanditgesellschaft auf Aktien*), whose stock is publicly traded on an "organized market" in Germany or anywhere within the European economic area. It gives management some instruments of defense.

---

[8] The proportions of acquirers are similar (data from Guillen 2000; quoted in Van den Berghe 2002: 68).

Similar to the "golden shares" in former French state-owned firms, Germany has a specific regulation, the so-called VW Law, that effectively protects the car maker Volkswagen from a hostile takeover. Lower Saxony's government owns just under 20 percent of VW's shares, and a special regulation prevents any other shareholder from controlling more than 20 percent of the company's voting rights. Accordingly, when he was governor of the federal state of Lower Saxony, Gerhard Schröder had a seat on the VW supervisory board. This regulation makes Volkswagen the only German company to enjoy protection similar to a golden share. In a landmark ruling of 2003, the European Court of Justice effectively banned the use of golden shares. This will call into question other ways in which governments within Europe have secured for themselves the right to intervene in the takeover process, including the VW law.

In order to foster corporate restructuring and capital market integration, the European Commission since the early 1990s has repeatedly attempted to introduce a EU-wide takeover regulation, but it has encountered strong resistance. A compromise was finally reached in late 2003, aiming to boost the power of shareholders and limit the rights of European companies to protect themselves from takeovers. The initial goal in crafting the EU-wide policy was to make merger and acquisition activity a more brisk process than previously. The German government, however, worried that such an outcome would spark a wave of hostile takeovers on German flagship companies (e.g., VW), a view that was echoed by the Nordic countries (especially Sweden, concerned about Ericsson). In these efforts to protect their corporations from takeover bids—efforts that were opposed by other EU members, e.g., the United Kingdom—Germany and other countries with similar preferences were successful in winning their agreement by making concessions in other areas, for example bans on "poison pills," which would have made hostile takeovers prohibitively complicated or expensive, and multiple voting rights, which would have allowed some shareholders to control a company without holding a majority share.[9] In exchange for backing Germany, the United Kingdom received reciprocal support in blocking Commission rules on employment rights for temporary workers.

GOVERNANCE OF THE UNIVERSITIES

The German university system, with nearly two million students in the winter semester 2002/03 and an annual budget of €28.6 billion for public

---

[9] Often there is a differentiation into type A (voting right) shares, for instance those tightly held by the founding family, and type B shares, limited to the right to participate in dividend payments.

and private universities in 2001, is administered by the Länder. It is financed from tax revenue, except for a very few private universities already established and a few new ones that are now coming into being at the periphery of the educational sector. The funds are allocated by the parliaments of the federal states. This system of governance, in which the respective ministry of culture of the federal state is in charge of administering the university more or less directly, is similar to that in central planning. Recently, the ministries of several states have attempted to draw up contracts with the universities defining university targets and providing funds for a planning period, thereby granting the universities more autonomy. These principal-agent contracts are reminiscent of a central agency like Gosplan, in the former Soviet Union. As a positive step, however, in quite a few cases a board of regents has now been introduced, endowed with the authority to decide on some of the issues that had previously been dealt with by the ministries.

As the universities are state-owned, each student who has obtained his high school diploma (*Abitur*) has a right of entry. There are no student fees; formal agreements among the federal states regulate that universities cannot take fees from their students.[10] Where student places are scarce, a nationwide allocation mechanism allocates the scarce places to the student candidates via a lengthy process, in which the universities' interest in obtaining motivated and qualified students does not play a role. Thus, a bureaucratic procedure determines who has access to the university. To date, student tuition fees are prohibited for any student's first degree studies by the Federal Framework Act for Universities (Hochschulrahmengesetz para. 24, sec. 4), so that scarcity of student places cannot be dealt with by a price mechanism. Some federal states now introduce extremely modest student fees (of €500 or €1000) for those students who decide to study a second discipline after having already received one degree, or who take longer to get their degree than the standard length of the study requires. But not even these modest fees are politically acceptable to the students, who view free access to university education as a fundamental entitlement, for which society has to bear the costs. Some federal states now are granting the universities the right to choose and recruit a part of their student body themselves, but the Federal Framework Act for Universities puts strict limits on the criteria that can be applied, and whenever capacity is limited the national allocation mechanism precedes any selection at individual university level.

An implicit aspect of the German university system is social equity, but, as has been explained in chapter 11, this has not been achieved. The

---

[10] Several states have now announced their intention to terminate this agreement.

government has not succeeded in opening the system to the lower strata of society. Ironically, since the working class contributes a large proportion of taxes that go into the financing of the universities, the middle-income groups get the education of their children for free. Comparing benefits and costs for the different social classes, the middle-income groups therefore benefit more from free access to university education than do the lower-income groups. Thus, the system is not really socially just. Moreover, it is not competitive internationally.

The administrative planning approach adopted with respect to German universities does not rely on the force of competition. Universities do not select their students, and students can select the university of their choice only within limits. Except for the intrinsic behavior of individual professors, universities and their departments are not really in competition with one another. Thus, competitive pressure is not used as a controlling device for German universities. Nor can the universities enjoy the options that competition entails. As they are unable to set fees, they cannot raise money for their day-to-day operation or for investment. For instance, they cannot cater to the international market for undergraduate and graduate degrees and benefit from the international willingness to pay with income that could be used for running expenses or investment. Germany has neither the imagination nor the courage to expose university education to competition. Given this history, and the strong opposition of the Social Democrats to student fees, it is amazing that, as of January 2004, the party is now favoring "elite universities."

OTHER INSTITUTIONAL SETUPS OF GROUP DECISION-MAKING

As has been illustrated, the German system of governance delegates decisions to groups and decision-making bodies. This applies to the role of the social partners in the labor market regarding decisions on the wage level, the wage structure, and other important aspects relevant for employment; to the banking industry with its intermediated products; to decision-making in firms, with codetermination on the boards of larger firms and with the participation of the workers' councils; and to codetermination in the universities. This consensus or corporatist approach places no trust in competition. When policy measures are taken the agreement of many groups in society is sought, instead of letting decisions emerge from diverse individuals and relying on the market as a mechanism to allocate incentives and impose control.

There are other important areas of society that are governed by self-administration, i.e., by the German approach of group-based decision-making relying on the consensus-inducing mechanisms of the institutional structure. One example is the associations of statuary health insurance physicians in the public health system (*Kassenärztliche Vereinigungen*). These organizations represent the doctors whose patients, about 90 percent of the population, are covered by the public insurers, and who are required by law to be members of the organization. According to the social law,[11] the role of these associations is to negotiate the doctors' fees with the public health insurers. They may be regarded as the doctors' trade union, albeit with mandatory membership. Although they can be interpreted as a countervailing power to the public health insurers, such associations nevertheless constitute a bargaining cartel with interests of its own. Thus, individual public insurers are forbidden to negotiate their fees directly with specific doctors and hospitals, legally preventing the creation of an integrated health management system, such as that found in Switzerland and in the United States. In such an integrated system, insurers offer their own medical services through a network of doctors and hospitals at a reduced insurance rate, in this way ensuring competition between public insurers.

The associations of statuary health insurance physicians in the public health system have the additional task of ensuring that sufficient medical services are provided throughout the country.[12] They also limit the geographical concentration of doctors in any field of specialization. In this area, then, an implicit distrust of market forces becomes evident—market failure is assumed a priori. Rather than applying countermeasures, such as monetary incentives for doctors to locate in rural areas where there are fewer medical services, an institutional planning system is set up for the entire economic activity, conferring decision-making power on organized professional groups. The patients, for whose benefit this system is supposedly set up in the first place, remain without representation.

Other areas in which decision-making is allocated to groups are the chambers of agriculture, commerce, craftsmen, and architects, and the regional bar associations, all of which require mandatory membership. These organizations represent part of the self-administration system in Germany, dealing with issues of common interest to their members—e.g., administering the apprenticeship system, standardizing apprenticeship profiles, and overseeing the examinations for these profiles by the chambers of commerce and craftsmen. While a case can be made for self-administration in these areas, in that problems are solved in a decentralized way according to the subsidiarity principle, such approaches drive

[11] SozialGesetzBuch V para. 82.
[12] SozialGesetzBuch V para. 99.

out market solutions. For example, the fees that architects and lawyers can charge are strictly regulated, and advertising is prohibited for them, as for other professions such as doctors, dentists, or pharmacists (all forming part of Freie Berufe), who are considered to operate in a sphere where competition is not desirable. Chambers of craftsmen also may be assumed to collude on price and on the control of access to the market by administering the exams taken to become a master craftsman. All chambers publicly express the joint interest of their constituents, participating as lobby groups in the political process. They represent interest groups that get support from the state for their organization through the device of mandatory membership and the transferal of exclusive norm-setting privileges, exempting their respective sectors from the rule of market forces.

Organized groups are also involved in self-administering important aspects of economic life in Germany's public sphere, including the social security systems. In 174 supervisory boards of the federal government, interest groups are overwhelmingly represented (Rudzio 2003: 104). Thus, representatives of these interest groups have seats in the supervisory boards of the Kreditanstalt für Wiederaufbau, the agricultural import and stock agencies, and the radio and television stations. Trade unions and employers' associations nominate assessors for the labor and the social courts. The public welfare organizations (*Wohlfahrtsverbände*)—the Red Cross, Workers' Welfare (Arbeiterwohlfahrt), Caritas (of the Catholic Church), and Diakonie (of the Protestant Church)—implement the laws of social welfare and youth welfare, for instance by running kindergartens, nursing homes, and hospitals.[13]

A common form of representation of organized groups is the one-third parity, whereby one-third of the seats in a supervisory board goes to the trade unions, one-third to the employers' associations, and one-third to government. Thus, the Labor Office (Bundesagentur für Arbeit) is supervised by a board in which the social partners have two-thirds of the votes; the remaining one-third goes to different layers of the government, i.e., the Bund and the states. As of 2004, a new setup applies to the Labor Office as part of the 2003 reform; whereas the Office used to be a governmental agency under the direction of the economics and labor minister, with more of the counseling function of the supervisory board, it will now be steered and controlled by the supervisory council. Although this new arrangement may be seen as an attempt to decentralize decisions and no longer have them taken by the respective ministry, it assigns additional power to the trade unions and the employers' associations. In a way, they

---

[13] All four organizations have 1 125 000 full-time and part-time employees (data for 1995/96: Rudzio 2003: 104). It is questioned whether this service sector is sufficiently controlled and whether its efficiency can be substantially increased.

now can influence unemployment policy more directly and thus control the policy that is needed because of the failure of their own behavior in wage-setting. They have control over instruments allowing them to shift the impact of their behavior to a third party, i.e., to the state and the taxpayer. In January 2004, they used this new power to oust Florian Gerster from his position as head of the management board of the Labor Office. Gerster, who had been installed only two years earlier by Schröder to modernize the Labor Office, had pushed for reforms. His policy fell victim to the opposition of the unions.

Other institutions of the German social security network are also self-administered in a manner that gives trade unions and other continuously organized interest groups a significant say. In both the pension system and the public health insurers, social elections (*Sozialwahlen*) are held every six years among all the current contribution-paying insured and pensioners to elect the supervisory council (*Verwaltungsrat*) of the health insurers and the assembly of representatives (*Vertreterversammlung*) of the pension system. These supervisory bodies comprise equal shares (30 members each) of the two groups that pay the contributions: the insured and their employers.[14] While the employers' associations determine their representatives independently, all insured persons and the pensioners can elect representatives from candidate lists, for which the right of proposal is restricted to employee associations with social policy objectives (mainly voluntary interest associations of insured) and trade unions. However, as the participation in these elections is rather meager (in 1999, of the more than 32 million insured and pensioners of the largest public pension institution, just over 10 million voted), the chances of motivated minorities gaining over-proportional representation are high.[15] These bodies have stark prerogatives similar to those of a parliament: they elect the board of directors (*Vorstand*) and a separate management board (*Geschäftsführung*), decide on the annual budget, approve the annual report, and have the power to set and change the autonomous statutes of the institution. Like the board of directors, they have two chairpersons who alternate yearly, one from the employers' representatives and the other from the representatives of the insured. While day-to-day operations are handled by the management board, the board of directors administers the institution's funds, decides on construction projects and extraordinary personnel and organizational

---

[14] Only in those statutory health insurers that have their origin in self-help associations of professional groups (*Ersatzkassen*) are there no employers' representatives.

[15] In the largest public pension insurer (Bundesversicherungsanstalt für Angestellte), 8 of 30 members in the assembly of delegates are trade union representatives, and one is a representative of the social organizations of the Catholic and Protestant Churches. The head of the board of directors also is a trade union representative.

issues, sets the budget, and represents the institution. Members of the supervisory bodies and the board of directors are unsalaried but have their expenses paid.

Without a doubt, these institutional arrangements endow the organized groups with additional power; not only do they have a role in overseeing the key institutions of Germany's social security system, but they also represent these institutions in the public sphere and the political process. They thus have the power to voice the structurally conservative interests of their groups through the megaphone of public institutions. It is possible, then, that, via the committee approach to reform proposals that is currently preferred by the Schröder administration, they may have two seats at the same table: one in their original function as interest group, and another in the guise of a representative of a public social security institution.

Another example of decision-making by groups concerns the voluntary sector agreements, which have been used to effect a reduction in emissions in environmental policy by sectors of the economy. The attempt to open up access to power and gas lines by voluntary sector associations is another case in point; it failed, so a new regulatory regime had to be introduced (chapter 8).

THE CONSENSUS APPROACH

In addition to these formalized institutional approaches of group decision-making, as written into law, more informal attempts to find a consensus have been tried. These included the "concerted action" between the relevant social groups, especially the trade unions and the employers' associations, by the economics minister Schiller in the 1960s, and Chancellor Schröder's round tables, representing different groups of society. An example of the latter was the "Alliance for Work," a forum including the trade unions, employers' associations, German industry, and the German Chamber of Commerce, whereby Schröder tried to reach some consensus in the years 1998–2000 on important questions concerning unemployment. This attempt failed, mainly because the unions were not willing to discuss the issue of wage-setting. Another such example relates to committees such as the "Hartz Commission" and the "Rürup Commission," which were created to develop blueprints for major reform steps and to secure the consent of the groups represented in the committees.

An implication of this approach is that the decisions taken reflect the interest of both the organized groups and the incumbents. Organized interest groups are endowed with bargaining power; they get a de facto

right of veto. Consequently, major changes are not accepted when important groups of society are negatively affected by them. For instance, the
trade unions have so far blocked important modifications in the system of
rules and regulations for the labor market; as another example, the
Riester reform of the pay-as-you-go pension system was possible only
after the unions agreed in December 2000 on the pension formula. In a
way, the consensus approach is an application of the Pareto criterion,
according to which an increase in welfare presupposes that at least one
agent wins and no one loses. The problem however is that, in a corporatist setting and in a static perspective, a relative improvement for one
group *is*considered a loss for the other groups. This prevailing mood
becomes even more severe in a situation in which all groups must cut
back their social absorption. The consensus approach implies that the
status quo will play a central role and development will become extremely path-dependent. This is not an institutional environment that is
conducive to leapfrogging. Consensus translates into risk aversion. A
standstill is the most likely outcome, and consequently economic
dynamics will be lost. Decisions tend to be blocked if consensus is sought
from all sides, effectively handing out veto rights to groups with a vested
interest in the status quo.

The consensus approach may have been appropriate in an environment
of high GDP growth rates such as the 8 percent that pertained in the
1950s and over 4 percent in the 1960s, when the German economy
was catching up with the United States, and welfare gains could be spread
widely. However, in a situation where the growth path is characterized by
a growth rate of only about 1.5 percent, as in the years 1995–2003,
restraints become more binding, goal conflicts more biting, and flexible
responses less likely. Negative external shocks are then hard to come by.
This suggests that the institutional setup for decision-making is part of the
German problem of low growth performance.

A serious shortcoming is that such an approach does not make use of
decentralized allocation through markets and competition, where
changes occur more or less automatically and where market participants
are expected to adjust to new economic conditions. Round tables do not
have an automatic and decentralized way of finding new technological
and organizational solutions. They are concerned with formally establishing and adjusting the rules. Such a system does not utilize the problem-
solving capacity of decentralized markets and competition. Creative
energy is lost, because the problem-solving potential of the market and
decentralized competition is not exploited.

In conclusion, what needs to be avoided is the empowerment of interest
groups by handing them the bargaining power over changes in the status
quo, as this institutionalizes obstacles to an evolutionary process of

economic and social change, given the conservative incentive structure of these incumbents.

"AD HOCKERY" IN THE GOVERNMENT'S APPROACH

The consensus approach in a corporatist setting means that government can take discretionary decisions. A politician who can focus such decisions into popular issues that make headlines in the press can use this approach to put himself into the limelight. The politician would like to think of himself as a fireman—if a fire breaks out, he can come to the rescue; if there is problem, he can step in and solve it; if a firm is threatened by a crisis, such as illiquidity or even insolvency, he can help it out. In this way he can demonstrate his indispensability to society. This activist approach is made easier in an environment in which corporatist decision-making is the rule.

Thus, the corporatist approach leads to interventionism, to adhockery, and to a short-run orientation. "In the long run, there is just another short run," as Abba Lerner once said. More fundamental restraints are likely to be put on the back burner, for instance long-run impacts of economic policy measures, issues of sustainability, and intergenerational budget constraints. In such an approach, the politician does not lead in the true sense of the word, and he is not a statesman. As Churchill replied when asked what makes the difference between a politician and a statesman: "A politician always thinks of the next election, a statesman considers the next generation." During his first term, Chancellor Schröder used this short-run approach when he attempted to prevent the collapse of the construction firm Holzmann in 1999 from illiquidity, presenting the rescue in the evening news and in front of cheering workers of the ruined company. Three years later, however, the firm was gone; its restructuring plan had failed, despite massive public loan guarantees and dumping prices that hurt the already strained German construction sector.

This ad hoc approach is likely to lead to different answers over time, i.e., to lead to time inconsistency, as it reacts to acute problems as and when they appear, regarding them as singular cases having no consistent line, and contradictory in the instruments used. During his two terms, Schröder has changed his position so much that laws passed on his initiative have had to be undone by his own government. In 1998 the size limit for firms for which the layoff restraint did not apply was lowered from more than ten to more than five employees—in 2003 this decision was reversed. In 1998 the demographic factor in the pension formula was suspended—now a similar factor has been reintroduced. In 2000 the tax allowance for commuting from home to the work place was enlarged—in 2003 the allowance was reduced. At the end of 2000 the options provided by law for employment contracts of limited duration were reduced—in 2003 newly founded firms were exempted from the regulation for the first four years. In 2001 the Business Constitution Act was tightened in the face of opposition from the entrepreneurs,[16] especially from the Mittelstand—now we are looking for ways to intensify the investment activity of the enterprise sector. Such varying concepts of economic policy are especially relevant as the state plays such a decisive role in the governance system of the German economy. Their effects are particularly damaging on the expectations of entrepreneurs and firms.

THE GOVERNANCE OF GOVERNMENT

Strong elements of cooperative decision-making can also be found in the institutional setup of government activity itself.

The Voting System

The electoral system in Germany is a combination of majority and proportional voting, whereby each citizen has two votes in the elections for the Bundestag and for the parliaments of most of the federal states. The voting procedures in the municipalities differ from state to state.[17] In the elections for the Bundestag, one vote is for the district representative, the other for the party list of candidates. The proportional vote for the party lists determines the relative size of parties in parliament. If a political party carries more districts than it attracts proportional votes, it obtains the direct parliamentary seats as excess seats (*Überhangmandate*), that is in excess of its proportional weight. The number of parliamentary seats of the federal parliament is expanded accordingly. In this case, the total number of seats is no longer allocated according to the proportional vote. For instance, in the 2002 parliamentary elections to the Bundestag, the Social Democrats won 171 seats by direct votes (41.9 percent) and 80 by party votes (38.5 percent); the SPD gained four additional seats thanks to the excess mandates in some of the federal states, which represent the geographical areas by which the representation and the excess mandates are determined in the federal elec-

[16] In the second part of his first term, Schröder leaned toward the interest of the trade unions.

[17] For example municipalities in some states, such as Bavaria, conduct a majority election, while in other states, such as Hessen, local politicians are elected from a party list via a proportional election.

tion. By contrast, in the same election the Greens won one district by direct vote and 55 by party votes (8.6 percent).

Importantly, however, every party must win at least 5 percent of the proportional votes; if it remains below this threshold, the party must carry at least three districts directly to gain party representation in the Bundestag according to the proportional vote. If it receives less than 5 percent and does not carry at least three districts, the plurality votes will be lost for the party; if it carries only one or two districts directly and remains below 5 percent, it will only have one or two directly elected members. The 5 percent threshold is used to avoid the known outcome of pure proportional voting, i.e., a great number of parties with rather specific focuses; under such conditions it is difficult to form a stable government, as the experience of the Weimar Republic has shown: its decline has been linked to the institutional arrangement of proportional voting (Hermens 1972). The 5 percent clause also makes it more difficult for extremist parties to become permanently established by way of a parliamentary representation as a bridgehead in public attention.

The choice of voting system has been influenced by attempts to avoid the failures of the past, both the political instability of the Weimar Republic and the concentration of power and disempowerment of democracy in the Nazi period. Whereas the voting system's main feature—the mixture of majority and proportional voting with a cutoff clause for parties failing to command 5 percent of the votes—prevents the weaknesses of pure proportional voting by adding elements of majority voting, the 5 percent clause means that the institutional arrangement tends not to produce clear majorities each legislative periods. Swings in the vote do change the composition of parliament and the relative strength of political parties, but they usually do not translate into a large swing of seats as in a majority voting system. Thus, a party may carry the overwhelming majority of the districts directly and another party may lose nearly of all its previously held districts, but the proportional vote prevents the same swing from becoming fully effective in parliament. A party losing most of the direct districts can remain partly protected in its parliamentary strength by the proportional votes. Compared with a system of majority voting, therefore, electoral swings are partly absorbed. Moreover, it does not lead to a two-party system but allows smaller parties like the Liberal Democrats and the Greens to exist as long as they remain above the threshold of 5 percent or directly carry three districts.

Only in 1957 did a single party—the Christian Democratic Union (CDU), together with its Bavarian sister party, the Christian Social Union—win the majority of seats in parliament. The consequence is that in the parliamentary system governments are usually formed by coalitions. Indeed, all German governments have been coalition governments, centered on the Christian Democratic Union in 1949–66 and 1982–98 and on the Social Democratic Party (SPD) in 1969–82 and from 1998 to the present (Goetz 2003: table 1.1). Until 1998, the Liberal Democrats (FDP) were the crucial second party in forming the government, in a triangular relationship with the two major parties. Thus, a change of government occurred when they formed a new government with the Social Democrats after the 1969 election, replacing the "grand coalition" of the both major parties (1966–69). Moreover, the FDP switched sides in 1982 during the legislative session by a constructive vote of confidence against Schmidt and the election of Kohl. Only in 1998 was a governing coalition (Christian Democratic Union and Liberal Democrats) voted out of power in favor of an alternative coalition (Social Democrats and Greens).

This system has the advantage of preventing abrupt shifts in policy. It apparently also allows new paradigms to be introduced by a new party, such as the ecological focus by the Greens. This can be seen as a stabilizing feature. But at the same time, the system tends only marginally to introduce potentially major changes. One structural reason for this is that in electoral competition the two major parties must take into account the fact that a change in the plurality vote in their favor will not transform into a clear majority enabling one of the parties to form the government alone, since it depends on a coalition. Another structural reason is that the two smaller parties in parliament cater to narrowly defined special interest or specific issue groups of voters at the margins of the political spectrum (and in its moderate center) by trying to put clear-cut reform initiatives at the core of the campaigns. These reform-seeking constituencies get skimmed off by either the Liberal Democrats or the Greens. The major parties, then, are left with constituencies both on the Left and on the Right that are more structurally conservative on average than the overall body of German voters. Accordingly, they have little incentive to try to appeal with a profile of change and reform.

Thus, in the 2002 elections the major parties were extremely reluctant to ask for a clear mandate for innovation or to focus on long-run necessities of change. The voting system makes it risky for the large parties to break away from the traditional lines. Consequently, the new Red–Green government was without a clear mandate and a clear concept for institutional innovations when it started the legislative period in 2002. This system leaves a void that has been partly filled by interest groups. Apparently, the voting system replicates an important feature of the German governance system whereby consensus among different actors has to be found. In the coalition government itself, a consensus among the parties forming the government has to be permanently established. The cooperative spirit or the consensus approach is enforced upon the government by the voting system.

The alternative would be to move to a majority voting system, where the elected members of parliament represent the majority of votes in the districts carried. In such a setting, a two-party system would likely evolve. Parties would be forced to orient themselves to the median voter. This approach would prevent extremist parties, and at the same time would lead to a government with a clear majority in a legislative period as well as a weakened opposition. However, the opposition would have the chance to win the next election by putting forward a clear alternative. In such a system, a decisive check would come not from the cooperation of parties in a coalition government in the face of a threat of new coalitions, but from the threat of the opposition taking over. It is a system that relies on party competition instead of a blurred system of party competition with coalition formation.

Germany is a representative democracy. It has been cautious introducing elements of direct democracy in the form of popular referenda. Thus, the president of the Republic is elected not in a referendum, but by a joint assembly of the Bundestag and the states. Elections of the parliaments of the Bund and the states are the exclusive means of legitimizing government; the German Constitution does not allow competing means of legitimacy (Rudzio 2003: 53). In the Constitution plebiscites on the federal level are inadmissible, even if they would only have the role of informing parliaments of the population's preferences. In 1958 the Federal Constitutional Court confirmed the federal system of representative democracy when it ruled against the use of referenda on federal issues by disallowing popular referenda on nuclear armament that were to be initiated by some states. The cautiousness stems from the historical experience of the Weimar Republic, where populist misuse aided the legal maneuvering to transform the parliamentary democracy into dictatorship. However, provision is made for a decision by referendum in the case of a new spatial delineation of the federal states (Article 29). Referenda in federal states also may be initiated by citizens according to the state constitutions. However, they have to pass two levels of collection of minimum votes before a binding decision referendum (*Volksentscheid*) must be held, where again a quorum is required. Referenda are also used in the municipalities (in all states except Berlin); they are valid only if a minimum quorum of voters has participated. Moreover, certain issues, such as the budget, fees and dues, and organizational and remuneration issues, are excluded from referenda.

Political Parties

Germany has a relatively stable pattern of two larger and a few smaller parties of political importance. The two larger parties both attempt to attract the median voter (*Volksparteien*) and have thus a very broad spectrum of not very precisely defined goals.[18] Both parties assign importance to the social question and to issues of distribution and equity, albeit from a different perspective. The *Christian Democratic Union* (CDU), with its Bavarian wing the Christian Social Union (CSU), founded after the war, stresses—from its own understanding—a Christian, social, conservative, and family orientation. Weight is put on "social" in the term "social market economy." The Mittelstand, the agricultural sector, and ownership of one's own home—especially for families with children—are important topics. The importance of the subsidiarity principle in social solutions and an orientation toward a Christian view of mankind are central concepts. The CDU/CSU can be viewed as a party that is in permanent search of a definition of a social market economy under conditions applying at a specific moment of time; it has been one of the driving forces of the expansion of the welfare state.

The *Social Democratic Party* (SPD), having a long tradition since its start in 1890 and its origins in 1863, has equity, solidarity, and the modernization of society as its central policy aims. Equity as a socially defined target plays a central role, so that the market is seen as needing to be corrected in some way by the state, on which some reliance is placed. The market is seen as a functional vehicle by which important goals of society are reached, but the market mechanism should be adjusted by government activity, for instance the state's administration of the university system. Cooperation of organized groups, as in the labor market through the social partners, is seen as a correction of the market mechanism. Whereas the CDU/CSU has its links to the employers, the Social Democrats are connected to the trade unions. They seek a "third way" between a pure capitalist market economy and a state-dominated planned economy, a Social Democratic version of the social market economy. In the 1970s the Social Democrats implemented major changes in Germany under Willy Brandt, resulting in an expansion of the welfare state.

Both parties have, in effect, segments closely wedded to a structurally conservative, interventionist notion of the social market economy with mechanisms of redistribution and social protection. Both introduced the issue of environmental protection into their programs.

Among the smaller parties, the *Free Democratic Party* (FDP) is more focused on the free market, stressing initiative, individual effort, indivi-

---

[18] On a detailed description of the party programs, see Rudzio (2003: table 3) and Conradt (2001: 112).

dual responsibility, civil rights, and the liberal constitutional state. They represented the free market partner of the CDU/CSU in the Kohl government and in the first two decades after the war; during the 1970s, however, when the Liberal Democrats formed the government together with the Social Democrats, they stressed "social liberalism," placing more weight on social issues.

The *Green Party* has as its primary policy aims protection of the environment and the pursuit of peace. They achieved political importance in the early 1980s, first in securing representation in several state parliaments and then in the 1983 Bundestag elections. In their anti-establishment history, two groups—the Fundamentalists (Fundis) and the more pragmatic Realists (Realos)—battled for dominance, with the pragmatic contingent gaining the upper hand in recent years. The Greens have lately shown more understanding of economic restraints, for instance with their concept of sustainability that extends beyond their traditional focus on environmental policy.

Finally, the *Party of Democratic Socialists* (PDS), the successor of the ruling communist party of East Germany, has been looking for an alternative approach to production and life-style and has gained support among the disappointed voters in eastern Germany.

Parliament and Government

Germany is a parliamentary democracy in which the chancellor as the head of government is elected by the federal parliament; he must be a member of parliament. He can be dismissed by parliament only through a "constructive vote of no confidence," meaning that parliament can elect someone else, with a majority of its votes. Within the government, the chancellor has a strong position because it is he, not parliament, who chooses and dismisses the ministers who are formally appointed and dismissed by the president of the republic. He also has the authority to set the policy objectives of the government (*Richtlininenkompetenz*). The chancellor needs the support of his party, so parliamentary democracy as defined by the Constitution is in fact a party democracy. Major political projects need the approval of the governing parties' national decision-making bodies. The political system is also a representative democracy in which, according to the Constitution, the will of the people finds its expression through the political parties, which are the institutional device by which individual preferences are aggregated.

Schröder has used the corporatist approach of finding consensus in round tables and committees in which the societal groups, i.e., associations of organized societal interest, were represented. The outcome of these round tables and committees then were more or less accepted by parliament, which did not have many other option since the decisions had been predetermined. In a way, parliament is circumvented by using round tables and committees to present the decisions that are to be made by the national decision-making bodies of the parties, i.e., the party assemblies, forming the government, and thereby designing the law projects outside of the genuine legislative process. This raises a constitutional question concerning the extent to which parliament has been disempowered by this approach, to the advantage of organized interest groups. These groups do not represent the common interest, nor are they in any way representative of the population, or of the preferences of the population as expressed in an election. They merely represent the interests of the specific interest group. Often not even the concerns of their members come first, but instead the interests of their organization. This raises the issue of how much power and influence interest groups should be allowed to hold in a parliamentary democracy. Corporatism, in fact, is not only an obstacle to economic efficiency, growth, and innovation, but also a stifling of the democratic process through an attempt to short-cut it by way of supposedly representative organized groups. That democracies are prone to influence by lobbying groups is a problem that arises per se out of the intricacies of collective action (Olson 1971). However, surrendering the decision-making processes directly to those interests with the power to organize the means to influence outcomes that run counter to the societal optimum may be simply a democratic façade to a rather oligarchic system.

The Bundesrat and Law-making

The federal character of Germany becomes apparent in the role that the Bundesrat, the decision-making body representing the 16 Länder, plays in law-making as defined by the German Constitution, in which one-third of the articles relate to aspects of federalism. The choice of a two-chamber system with an important role for the Länder in political decision-making, and with the Länder acting as check to the federal government—together with the country's chosen voting system—can be seen as a lesson drawn from Germany's past.

In principle, law-making competences rest with the Länder unless otherwise specified (Article 30). An important concept is how the legislative competence is allocated to federal and state levels. The federal level has the exclusive legislative competence in foreign affairs, defense, citizenship, the free movement of people, immigration (subject to the conditions of Article 74), the organization of the monetary system, the postal system, telecommunications, the railroads and air traffic, and some other areas (Article 73). Where there is competition among legislative competences, the federal states, i.e., the Länder, and the federal government, i.e., the Bund, must cooperate. As a principle, the competence lies with the Länder unless the Bund takes the initiative; then the Bundesrat has to agree. It thus has a veto. The competing competences extend to civil and criminal law, the legal system, the registration system of citizens, the right of domicile for foreigners (see immigration above), labor law, the Labor Office, unemployment policies, social insurance, the constitution of firms, expropriation, public welfare politics, labor law, scientific research, and other areas (Article 74). Schools and universities, culture, and broadcasting (all three subject to the framework competence of the federal layer; see below), regional economic policy, and local government belong to the competence of the states; this follows from Article 30. In addition to these two forms of law-making competence, the federal government has the right to establish a common institutional framework for the country in order to ensure similar conditions and to guarantee the legal and economic unity of the country. This framework competence relates to higher education, the legal system, the media, the protection of nature, and other areas (Article 75).

Historically, the Länder have lost power through two developments. In 1969 and the early 1970s, the cooperative element in federalism was expanded by some constitutional changes (Jeffery 2003). In 1969 the income tax, the corporate income tax, and the value added tax became shared taxes whose revenue is distributed between the federal government and the Länder according to proportions agreed upon (see chapter 10). A revenue-sharing mechanism among the Länder was also introduced. Moreover, a number of tasks were defined as joint tasks, with co-financing in such areas as university construction, regional economic policy, and agriculture (Article 91a). Co-financing became possible for major infrastructure projects. Such changes meant joint planning, and thus a loss of autonomy for the states. In a second development, which occurred in the late 1980s and in early 1990s, many national powers had to be transferred to the European level in the process of establishing the single market. These transfers included some powers of the Länder, meaning that they lost part of their competence to the EU level. During the Maastricht negotiations the Länder succeeded in introducing a new article into the German Constitution (Article 23) giving them a veto over the transfer of power to the European level, so that they now have a say in whether parts of their sovereignty can be assigned to the EU level.

The Bundesrat is composed of representatives of the governments of the Länder. Each of the states has a number of votes in proportion to its population; the votes of a Land have must be cast en bloc. The Bundesrat can initiate laws, and is involved in law-making in several other respects. It has to be informed of the laws passed in the Bundestag, and if it does not agree with the law it can request the creation of a mediating commit-tee (*Vermittlungsausschuss*) consisting of 16 members each from the Bundestag and the Bundesrat in proportion to the political majorities. The creation of a mediating committee can also be requested by the government and by parliament; this applies when a law has been initiated by the Bundesrat. If the mediating committee proposes a change to the law, the Bundestag has to vote again. In this context, two different type of law have to be distinguished. Where the consent of the Bundesrat is not required and where it does not have a veto, the Bundesrat can express its objection. This objection, however, can be overruled by the majority of the members of the Bundestag. (This is not the majority of the members present, but the majority of all members elected—chancellor majority.) The qualified majority of two-thirds of the members of the Bundestag is needed if the vote of the Bundesrat was taken with two-thirds of the votes of the Bundesrat. With respect to laws for which the majority of the Bundesrat is required according to the competing law-making compe-tence, the veto of the second chamber cannot be overruled. If no agree-ment in the mediating committee can be reached after three attempts, the law is not passed. When the majority in the Bundestag, i.e., of the parties forming the government, is identical to that of the Bundesrat, the role of the second chamber is to express the interest of the federal states and require changes that run counter to their interest. When the majorities differ, party considerations play a major role (Figure 14.3).

A Reform of Federalism

This institutional setup of decision-making in which the federal govern-ment and the Länder have to agree on new laws has been expanded over the years. It is estimated that the competing competence has applied to 60 percent of all the federal laws passed. This institutional arrangement, which was intended to bring about a consensus, has blurred the clear responsibilities of the different layers of government. It has taken away responsibilities and autonomy from the Länder. At the same time, when political majorities in the Bundestag and the Bundesrat diverge, the proce-dure's intent of mediating between the interest of the federal government and the interest of the Länder changes into a bargaining setup between the two major parties. If decisions are arrived at, the setup can be viewed as a grand coalition trying to find a compromise along the lowest common denominator. It may be seen as a cooperative government, superseding the existing system, as the president of the Constitutional Court, Papier (2003), wrote.

An example of this role relates to negotiations in the mediating committee in December 2003, where 16 reform laws of the Red–

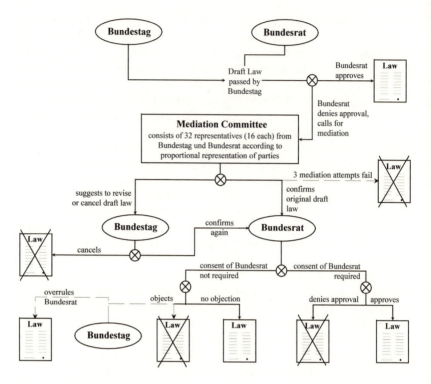

Figure 14.3   Law-making by the Bundestag and the Bundesrat.

Green coalition were dealt with. Under such circumstances, a major change of orientation in response to changed external conditions or external shocks is difficult to effect. Modernization becomes less likely, and the system tends to stall. A grand coalition may be one way of approaching this situation. An alternative one, which also represents a possible outcome, is for the opposition in the Bundestag to use the intermediating committee to block reforms proposed by the national government. For the country, this means a deadlock. When voters hold the national government liable for the policy failures that they observe, the institutional setup acts as a lever for the opposition to remove the acting government from power by blocking the reforms that would have alleviated the situation. This happened prior to the 1998 election, when in 1997 Lafontaine, then prime minister of the Saarland and leader of the Social Democrats, used the Bundesrat to block the tax proposals—the Petersberger Beschlüsse—passed by the Bundestag during the Kohl government.

The difficulties created by this system of governance necessitate reforms. The changes of 1969 and the early 1970s which led to a more intense cooperative federalism have to be corrected. The mixed responsibilities of the federal government and the Länder should be disentangled by returning competences to the Länder according to the subsidiarity principle. The domain of the competing law-making competence should be relegated to a few clearly defined problem areas, while the framework competence of the federal level should be curtailed to allow competition among the Länder. Then the federal states would be in a better position to pursue their independent policies. They must levy their own taxes, which should generate enough revenue to enable them to fulfill their clearly defined tasks. This means that the notion of "joint tasks" should be abandoned, and the revenue-sharing from the federal taxes should be reduced. Horizontal revenue-sharing should also be downgraded. A precondition for this change, however, is that the Länder are viable units. This implies that the geographical delineation of the Länder must be revised so as to produce a smaller number of federal states.

An alternative to this approach would be to replace the Bundesrat, as a representation of the Länder, by a senate whose members are directly elected and thus are not representatives of the Länder governments, as was proposed by Papier (2003). The governments of the federal states would then lose their direct influence on federal policy.

The Constitutional Court

Whereas it has been the role of the Constitutional Court to examine the constitutionality of laws passed (and the of the decisions of the lower courts), the Court has increasingly assumed the role of resolving problems that the political process is unable to tackle. Thus, in its 1999 ruling it has compelled the political parties, as well as the federal government and the states, to set up criteria to enable them to find a new formula for the revenue-sharing among states. It also defined an upper limit for taxation in its 1995 ruling, in that the state is not allowed to take more than a half of a citizen's income in the form of taxes. Such rulings are the consequence of a stalemate of the political process in Germany. Politicians, when unable to come up with a solution to a specific issue, have a tendency to wait until the Constitutional Court has spoken. This then imposes the need for a political compromise; it also serves as a constraint for interest groups. Thus, the Constitutional Court assumes the role of shaping important aspects of the economy. It becomes a substitute for parliament and disempowers it. This is an additional disempowerment to that enforced by the interest groups. The role of defining the upper and lower bounds of practical solutions, or even of predetermining practical economic answers, is problematic for a constitutional court, since it is not in the position to evaluate all the implications of its suggestions in a general equilibrium framework. Here a critical economic evaluation of the Constitutional Court's decisions is still lacking.[19]

THE RESTRAINED MARKET ECONOMY

Looking at the governance approach used in Germany, the social market economy is a restrained market economy. In many areas, the institutional setup removes decisions from the market process and from competition and assigns them to the government, to social groups, to organizations, and to informal relationships (table 14.1).

Decision-making in many sub-spheres of the economy are taken away from the market mechanism. The institutional arrangements interact with each other. Thus, strong product market regulations are likely to entail strong labor market regulations and vice versa. In a diagram with employment protection on the vertical axis and product market regulation on the horizontal axis, Germany lies to the right and above the Anglo-Saxon countries (German Council of Economic Advisers 2002: figure 57). In another diagram with the same vertical axis and stock market capitalization, it has a low stock market capitalization (Hall and Soskice 2001: figure 1.1). If full-time equivalent employment is considered, Germany exhibits a relatively low figure, together with the Scandinavian countries (Hall and Soskice 2001: figure 1.2).

Instead of letting decisions take place in a decentralized way in the markets and by competition, the German approach seeks to establish consensus and relies on non-market processes. Unlike in the United States, when a new problem arises German public opinion does not ask first "Where is the market solution?" but instead, nearly instinctively, looks to the intervention of the politician for a solution. Non-market approaches receive an implicit preference; there is even a deeply rooted mistrust of markets and competition, which possibly increased after German unification. The non-market processes are often thought of as protecting the collective interest, including the aspect of equity, whereas it seems difficult for the public to understand that the aggregation of decentralized market decisions and competitive processes lead to efficient economic results and stimulate the dynamics of the economy. Thus, whereas the western German type of economy has prevailed over an extreme form of collectivism in eastern Germany, soft forms of collective decision-making continue to exist.

It is the hypothesis of this book that Germany has lost economic dynamics because of its institutional setup. Its institutions favor the status

---

[19] Compare the annual reviews of the US Supreme Court decisions by the Cato Institute.

TABLE 14.1
Cooperative decision-making versus markets and competition

Area	Cooperative decision-making	Markets and competition
Employment	Wage formation and institutional setting by social partners	Labor markets determining the equilibrium wage
Banking	Bank-intermediated products; relationship-banking	Capital market intermediated products
	Public guarantees; protection against takeover	Market control by the threat of takeover
Governance of firms	Two-tier board system, control by the supervisory board	Strong reliance on the capital market and the threat of takeover
	Codetermination in the supervisory board	No formal restraint on the decision space
	Workers' councils	Self-interest of the firm to be attractive to its employees
Health	Associations of statuary health insurance physicians in the public health system	Competition of integrated systems of insurers and health service providers
Universities	Governmental administrative planning of the university sector	Competition among universities
	Entitlement to free access	Scarcity prices for students
Steering the economy	Round tables and committees (consensus approach)	Decentralized decisions via markets
Governance of government	Cooperative federalism	Competitive federalism
	Mix of majority and plurality voting	Majority voting

quo and consequently make economic development extremely path-dependent. Given technological trajectories and long-practiced organizational approaches dominate the road to the future, allowing marginal improvements in the familiar areas of production; but the conditions are not incentive-compatible for leapfrogging. In contrast, other countries, especially the small and foreign trade-oriented economies in Europe, have changed their institutional arrangements in response to new challenges in the world economy.

This leads to the fundamental question of whether, and to what extent, Germany has become immobile with respect to institutional modernization. One answer is that a country's institutional arrangement is the expression of its political preferences. Given these preferences, a trade-off exists between the wish for collective decisions and the performance of the economy. Those who want more collective choices instead of markets and competition have to pay the price of a less economically dynamic system. This may well be the decision of a mature economy, having reached a satisfactory level of income to allow itself the luxury of consensus-seeking solutions.[20] At that point a relative decline in economic performance compared to other countries is certain to come, and absolute economic decline cannot be ruled out.

The other answer is that the institutional structures have become so rigid that institutional adjustment can no longer take place, and that vested interests have captured the institutional setup and now control it to such an extent that the political process has lost its problem-solving capacity. In that case a country like Germany must rely more and more on decisions of the Constitutional Court to unblock political deadlocks. In such a scenario, Germany can indeed be compared to Japan as another mature economy,[21] facing problems similar to those of the latter. These countries' institutional systems were appropriate for expanding economies, but no longer seem to be appropriate for solving structural issues. We then have the new category of NDCs in the world economy—the newly declining countries.

I do not believe that this is the inevitable answer for Germany. The institutions have not been completely captured by political groups, and with enough energy and resilience, the country should be able to find a way out of deadlock in which it finds itself. This is the topic of the concluding chapter.

---

[20] As an indication of this conflict see Hall and Soskice (2003: figure 1.2), with a similarly low Gini coefficient as the Scandinavian countries indicating a more equal distribution, but also a low full-time employment equivalent.

[21] For Japan, the reason for political immobility is seen in the relative over-representation of agricultural voting districts to the city districts; this finds its analog in the consensus approach in Germany.

CHAPTER FIFTEEN

The Need for a Renaissance of the Market Economy

Looking at Germany's poor performance in terms of high unemployment, low economic growth, the near-insolvency of the social security systems, and the deterioration of the public finances, it must be concluded that the country needs a major change—an institutional big bang, similar to the Erhard reform of western Germany in 1948. The task of restructuring Germany would be much easier if the country were in a win-win situation, in which not only would the country's economic position improve as a consequence of measures taken, but all groups would benefit from the change. Unfortunately, Germany is not in such a situation. Without a doubt, there will be losses for some groups if the present economic state of affairs is to be amended.

The country faces three tradeoffs. The first is the choice between equity and dynamics, the second, the choice between the collective interest and individual liberty, and the third, the choice between corporatist decision-making and competition. These decisions require political leadership. Although Germany is not yet in as dire a situation as the United Kingdom was in its Winter of Discontent in 1979, when the general conditions of life were deteriorating before the eyes of the average citizen—for instance through the subway strikes—the conditions in which Germany finds itself are serious enough to require a systematic overhaul of its institutional system.

EQUITY OR DYNAMICS

Germany has reached a level of social absorption that is affecting the foundation of the economy negatively. Its policy failures are linked to the priority that has been given to social protection and equity. Thus, a major issue for Germany is how the tradeoff inherent in the concept of the "social market economy," i.e., between an efficient and dynamic economic system—based on decentralized decisions, effort, and initiative of the individual—and social protection and equity—relying on distribution by government—can be resolved.

An important aspect in this normative debate is how equity should be defined. In the first place, the term "equity" cannot be a catch-all, in which woolly perceptions and stirred-up emotions play a role. The concept of equity must be defined explicitly, and not used merely as an expression of people's feelings. What may at first sound just and equitable may come to be seen as unjust and inequitable after some reflection. Second, equity should not be given a static interpretation, i.e., as the outcome of economic processes at a given moment of time. Equity considerations have to take into account how a measure for distribution, or for allocation and dynamics, influences the decisions of economic agents and the outcome of economic processes that will prevail after all adjustments have played out in the economy. For economists, this is the idea of a change from one general equilibrium to another. For instance, there is a surprisingly high vertical mobility in the income hierarchy of people in Germany: 40.7 percent of the households of the dependently employed who were in the lowest income segment in 1997 had moved to a higher level three years later, and of those 12.9 percent had moved up further than the next level.[1] Interpreting equality in a strictly static sense would neglect such upward mobility.

Third, taking into account the intertemporal aspect, equity cannot be defined in the eyes of the present generation alone, but must include the interests of future generations. The present generation will hand down the environment, other stocks, and durable consumer goods to the next generation. In order to do this, a country has to save and accumulate capital, thereby producing a larger output and enjoying higher welfare later on. This means renouncing some present consumption. The same argument applies to knowledge capital, to the conservation of nature,[2] or to other goods[3] that are to be bequeathed to the next generation.

Equity considerations may lead us to conclude that a given sector should be protected; but over time, this sector may then become less competitive, requiring more subsidies, and resources will thereby be wasted, eventually making everybody in the economy worse off. These aspects cannot be neglected in the definition of equity.[4] But in addition,

[1] "Lowest segment" defined as between 0 and 50 percent of the median, "highest segment" as 200 percent and over of the median; seven segments altogether (German Council of Economic Advisers 2002: table 70).

[2] For instance, when it was first opened Yellowstone National Park could be used only by the rich, but now it can be enjoyed by everybody.

[3] For example Cologne Cathedral.

[4] Economists have to study the impact of equity measures, including all the ramifications and changes in incentives, in a general equilibrium context. It is a fascinating question whether this proposition applies to ethical norms as well. Are ethical norms evaluated at a *prima vista* point of view, or are they judged in a general equilibrium including all ramifications in a social system?

the present generation may place a burden on future generations in the form of government debt, or entitlements of the retired vis-à-vis the producing generation. The issue of equity between the generations will become a major concern in the larger European continental economies. In all of these considerations, the present interest of future generations should be introduced more explicitly, so that their utility and preference functions can be taken into account. To put it differently, if adjustments are needed in the public systems, the issue is how to split the burden of adjustment between the generations. It is clear that society and the political process must arrive at a solution to this problem that is fair between the generations. Political parties are now taking up that issue in their programs.

Fourth, it has to be decided to which group the goal of equity should refer—family, friends, the neighborhood, the region, the nation, the continent, or the world? In practice, equity considerations are more important the closer the personal relationship; they fade in importance the larger the group of people taken into consideration. The ethical issue is whether this is justified. With respect to the nation state, the issue is whether distribution and social protection should focus on the low-income groups and those who desperately need such help, such as the ill and the handicapped, or should be spread more widely, as is the case in the German welfare state. Another issue is whether the protection of one group of the population might give rise to the discrimination of another group. Thus, layoff restraints for the employed introduce an incentive for firms not to hire workers because they will then be constrained from laying them off; thus, the insiders are protected, but the outsiders will find fewer jobs. Equity should not be defined just from the perspective of the incumbents.

Fifth, equity should not be understood as an equality of the economic *outcome*, but rather as an equal starting condition and an equality of *opportunities* (unless a specific group is addressed, such as the handicapped or those who are ill). Since outcomes are the result of individual effort and remuneration, people will not have sufficient incentives if outcomes are equalized. Because individuals have different predispositions and qualifications, neither jobs nor incomes can be equal for all. What is important is that there is no preferential treatment or discrimination from government.

Finally, equity differs with respect to the variables to which it refers and the instruments used. Equity can mean the coverage of risks, e.g., income risks in case of illness or unemployment, distribution of contribution rates to the insurance system, distribution of income, and access to goods. Accordingly, policy recommendations differ.

Once a definition of equity is decided upon, the tradeoff between equity and dynamics can be considered. This is the essence of the conflict. It seems that Germany is on the right-hand tail of the bell-shaped curve between efficiency or growth and equity, so, by reducing some of the distribution, efficiency and growth will be enhanced. This tradeoff depends, of course, on the definition of equity. Thus, a stricter and more ambitious definition of equity will convey more severe opportunity costs in terms of forgone employment and growth. Moreover, if the government introduces many single equity restraints into the economic system, the solution space for the economy is reduced, and efficiency and dynamics are lessened. Some of the properties of the tradeoff can be brought to light by looking at specific aspects of this goal conflict in more detail. This should lead to specific recommendations for resolving Germany's problems.

Distribution and social protection should not violate the financing constraint. In any given period, an economy must not distribute more than it has produced. The financing of social policies through deficits, as now happens in Germany, creates a burden for future generations. This is the first reason why the level of social absorption must be brought down instead of following an approach that simply raises revenues when the desired absorption increases. But it is not only a matter of being able to finance the social systems. Distribution and social protection affect the economic base negatively. Contributions to these systems represent a tax on employees, weakening the demand for labor. The system also confers a disincentive for effort. Moreover, the implicit minimum wage—an important instrument of social protection—represents a lower floor to the wage structure, resulting in a drying up of the lower segment of the labor market. This is the second reason why reforms are necessary for the achievement of a more efficient economy on a higher growth path with lower unemployment. Finally, given the ageing of the population and the future financing restraints of the social security systems, adjustments are needed to keep these systems viable in the future, and this is the third reason for reducing the level of social absorption.

Under these circumstances, increasing transfers from the public budget to the social security systems in order to avoid lowering the level of social absorption is not advisable, for several reasons. First, the link between benefits and contributions will thereby be seen to be further weakened. Thus, a tax-financed pension system will destroy what remains of equivalence in the existing system. Second, such transfers will increase the share of government in an ageing economy. Third, the opportunity costs of financing the transfers will lead to a higher tax wedge. And fourth, fiscal policy, which has to pick up the deficit of social policy, will become even more unreliable.

In order to reduce the level of social absorption, benefits have to be redefined. First, the retirement age should be increased to 67 years.

Second, the unusually long period of university education before students enter the labor force must be reduced. Furthermore, a distinction should be made in the four social security systems between what represents a large risk for an individual and what represents a small risk; large risks should be covered by the social security systems, while small risks should be borne by the individual himself. This means that part of the risks covered by the public system at present should be shifted to the individual; he then can decide himself how much insurance coverage he wants for the small risks—say, in the voluntary additional funded system for his pension.

A major problem in the reform of the welfare state concerns the income floors established by social welfare and by the social security systems. These represent a lower floor of social absorption, limiting the possibilities of reform and affecting the reservation wage. With respect to the reforms passed in December 2003 and becoming effective in 2005, it remains to be determined whether the reservation wage was actually reduced for the low-skilled, long-term unemployed. It seems that this may not have occurred, since they had relatively low incomes when they were in employment. If this does indeed turn to be the case, then it may be necessary to make another correction of the reservation wage, with an automatic reduction of the support level by one-third for those capable of working, and a more generous phasing-in period during which market income is not lost. Meanwhile, after the Social Democrats lost in the elections for the European Parliament and in Thuringia, the first voices can be heard that the reforms should be partly undone.

In the social security system, the income floors consist of the basic pensions, introduced in 2003 and guaranteeing a minimum pension irrespective of contributions. There are also proposals for completely tax-financed pension or health services. In these approaches, the still existing, albeit weak, link between benefits and contributions would be completely destroyed. In addition to the income floors, the actual level of social protection has come to be seen as an entitlement: people expect it. A possible response to this attitude is to take redistribution out of social security systems and to deal with it through a tax-transfer mechanism. Persons with a low income would receive a transfer enabling them to pay their health insurance contributions. Contributions would be determined by assessing the total health costs of the economy, excluding smaller risks that the individual would carry himself, and then dividing the remaining costs by the number of people to be insured. Their contributions would reflect the average health risk and would be independent of income, including labor income.

Such a concept would more or less automatically remove contributions from labor income as a base for payment. The solidarity of this system lies in the sharing of the health costs. The separation of insurance and distribution would make the redistributive dimension explicit, showing the costs of financing in a transparent way and allowing a better targeting of equity. At the same time, a decentralized mechanism would be established by which the financing constraint would be expressed to individuals. However, since this approach would take the costs of the health system as given and then allocate the financing of the costs to the insured, it would not be an incentive-compatible system of cost control and efficiency enhancement. Consequently, it would have to be combined with other approaches, for instance the distinction between large and small risks. Note that this remains far from a market solution, in which health expenditures are determined solely by the individual decisions of patients, health service suppliers, and insurers: the German system, by contrast, defines health standards, regulates the behavior of service suppliers, and requires mandatory insurance.

For the old-age pension system, a tax-transfer mechanism can be less readily applied because pensions are the result of precautionary savings, and these are the consequence of individual decisions. The concept of a minimum pension should not have been introduced; instead, the problem should have been dealt with as a social welfare problem, as in the past. Now it hardly can be undone, although possibly its level could be scaled down. Distributive schemes for contributions should not destroy incentives to save for old age: in fact, this should be a requirement, especially for the pay-as-you-go system.

With respect to the social budget, where the welfare state has distributed benefits to nearly all of the population, giving entitlements to high-income groups as well as low,[5] support should now be focused on those on lower incomes. In addition, it should be recognized that opportunities for income redistribution are limited. A realistic assessment of the possibilities of redistribution is therefore in order. About 80 percent of net national income is income to labor; 70 percent is income to the dependently employed; the remaining 20 percent is income to firms, i.e., profits, and income deriving from wealth, i.e., interest and dividend income, of which about 3–5 percent is interest income. Profits represent a residual, varying with the economic situation. Thus, redistribution can occur predominantly, if not exclusively, only within labor income, from the higher wage earners to the lower wage earners. In addition, the negative impact of redistribution on effort has to be considered. Moreover, capital has the exit option in a global market. If capital is driven out by redistributive taxation, labor will end up with a lower and possibly less inno-

---

[5] For example the free access to university of well-to-do students, or the child allowance up to the age of 27 years.

vative capital stock, causing weaker growth in its productivity and thus a smaller increase in real wages or a reduced employment outlook. Finally, distribution itself is not without costs. Okun (1975) has expressed this in the picture of the "leaky bucket": by redistributing from people with higher incomes to people with lower incomes, a bucket is used—but the bucket leaks, so that part of the income that is to be redistributed does not arrive at its destination.

The above considerations put into perspective the issue of "a distorted income distribution" (*Schieflage*), which is a topic of public discussion from time to time. Whereas the question of how much distribution is desirable remains a value judgment, it is fair to say that in the German situation less equity and a lower, redefined level of protection are needed if a higher growth path and a higher rate of employment are to be achieved. How difficult it is to implement such a reorientation can be seen by the unrest and protest that arose in the Social Democratic Party at the beginning of 2004, when the first effects of some of the reforms, such as paying a fee to see a doctor, were felt. The Social Democratic Party was unable to raise its very low acceptance ratings in the population above 30 percent. The protest in the party was so strong that Chancellor Schröder had to resign as chairman of the party. Since the Christian Democrats are similarly hesitant to implement reforms, this indicates the difficulties that Germany will face in trying to reform its economy.

COLLECTIVITY OR INDIVIDUAL LIBERTY

On a more fundamental, or even philosophical, level, the choice is between the collective interest and individual liberty. Collective solutions play an important role in Germany's economic system. The high share of government of nearly half the GDP; the mandatory system of social security, with an implicit tax on labor; the other elements of the social budget, with the distributive role of the state, the delegation of vital decisions to interest groups, the support by subsidies, and the administrative approach in such fields as universities—all indicate that the collective interest finds a strong expression in Germany's economic system. The common wheal, the consensus of society, the essence of community (*Gemeinschaft*), a caring and paternalistic interpretation of the state and solidarity—all have been central notions in Germany's economic approach, and still are. Collective solutions arise from the way of life and from an implicit understanding in society, but they also stem from the wish for distribution and for equity.

In contrast, individual liberty—the maneuvering space of the individual citizen, his personal protected sphere, his basic right as a sovereign vis-à-vis the administration and government—though present in periods of German history and, of course, addressed by the Constitution, seem to be less pronounced than in countries such as Switzerland, the United Kingdom, and the United States.

The tradeoff between equity and efficiency has many facets (Siebert 2003: 235). Apparently, if collectivism goes too far the desire for individual liberty takes over, as the East German silent revolution of 1989 has illustrated. But within that threshold, collective solutions are important in the German system. When new solutions to a problem have to be developed, the average German tends to find a collective approach sympathetic. Consequently, an important prerequisite to the necessary changes in Germany is a change in mind-set. When confronted with a problem, it would be desirable for the average German to first ask the question, "What does a market solution for a problem look like, and how can individuals themselves find an answer to a problem instead of calling for the government to fix it?" It seems that the economics profession has not succeeded in educating the German population on the paradigm of competition.

In this reorientation, the principles of subsidiarity and individual responsibility should receive more emphasis. Only when it has been established that the individual, the family, the firm, and/or the region cannot solve a problem should the government be asked to step in. The system has to rely more on the responsibility of each individual to solve problems. This means that Germans need to think in terms of opportunities and options provided by a decentralized institutional framework. It is important that an institutional framework provide options and space to the individual. Society should not be "closed," but rather should be open in the sense of Karl Popper (2003), where "individuals are confronted with personal decisions" (Popper 2003: 186), "in which institutions leave...room for personal responsibility" (p. 185), "...which sets free the critical powers of man" (p. xvii).

This leads to specific recommendations for solving Germany's problems. Subsidiarity and responsibility of the individual imply, for instance, that persons who are capable of working should not rely on social welfare provided by the state, but should take an active part in finding employment and in enhancing their qualification and employability. Subsidiarity and responsibility also mean that some of the risks covered by social security that have been socialized in the past should be privatized, leaving just those risks that are too large for an individual to bear himself. Subsidiarity and responsibility mean, furthermore, that in a federal structure decisions should be assigned to the lowest level of government whenever that is feasible.

Incentives should be set in such a way that effort is rewarded. They should avoid, wherever possible, an agent receiving benefits or services without making effort or contributions. Costs should not be socialized; i.e., an individual should not have the option of shifting the opportunity cost of using a good or service on to someone else. We know only too well that wrong incentives create long-run distortions.

The state should allow room for the development of the personality, and maneuvering space for the individual. This relates to consumer sovereignty, to the freedom of education and work, to the guarantee of individual property, to entrepreneurial freedom, and to the limits of taxation. A case in point is the principle developed by the 1995 ruling of the German Constitutional Court that the state should not take more than half of an individual's income over a given period (*Halbteilunsggrundsatz*) in the form of direct taxes (including property taxes); another is that employees should be allowed to deviate from the collective wage contract if a firm offers a choice between job security and lower wages or longer working time.

To give more weight to individual liberty, Germany needs to develop a culture in which self-reliance and the individual's own initiative are encouraged. Entrusting the younger generations with responsibility and exposing them to a more competitive environment in the universities will help to foster such a culture.

CORPORATIST DECISION-MAKING OR COMPETITION

Germany's third major choice refers to its institutional approach to economic governance. This becomes apparent if one takes markets and competition as a frame of reference and then considers how much Germany has deviated from that concept (Siebert 2004b). Germany has established an economic governance in which non-market mechanisms play a vital role in many areas. They affect decisions on employment and unemployment, the allocation of capital, the governance of firms, the formation of human capital, the role of the state, and the federal structure. This approach gives much authority to interest groups and incumbents, who can prevent changes and thereby preserve the status quo. In the labor market it protects the insiders at the expense of the outsiders. Market exit is made more difficult, so that market entry is restricted. The government and social justice play an overwhelming role in the formation of human capital, and distributive federalism does not make use of competition as a method of organization. Here the choice is between the corporatist approaches actually used, and greater governance through markets and competition. This is the central issue in Germany's reforms.

In the reformation of Germany, the political task is to assign more decisions to markets and competition. Then adjustments will take place more or less automatically by a set of decentralized decisions of households and firms. Markets and competition represent mechanisms of discovery, in which new solutions can be found. They command a huge potential to reduce costs, to invent new products, to find new production processes, and to come up with new organizational ideas. This must be the new central orientation of economic policy.

Germany always has had a consensus that firms should not be shielded behind walls of protectionism, but should have to adjust to world markets, so that production, investment, and innovation of the enterprise sector respond automatically to changing international conditions of supply and demand. This concept of decentralized decision-making under competition will have to be applied comprehensively to other sectors of the economy.

The groups that have benefited from Germany's corporatist approach will fight these changes. But their position will weaken when it becomes apparent that their positions are unsustainable, that the forces of change throughout the world are so strong that it is impossible to continue in the former way. Thus, if other industrial countries can digest economic shocks more easily, and if external shocks now affect Germany for longer than other countries and longer than in the past, changes become inevitable. The position of interest groups will weaken if goal conflicts with other countries are seen to dominate national conflicts. For instance, closing European agricultural markets to the exportable products of developing countries is difficult to defend on moral grounds; and it becomes increasingly difficult to justify politically the current practice of protecting or subsidizing domestic products. When developing countries catch up and improve their comparative advantage in the production of manufactured goods, the former comparative advantage in industrial countries must be eroded. Positions of interest groups are also harder to defend if the inconsistencies of economic policy become too obvious; politics cannot at the same time pay subsidies to the coal industry (or tobacco farmers) and reduce CO_2 emissions (and forbid cigarette advertising because of health risks).

Nevertheless, it will be a difficult task to break up the distributional alliances of the status quo. A mechanism must be found that will weaken the position of the interest groups. One possibility is for the national government to make distribution more transparent and financing constraints more explicit, thereby putting pressure on the status quo. The social security systems are already financed by deficits, and this cannot be continued. Moreover, present social absorption is no longer sustainable because it is placing an increasingly heavy burden on future generations. Another possibility is to deregulate the product markets, which would put pressure on the rents that arise and are distributed in the factor market. Here the European Union can play an important role. With the single market concept and with mutual recognition, the EU has already put pressure on traditional national solutions. Indeed, its directives on the privatization of public monopolies and on new regulatory regimes for the network industries have already affected the position of the German trade unions in these sectors.

In this approach, it is paramount not to increase the power of interest groups. This requirement is in contrast to what the Schröder government has done, e.g., by giving the social partners a greater say in the supervisory board of the Labor Office as of 2004, by redoing the law on the workers' councils (Business Constitution Act) in 2001, or by requiring by law in 2003 that the private agencies for temporary employment must negotiate a labor contract with the unions; this was done to get the unions' political permission to introduce official agencies for temporary jobs.[6]

If Germany wants to move to a higher growth path with lower unemployment, quite a few changes are needed in its system of governance. In the institutional setup relevant for employment and unemployment, decentralized decisions on wage formation should be allowed. Firms should be given the option to deviate from the collective wage contract if an overwhelming majority of their employees agree to it; the concurrence of the workers' council might also be required, possibly not in the form of a mandatory agreement for all employees of a firm, but as a recommendation for individual contracts (*Regelungsabrede*). If such an agreement could not be reached, the collective contract would remain in force, and so would be a fall-back position. Individual employees and unemployed persons should also be given the explicit right to determine for themselves whether a deviation from the collective contract, containing for instance a no-layoff guarantee of the firm for some years, is desirable.

In the capital market, public guarantees backing the savings banks and their central institutions would have to go. There is no reason why these institutions should be owned by the municipalities and the states; they should be completely privatized. In developing the institutional setup for the financial sector, greater reliance should be placed on market processes instead of on bank-intermediated products.

With regard to the governance of firms, codetermination can hardly be defended in the institutional environment of the European Union. It will have to be scaled down and eventually given up. The role of workers' councils should be examined in light of the experience that has been garnered after the 2001 change of the law.

In the university system, competition should be introduced. The allocation of students to universities should be conducted via a decentralized market process of demand and supply. Students should be able to express

---

[6] Whereas the official agencies have arranged 50 000 jobs in 2003 according to estimates, the private agencies procure 750 000 positions annually.

their preferences, universities should be given the right to recruit their students. The financing of universities should then be linked to the number of students. Institutions that do not succeed in attracting a sufficient number of students would have to be closed. Codetermination in the university system in its present form should be given up. This is an important precondition for future innovation.

Germany's expenditures on research and development, amounting to 2.5 percent of GDP in 2001 and financed by both government and the private sector, should be increased to a level of around 3 percent, comparable to that of the United States and Japan. The role of the state in generating more innovation is to finance basic research and define its institutional conditions; it should also help organize the diffusion of basic knowledge. Otherwise, its role should be limited. Mission technologies promoted by the state have often been a failure. The state does not have a priori information on future technologies, and may well be the victim of political capture by rent-seeking firms, which use their technological information advantage strategically to their own profit. This argument also holds for the European Union.

Policy cannot generate more innovation and dynamics by working against the entrepreneurs, but only by working with them. Policy therefore will have to focus on how policy measures affect the production, investment, and innovative behavior of firms, instead of on seeking union consent to introduce any such measures. Society must be prepared to accept the role of the entrepreneur. German enterprise taxes, an important aspect in the incentives for investment and innovation in firms, are high by international comparison and should be reduced. Society should accept high profits, if the ex ante risks are high. Profits should be judged not ex post, when uncertainty is no longer there, but ex ante. Investment opportunities too will depend on the preparedness to accept technological risks.

Major changes are needed in government. Its role has to be redefined. The share of government in GDP should be reduced considerably, say from nearly 50 percent to 40 percent. Subsidies amounting to 7.5 percent of GDP should be eliminated. New subsidies should not be introduced, not even in the area of environmental protection. The consumption part of government's expenditures should come down in favor of investment.

An important aspect of reducing the government's share in GDP is a reform of the social security systems. Fiscal policy cannot be assigned the role of permanently taking over the deficits of social security. The government should give up its ad hoc approach, addressing predominantly acute economic policy problems, and instead should take a long-run view of its actions. Its fundamental task should be to set incentives so that the economic decisions of households and firms lead to optimal results—or, put differently, to results satisfying the policy targets.

The federal structure of government needs serious reform. Distributive federalism should be renounced in favor of competitive federalism. This implies that the states should have the appropriate instruments, including a set of own taxes, to compete geographically. Competing law-making competences and joint financing should be disentangled so that clear responsibilities are defined for the federal and state levels. In the end, this implies a new geographic delineation of the federal states to create viable units.

Blockades of decision-making can be prevented if the voting system is amended in the direction of majority voting.

Beyond the Social Market

Over the last forty years, Germany has gone astray in its economic governance. It has expanded its social security systems to such an extent that they are now weakening the country's economic foundations and negatively affecting its economic performance. But the economic base has to finance social absorption, and the country's social absorption is exceeding the possibilities of its social production. Germany has an institutional incentive system that has caused unemployment to ratchet upward in each recession, and negative economic shocks to last longer and be more severe each time. It has moved onto a lower growth path since the mid-1990s. Europe's largest economy is having to rely on external stimulus for an improved production and employment performance through exports, instead of being able to promote economic growth endogenously. Unlike other countries, it has not succeeded in modernizing its institutional setup according to the changing international conditions.

To conclude, Germany faces severe economic policy challenges. At heart I am optimist, and of course I hope that Germany will find solutions for all its problems. The optimistic response to Germany's ills is a reminder that the Germans as a people are resilient, and that in terms of economics they are good when they are under pressure. To bring this strength—if it still exists—to the forefront, Germany needs a renaissance of the market economy; a redefinition of the social market.

The country has come to a crossroads. If it chooses to make the necessary changes in its institutional framework and to set new incentives, it will reach a higher growth path with lower unemployment again. If not, i.e., if it chooses to keep its corporatist approach of decision-making, if it opts for the equity target, and if Germans continue to believe in the merit of government intervention, then a lower growth path with less dynamics, high unemployment, and structural problems in the social security systems will be the likely outcome.

Acemoglu, Daron (2002). Technical Change, Inequality, and the Labor Market. *Journal of Economic Literature* 40: 7–72.

———— (2003). Cross-Country Inequality Trends. *Economic Journal* 113: F121–F149.

Afhüppe, Sven, Julia Leendertse, and Volker Müller (2002). Neuer Schub. *Wirtschaftswoche* 19: 46–48.

Aschauer, David A. (1989). Is Public Expenditure Productive? *Journal of Monetary Economics* 23: 177–200.

Baldwin, Richard and Mika Mildgren (2003). *The Draft Constitutional Treaty's Voting Reform Dilemma.* CEPS Policy Brief no. 44, November 2003.

Bank for International Settlements (2003). *73rd Annual Report.* Basel. Available from http://www.bis.org/publ/arpdf/ar(2003e.pdf.

Barca, Fabrizio, and Marco Becht (2001). *The Control of Corporate Europe.* Oxford: Oxford University Press.

Baumert, Jürgen, Wilfried Bos, and Rainer Lehmann (eds.) (2000). *TIMSS/III. Dritte Internationale Mathematik- und Naturwissenschaftsstudie - Mathematische und naturwissenschaftliche Bildung am Ende der Schullaufbahn*, 2 vols. Opladen: Leske & Budrich. A survey is available from http://www.timss.mpg.de/TIMSS_im_Ueberblick/TIMSSIII-Broschuere.pdf.

Baumol, William J., John C. Panzar, and Robert D. Willig (1988). *Contestable Markets and the Theory of Industry Structure*, rev. edn. San Diego: Harcourt, Brace, Jovanovitch; originally published 1982.

Baums, Theodor (2003). Unternehmensführung und Unternehmenskontrolle: Brauchen wir eine neue Konzeption für Corporate Governance? In *Die Weltwirtschaft vor den Herausforderungen von morgen.* Vortrags- und Diskussionsveranstaltung des Instituts für Weltwirtschaft am 23, January 2003, Frankfurt am Main. Kiel: Kiel Institute for World Economics, pp. 31–41.

Becht, Marco, Patrick Bolton, and Alisa Röell (2002). *Corporate Governance and Control.* NBER Working Paper no. 9371, Cambridge, MA: NBER. Available from http://papers.nber.org/papers/w9371.pdf.

Belaisch, A., L. Kodres, J. Levy, and A. Ubide (2001). *Euro Banking at the Cross Roads.* IMF Working Paper no. 01/28. Washington, DC: IMF. Available from http://www.imf.org/external/pubs/ft/wp/2001/wp0128.pdf.

Belitz, H. (2004). Forschung und Entwicklung in multinationalen Unternehmen. *Studien zum deutschen Innovationssystem* no. 8-2004, Deutsches Institut für Wirtschaftsforschung.

Bernholz, Peter (1979). Freedom and Constitutional Economic Order. *Zeitschrift für die gesamte Staatswissenschaft* 135: 520–32.

Beyer, Juergen (2002). *Deutschland AG a.D.: Deutsche Bank, Allianz und das Verflechtungszentrum großer deutscher Unternehmen.* MPIfG Working Paper no. 02/4, Cologne.

Blanchard, Olivier, and Justin Wolfers (2000). The Role of Shocks and Institutions in the Rise of European Unemployment: The Aggregate Evidence. *Economic Journal* 110: C1–C33.

Bleaney, Michael F., Norman Gemmel, and Richard Kneller (1999). Fiscal Policy and Growth: Evidence from OECD Countries. *Journal of Public Economics* 74: 171–90.

Boehmer, Ekkehart (1999). *Corporate Governance in Germany: Institutional Background and Empirical Results.* Working Paper no. 78 of the Institute for Commercial and Business at the University of Osnabrueck.

Börsch-Supan, Axel H. (1998). Germany: A Social Security System on the Verge of Collapse. In Horst Siebert (ed.), *Redesigning Social Security.* Symposia and conference proceedings, Kiel Week Conference 1997. Tubingen: Mohr, pp. 129–59.

_____ (2000a). A Model under Siege: A Case Study of the Germany Retirement Insurance System. *Economic Journal* 110: 24–45.

_____ (2000b). Incentive Effects of Social Security on Labor Force Participation: Evidence in Germany and Across Europe. *Journal of Public Economics* 78: 25–49.

Boss, Alfred (1999). *Sozialhilfe, Lohnabstand und Leistungsanreize.* Kiel Working Papers no. 912. Kiel: Kiel Institute for World Economics.

_____ (2002). *Sozialhilfe, Lohnabstand und Leistungsanreize. Empirische Analyse für Haushaltstypen und Branchen in West- und Ostdeutschland.* Kiel Studies no. 318. Berlin and Heidelberg: Springer.

_____ (2003). *Arbeits- und Investitionsanreize in Deutschland: Die Rolle der Abgaben- und Transferpolitik als Determinante des Wachstums des Produktionspotentials.* Kiel Working Paper no. 1148. Kiel: Kiel Institute for World Economics.

Boss, Alfred, and Thomas Elendner (2003). *Steuerreform und Lohnsteueraufkommen in Deutschland. Simulationen auf Basis der Einkommenssteuerstatistik.* Kiel Working Paper no. 1185. Kiel: Kiel Institute for World Economics.

Boss, Alfred, and Astrid Rosenschon (1996). *Öffentliche Transferleistungen zur Finanzierung der deutschen Einheit: eine Bestandsaufnahme.* Kiel Discussion Paper no. 269. Kiel: Institute for World Economics.

_____ (2002). *Subventionen in Deutschland: Quantifizierung und finanzpolitische Bewertung.* Kiel Discussion Paper no. 392/93. Kiel: Kiel Institute for World Economics.

Brauer, Holger (2003). *The Real Exchange Rate and Prices of Traded Goods in OECD Countries.* Kiel Studies no. 322, Kiel Institute for World Economics. Berlin: Springer.

Breyer, Friedrich (2001). *Why Funding is not a Solution to the "Social Security Crises".* IZA Discussion Paper no. 328, Bonn. Available from ftp://ftp.iza.org/dps/dp328.pdf.

Breyer, Friedrich, and Volker Ulrich (2000a). Demographischer Wandel, medizinischer Fortschritt und der Anstieg der Gesundheitsausgaben. In: *DIW Wochenbericht* 24/2000, Berlin. Available from http://www.diw.de/deutsch/publikationen/wochenberichte/docs/00–24–2.html.

_____ (2000b). Gesundheitsausgaben, Alter und medizinischer Forschritt: eine Regressionsanalyse. *Jahrbuecher fuer Nationaloekonomie und Statistik* 1/220: 1–12.

Breyer, Friedrich, Wolfgang Franz, Stefan Homburg, Reinhold Schnabel, and Wille Eberhard (2004). *Reform der sozialen Sicherung*. Berlin: Springer-Verlag.

Buch, Claudia M., and Stefan M. Golder, (2002). Domestic and Foreign Banks in Germany: Do They Differ? *Kredit und Kapital* 35: 19–53.

Buchanan, James M. (2000). *The Limits of Liberty: Between Anarchy and Leviathan. The Collected Works of James M. Buchanan*, vol. 7. Indianapolis: Liberty Fund. First published in Chicago: University of Chicago Press, 1975.

Christensen, Bjoern (2001). *The Determinants of Reservation Wages in Germany: Does a Motivation Gap Exist?* Kiel Working Paper no. 1024. Kiel: Kiel Institute for World Economics.

_____ (2002). *Reservation Wages, Offered Wages, and Unemployment Duration: New Empirical Evidence*. Kiel Working Paper no. 1095. Kiel: Kiel Institute for World Economics.

_____ (2003). Die Entwicklung der qualifikatorischen Lohndifferenzierung in Deutschland. *Die Weltwirtschaft* 3: 313–22.

_____ (2004). *Reservationslöhne und Arbeitslosigkeit in Deutschland*. Kiel Studies. Berlin and Heidelberg: Springer, Forthcoming.

Christensen, Bjoern, and Axel Schimmelpfennig (1998). Arbeitslosigkeit, Qualifikation und Lohnstruktur in Deutschland, *Die Weltwirtschaft* 2: 177–86.

Coase, Ronald H. (2001). The Problem of Social Cost. Reprinted in Ulaganathan Sankar, *Environmental Economics*. New Delhi: Oxford University Press, pp. 21–56. First published in 1960 in the University of Chicago Law School *Journal of Law and Economics* 3: 1–44.

Conradt, David P. (2001). *The German Polity*, 7th edn. New York: Addison-Wesley Longman.

Creditreform (2003). *Insolvenzen, Löschungen, Neugründungen, Jahr 2003*. Neuss: Creditreform AG. Available from http://www.creditreform.de/angebot/Downloads_Analysen/Wirtschaftsanalysen/Insolvenzen4.pdf

Deregulierungskommission (1991). *Marktöffnung und Wettbewerb: Deregulierung als Programm?* Unabhängige Expertenkommission zum Abbau Marktwidriger Regulierungen. Stuttgart: Poeschel.

Deutsche Bundesbank (1975). *Monthly Report, November 1975*.

_____ (1976). *Deutsches Geld- und Bankwesen in Zahlen 1876–1975*. Frankfurt am Main: Knapp.

_____ (1996). Zur Diskussion über die öffentlichen Transfers im Gefolge der Wiedervereinigung. In *Monatsbericht Oktober 1996*, pp. 17–31.

_____ (2000). *Monthly Report, December 2000*. Available from http://www.bundesbank.de/vo/download/mb/2000/12/(200012mb_e.pdf

_____ (2003a). *Monthly Report April 2003*. Available from http://www.bundesbank.de/vo/download/mb/2003/04/200304mb_e.pdf.

_____ (2003b). *Monthly Report, September 2003*. Available from http://www.bundesbank.de/vo/download/mb/2003/09/200309mb_e.pdf.

_____ (2004). Kreditzinsen in der EWU und in Deutschland. *Monthly Report, February 2004, 32-33*. Available from World Wide Web: (http://www.bundesbank.de/vo/download/mb/2003/09/200309mb_e.pdf).

Deutsches Institut für Wirtschaftsforschung (2001). Wirtschaftliche Aspekte der Märkte für Gesundheitsdienstleistungen, http://www.diw.de/deutsch/publikationen/gutachten/docs/diw_GesundheitsDL_200112.pdf

Deutsches Pisa-Konsortium (eds.) (2001). *PISA 2000: Basiskompetenzen von Schülerinnen und Schülern im internationalen Vergleich*. Opladen: Leske & Budrich. A summary is available from http://www.pisa.oecd.org/NatReports/PISA2000/Germanynatrepshortversion.pdf

Dohse, Dirk (2000). Technology Policy and the Regions: The Case of the BioRegio Contest. *Research Policy* 29: 1111–33.

Donges, Juergen B., and Klaus-Werner Schatz (1986). *Staatliche Interventionen in der Bundesrepublik Deutschland. Umfang, Struktur, Wirkungen*. Kiel Discussion Paper no. 119/120, Kiel Institute for World Economics.

Ebbinghaus, Bernhard (2002). *Dinosaurier der Dienstleistungsgesellschaft? Der Mitgliederschwund deutscher Gewerkschaften im historischen und internationalen Vergleich*. MPIfG Working Paper no. 02/3. Cologne: Max Planck Institute for the Study of Societies.

Egeln, J., T. Eckert, H. Griesbach, C. Heine, U. Heublein et al. (2003). *Indikatoren zur Ausbildung im Hochschulbereich: Studie zum Innovationssystem Deutschlands No. 10-200)*. Mannheim: Center for European Economic Research. Available from ftp://ftp.zew.de/pub/zew-docs/docus/dokumentation0303.pdf.

Ehrmann, M., L. Gambacorta, J. Martinez-Pages, P. Sevestre, and A. Worms (2002). *Financial Systems and the Role of Banks in Monetary Policy Transmission in the Euro Area*. ECB Working Paper no. 105. Paris: European Central Bank. Available from http://www.banque-france.fr/gb/telechar/ner93.pdf.

Eucken, Walter (1990). *Grundsätze der Wirtschaftspolitik*. UTB für Wissenschaft: Uni-Taschenbücher 1572, 6th rev. edn. Tübingen: Mohr Siebeck. First published in Bern, Tübingen: Francke und Mohr Verlag, 1952.

European Central Bank (ECB) (2002a). *Report on Financial Structures*. Frankfurt: ECB.

_____ (2002b). *Structural Analysis of the EU Banking Sector. Statistical Annex*. Available from http://www.ecb.int/pub/pdf/eubksectorstructure.pdf

European Commission (2002). *Report of the High Level Group of Company Law Experts on A Modern Regulatory Framework for Company Law in Europe*. Available from http://europa.eu.int/comm/internal_market/en/company/company/modern/consult/report_en.pdf

FAZ Institut für Management-, Markt- und Medieninformationen GmbH. (2002). *Germany's Top 500: Edition 2003: A Handbook of Germany's Largest Corporations*, Frankfurt am Main.

Federal Ministry of Education and Research (2003). *Zur technologischen Leistungsfähigkeit Deutschlands 2002*. Verhandlungen des Deutschen Bundestages: Drucksachen no. 15/788. Berlin: Heenemann/Bonn: Bundesanzeiger.

Federal Ministry of Education and Research and Center for Research on Innovation and Society (eds.) (2001). *Deutsche Nachwuchswissenschaftler in den*

USA. Perspektiven der Hochschul- und Wissenschaftspolitik. Project Talent, Bonn. Available from http://www.bmbf.de/pub/talent.pdf.

Federal Ministry for the Environment, Nature Conservation and Nuclear Safety (1998). *Bericht der Bundesregierung nach dem Übereinkommen über die biologische Vielfalt: Nationalbericht biologische Vielfalt*. Neuss: Neusser Druckerei und Verlag GmbH. Available from http://www.gtz.de/listra/documents/beratung/vielfalt.pdf

Federal Ministry of Health and Social Security (2002). *Sozialbericht 2001*. Available from http://www.bmgs.bund.de/download/broschueren/A101.pdf.

Federal Statistical Office (1989). *Fachserie 18: Volkswirtschaftliche Gesamtrechnungen, Reihe 1.2: Kosten und Standardtabellen*. Wiesbaden: Vorbericht.

———— (2002). *Fachserie 18: Volkswirtschaftliche Gesamtrechnungen, Reihe S21: Revidierte Ergebnisse: 1970 bis 2001*. Stuttgart: Metzler-Poeschel.

———— (2003a). *Bericht zur finanziellen Lage der Hochschulen*. Wiesbaden. Available from http://www.destatis.de/download/d/veroe/fach_voe/gesamtbericht04.pdf.

———— (2003b). *Population of Germany today and tomorrow, 2002–2050*. Wiesbaden: The Spotlight. Available from http://www.destatis.de/download/e/veroe/population.pdf

———— (2003c). *Sozialhilfe in Deutschland. Entwicklung, Umfang, Strukturen*. Wiesbaden. Available from http://www.destatis.de/presse/deutsch/pk/2003/sozialhilfe_2003i.pd.

———— (2004a). *Fachserie 7: Außenhandel, Reihe 1: Zusammenfassende Übersichten für den Außenhandel*. Stuttgart: Metzler-Poeschel.

———— (2004b). *Fachserie 1: Bevölkerung und Erwerbstätigkeit. Reihe 4.1.1: Stand und Entwicklung der Erwerbstätigkeit*. Stuttgart: Metzler-Poeschel.

Feldstein, Martin (1992). The Case against EMU. *The Economist*, June 13, pp. 19–22.

———— (1995). *Would Privatizing Social Security Raise Economic Welfare?* NBER Working Paper no. 5281, Cambridge, MA.

———— (1997). EMU and International Conflict. *Foreign Affairs* 76: 60–73.

———— (2003). Germany's Economic Ills. In Rüdiger Pethig and Michael Rauscher (eds.), *Challenges to the World Economy: Festschrift to Horst Siebert*. Berlin: Springer, pp. 7–16.

Feldstein, Martin S., and Andrew A. Samwick (1996). *The Transition Path in Privatizing Social Security*. NBER Working Paper no. 5761. Cambridge, MA.

Fier, Andreas (2002). *Staatliche Förderung industrieller Forschung in Deutschland: Eine empirische Wirkungsanalyse der direkten Projektförderung des Bundes*. ZEW-Wirtschaftsanalysen, vol. 62, Baden-Baden: Nomos-Verlagsgesellschaft.

Fischer, Wolfram (ed.) (1997). *The Economic Development of Germany since 1970*. Cheltenham, UK: Edward Elgar.

Fitzenberger, Bernd (1999). *Wages and Employment Across Skill Groups: An Analysis for West Germany*. ZEW Economic Studies no. 6. Heidelberg: Physica/Springer.

Fitzenberger, Bernd, and Wolfgang Franz (2000). *Jobs. Jobs? Jobs! Orientierung-*

shilfen für den Weg zu mehr Beschäftigung. ZEW Discussion Paper no. 00–49. Mannheim: ZEW. Available from ftp://ftp.zew.de/pub/zew-docs/dp/dp0049.pdf

Fitzenberger, Bernd, Isabelle Haggeney, and Michaela Ernst (1999). Wer ist noch Mitglied in den Gewerkschaften? Eine Panelanalyse für Westdeutschland. *Zeitschrift für Wirtschafts- und Sozialwissenschaften* 119: 223–63.

Fölster, Stefan, and Magnus Henrekson (2001). Growth Effects of Government Expenditure and Taxation in Rich Countries. *European Economic Review* 45: 1501–20.

Freeman, Richard, and Ronald Schettkat (2000). *Skill Compression, Wage Differentials and Employment: Germany vs. the .S.* NBER Working Paper no. 7610, Cambridge, MA.

Friedman, Milton (2002). *Capitalism and Freedom*, 40th anniversary edn. Chicago: University of Chicago Press. First published in 1962.

German Advisory Council on the Environment (2002a). *Towards a New Leading Role*. Environmental Report 2002, Bundestag Publication 14/8792. Stuttgart: Metzler-Poeschel. Available from http://www.umweltrat.de/02gutach/downlo02/umweltg/UG_2002.pdf; abbreviated version in English: http://www.umweltrat.de/english/edownloa/envirrep/UG_2002_summary.pdf

——— (2002b). *Towards Strengthening and Reorienting Nature and Landscape Conservation*. Special Report. Bundestag Publication 14/9852. Stuttgart: Metzler-Poeschel. Available from http://www.umweltrat.de/02gutach/downlo02/sonderg/1409852.pdf; abbreviated version in English: http://www.umweltrat.de/english/edownloa/specrepo/SG_Towards_Strengthening_2002_summary.pdf.

German Council of Economic Advisers (1988). *Arbeitsplätze im Wettbewerb*. Annual Report 1988/89. Stuttgart and Mainz: Kohlhammer.

——— (1990). *Auf dem Wege zur wirtschaftlichen Einheit Deutschlands*. Annual Report 1990/91. Stuttgart: Metzler-Poeschel.

——— (1995). *Im Standortwettbewerb*. Annual Report 1995/96. Stuttgart: Metzler-Poeschel.

——— (1996). *Reformen voranbringen*. Annual Report 1996/1997. Stuttgart: Metzler-Poeschel.

——— (1997). *Wachstum, Beschäftigung, Währungsunion: Orientierungen für die Zukunft*. Annual Report 1997/98, Stuttgart: Metzler-Poeschel.

——— (1998). *Vor weitreichenden Entscheidungen*. Annual Report 1998/99. Stuttgart: Metzler-Poeschel.

——— (1999). *Wirtschaftspolitik unter Reformdruck*. Annual Report 1999/2000. Stuttgart: Metzler-Poeschel.

——— (2000). *Chancen auf einen höheren Wachstumspfad*. Annual Report 2000/2001. Stuttgart: Metzler-Poeschel.

——— (2001). *Für Stetigkeit: Gegen Aktionismus*. Annual Report 2001/2002. Stuttgart: Metzler-Poeschel.

——— (2002). *Zwanzig Punkte für Beschäftigung und Wachstum*. Annual Report 2002/2003. Stuttgart: Metzler-Poeschel.

——— (2003). *Staatsfinanzen konsolidieren: Steuersystem reformieren*. Annual Report 2003/04. Stuttgart: Metzler-Poeschel.

German Economic Research Institutes (2003a). *The State of the World Economy and the German Economy in the Spring of 2003*. Available in German from http://www.diw.de/deutsch/produkte/publikationen/wochenberichte/docs/03–16.pdf

‗‗‗‗‗‗ (2003b). *The State of the World Economy and the German Economy in the Autumn of 2003*. Halle: German Institute for Economic Research. In German available from http://www.uni-kiel.de/ifw/konfer/gd/gd03_2.pdf

Gern, Klaus-Juergen (1999). *Auswirkungen verschiedener Varianten einer negativen Einkommensteuer in Deutschland: Eine Simulationsstudie*. Kieler Studies no. 294. Tübingen: Mohr Siebeck.

Giersch, Herbert (1991). *Allgemeine Wirtschaftspolitik: Grundlagen*, reprint. Wiesbaden: Gabler. First published in 1961.

Giersch, Herbert, Karl-Heinz Paque, and Holger Schmieding (1994). *The Fading Miracle: Four Decades of Market Economy of Germany*. Cambridge Surveys in Economic Policies and Institutions, rev. and updated edn, Cambridge (UK): Cambridge University Press.

Gottschalk, Peter T., and Mary Joyce Gottschalk (1998). Cross-national Differences in the Rise in Earnings Inequality: Market and Institutional Factors. *Review of Economics and Statistics* 80: 489–579.

Gruber, Jonathan, and David A. Wise (2002). Different Approaches to Pension Reform from an Economic Point of View. In Martin S. Feldstein and Horst Siebert (eds.), *Social Security Pension Reform in Europe*. National Bureau of Economic Research Conference Report. Chicago: University of Chicago Press, pp. 49–77.

Guillen, Mauro F. (2000). Corporate Governance and Globalization: Is There Convergence across Countries? *Advances in Comparative International Management* 13: 175–204.

Hackethal, Andreas (2003). German Banks and Banking Structure. In Jan Pieter Krahnen and Reinhard H. Schmidt, *German Financial System*. Oxford: Oxford University Press, forthcoming.

Hall, Peter A., and David Soskice (eds.) (2001). *Varieties of Capitalism: The Institutional Foundations of Comparative Advantage*. Oxford: Oxford University Press.

Hancké, Bob and David Soskice (2003). Wage-setting and Inflation Targets in EMU. *Oxford Review of Economic Policy* 19: 149–60.

Hansjürgens, Bernd (2000). Umweltpolitik in den USA und in der Bundesrepublik Deutschland: ein institutionenökonomischer Vergleich. In Bettina Wentzel and Dirk Wentzel (eds.), *Wirtschaftlicher Systemvergleich Deutschland/USA: anhand ausgewählter Ordnungsbereiche*. UTB für Wissenschaft no. 2121. Stuttgart: Lucius & Lucius, pp. 181–222.

Hayek, Friedrich A. von (1968). *Wettbewerb als Entdeckungsverfahren*. Kieler Vorträge, N.F. 56. Kiel: Kiel Institute of World Economics.

‗‗‗‗‗‗ (2001). *The Road to Serfdom*. London: Routledge. First published in London: George Routledge, 1944.

Heckman, James J. (2002). *Flexibility and Job Creation: Lessons for Germany*. NBER Discussion Paper no. 9194, Cambridge, MA.

Heilemann, Ulrich, Heinz Gebhardt, and Hans Dietrich von Loeffelholz (2003).

Wirtschaftspolitische Chronik der Bundesrepublik 1949–2002, 2nd newly arranged and extended edn. UTB für Wissenschaft: Uni-Taschenbücher 2495. Stuttgart: Lucius & Lucius.

Hermens, Ferdinand A. (1972). *Democracy or Anarchy? A Study of Proportional Representation*. New York: Johnson Reprint Corporation. First published in German in 1951, Wissenschaftliche Schriften des Instituts zur Förderung öffentlicher Angelegenheiten in Frankfurt am Main, vol. 8. Frankfurt am Main: Metzner.

Holmström, Bengt (1999). Managerial Incentive Problems: A Dynamic Perspective. *Review of Economic Studies* 66: 169–82.

Hopt, K. J., H. Kanda, M. J. Roe, E. Wymeersch, and S. Prigge (eds.) (1998). *Comparative Corporate Governance: The State of the Art and Emerging Research*. Symposium at the Max Planck Institute for Foreign Private and Private International Law in Hamburg, May 15–17, 1997. Oxford: Oxford University Press.

Hunt, Jennifer (1995). The Effect of Unemployment Compensation on Unemployment Duration in Germany. *Journal of Labor Economics* 13: 88–120.

Hutchison, Terence W. (1979). Notes on the Effects of Economic Ideas on Policy: The Example of the German Social Market Economy. *Zeitschrift für die gesamte Staatswissenschaft* 135: 426–41.

———— (1981). Walter Eucken and the German Social-Market Economy. In *The Politics and Philosophy of Economies: Marxians, Keynesians and Austrians*. Oxford: Blackwell, pp. 155–75.

Institut der Deutschen Wirtschaft (2003). Belastungsneutrale Abschläge bei Frühverrentung. *iw-Trends* 4/2003. Available from http://www.iwkoeln.de/data/pdf/content/trends04–03–4_v2.pdf

Institut für Weltwirtschaft (2004). Thesen zum Kieler Konjunkturgespräch: March, Kiel.

International Monetary Fund (2003). *Germany: Selected Issues*. Country Report no. 03/342. Washington: IMF.

Jeffery, Charlie (2003). Federalism and Territorial Politics. In Stephen Padgett, William E. Paterson, and Gordon Smith (eds.), *Developments in German Politics*, vol. 3. Basingstoke: Palgrave Macmillan, pp. 38–59.

Jones, Erik (2003). New Dynamics of "Old Europe." *French Politics* 1: 233–42. Available from http://www.jhubc.it/facultypages/ejones/FP-07–03.pdf.

Kahn, Lawrence M. (2000). Wage Inequality, Collective Bargaining, and Relative Employment from 1985 to 1994: Evidence from Fifteen OECD Countries. *Review of Economics and Statistics* 82: 564–79.

Kamps, Christophe (2004). The Dynamic Macroeconomic Effects of Public Capital: Theory and Evidence for OECD Countries. Kiel Studies. Kiel Institute for World Economics, forthcoming.

Katz, Lawrence F., and David H. Autor (1999). Changes in Wage Structure and Earnings Inequality, in: Orley C. Ashenfelter (ed.) *Handbook of Labor Economics*. no. 5, vol. 3A. Amsterdam: Elsevier, 1463–1555.

Katz, Lawrence F., and Kevin M. Murphy, (1992). Changes in Relative Wages 1963–1987: Supply and Demand Factors. *Quarterly Journal of Economics* 107: 35–78.

Kirkpatrick, Grant, Gernot Klepper, and Robert Price (2001). *Making Growth More Environmentally Sustainable in Germany*. OECD Economics Department Working Paper no. 276. Available from http://www.olis.oecd.org/olis/2001doc.nsf/linkto/eco-wkp20012.

Kirchhof, Paul (2004). *Der sanfte Verlust der Freiheit.Für ein neues Steuerrecht: klar, verständlich, gerecht*. Munich: Hanser.

Klepper, Gernot and Sonja Peterson (2004). *The EU Emissions Trading Scheme: Allowance Prices, Trade Flows, Competitiveness Effects*. Kiel Working Paper no. 1195.

Klodt, Henning (2003). Das Telekommunikationsgesetz vor der Novellierung. *Die Weltwirtschaft* 2: 196–214.

_____ (2004). Alte Industriepolitik in neuen Schläuchen. *Frankfurter Allgemeine Zeitung* no. 18, January 22, 2004, p. 10.

Klodt, Henning, Alfred Boss, Jens Oliver Lorz, Rainer Maurer, Axel D. Neu, Karl-Heinz Paqué, Astrid Rosenschon, Jürgen Stehn, and Christine Walter (1994). *Standort Deutschland: Strukturelle Herausforderungen im neuen Europa*. Kiel Studies no. 265. Tübingen: Mohr Siebeck.

Kloten, Norbert (1989). *40 Jahre "Soziale Markwirtschaft"*. In Deutsche Bundesbank, *Auszüge aus Presseartikeln*, no. 50, June 22, S10–16.

Klump, Rainer (1985). *Wirtschaftsgeschichte der Bundesrepublik Deutschland. Zur Kritik neuerer wirtschaftshistorischer Interpretationen aus ordnungspolitischer Sicht*. Beiträge zur Wirtschafts- und Sozialgeschichte, vol. 29. Wiesbaden: Steiner.

Krahnen, Jan Pieter, and Reinhard H. Schmidt (2004). *The German Financial System*. Oxford: Oxford University Press.

Krugman, Paul R. (1994). Past and Prospective Causes of High Unemployment. *Economic Review* (Kansas City, Mo.) 79: 23–43.

Layard, Peter R. G., Stephen J. Nickell, and Richard A. Jackman (1997). *Unemployment: Macroeconomic Performance and the Labour Market*. Oxford: Oxford University Press.

Lindbeck, Assar (1994). *Turning Sweden Around*. Sverige Ekonomikommissionen. Cambridge, MA: MIT Press.

Machin, Stephen, Alan Manning, and Lupin Rahman (2003). Minimum Wage Effects where the Minimum Bites Hard: Introduction of Minimum Wages to a Low Wage Sector. *Journal of the European Economic Association*, 1: 154–80.

Mankiw, N. Gregory, David H. Romer, and David N. Weil (1992). A Contribution to the Empirics of Economic Growth. *Quarterly Journal of Economics* 107: 407–37.

Maurer, Raimond (2003). *Institutional Investors in Germany: Insurance Companies and Investment Funds*. Centre for Financial Studies, Working Paper no. 2003/14. Available from http://www.ifk-cfs.de/papers/03_14.pdf

Mayer, Colin P. (1988). New Issues in Corporate Finance. *European Economic Review* 32: 1167–83.

Miksch, Leonhard (1947). *Wettbewerb als Aufgab: Grundsätze einer Wettbewerbsordnung*, 2nd (extended) edn. Godesberg: Küpper. First published in Stuttgart, Berlin: Kohlhammer, 1937.

Mises, Ludwig von (1929). *Kritik des Interventionismus. Untersuchungen zur Wirtschaftspolitik und Wirtschaftsideologie der Gegenwart.* Jena: Fischer.

Müller-Armack, Alfred (1971). Genealogie der Wirtschaftsstile. Die geistesgeschichtlichen Ursprünge der Staats- und Wirtschaftsformen bis zum Ausgang des 18. Jahrhunderts. In Hans G. Schachtschabel (ed.), *Wirtschaftsstufen und Wirtschaftsordnungen.* Wege der Forschung, vol. 176. Darmstadt: Wiss. Buchges, pp. 156–207. First published in Stuttgart: Kohlhammer, 1941.

_____ (1978). Social Market Economy as an Economic and Social Order. *Review of Social Economy* 3: 325–31.

_____ (1982). *Wirtschaftsordnung und Wirtschaftspoliti: Studien und Konzepte zur sozialen Marktwirtschaft und zur europäischen Integration.* Beiträge zur Wirtschaftspolitik, vol. 4. Freiburg: Rombach. First published 1966.

_____ (1999). *Wirtschaftslenkung und Marktwirtschaft.* Die Handelsblatt-Bibliothek "Klassiker der Nationalökonomie." Düsseldorf: Verlag Wirtschaft und Finanzen. First published in Hamburg: Verlag für Wirtschaft und Sozialpolitik, 1947.

Musgrave, Richard A., and Peggy B. Musgrave (1989). *Public Finance in Theory and Practice,* 5th edn. New York: McGraw-Hill. First published as Richard A. Musgrave, *The Theory of Public Finance. A Study in Public Economy.* New York: McGraw-Hill, 1959.

Nicoletti, Guiseppe, and Stefano Scarpetta (2003). *Regulation, Productivity and Growth: OECD Evidence.* World Bank Policy Research Working Paper no. 2944. Washington, DC: World Bank. Available from http://econ.worldbank.org/files/22970_wps2944.pdf

Nicoletti, Guiseppe, Stefano Scarpetta, and Olivier Boylaud (1999). *Summary Indicators of Product Market Regulation with an Extension to Employment Protection Legislation.* OECD Working Paper no. 226, Paris. Available from http://www.oecd.int/dataoecd/21/13/1880867.pdf

Niedenhoff, Horst-Udo (2000). *Mitbestimmung in der Bundesrepublik Deutschland,* 12th supplemented edn. Cologne: Dt. Instituts-Verlag.

O'Brien, Paul S., and Ann Vourc'h. (2001). *Encouraging Environmentally Sustainable Growth: Experience in OECD Countries.* OECD Economics Department Working Paper no. 293. Available from http://www.olis.oecd.org/olis/2001doc.nsf/linkto/eco-wkp200119

Okun, Arthur M. (1975). *Equality and Efficiency: The Big Tradeoff.* Washington DC: Brookings Institution.

Olson, Mancur (1969). The Principle of "Fiscal Equivalence": The Division of Responsibilities among Different Levels of Government. *American Economic Review* 59: 479–87.

_____ (1971). *The Logic of Collective Action: Public Goods and the Theory of Groups,* rev. edn. Cambridge, MA: Harvard University Press. First published in 1965 as Harvard Economic Studies, vol. 124.

_____ (1982). *The Rise and Decline of Nations: Economic Growth, Stagflation and Social Rigidities.* New Haven: Yale University Press.

Organisation for Economic Co-operation and Development (OECD) (1997).

Maintaining Prosperity in an Ageing Society: The OECD Study on the Policy Implications of Ageing—Fiscal Alternatives of Moving from Unfunded to Funded Pensions. Working Paper no. AWP 5.2. Paris: OECD. Available from http://www.oecd.org/dataoecd/21/41/2429222.pdf

———— (2001a). *Bank Profitability 2000.* Paris: OECD.

———— (2001b). *OECD Environmental Performance Reviews: Germany.* Paris: OECD.

———— (2002). *Education at a Glance: OECD Indicators 2002.* Paris: OECD. Available from http://www1.oecd.org/publications/e-book/9603061E.PDF

———— (2003a). *Education at a Glance: OECD Indicators 2003.* Paris: OECD. Available from http://www1.oecd.org/publications/e-book/9603061e.pdf

———— (2003b). *OECD Economic Outlook* no. 73, June 2003. Paris: OECD.

Padgett, Stephen, William E. Paterson, and Gordon Smith (eds.) (2003). *Developments in German Politics*, vol. 3. Basingstoke: Palgrave Macmillan.

Papier, Hans-Jürgen, (2003). Überholte Verfassung. *Frankfurter Allgemeine Zeitung* no. 276, November 27, p. 8.

Popper, Karl R. (2003). *The Open Society and its Enemies*, 5th edn. London: Routledge. First published in London: Routledge & Sons, 1945.

Posen, Adam S. (1998). *Restoring Japan's Economic Growth.* Washington, DC: Institute for International Economics.

———— (2003). *Is Germany Turning Japanese?* Working Paper of the Institute for International Economics. Available from http://www.iie.com/publications/wp/(2003/03–2.pdf

Puhani, Patrick A. (2003). *A Test of the "Krugman Hypothesis" for the United States, Britain, and Western Germany.* Discussion Paper no. 2003–13, Department of Economics, University of St Gallen; IZA Discussion Paper no. 764, Bonn; ZEW Discussion Paper no. 03–18, Mannheim. Available from ftp://ftp.iza.org/dps/dp764.pdf and ftp://ftp.zew.de/pub/zew-docs/dp/dp0318.pdf

Rammer, Christian (2002). *Unternehmensdynamik in forschungs- und wissensintensiven Wirtschaftszweigen.* ZEW Studien zum deutschen Innovationssystem no. 13-2003. Mannheim. Available from http://technologische-leistungsfaehigkeit.de/_downloads/SDI_13–03).pdf

Rawls, John (1971). *A Theory of Justice.* Cambridge, MA: Harvard University Press.

Röpke, Wilhelm (1958). *Ein Jahrzehnt Sozialer Marktwirtschaft in Deutschland und seine Lehren. Aktionsprogramm der Aktionsgemeinschaft Soziale Marktwirtschaft.* Cologne–Marienburg: Verlag für Politik und Wirtschaft.

———— (1994). *Economics of the Free Society*, new printing. Grove City, PA: Libertarian Press. First published in German as *Die Lehre von der Wirtschaft* in Vienna: Springer, 1937; first published in English in Chicago by Henry Regnery Company, 1963.

———— (2002). *Die Gesellschaftskrisis der Gegenwart.* Die Handelsblatt-Bibliothek "Klassiker der Nationalökonomie." Düsseldorf: Verlag Wirtschaft und Finanzen. First published in Erlenbach-Zürich: Rentsch, 1942.

Rudzio, Wolfgang (2003). *Das politische System der Bundesrepublik Deutschland*, 6th rev. edn. UTB für Wissenschaft no. 1280. Opladen: Leske & Budrich.

Rüstow, Alexander von (1932). Untitled contribution to a discussion. *Deutschland und die Weltkrise, Schriften des Vereins für Socialpolitik* 187: 62–69.

Sachverständigenrat: *see* German Council of Economic Advisers.

Saint-Paul, Gilles (2000). *The Political Economy of Labour Market Institutions.* Oxford: Oxford University Press.

Sapir, André, et al. (2003). *An Agenda for a Growing Europe: Making the EU Economic System Deliver.* Report of an Independent High-Level Study Group established on the initiative of the President of the European Commission. Available from http://europa.eu.int/comm/dgs/policy_advisers/experts_groups/ps2/docs/agenda_en.pdf

Sauve, Annie, and Manfred Scheuer (eds.) (1999). *Corporate Finance in Germany and France: A Joint Research Project of the Deutsche Bundesbank and the Banque de France.* Frankfurt am Main: Deutsche Bundesbank.

Scarpetta, S., P. Hemmings, T. Tressel, and J. Woo (2002). *The Role of Policy and Institutions for Productivity and Firm Dynamics: Evidence from Micro and Industry Data.* OECD Working Paper no. 329, Paris. Available from http://appli1.oecd.org/olis/(2002doc.nsf/linkto/eco-wkp((2002)15/$file/JT00125006.pdf

Schewe, Dieter, Karlhugo Nordhorn, and K.-W. Hermsen (1975). *Übersicht über die soziale Sicherung,* 9th edn. Bonn: Federal Minister for Labor and Social Affairs. First published 1956, Cologne.

Schimmelpfennig, Axel (2000). *Structural Change of the Production Process and Unemployment in Germany.* Kiel Studies no. 307. Tübingen: Mohr Siebeck.

Schmidt, Reinhard H., Andreas Hackethal, and Marcel Tyrell (2001). *The Convergence of Financial Systems in Europe.* Working Papers on Finance and Accounting, no. 75, Frankfurt am Main: Johann Wolfgang Goethe-Universität, Fachbereich Wirtschaftswissenschaften. Available from http://finance.uni-frankfurt.de/schmidt/WPs/wp/wp75.pdf

Siebert, Horst (1973). *Das Produzierte Chaos. Ökonomie und Umwelt.* Stuttgart: Kohlhammer.

———— (1980). Allokation zwischen Generationen. In Dieter Duwendag and Horst Siebert (eds.), *Politik und Mark: Wirtschaftspolitische Probleme der 80er Jahre.* Stuttgart: Fischer Verlag.

———— (1993a). *Das Wagnis der Einheit: Eine wirtschaftspolitische Therapie,* 2nd edn. Stuttgart: Deutsche Verlags-Anstalt. First published in 1992.

———— (1993b). *Principles of the Economic System in the Federal Republic. An Economist's View.* Vol. 14 of the Dräger Foundation Series, *Germany and its Basic Law, Past, Present and Future: A German–American Symposium,* pp. 291–310. Baden-Baden: Nomos Verlagsgesellschaft.

———— (1994a). *Geht den Deutschen die Arbeit aus? Wege zu mehr Beschäftigung.* Gütersloh: Bertelsmann.

———— (ed.) (1994b). *The Ethical Foundations of the Market Economy.* International Workshop, Kiel Institute for World Economics, Tübingen: Mohr.

———— (ed.) (1995). *Locational Competition in the World Economy.* 1994 Symposium: Kiel Institute for World Economics, Tübingen: Mohr.

———— (1997). Labor Market Rigidities: At the Root of Unemployment in Europe. *Journal of Economic Perspectives* 11: 37–54.

_____ (1998a). *Arbeitslos ohne Ende? Strategien für mehr Beschäftigung.* Wiesbaden: Gabler Verlag/FAZ.

_____ (1998b). Pay-As-You-Go versus Capital-Funded Pension Systems: The Issues. In Siebert (1998c).

_____ (ed.) (1998c). *Redesigning Social Security.* Symposia and Conference Proceedings, Kiel Week Conference 1997, Kiel Institute for World Economics, Tübingen: Mohr.

_____ (2000). *Zum Paradigma des Standortwettbewerbs.* Walter Eucken Institut, Beiträge zur Ordnungstheorie und Ordnungspolitik 165. Tübingen: Mohr Siebeck.

_____ (2001). *How the EU Can Move to a Higher Growth Path: Some Considerations.* Kiel Discussion Paper no. 383. Kiel: Kiel Institute for World Economics.

_____ (2002a). Economic Perspectives for Aging Societies: The Issues. In Horst Siebert (ed.), *Economic Policy for Aging Societies.* Kiel Week Conference 2001, Kiel Institute for World Economics. Berlin: Springer.

_____ (2002b). Europe: Quo Vadis? Reflections on the Future Institutional Framework of the European Union. *World Economy* 25: 1–32.

_____ (2002c). *The World Economy,* 2nd edn. London: Routledge. First published in 1999.

_____ (2002d). *Verliert der deutsche Industriestandort?* Available from www.uni-kiel.de/ifw/pub/siebert/siebess.htm

_____ (2002e). *Verliert die deutsche Wirtschaft Wettbewerbsfähigkeit?* Available from www.uni-kiel.de/ifw/pub/siebert/siebess.htm

_____ (2003). *Der Kobra Effekt: Wie man Irrwege der Wirtschaftspolitik vermeidet,* reprint of the 2nd rev. edn. Munich: Piper. First published in 2001.

_____ (2004a). *Economics of the Environment: Theory and Policy,* 5th rev. edn. Berlin: Springer. First published in 1981 in Lexington, MA: D. C. Heath.

_____ (2004b). Mehr Markt für mehr Wachstum. *Frankfurter Allgemeine Zeitung* no. 20, January 24, 2004, p. 13.

Siebert, Horst, and Martin Feldstein (eds.) (2002). *Social Security Pension Reform in Europe.* A National Bureau of Economic Research Conference Report. Chicago: University of Chicago Press.

Siebert, Horst, and Michael Stolpe (2002). Germany. In Benn Steil, David G. Victor, and Richard R. Nelson (eds.), *Technological Innovation and Economic Performance.* Princeton and Oxford: Princeton University Press, pp. 112–47.

Sinn H.-W., Ch. Holzner, W. Meister, W. Ochel, and M. Werding (2002). Aktivierende Sozialhilfe: Ein Weg zu mehr Beschäftigung und Wachstum. Sonderausgabe, ifo Reformvorschlag. *Ifo-Schnelldienst* 55: 3–52.

Smith, Adam (1998). *The Wealth of Nations.* Oxford: Oxford University Press. First published as *An Inquiry into the Nature and Causes of the Wealth of Nations,* London, 1776.

_____ (2002). *The Theory of Moral Sentiments,* ed. Knud Haakonssen, Karl Ameriks, and Desmond M. Clarke. Cambridge Texts in the History of Philosophy. Cambridge (UK): Cambridge University Press. First published in London 1759.

Smith, Eric O. (1994). *The German Economy.* London: Routledge.

Smyser, W. R. (1993). *The German Economy. Colossus at the Crossroads*, 2nd edn. New York: St Martin's Press.

Soltwedel, Ruediger, Axel Busch, Alexander Gross, and Claus-Friedrich Laaser (1986). *Deregulierungspotentiale in der Bundesrepublik*. Kiel Studies, no. 202. Tübingen: Mohr.

Statistisches Bundesamt: *see* Federal Statistical Office.

Steiner, Viktor (1998). Extended Benefit-Entitlement Periods and the Duration of Unemployment in West Germany. In John T. Addison and Paul J. Welfens (eds.), *Labor Markets and Social Security: Wage Costs, Social Security Financing and Labor Market Reforms in Europe*. Heidelberg: Springer.

Stifterverband der deutschen Wissenschaft. (2002). *Brain Drain–Brain Gain: Eine Untersuchung über internationale Berufskarrieren*. Berlin. Available from http://www.stifterverband.org/pdf/braindrain_studie.pdf

Story, Jonathan, and Ingo Walter (1997). *Political Economy of Financial Integration in Europe: The Battle of the Systems*. European Policy Research Unit series. Manchester: Manchester University Press.

Tuchtfeldt, Egon (1973). Soziale Marktwirtschaft und Globalsteuerung – zwei wirtschaftspolitische Experimente. In Institut für Wirtschaftspolitik an der Universität zu Köln, *Wirtschaftspolitische Chronik*, vol. 1, pp. 7–38. Reprinted in Wolfgang Stützel, Christian Watrin, Hans Willgerodt, and Karl Hohmann (eds.), *Grundtexte zur Sozialen Marktwirtschaft: Zeugnisse aus zweihundert Jahren ordnungspolitischer Diskussion*. Ludwig–Erhard–Stiftung. Stuttgart: Fischer, 1981, pp. 83–104.

United States Department of Labor (2003). *International Comparisons of Manufacturing Productivity and Unit Labor Cost Trends, 2002*. Washington, DC: US Bureau of Labor Statistics.

Van Den Berghe, Lutgart (2002). *Corporate Governance in a Globalising World: Convergence or Divergence? A European Perspective*. Boston, MA: Kluwer Academic.

Van der Elst, Christoph (2001). *Scale of Corporations, Industry Specifications and Voting Blocks: A Private Benefit Approach*. Working Paper no. 2001–10, Financial Law Institute, Ghent University. Available from http://www.law.rug.ac.be/fli/WP/WP(2001-pdf/WP2001–10.pdf

Vanberg, Viktor J. (1988). "Ordnungstheorie" as Constitutional Economics: The German Conception of a "Social Market Economy." *Ordo: Jahrbuch für die Ordnung von Wirtschaft und Gesellschaft* 39: 17–31.

Verband der Vereine Creditreform (2003). Insolvenzen, Neugründungen, Löschungen: eine Untersuchung zur Unternehmensentwicklung der Creditreform Wirtschafts- und Konjunkturforschung, 1 Halbjahr 2003. Neuss.

Wassermann, Wolfram (2002). *Die Betriebsräte: Akteure für Demokratie in der Arbeitswelt*. Schriftenreihe Hans Böckler Stiftung. Münster: Westfälisches Dampfboot.

Watrin, Christian (1979). The Principles of the Social Market Economy: Its Origins and Early History. *Zeitschrift für die gesamte Staatswissenschaft* 135: 405–25.

Weber, Max (2001). *Soziologie. Weltgeschichtliche Analysen. Politik*, ed. Johannes Winckelmann. Stuttgart: Kröner Verlag. First published 1956.

Willgerodt, Hans (1988). Die Krise der Wirtschaftspolitik. *Zeitschrift für Wirtschaftspolitik* 37: 5–12.

Wößmann, Ludger (2002). *Schooling and the Quality of Human Capital*, Kiel Studies no. 319. Berlin: Springer.

_____ (2003). Returns to Education in Europe. *Review of World Economics* 139: 348–76.

World Bank (2002). *World Development Report 2002: Building Institutions for Markets*. Available from http://econ.worldbank.org/wdr/WDR2002/